W9-APZ-048

WELCOME!

Bake A Cake Memory

BUNDT CAKES

SHEET CAKES

BROWNIES

POUND CAKES

BARS

LAYER CAKES

CUPCAKES

. . . AND A WEDDING CAKE

FROSTINGS

MUFFINS

COOKIES

A Better Banana Cake, PAGE 27

Fresh Strawberry Cake, PAGE 30

Strawberry Refrigerator Cake, PAGE 34

Fresh Orange Birthday Cake, PAGE 37

Williamsburg Orange Cake, PAGE 42

Blueberry Muffin Crumble Cake, PAGE 47

Lemonade Chiffon Layer Cake, PAGE 50

Lemon Lover's Layer Cake, PAGE 53

Old-Fashioned Pear and Ginger Cakes, PAGE 57

Apple Butter Spice Cake, PAGE 59

Cinnamon Apple Spice Cake, PAGE 62

Pineapple Carrot Cake, PAGE 64

Classic Yellow Cake, PAGE 67

Marsha's Lively Lemon Cake, page 165

Key Lime Pound Cake, page 168

Orange Poppy Seed Pound Cake, page 171

Apricot Cake with Lemon Cream Cheese Filling, page 174

Carolyn's Mango Cake, page 177

Apple Cider Cake, page 179

Ruth's Applesauce Spice Cake, page 181

Red Peach Nectar Cake, page 183

Cathy's Marbled Spice Cake, page 186

A New Zucchini Cake, page 188

Kathy's Cinnamon Breakfast Cake, page 191

Cinnamon Sour Cream Coffee Cake, page 194

Maple Cream Cheese Pound Cake, page 196

Almond Pound Cake, page 199

Butter Pecan Bundt Cake, page 202

Pumpkin Spice Cake, page 205

Chocolate Flan Cake, page 207

Fudge Brownie Pound Cake, page 209

Chocolate Chip Cappuccino Coffee Cake, page 212

A Lighter Stacy's Chocolate Chip Cake, page 215

Chocolate Chip Zucchini Cake, page 218

Jewish Pound Cake, page 220

Aimee's Almond Chocolate Chip Cake, page 222

More Amazing German Chocolate Cake, page 224

German Chocolate Darn Good Cake, page 226

Classic Darn Good Chocolate Cake, page 228

White Chocolate Macadamia Darn Good Chocolate Cake, page 231

Double Coconut Macadamia Cake, page 233

Chocolate Espresso Pound Cake, page 236

Apricot Amaretto Cake, page 238

Baileys Irish Bundt Cake, page 240

Banana Buttered Rum Cake, page 242

Cream Cheese Pound Cake, page 70

Penny's Mom's Cake, page 73

Sour Cream Cake with Lemon Filling, page 75

Easy Coconut Refrigerator Cake, page 78

Butter Pecan Cake, page 81

Hawaiian Wedding Cake, page 84

Pumpkin Spice Cake, page 88

Kentucky Blackberry Jam Cake, page 90

Cinnamon Streusel Layer Cake, page 92

Elegant Almond Amaretto Cake, page 95

Holiday Eggnog Cake, page 98

Toffee Cake, page 101

The Best Red Velvet Cake, page 104

Maryann's Chocolate Layer Cake, page 107

Sour Cream Chocolate Cake, page 109

Chocolate Chip Layer Cake, page 111

Chocolate Cake with Chocolate Mint Ganache, page 114

The Chocolate Raspberry Cake, page 117

Favorite German Chocolate Cake, page 120

Miami Beach Birthday Cake, page 123

Smith Island Cake, page 126

For That Extra Special Day

A Basic and Beautiful Wedding Cake, page 149

Chocolate Swirled Cannoli Cake, page 130

Tiramisu Cake, page 133

Triple Decker Chocolate Icebox Cake, page 136

Chocolate Rum Icebox Cake, page 140

Double Chocolate Kahlua Cake, page 144

Lemon Cake with a Blueberry Crown, page 159

A Lighter Susan's Lemon Cake, page 162

Pumpkin Cranberry Christmas Cake, page 245

Pina Colada Cake, page 249

Margarita Cake, page 252

Chocolate Rum Raisin Cake, page 255

Hot Lemon Poke Cake, page 259

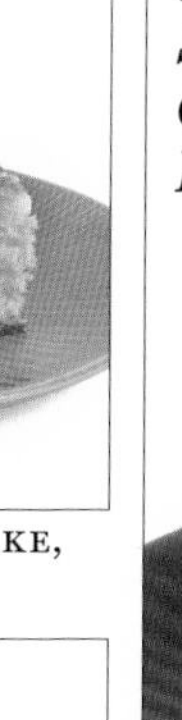

Lemon Streusel Cake, page 262

Topped with a Sherry-Flavored Cream Cheese Frosting

Mandarin Orange Cake, page 270

Lemon Curd Icebox Cake, page 265

Pink Lemonade Party Cake, page 268

Orange Cranberry Coffee Cake, page 273

Chunky Applesauce Cake, page 275

Sour Cream and Cinnamon Raisin Cake, page 277

Hummingbird Cake, page 280

Banana Chocolate Chip Cake, page 282

Pineapple Dump Cake, page 284

Pineapple Upside-Down Cake, page 286

Brandied Peach Upside-Down Cake, page 288

Brown Sugar and Rhubarb Upside-Down Cake, page 291

Carrot and Raisin Spice Cake, page 293

Gingerbread Spice Cake, page 295

Pumpkin Cranberry Cake, page 297

Hot Prune Cake, page 300

Nancy's Cinnamon Swirl Coffee Cake, page 302

Birthday Cake for a Crowd, page 305

Broiled Peanut Butter Crunch Cake, page 308

Mindy's Jack Cake with Tennessee Drizzle, page 310

LEMON-LIME CAKE, PAGE 312

MOIST AND CREAMY COCONUT CAKE, PAGE 315

CARAMEL TRES LECHES CAKE, PAGE 317

GERMAN CHOCOLATE CAKE WITH CHEESECAKE POCKETS, PAGE 320

FAST FIXING CHOCOLATE CHIP CAKE, PAGE 322

CHOCOLATE BAYOU CITY CAKE, PAGE 324

A NEW CHOCOLATE-COVERED CHERRY CAKE, PAGE 326

CHOCOLATE PEANUT BUTTER MARBLE CAKE, PAGE 328

OLD-FASHIONED CHOCOLATE SHEET CAKE, PAGE 330

WARM CHOCOLATE PUDDING CAKE, PAGE 333

OVERNIGHT CHOCOLATE CARAMEL CAKE, PAGE 335

COOKIES AND CREAM CHEESECAKE, PAGE 337

KEY LIME CHEESECAKE, PAGE 340

A BETTER CHOCOLATE CHIP COOKIE DOUGH CUPCAKE, PAGE 345

PEANUT BUTTER COOKIE DOUGH CUPCAKES, PAGE 348

CREAM-FILLED CHOCOLATE CUPCAKES, PAGE 352

Chocolate Marbled Cupcakes, page 355

Chocolate Buttermilk Cupcakes, page 358

German Chocolate Cupcakes, page 360

Red Velvet Peppermint Cupcakes, page 363

Strawberry Cheesecake Cupcakes, page 366

Lemon Cupcakes, page 369

White Sour Cream Cupcakes, page 371

Bake Sale Caramel Cupcakes, page 375

Sock-It-To-Me Muffins, page 377

Chocolate Chip Muffins, page 379

Apple Spice Muffins, page 381

Cake Mix Cinnamon Rolls, page 383

Whoopie Pies, page 386

Old-Fashioned Pan Brownies, page 391

Mireille's Brownies, page 393

Cookies and Cream Brownies, page 396

Gooey Pecan Pie Brownies, page 398

Cranberry Almond Brownies, page 401

Music To My Mouth Brownies, page 403

Marbled Ricotta Cheesecake Brownies, page 405

Chocolate Mint Brownies, page 407

Peanut Butter Brownies, page 409

Rum-Soaked Apricot Brownies, page 412

Tiramisu Brownies, page 414

Night and Day Brownie Bites, page 417

Slow Cooker Brownie Peanut Butter Pudding, page 420

Fudge Brownie Torte, page 422

Chocolate Chip Cookie Bars, page 424

Orange Chocolate Chip Bars, page 426

Our Favorite Peanut Butter Chocolate Bars, page 429

Houdini Bars, page 431

Turtle Bars, page 433

Butterscotch Bars, page 435

Aimee's Chess Cake, page 437

Lemon Gooey Butter Cake, page 439

Chocolate Walnut Gooey Butter Cake, page 441

Pineapple Coconut Bars, page 444

Applesauce Bars, page 446

Pumpkin Spice Bars, page 449

Chocolate Italian Cookies, page 451

Easy Chocolate Cookies, page 453

German Chocolate Thumbprint Cookies, page 455

Chocolate Espresso Biscotti with Walnuts, page 457

Laura's Fudgy Rum Balls, page 459

Butterscotch Walnut Brownie Drops, page 461

Spice Drop Cookies, page 463

Angel Food Macaroons, page 465

The
Cake
mix
Doctor®
RETURNS!

BY ANNE BYRN

PHOTOGRAPHY BY BEN FINK

WORKMAN PUBLISHING • NEW YORK

For my readers,

Cakes are meant to be shared.

Thank you for sharing them with me.

COVER CAKE:

If you'd like to bake the cover cake, see page 109.

Published simultaneously in Canada by Thomas Allen & Son Limited.

Library of Congress Cataloging-in-Publication Data
Byrn, Anne.
The cake mix doctor returns! / by Anne Byrn.
p. cm.
Includes index.
ISBN 978-0-7611-2961-5 (alk. paper) — ISBN 978-0-7611-5694-9 (hard cover)
1. Cake. I. Title.
TX771.B9735 2009
641.8'653—dc22 2009024901

Cover design: David Matt
Interior design: Lisa Hollander
Author photograph: Deborah Ory
Interior photographs: Ben Fink

Workman books are available at special discounts when purchased in bulk for premiums and sales promotions as well as for fund-raising or educational use.
Special editions or book excerpts can be created to specification.
For details, contact the Special Sales Director at the address below.

Workman Publishing Company, Inc.
225 Varick Street
New York, NY 10014-4381
www.workman.com

Printed in the United States of America
First printing August 2009
10 9 8 7 6 5 4 3 2 1

ACKNOWLEDGMENTS

I'd like to think of this book project as a luscious layer cake. I couldn't bake it without the right ingredients, labor, love, creativity, dedication, and wisdom. And the ingredients that make my books sweet and rich, and allow them to rise way up? Readers just like you, from all parts of this wonderful country and all parts of the globe. You have baked my cakes, shared them with your friends and families, and have e-mailed me feedback. Thank you. Thanks also to my friends in Nashville and beyond who have contributed recipes and fresh ideas.

My book couldn't be baked and frosted without the labor of Martha Bowden, Mindy Merrell, and Diane Hooper here in Nashville. You are dear to me. Many thanks go to Marybeth and Kathleen for typing and testing recipes during your summer before college. And in New York, thanks to Barbara Mateer for her expert copy editing and Carol White for her production editing.

What are cakes and books without love? Thanks once again to my husband John for his calm as I cooked up another project. And thanks to my children Kathleen, Litton, and John who have shared their mom, the Cake Mix Doctor, all these years with many avid bakers. I've told them to look on the bright side—not every family has all their favorite recipes in print!

Cakes need creativity, and books surely do. When I hit an idea-block and need titles, stories, cake mix packaging ideas, a speech, or just want to jazz up my television wardrobe I reach out to the creative minds of Katy Varney, Mindy Merrell, R.B. Quinn, Susan Puckett, my agent Nancy Crossman, friends Beth Meador and Judy Wright, sister Susan Anderson, and Jenny Mandel of Workman Publishing. Thank you. Many thanks, too, go to Lisa Hollander at Workman for her new design of this book and David Matt for the cover. And thanks to photographer Ben Fink and food stylist Susan Sugarman for making my cakes look great on camera. Plus, the many appearances I've made on QVC would not have been doable without Lucille Osborn because she makes the humblest cake look ready for the runway. And thanks to the many media escorts I've come to know and trust on book tour.

So many of you have been dedicated to my cake mix books. You've bought them all, you've given them as gifts, and you've hounded book store clerks when you couldn't find them on the shelves. I am fortunate to have so many cheerleaders, but I'll name just a few—Mary Jo, Elizabeth, Ginger and Susan, Joe, Cindy, Mary, Becky, Flowerree and Flowerree, and Janet. Thanks to Rusty Bowden for his enthusiasm and feedback. Thanks to the Regions Bank employees who always beg for cake. And hugs to the students at Harpeth Hall here in Nashville who have been eager recipients of cake brought to advisory by one of my girls.

What I have learned about baking and writing books is that with practice you do get better. That is why I say cooking and baking are things that improve as you age! They benefit from trial and error. I know this book and all my books would never have been possible without the wisdom of Peter Workman, who understood the cake mix idea from the moment he saw it. Thanks also go to Suzanne Rafer, my editor, from whom I have learned much. And thanks to Nancy Crossman, who is wise not only about books and publishing but about cooking and being a mom.

When you combine all of the above and bake, you have a book and a cake truly worth savoring. And you have friendships that last a lifetime. Thank you!

Anne Byrn

Contents

Sheet Cakes

PAGE 257

When you're baking for a crowd, sheet cakes come to the rescue—there's little prep, little assembly, but big flavor results. Just slice and serve. Dazzle friends with a Pink Lemonade Party Cake, Chocolate Bayou City Cake, Brown Sugar and Rhubarb Upside-Down Cake, or the Birthday Cake for a Crowd.

Cupcakes and Muffins

PAGE 343

Longtime favorites of kids (and kids at heart), these miniature cakes pack a lot of flavor into their small size. Bake up Peanut Butter Cookie Dough Cupcakes, Strawberry Cheesecake Cupcakes, or Apple Spice Muffins. And if you're feeling nostalgic, there's even a recipe for Whoopie Pies.

Brownies, Bars, and Cookies

PAGE 389

Whether they're for a school, church, or Girl Scout troop fundraiser, expect these bake sale favorites to fly off the table. Gooey Pecan Pie Brownies, Angel Food Macaroons, Pineapple Coconut Bars, and German Chocolate Thumbprint Cookies are just a few favorites.

Frostings

PAGE 467

Homemade frostings, icings, and glazes are the heart and soul of this book. Classic Buttercream Frosting, rich Orange Cream Cheese Frosting, delicious Chocolate Pan Frosting, Caramel Glaze—these are easy, no-fail recipes that will turn a good cake into a great cake.

Conversion Tables

PAGE 490

Index

PAGE 491

INTRODUCTION

I'm Back . . . So Let's Bake!

My mom might have fried up chicken, stocked our freezer with soups, breads, and casseroles, carved watermelons into fruit baskets, and baked birthday cakes in the blink of an eye, but she admitted she couldn't do everything. The cakes, she later revealed, were a lot easier to assemble if they began with a mix. Then she'd slather them with her signature from-scratch, easy Chocolate Pan Frosting!

Her casual approach would transform how my on-the-go family made birthday cakes, and later it gave me the idea to write a newspaper story about doctoring up a box of cake mix to make it taste better than if you just followed the package directions. I received so much feedback from that one story that I decided to take my mom's approach to another level. The result was *The Cake Mix Doctor*, a book that gave busy cooks everywhere hundreds of yummy baking solutions.

That was ten years ago. Since the first book, I've gone on to write four more cookbooks—*Chocolate from the Cake Mix Doctor, The Dinner Doctor, Cupcakes! from the Cake Mix Doctor*, and the *What Can I Bring? Cookbook.* And as a result, a wonderful cooking community has formed. Through the books, my website (www.cakemixdoctor.com), and my personal appearances, people have connected with each other in and out of the kitchen. Their recipes have been shared endeavors via my website's online community board. Whether it involves shipping a cake to a son in the military, staging a bake sale at school, baking for the local soup kitchen, or baking a daughter's wedding cake, these cooks have embraced one another.

I'm really overwhelmed that our family's simple approach has turned into a way of baking cakes for so many. It's staggering and joyous at the same time to think that millions of you have celebrated birthdays and anniversaries with cakes you've discovered in my books, and have taught your children and grandchildren how to cook using my recipes. You have baked these cakes for aging parents. You have baked them to celebrate the birth of a baby.

Here in Nashville, I have baked right along with you, and this new book is the result. I've answered many of your requests with the recipes on these pages, specifically a wedding cake, and your desire for a photo, once again, for every recipe.

Over the years, my recipes have evolved, the changes indicative of how we bake today. For example, these days I add half as much cream cheese to a frosting as I used to, not only to save calories and fat but also to make the cake taste lighter. I might omit the added sugar in a recipe because the glaze makes the final cake sweet enough. Or I might reduce the oil or replace some of it with applesauce. You will see some golden-oldie recipes in this book, such as the Darn Good Chocolate Cake and my sister Susan's lemon cake, but they have been lightened or altered slightly because this is the way I bake them today.

And because my first recipes were road tested in cities across the country as I have traveled on book tours, I have learned new and better methods for prepping, baking, frosting, and presenting the finished cakes. Many of you have suggested these new methods as well as new ingredients to try, and I share all of these in the pages that follow. You'll find this book fresh with new ideas, but loyal to the original tried-and-true *Cake Mix Doctor* concepts.

For some things don't change. Now more than ever, with the stresses and demands of the outside world, the home—and specifically the kitchen—is a refuge. Baking and sharing good food with those we love strengthens and renews us.

When we preheat the oven and grease and flour the pan, we anticipate something hot, fragrant, moist, and memorable. Our family and work lives may change, but baking is always a constant. Year after year, decade after decade, we look forward to cakes—new and old recipes—to bake and share with others.

Thank you for baking my cakes, for doctoring them up, and for requesting recipes I wasn't aware existed so that I might go looking for them. You have kept me happily curious and in the kitchen.

Bring on the milk!

Anne Byrn
Nashville, Tennessee

◆◆◆◆◆

Take a Cake Break

HOW TO USE THIS BOOK

◆◆◆◆◆◆◆

In the ten years since the first *Cake Mix Doctor* was published I've learned a lot. I've taught cooking classes and learned about ingredients in other parts of the country. I've figured out the best ways to present cakes for the camera. And I've learned which recipes from the first book you liked the best, and how *you* doctored my recipes, and kept track by writing notes in the margins of the book. Well, I've written notes, too, so it seemed the right time for a follow-up.

And as much as we all enjoy baking cakes that begin with a cake mix, just as we did ten years ago, times have changed a bit since then. Dessert portions have gotten smaller, which is a good thing. (I've got plenty of smaller cakes in this book, as well as strategies for freezing leftovers for another meal—perfect for smaller families and for providing you with last-minute desserts.)

People expect more than a plain cake, so the generic chocolate layer cake of a decade ago has given way to what might be called the Starbucks cake—a triple-decker mocha or chocolate-cinnamon latte. And what used to be just cream cheese frosting now contains all kinds of fold-ins, from berries to lemon zest. Fresh cherries have replaced maraschinos. Yesterday's caramel is now *dulce de leche*. But I still love the plain and simple, and hope I've struck a balance in this collection between the razzle-dazzle recipes and simple ones like chocolate on chocolate. These are to cake what your favorite jeans and a plain white T-shirt are to your wardrobe—timeless and comfortable.

I stick by my original philosophy that you can fool everyone by doctoring up a cake mix but you must make your own frosting. Yes, we're busier than ever. So it's good to know that you don't need to bake a cake from scratch for it to be good. But canned frostings? You can easily make better frostings in your own kitchen, and I will show you how.

Join me as I take you through a new and improved baking process. Preheat your ovens. As my son says, "The Cake Mix Doctor Returns!"

The Older We Get . . .

Believe it or not, baking improves as we age. As we taste new foods, travel, try a new pan, weigh tried-and-true ingredients against newer options, take cooking classes, and sample new recipes, we bake better. We cook better. With mixing bowl in hand, practice does make perfect. Or to paraphrase the wonderful Julia Child, you can learn something from everybody you meet. If you take this attitude, you'll never grow old, you'll just be a better baker!

Experienced cooks know a cake is done because they smell the aroma. They can tell a frosting is ready to be spread onto a cake just by looking at how it clings to the wooden spoon. They can recognize the better cocoa, unsalted butter, the best vanilla. No wonder our grandmothers were such skilled bakers. They just had more experience.

Choosing a Cake Mix

Why are cake mixes so popular? People are comfortable with them, more comfortable than they are measuring flour and other dry ingredients into a bowl. There are just too many variables in a cake made from scratch—little land mines waiting to be detonated. You need to use the right type of flour, sift in the leavening, measure ingredients properly, let the eggs come to room temperature, and on and on. It can be a hassle even for the more accomplished cook. Add a busy schedule or an unexpected phone call or a missing ingredient, and that cake is toast. Cake mixes are successful largely because the variables are removed. They bake, they rise, they turn out of the pan. You just need to make the results interesting, but that's where I come in.

The shortcomings of cake mixes are their use of artificial coloring and flavoring. Let's face it, reading the ingredient list is a little like being back in chemistry lab. I have always said a perfect mix would have all-natural ingredients and still turn out moist and light the way current cake mix cakes do. At this writing, I am working on such a mix. Until then, let's look at what's on the shelf and select the right cake mix for the recipe.

Plain Cake Mix or Cake Mix with Pudding?

The question I have heard the most often through the years has been "Which brand is plain cake mix and which brand has pudding in it?" Duncan Hines makes plain cake mixes, even though the packages are labeled "moist deluxe." There are some store brands that are also plain cake mix. Betty Crocker and Pillsbury, on the other hand, put pudding in their cake mixes. If you are in doubt as to just what's in the box, call the 800 number on the cake mix package and ask.

I find plain cake mix cakes tend to rise higher in the pan. That said, I do like the moist consistency and rich flavor that result from a chocolate cake mix with pudding. So, many times it's the recipe that dictates the particular type of cake mix I use. And some recipes in this book are very specific in calling for a plain butter recipe golden cake mix—that is cake mix *without* pudding.

Unfortunately, the availability of cake mixes differs across the United States, and often you just have to bake with what you find on the store shelf. You can always add instant pudding mix to a plain cake mix, but you should not add more pudding if the cake mix you are using already has pudding in it.

A drawback to pudding in a cake mix is that it may cause the cake to shrink as it cools. This is especially true when the recipe calls for additional moist ingredients, such as applesauce, sour cream, or buttermilk. But, you can always cover a shrunken cake with frosting! Martha Bowden, who tests recipes for me, has come up with a brilliant idea for adding instant pudding mix; she uses just a few tablespoons, about half a package, saving the remaining pudding for the next cake. She finds that this is not only economical, it also makes a moist cake that does not shrink. One benefit of having pudding in the mix that is often overlooked is that it helps suspend chocolate chips in the batter, so that they do not sink to the bottom of the pan. About three tablespoons of instant pudding mix will do the trick if the recipe calls for this.

Brands, Flavors, and All That Jazz

Okay, how can I be honest without stepping on any toes? The flavor and quality of cake mixes do vary from brand to brand. And generally you get what you pay for. So, I am all for trying new mixes and baking them following the instructions on the package; if you like the look and flavor, then decide if this is the cake mix for you. And if you watch the store specials, your favorite cake mix might go on sale, which means that you can stock up with a half-dozen boxes to place in your pantry where they will keep for nearly a year. That was a long-winded answer to another frequently asked question: How long do cake mixes last? No longer than one year.

As for the flavor, yellow (or vanilla), white, and chocolate cake mixes have been the most popular through the years. Most of the recipes in this book are based on these mixes. I may call for a white mix when the white color is essential, but I prefer the flavor of a yellow mix. Lately I am a bit miffed at how much food coloring is going into the yellow mixes. What are labeled butter recipe mixes are not as brightly colored as the yellow cake mixes, and I find these create more natural looking and tasting cakes.

The Cake Baker's Basic Pantry

Here's a list of the ingredients I turn to again and again for baking. Keep them on hand and baking will be a lot easier when you are busy.

Cake mixes: My favorite flavors of cake mix to keep in the pantry are a couple packages of yellow, a couple of golden butter recipe, a couple of deep chocolate (devil's food), a couple of German chocolate, and a couple of spice. And I love to work with a good brownie mix, as well as a gingerbread mix.

Flour: All-purpose flour is always in my pantry. I shake some into a cake pan after misting it with vegetable oil spray or greasing it with solid vegetable shortening. This way of preparing the pan prevents the cake from sticking. Often I add all-purpose flour to a batter to make the batter more sturdy. In the case of the new version of the More Amazing German Chocolate Cake (see page 224), I added a third of a cup of flour to the recipe because I found the cake was sinking as it cooled and needed more structure. Living in the South, I tend to buy White Lily flour, but any all-purpose flour will do the job. Once opened, place the flour bag in a large resealable plastic bag to keep it fresh.

Sugar: Since sugar is an ingredient in cake mixes, I don't add it to many of my recipes. If I do, it is because it will improve the

Easiest Tricks in the Book

A little trial and error (and learning from your suggestions) has produced this list of baking essentials. What I know now that I didn't know then . . .

1. Most of my cakes call for vegetable oil. But if they call for butter, use unsalted butter in the cake and lightly salted butter in the frosting.

2. For everyday recipes, Nestlé semisweet chocolate chips are great. Upgrade to Ghirardelli bittersweet or other premium chips if you are making a ganache frosting for a special occasion.

3. If you don't grease the side of layer pans, you'll have a slightly taller cake.

4. Paint Bundts and decorative pans with vegetable shortening (Crisco), then dust them with flour and your cakes will not stick to the pan.

5. The refrigerator is your friend. Cool layers there in a hurry. Let a cake frosted with cream cheese frosting set before wrapping it for storage or travel.

6. You can easily reduce the oil in a fruit-based cake by just upping the fruit a bit and decreasing the oil by the same amount.

7. Instead of an 8-ounce package of cream cheese and a stick of butter, use half the cream cheese to reduce fat and heaviness.

8. Use half a package of instant pudding mix to prevent cakes from shrinking as they cool.

9. Even if the package directions call for it, you can use some other liquid instead of water—milk, buttermilk, orange juice, or brewed coffee (especially in brownies).

10. If the layer, Bundt, or sheet cake recipe calls for chocolate chips and you're worried that they might sink to the bottom as the cake bakes, use miniature chips.

11. Buttermilk, plain yogurt, and sour cream are amazingly interchangeable in recipes. If the recipe calls for one of these, you can easily use another one or a little bit of two to make up for what's in the recipe. When substituting buttermilk for milk or water, use slightly more buttermilk, as it tends to be thick.

12. Keep evaporated milk in your pantry. You can substitute it for heavy cream in recipes where the cream is either baked in the batter or where it is intensely flavored with coffee, which will take away the "canned" taste.

13. Keep chopped nuts and grated citrus zest in your freezer. This way they are at your fingertips when you need them.

14. You can turn a yellow cake mix into a spice mix by adding one teaspoon of cinnamon, a half teaspoon of allspice, and a quarter teaspoon of nutmeg.

15. Don't throw away a cake that falls, cracks, or overbakes. Crumble it into wine glasses, drizzle Kahlúa or rum over it, and add a scoop of vanilla ice cream.

flavor and texture of the cake. However, brown sugar and confectioners' sugar are key ingredients in my frostings. To measure brown sugar, lightly press it into a cup measure with a spoon. Only sift confectioners' sugar if the recipe calls for it. If stored in

How to Have Your Cake and Be Healthy, Too

I'm often asked how it is that my career revolves around cake baking and yet I am not fat. I guess I have learned how to live with my work—enjoy it but don't let it get the best of me. Honestly, I've never fancied doing without the foods I love, like chocolate cake, because whenever I've tried, I just think more about them. That does not mean I've never dieted, because I often did in my teens, twenties, and not too long ago, after returning from Italy ten pounds heavier. But when faced with the choice of dieting or not to stay trim, I would rather eat sensibly and moderately and get exercise day-to-day so I can have my chocolate cake.

There should be a place in our lives for cake, for goodness sake. Cake plays a part in celebrations, birthdays, anniversaries, weddings, big events. It's a joyous food and too much fun to do without. So what I do is have one reasonable slice, not two. If I have leftover cake in the house, I either give it to friends to take home with them, send it to the office with my husband, or freeze it for future meals. If a chocolate cake sits on my kitchen counter, I will carve off a slice two or three times a day, so my solution is to simply get it out of my sight—which is really hard during recipe testing for a new book. During times like these I just plan on eating more cake than usual, getting more exercise than usual—running—and cutting back on other carbs like bread and potatoes because I'm eating more cake.

Through the years I have come up with ways to slim down my cakes without sacrificing flavor. I buy reduced-fat sour cream and reduced-fat cream cheese almost all the time. The exception is when making cream cheese frostings, where whole-fat cream cheese is less watery and makes a nicer and creamier frosting. I cut back on oil and up the liquid in a cake whenever possible. Say a cake recipe calls for one cup of oil and a half cup of milk. I would change that recipe right off the bat to a half cup of oil and one cup of skim milk. I often add pumpkin and mashed bananas and applesauce to cakes. And when our family needs a lighter dessert, I'll bake a Bundt cake and simply dust it with confectioners' sugar instead of frosting it.

These little changes allow me to bake, eat, and enjoy cake. I think it's important that my children see me savoring dessert and having a healthy relationship with it, too.

a tightly closed bag, confectioners' sugar will not lump up and need sifting. Moisture makes brown sugar hard and confectioners' sugar lumpy, so close the bags tightly.

Eggs: To keep things simple I use only large eggs. And to make things even simpler I add these eggs straight from the refrigerator. The beauty of my recipes is that eggs do not need to be at room temperature as they must be when making cakes from scratch. Egg substitutes work well in all my recipes where eggs are needed. Consult the egg substitute package for how much to use for each egg called for in the recipe.

Butter: Lightly salted butter is still my favorite choice for frostings because that bit of salt plays nicely with the sugar and creates a frosting that seems less sweet. However, if I am using butter in a cake recipe, I now prefer unsalted. And I'll tell you why. Mostly I suggest adding butter to cake mixes when making bars, brownies, and cookies. When I used salted butter, they started tasting too salty to me. When I made them with unsalted butter, they were better, with more of a from-scratch taste. I still veto margarine. Sorry, just don't like the flavor. It's either butter or vegetable oil for me.

Vegetable oil: An indispensable ingredient in my recipes, vegetable oil makes a cake moist and tender. It partners well with chocolate, letting the flavor come through and making the cake seem more chocolaty. I prefer light oils, such as canola or soybean.

Milk: In my first book I was adamant about using whole milk in frostings and many cake recipes because of the added richness. But in reality you are not going to run out and buy milk specifically for a recipe, and I know that. You want to use the milk that's in the refrigerator! So, now if a recipe calls for milk almost 99 percent of time I just say milk. The only exception is in caramel frosting, which really is better if you make it with whole milk. Feel free to add the milk cold, straight from the fridge.

Chocolate: I have a kitchen drawer dedicated to chocolate—chips, chocolate bars, and cocoa powder. They all have a place in my recipes. And having them on hand makes me a happier and more creative cook. For chocolate chips, I prefer regular-size chips for frostings, bars, and cookies. I like miniature chips for folding into layer and Bundt cakes because they don't sink to the bottom when baking. Bar chocolate—be it bittersweet, semisweet, white, or German's—is handy to chop and fold into batters, turn into a frosting, or scrape into curls or shavings to decorate the top of a cake. And cocoa powder adds a little depth to an already chocolate cake batter or forms the foundation for a decadent frosting. I buy both regular and Dutch-process cocoas. The former is more ruddy brown in color and has that mild cocoa flavor most people are accustomed to whereas Dutch process has a deeper flavor and a darker color. Add a little Dutch-process cocoa and it will turn some frostings a grayish brown. Add a lot and it will make them really dark brown. Experiment with each and suit yourself. Yum!

Extracts: Vanilla, almond, lemon, orange, and peppermint are bottled as pure extracts. Maple, coconut, and rum come in the form of synthesized flavorings. I love to add all of these to cakes and frostings. I use so much vanilla that I buy it in a large bottle at the warehouse club store because it's much cheaper that way. And I keep my little bottles of extracts and flavorings in a metal tin in the baking drawer and replenish them as they run dry. Just a half teaspoon of any of these can transform a cake. Peppermint, citrus, and almond extracts tend to be the strongest in flavor.

Nuts: My nut cabinet is my freezer door where I have sacks of pecan halves, walnuts, and whole and sliced almonds ready for baking. The freezer can keep nuts fresh for six months or more. How long they last really depends on how fresh the nuts were in the first place, how they are packaged, and how many times you open your freezer. Take nuts out of thin plastic bags and store them in heavier resealable plastic bags. Nuts can be chopped and added right to the batter, but nuts will always have more flavor if you toast them first in a 350°F oven until deep brown and fragrant. For brownies, I scatter walnuts or pecans on top of the batter before baking. For Bundt cakes I might place the chopped nuts in the bottom of the pan and pour the batter on top. As the cake bakes, the nuts toast on the bottom, and when the cake is turned out of the pan, the nuts form a crisp and attractive crust on top. Since I don't use macadamia nuts too often, I buy them just when I plan to make a particular recipe.

Spices: My spice drawer is well stocked for cooking dinner, but my baking needs are simpler. Ground cinnamon, nutmeg, and ginger are my favorite baking spices. Buy spices in small amounts and replenish them as needed for they lose their pungency over time.

The Cake Baker's Expanded Pantry

Cream cheese: A necessary add-in for sturdy pound cakes and cupcakes, cream cheese makes many cake batters richer and just better! When making cakes, I use reduced-fat cream cheese with no regrets. I don't buy fat-free, and I prefer regular cream cheese for frostings. That's because the reduced-fat kind has more moisture and can make the frosting wetter, a disadvantage if you add strawberries to it or are frosting a cake to be served in the summertime in Atlanta humidity.

Make sure cream cheese has had time to come to room temperature so it will blend evenly and not lump up in your cake or frosting. If in doubt, place it in the microwave for ten to thirty seconds. Or just dump it in the mixing bowl by itself and beat it until it softens and is creamy. While cream cheese can be frozen, it gets watery when thawed, so I only buy what I need and store it in the fridge.

Evaporated milk and heavy cream: Keep a can or two of evaporated milk on the pantry shelf. Buy heavy cream when you need it and use it by the date on the carton. In a pinch you can substitute evaporated milk for heavy cream, especially in frostings and fillings.

Buttermilk, sour cream, and yogurt: These are some of my favorite add-ins. They contribute moisture, richness, and character to a cake. Shake buttermilk well before pouring it. I use buttermilk for making pancakes and banana bread, but if you don't think your family will use up a quart of it, buy buttermilk powder instead and store it in your refrigerator.

Sour cream is a mainstay at our house, and I use full-fat sour cream in rich fillings and frostings and the reduced-fat kind in cake batters. Plain nonfat yogurt is a great substitute wherever sour cream is called for, and it is a lot lower in fat and calories. Flavored yogurts are also fun to bake with—add them to recipes instead of some of the oil and liquid, using lemon yogurt in lemon cakes, coffee in chocolate, and so on—pairing flavors that are compatible.

Coconut: Coconut has moved down on my pantry list this go-round. In the South we can readily find the frozen unsweetened coconut that is so delicious in coconut cake and coconut cream pie. But this ingredient is hard to find outside the South, something I learned after the publication of the first book. Now I simply call for sweetened flaked coconut, found in the baking aisle most everywhere. If you can find unsweetened flaked coconut at the supermarket, buy it because the flavor is fresher. And here's a trick passed along to me from a reader: Pulse the flaked coconut in a food processor until it is half the size and it will resemble freshly grated coconut, making a nice garnish for the top of a cake.

Lemons and oranges, orange juice: Keep citrus fruit in the drawer of your refrigerator for cooking and baking. Rinse and dry them before removing the zest with a Microplane grater. Any leftover zest can be placed in a small plastic bag and frozen. Cut the fruit in half and squeeze out the juice. You will get about a teaspoon of zest and from two to three tablespoons of juice per medium-size lemon. Oranges yield more. A carton of orange juice is handy to have on hand to add to cake batters instead of water. Or add orange juice to butter and confectioners' sugar for a quick buttercream frosting.

Peanut butter: Creamy or chunky, I love peanut butter as a doctoring ingredient. Add it to cake batters or to frostings.

Canned fruits: Canned apricots, pineapple, applesauce, mandarin oranges, peaches, and pears are all nice to have on hand to use in cake recipes. You can drain, chop, and add the fruit to the cake batter or puree apricots and pears first.

Pumpkin: Plain and simple, canned pumpkin is a great add-in; you'll find it in many of my recipes. It is low in fat and high in fiber and makes a moist cake.

Butterscotch chips, white chocolate chips, toffee bits: Keep these in a baking drawer for folding into cupcake batters, topping brownies before baking, or decorating cakes.

Coffee: Leftover brewed coffee is delicious as a substitute for water in brownie recipes. Use instant coffee granules or espresso powder in batters and in frostings. Store the coffee powder on the pantry shelf.

The Cake Baker's Equipment Essentials

Bowls: Whether you use stainless steel, ceramic, glass, or plastic bowls really depends on what you have on hand. All work. A variety of sizes is nice: Two large, a medium-size, and a few small bowls will be useful. But should you be looking to buy new bowls, I have my preferences. Choose stainless steel bowls that nest inside each other for ease of storage. These bowls are lighter in weight than glass or ceramic ones, which makes pouring batter into cake pans a lot easier. And these bowls go right into the dishwasher. The benefit of a glass bowl is that it can be placed in a microwave oven, convenient when a recipe calls for melted butter or chocolate or when the cream cheese is still cold and needs to be briefly zapped and softened.

Pans: If you've read my books or heard me quoted you know I am adamant about using shiny bakeware. Dark pans cause the edges of cakes to darken. They cause those edges to bake more quickly and thus the cake doesn't cook evenly. Shiny baking pans reflect heat, resulting in even baking. There are several good brands out there made from either aluminum or aluminized steel. Invest in good pans because they'll last you a lifetime. I am still baking strong with my 9-inch rounds, sheet pans, and Bundts.

What to Give the Cake Baker

About to buy a gift for a friend who loves to bake? Here are a few gifts all bakers would love to open.

A new cake saver. Pick out a durable one with a handle and a locking lid. Tie a bow on the handle and place a freshly baked cake inside.

A cake stand. Like shoes, you can't have too many. Your first cake stand needs to be stainless steel or glass. These are the most durable and any cake looks great on them. Then move into ceramics in basic colors or brights—one of my favorites is a pink scalloped stand, on which I place cupcakes or a chocolate layer cake. Search flea markets for antique glass stands. Also fun are stackable stands for a multitiered look when the baker entertains.

Bowls. Bakers always love a new bowl—a large stainless steel or a retro glass one. Maybe it's a set of nesting bowls, which are perfect for small kitchens. Maybe it's a bright orange ceramic bowl to be used for mixing and also holding goodies on Halloween.

Metal icing knives. Again, the more the merrier. I love the short chubby ones for icing cupcakes. And the long professional ones frost an attractive cake.

Baking supplies. No one can pass up pretty cupcake liners, fun sugar sprinkles, sanding sugars in glorious colors, or a fine bottle of vanilla extract. Chocolate, espresso powder, good cinnamon—the list could go on and on. Package these in a reusable plastic storage bin or an antique basket.

You will need three 9-inch pans, a 12-cup Bundt, possibly a 10-inch tube pan for pound cakes, a 13 by 9–inch metal baking pan, and a 9- or 10-inch springform pan for cheesecakes, if you like. The rectangular springform is a wonderful new pan in which you can bake sheet cakes, then release the sides for easy frosting. Serve the cake right on the base of the pan. If possible, buy rectangular pans that have snap-on plastic lids because these come in so handy for toting. You'll also want to have two cupcake or muffin pans, each with twelve wells, and two baking sheets.

Mixer: Any electric mixer you have will work with my recipes. I prefer an electric hand mixer for cake batters because you are not as likely to overbeat the batter. Overbeating batters that are based on cake mix can cause tunneling and tough cakes. If you use a stand mixer for cake batters be sure to beat them on low speed and watch the clock so you don't overbeat. Sturdy

These Pans Are a-Changin'

If you want to bake a layer cake using a recipe for . . .

A BUNDT OR TUBE CAKE: Choose a lighter-weight cake made with 3 eggs and that has few added ingredients. Bake the layers for 28 to 32 minutes at 350°F. Add a compatible frosting. Depending upon how full you fill the pans, a Bundt cake recipe can be used for a two- or three-layer cake.

CUPCAKES OR MUFFINS: Choose lighter-weight cupcakes or muffins made with 3 eggs and that have few added ingredients. Bake the layers for 28 to 32 minutes at 350°F. Omit any fillings.

A SHEET CAKE: Make sure you pick a sheet cake that doesn't have a lot of add-ins, like chocolate chips; these will weigh down a layer cake and cause it to sink. You may need more frosting than the recipe makes.

If you want to bake a Bundt or tube pan cake using a recipe for . . .

LAYERS: Choose a sturdy cake containing 3 or 4 eggs. The cake will be baked in 45 to 55 minutes at 350°F. You can use a recipe for either a two- or a three-layer cake.

CUPCAKES OR MUFFINS: Look for a moist recipe with plenty of oil or liquid and that contains 3 to 4 eggs. The cake will be baked in 20 to 25 minutes at 350°F. A recipe that makes 18 to 24 cupcakes will make one Bundt cake.

A SHEET CAKE: Look for a moist recipe with plenty of oil or liquid and that contains 3 to 4 eggs. The cake will be baked in 50 to 60 minutes at 350°F.

If you want to bake cupcakes or muffins using a recipe for . . .

A BUNDT OR TUBE CAKE: This will result in a good conversion. Bake the cupcakes or muffins for 20 to 24 minutes at 350°F. Add your favorite frosting.

LAYERS: If the cake batter is a light one, without cream cheese or sour cream, or does not contain nuts, chocolate chips, or fruit, the baking time will be only about 20 minutes at 350°F. You may have leftover frosting.

A SHEET CAKE: This also makes a good conversion. Bake the cupcakes or muffins for 20 to 25 minutes at 350°F. They will need the same amount of frosting.

(Converting the recipes in this book will yield 18 to 22 cupcakes or muffins.)

If you want to bake a sheet cake using a recipe for . . .

A BUNDT OR TUBE CAKE: Look for a cake that isn't heavy with sour cream, oil, or chocolate chips—these tend to sink in the center. Bake the cake for about 40 minutes at 350°F. You may need to increase the amount of frosting if the Bundt cake has a light glaze. Or, you can drizzle that light glaze over the sheet cake or even just dust it with confectioners' sugar.

LAYERS: Use a 3-egg cake for a sheet cake; even a 2-egg cake will work well. The cake will be baked in 35 to 45 minutes at 350°F. You may have about a cup of frosting left over.

CUPCAKES OR MUFFINS: Use a less heavy recipe, and scatter the add-ins or topping over the top before baking. You can also spread the add-ins or topping in the bottom of the pan before pouring in the batter to create an upside-down cake. Bake the cake 35 to 45 minutes at 350°F.

restaurant-style stand mixers are best for frostings and for whipping cream.

Racks: Just as you invest in nice pans, you should also choose stainless steel racks that will not rust. I like two sizes of racks—one large enough for two cake layers to cool on it and a smaller one for flipping the layers. If you are baking a 12-inch round layer cake (see my Wedding Cake on page 149), you'll need a 19 by 13–inch rack.

Spoons and spatulas: My brownie recipes can be stirred together with a wooden spoon. Make sure you've got an assortment of long-handled wooden spoons for stirring batters and cooked frostings. Rubber spatulas are essential for scraping down the side of a mixing bowl and for scraping the last bit of batter or frosting out of the bowl. Heat resistant silicone spatulas are handy for blending ingredients on the stove. Set aside a few small rubber spatulas and a few larger ones, including cupped spoonlike spatulas for thick batters.

Metal icing spatulas are incredibly handy, not only for frosting cakes but for lifting cakes out of a pan. Offset spatulas have a bend in them and allow you to frost a sheet cake while it's still in the pan. And small metal spatulas are perfect for frosting cupcakes.

Other Handy Things

◆ A vegetable oil mister makes prepping pans for baking an easy task. I like to use a nonaerosol sprayer into which I pour my own vegetable oil. You pump the container twelve to fifteen times to build up pressure and then spray. You can also buy the oil in nonaerosol containers in the supermarket, and they are handy as well. I do not like vegetable oil sprays with propellants because they make a dark and heavy crust on the cake that looks dreadful when sliced.

◆ A stainless steel shaker filled with flour makes the job of dusting pans a lot simpler. The same shakers filled with confectioners' sugar are handy for dusting the top of a baked cake. Be sure to mark which shaker contains flour and which sugar—I have accidentally dusted a cake with flour!

◆ I love a serrated knife for slicing layers in half horizontally to make more layers.

◆ A wooden skewer is useful for poking holes in a cake so a glaze can seep down into it.

◆ Filling a plastic squirt bottle with glaze makes it easy to drizzle the glaze onto Bundt cakes and cookies.

◆ Don't forget a Microplane grater for zesting citrus.

◆ A pastry bag is nice but not essential for decorating cakes. In a pinch, create your own pastry bag by placing the frosting in a gallon-size resealable plastic bag and snipping off one corner.

◆ A sharp vegetable peeler makes nice chocolate curls if you drag it across the surface of a room-temperature bar of chocolate.

The Cake Baker's Storage

You've undoubtedly got a drawer dedicated to aluminum foil, plastic wrap, and waxed or parchment paper. They all have a place in cake storage. Aluminum foil is the best freezer wrap, especially heavy-duty foil. But when wrapping cakes containing acidic ingredients, such as lemon, wrap the cake first in waxed paper or plastic and then in foil. Foil covers cake pans well, too, for storing on the counter or in the refrigerator. Plastic wrap is an all-purpose covering good for an unfrosted Bundt cake or slices of cake laid out on a platter. It works best in cool weather, when the frosting on a cake is not sticky. And waxed paper is great to lay on top of a cake frosted with cream cheese frosting that needs to be refrigerated in order for the frosting to set up for longer storage. I use waxed paper or parchment paper to line plastic storage containers before filling them with bars and cookies. You can use waxed paper or parchment paper to line baking pans before pouring in the batter. Lightly mist the pan first so the paper will stick to it.

After baking pans, cake savers are one of the great essentials when you are doing a lot of home baking. If you've got to store or transport a cake, you cannot beat a plastic plate with a snap-on lid for doing the job well. These are sold in all sorts of designs at all price points. My advice is to invest in a good one with a handle and to write your name on the bottom of it. Buy several other less expensive versions if you bake and tote a lot of cake. Just make sure the lid fits snugly before you pick up the cake. The beauty of a cake saver is not only in the ease of transport but in that once you arrive at your destination you can open the lid and the cake can be beautifully presented on the plastic base. If the gathering is a little dressy, I'll tape a paper doily to the base, then place the cake on top. You can store refrigerator cakes in these plastic containers, and you can freeze cakes in them, too, should your freezer be large enough.

In a pinch you can still cover a cake if you don't have a cake saver. Use a large soup pot, placing it upside-down over the cake on a plate. Glass cake domes are nice because they will fit over any size plate or cake stand. And a cake on a plate under the dome looks pretty on the kitchen counter.

Let's Bake!

The recipes in this book were tested in Thermador and General Electric ovens. Most of the recipes were baked at 350°F, but a good number were baked at 325°F. I have come to like the lower temperature when baking some brownies and chocolate cakes. For me arriving at the lower temperature was a result of trial and error. How do you know what is the best temperature for baking in your oven and for your cake?

As ovens age they have a tendency to bake hotter. You may be sensing this to be the case if the cookies you baked at 350°F for as long as you can remember are now burning before their baking time is supposed to be up. One appliance repairman actually told me the best way to determine if your oven is baking hot is to make a batch of chocolate chip cookies and to bake them at 350°F. If they are burned in ten minutes time, they are baking higher than 350°F, more like 375° to 400°F. Repairmen have fancy thermometers that can test the true temperature of your oven and the time it takes to preheat. If you've just moved into a new house, or if your oven seems to be baking funny, paying for this one-time service is well worth it. A less expensive method is to place an oven thermometer in the back of the oven and then set the oven to 350°F. If the thermometer doesn't register this temperature within 10 to 15 minutes, your oven thermostat might be incorrect. Learning to

10 Secrets for Sensational Cakes

I know it's tempting to just race through all this introductory advice and get to the recipes. But honestly, your cakes, whether they're from a box or from scratch, will turn out more successfully if you follow these tips.

1. Read through the recipe before you bake. Errors occur because you skip an ingredient, measure incorrectly, don't have the right size pan, or set the oven at the wrong temperature. Pan sizes are often marked on the bottom.

2. Place the oven rack in the center for good heat distribution and even browning.

3. Preheat your oven for ten to fifteen minutes before baking.

4. Check your oven temperature routinely with an oven thermometer. Call an appliance repairman to have the temperature tested if you feel the oven runs hot or cold. Cakes that are not done by the maximum time might be baking at too low a temperature, and cakes that brown too quickly or are done too quickly might be baking in too hot an oven.

5. Measure correctly. Measure dry ingredients, such as sugar, cocoa, flour, and so on, in measuring cups for dry ingredients. Spoon soft ingredients like flour and confectioners' sugar into measuring cups, then sweep the top level with a knife. Brown sugar should be packed lightly into a measuring cup, then leveled. Liquids should be measured in pourable measuring cups where you can read the measure at eye level.

6. Use an electric mixer for beating cake batters. A hand-held mixer is perfect, as you don't need to beat the batter for long. When using a stand mixer make sure you beat at a low to medium-low speed for only as long as the recipe suggests. A wooden spoon is fine for mixing brownies, bars, and cookies, stirring between forty and fifty strokes until the batter is smooth.

7. Prep cake pans with vegetable oil or shortening, then dust them with flour to make cakes easier to remove. Pour the batter into the pan, smoothing the top with a rubber spatula.

8. Use your senses when testing a cake for

live with an oven that is not calibrated perfectly has become a way of life for many. I remember an oven I once had in an apartment in Atlanta. It was more like a blazing pizza oven! I'd just lower the temperature no matter what the recipe so the food wouldn't incinerate.

Where the rack is positioned in the oven affects how your cake bakes. My recipes suggest it be in the centermost position—and

doneness. Light-colored cakes are done when they are golden brown, begin to pull away from the side of the pan, and spring back when touched lightly in the center. Chocolate cakes are done when they smell done, begin to pull away from the side of the pan, and spring back when touched lightly in the center.

9. Let the cake cool in the pan set on a rack before turning the cake out. Layers need five to ten minutes, Bundts and pound cakes require about fifteen minutes, and cupcakes can be removed as soon as they are cool enough to handle, after three to four minutes. Run a knife around the edge of a cake to loosen it. Give the pan a gentle shake to help loosen the cake. Then, invert Bundts onto a rack to cool. Invert cake layers and pound cakes from a tube pan twice so they cool right side up.

10. As a rule, spoon glaze over warm cake if you want it to soak into and flavor the cake. Poke holes in the cake with a wooden skewer or even a fork before slowly spooning on the glaze. Spoon glaze over cooled cakes if you want the glaze to show and have decorative drips.

I know with some oven models it seems one rack is slightly above center and one is slightly lower than center. Do the best you can to find the middle. For recipes with three layers you may need to use two racks—no problem if you have two ovens. If not, you'll need to place two cake pans on the center rack and one in the center of the top rack. Just make sure the pans are far enough apart that air can circulate. The cake on the top rack will brown and bake more quickly than those in the center, so rotate the layers if needed so that they bake evenly. And always when baking, if the cake browns on top before it has cooked through, lightly tent the top with aluminum foil to shield it.

One last word about oven temperature has to do with the pans you use. Glass pans and those metal pans with a dark finish bake better at a lower temperature, say 325°F, to prevent the edges from overbrowning. When baking layers larger than nine inches, for a wedding cake for example, you need to bake at 325°F; the layers will bake more evenly, producing flat tops that will stack well.

Prepping the Pans

Oh, to grease or not to grease—that is the question! In the beginning I greased pans with solid vegetable shortening and dusted them with flour. Then I got lazy and misted with oil and dusted with flour. Then I tried only greasing and flouring the bottom and leaving the sides untouched. Then I placed parchment or waxed paper in the bottom and didn't prep the pan at all. So, I've tried it all. And my advice is that how you prep a pan for baking depends on the pan.

For layers: These are the most adaptable cakes. They're happy if you take the time to brush the pans with solid vegetable shortening and dust them with flour. The pastry brush is an effortless way to coat the bottom and side with shortening. This method creates a nice crust and makes the cake easy to remove from the pan and easy to frost, with no crumbs messing up the frosting. But layer cake pans will also be content with a misting of vegetable oil spray and a dusting of flour. The crust will be a little softer, a little touchier to get out of the pan and you will need a gentle hand at frosting. Using soft butter instead of shortening or oil produces an even more crumbly crust, delicious, but messy when frosting. Either way, shake out the excess flour from one pan into another for the second layer or into the trash can or over the sink.

With no prep—oil, shortening, butter, flour, nothing—on the pan side, you may see a taller layer after baking than if you had prepped the side. I tried this with a number of the layer cakes in this book and I found that when I wanted the tallest cake it was best to grease and flour only the bottom of the pans. Or, to place rounds of parchment or waxed paper in the pan bottoms (you can oil the bottoms of the pans to secure the paper). As with angel food cakes, the batter seems to cling to the bare side of the pans and work its way up, making taller layers.

For Bundts: It only takes one time for a Bundt cake to stick to the pan and you will gladly prep it with vegetable shortening and flour the next time. I learned this the hard way when I was trying to turn out a fancy Bundt cake while promoting my first book on TV. The camera wasn't rolling but I could not get the top of that cake out of the pan. Fortunately, with many years of repair work under my belt, I spooned the top in pieces and placed them back on the cake, pressing them together gently with my fingers. I then poured a glaze on top to cover up the blemishes and the cake looked like a dream for the camera. But I was a wreck! Now, especially when making decorative Bundts with all those grooves and crevices, I paint the pan with shortening, using a small pastry brush, and I dust it well with flour. For me, it is worth it to know the cake will release from the pan. And it does every time!

For tube pans: Angel food cakes don't need a greased pan. Love them! But if you bake a pound cake or any Bundt cake recipe in a tube pan, you'll need to prep it. Fortunately the sides of a tube pan are flat, so a misting of vegetable oil and dusting of flour is sufficient.

For sheet pans: A light misting of vegetable oil spray and a dusting of flour is all you need for cakes baked in sheet pans.

For brownies and bars, I often mist and don't flour. And in some recipes where there is a high proportion of butter in the crust, just line the pan with parchment paper before baking. Remove the bars from the pan by lifting up the paper.

For cupcakes and muffins: If you are using paper liners, just place them in the wells of the cupcake pan—no prepping needed. But baked without liners, cupcakes and muffins take on a more homemade taste and appearance. I love the crunch you get when a muffin is baked without a liner. Just mist the pans with vegetable oil spray and dust them with flour if you like. For a more crumbly crust, rub the wells with soft butter and dust them with flour.

Mix It Up

The real beauty of baking cakes that begin with a mix is that it takes just a few simple steps to whip up a batter.

1. Dump the mix and other recipe ingredients in the bowl. The temperature of ingredients like eggs or milk doesn't matter—they can come straight from the refrigerator. The exception is cream cheese, which needs to be soft when added.

2. Beat the batter with an electric mixer on low speed for 30 seconds. Then, increase the speed to medium and beat the batter until it is smooth and thickened, 1 to 1½ minutes longer.

3. Fold in any add-ins, such as chocolate chips, nuts, or dried fruit, then pop the cake pan in the oven.

That's it! You may want to scrape down the side of the bowl as you mix and stir the batter on the bottom of the bowl once or twice as you scrape the side. With the exception of baking at high altitudes, where you should beat the batter a total of three minutes, you really don't need to beat a cake mix cake any longer than two minutes.

Tests for Doneness

Come in my kitchen on baking day and the light in the oven will be on. I like to peek at things as they bake just to make sure I don't overbake them. And there are other signs of doneness that I look for.

1. There should be spring in the texture of the cake. I press lightly with my fingertips on the center of the cake. When done, the cake should spring back and not leave an indentation.

2. Vanilla and yellow cakes should be golden in color, and chocolate cakes should look darker than when they were put in the oven.

3. The cake should just begin to pull away from the side of the pan.

4. The cake should smell done. Train your nose. I can smell a baked chocolate cake the moment I walk in the door.

High-Altitude How-To

Since I've never lived at a high altitude it was hard for me to fully understand the frustration felt by cooks who try to bake cakes above 3,500 feet. But, then I visited Denver on book tour and baked cakes with food writer Marty Meitus. In her kitchen I saw firsthand the cake wrecks that can come out of an oven this high above sea level. Bundts didn't rise as high as I am used to in Nashville. Sheet cakes had big dips in the center. Everything needed frosting as a cover-up!

Before baking in the clouds you need to select your recipe carefully. Bonnie West, a Denver home economist, tested recipes for me a while back and came to some conclusions of her own about how to bake well at high altitude. Avoid instant pudding, she said. That goes for both cake mixes with pudding in them, and adding extra pudding mix to a recipe. If you must use a mix with pudding in it, don't doctor it up, just follow the directions on the package for high altitude baking.

Because there is less air pressure at high altitudes, you need to choose cakes that have good structure. Sugar, peanut butter, and cocoa tenderize cakes and reduce their structure. So do sweetened gelatin, chocolate syrup, and marshmallows. Avoid recipes containing too much of these ingredients because they cause havoc at high heights. And, while cakes need oil, it also reduces the structure of a cake, so you have to cut back on it, for example adding a third of a cup plus a tablespoon instead of the half cup called for in the recipe.

The cake pan really affects baking success at these altitudes. Bundts are a good choice, giving the batter something to cling to even if the cakes don't bake as tall as they might at sea level. Long rectangular cakes do not bake well. Layers need to be at least nine inches in diameter—anything smaller and the batter will flow over the side of the pan.

Again, read the high altitude directions on the side of the cake mix box and apply them to my recipes. In addition, here are my basic rules for high-altitude baking.

◆ Add a little flour (two tablespoons to layers, up to a quarter of a cup for Bundts) to increase the batter weight and keep the cake from rising too quickly and then falling. In addition, add one tablespoon more liquid for layers and two tablespoons more for Bundts.

◆ Set the oven 25°F higher than the recipe calls for because this higher temperature makes batter set more quickly. Then it won't rise and overflow the pan.

◆ Blend the batter well with a mixer, beating for at least three minutes to build structure.

◆ Prep the pan well. Grease and flour the pan because cakes at these heights tend to stick.

◆ Don't worry if the cake cracks. The air is dry at high altitudes. Try and bake on a humid day, says Bonnie West. Interestingly most of the e-mails I have received about high altitude baking have been from readers who used to live in Florida and other places closer to sea level who can't make their favorite recipes work in the mountains. Cover the dips and cracks with frosting.

◆ Don't overbake the cake. A dry cake tastes worse than a moist cake that falls flat.

◆ Relax. Don't take high altitude too seriously, says Bonnie. You can also do as Barbara Lyons of Denver does. She bakes cakes in her seven-cup electric rice cooker. She uses half a box of cake mix and half of the add-in ingredients, greases the removable bowl, lines it with a circle of parchment paper, and greases the parchment. She pours in the batter and bakes the cake in the cooker with the small vent in the lid open for steam to escape. The cake will bake in thirty to forty minutes, says Barbara, is fun to make, does not heat up the kitchen, and best of all, doesn't sink at high altitude!

As far as the toothpick test, I know a lot of people rely on this as a test for doneness (the toothpick should come out clean when inserted into a cake that is done, but have some crumbs clinging to it in the case of brownies). Still, I don't like it because it can cause the cake to sink in the center if you test too soon.

Out of the Pan and onto the Rack

When a cake is done, transfer it to a wire rack or a burner on the stove that you know is turned off. Ideally, the cake pan needs to be elevated a bit for air to circulate around and cool the cake. You can cool cakes in a hurry by placing them in the refrigerator, and I have even placed them outside in the snow to cool. This dramatic plunge in temperature will cause a cake to flatten and often shrink more than if you have eased it into cooling. Covered with frosting, however, no one ever knows.

What is more critical is how long cakes stay in the pan before you invert them onto a rack. I usually allow five minutes for layers, fifteen minutes for Bundt and pound cakes, and fifteen to twenty minutes for sheet cakes you want to turn out and frost. I allow a little extra time for heavy Bundts with lots of nuts and chocolate chips. If the cake spends too little time in the pan, or too much, it may stick. Figuring out the right cooling time for the pans you use and the recipes you enjoy is really helpful.

Before you invert a cake onto a rack, be sure to run a knife around the edge to loosen the cake from the pan. I like to give the pan a few gentle shakes to loosen the cake, too, before turning the pan over onto the rack.

For both layers and cakes baked in a tube pan, turn the cake out upside down on a rack, then invert it again so that it is right side up. Bundts need to be inverted just once because it is their fluted top that should be displayed.

For a layer cake that will be frosted, you need to allow anywhere from twenty to thirty minutes for it to cool completely before frosting. The cooler the layer, the easier it will be to frost. Bundts, on the other hand, and sheet cakes, too, can be frosted or glazed while still a little warm.

Frosting the Cake

You *can* make each and every frosting in this book. They may sound fancy and complicated but really they are quite simple. My advice is to begin with a buttercream frosting. Move up to a cream cheese frosting. Try a ganache. Then aim for cooked icings, which you will find less stressful if you're not in a hurry.

There was a time when if someone in my family came into the kitchen while I was frosting a caramel cake I'd say to them please make your own snack, hold off on the questions, and just wait until I finish. Any distractions caused that frosting to harden before I got it on the cake. But now, when I'm making icing during a chaotic time, I know to remove the icing from the stove a little sooner or to add a little more milk so that it's a little runnier to begin with. It gives me a little extra distraction leeway. If it winds up too runny, I can always place the cake or the icing in the refrigerator to set for a minute or two.

It is important to have the right ingredients, measured correctly and at the correct temperature, for these frostings. For buttercreams and cream cheese frostings, the butter and cream cheese must be at room temperature. If they are not, soften them in the microwave oven. Make sure you measure the right amount of chocolate for a ganache. The recipe may call for one cup of chocolate chips, but this equals six ounces of chocolate not eight ounces.

If the frosting seems to need more sugar or more liquid, use your instincts. Baking is a science, but you need to take some creative license every now and then because things like humidity come into play. In your region of the country—whether in a high altitude like Denver or the humid South—a recipe may need to be amended a bit.

Ready to frost?

For the classic two-layer cake, I stack the layers top side up. This also works for most three-layer cakes. But if the layers are deep and heavy you may want to stack them bottom sides together, so the flat surfaces are next to each other. Frost the side and top as you would for any cake.

Veteran cake bakers work with flat cake layers. To do this they will either gently press down on a cake in the pan after it has been removed from the oven, or they will slice the domed top off a layer after it has cooled. You can also use the baking strips found in baking supply stores. These are cloth strips that you soak in water and attach to the outside of the baking pans before putting them in the oven. As the cake layers bake the outside stays cool and the cakes bake more evenly and don't dome in the center. And lastly, baking cakes at 325°F instead of the usual 350°F will produce a slightly flatter cake.

In this book I have tried to provide just the right amount of frosting for the job so you don't have too much left over. You'll see the Chocolate Pan Frosting on page 476 has several variations depending upon how much you need when you are using it on a Bundt cake, cupcakes, or a layer cake.

To keep a cake neat and tidy before frosting, place strips of waxed paper—about 3 inches by 12 inches—under the bottom layer to form a square and catch frosting run-offs. Gently pull the waxed paper out from underneath after the cake is frosted. Or you can just wet a piece of paper towel and wipe up the plate or stand after you are done frosting.

When frosting, my advice is to go lightly and sparingly at first. It's better to wind up with a little extra frosting in the bowl that you can pile on top than no frosting left and a top that needs to be frosted. Be gentle when frosting your layers so they don't split and crumb up. Crumbs can get pretty messy in the frosting—especially red velvet crumbs! They can turn a white frosting pink.

I'm a big believer in skim coats, that first thin coat of frosting that seals in the crumbs. Once the crumbs are sealed, go back and be more generous with frosting on top and around the side—you can be decorative and daring. Pastry chefs will put a skim coat on a cake, then chill it so the cake is even easier to frost with a second coat. In a humid summer home kitchen, this is a great trick as well.

Such sticky frostings as those made with cream cheese need to be refrigerated briefly, uncovered, before storing. Iced cakes need to rest ten to twenty minutes for the frosting to harden before wrapping. And cakes with a whipped cream frosting will need to be stored in the refrigerator in a cake saver or under a glass cake dome.

Freezing Cake

One of my favorite ways to work ahead on a busy schedule is to bake and freeze. Most cakes are great keepers, especially Bundts and pounds. Layer cakes, too, can be frozen, but you'll have better results if you freeze the layers, then thaw, and frost them later. Cream cheese frostings, in particular, get watery after being frozen.

Freezing is also a great way to extend the life of a favorite cake and to keep you from eating too much! I freeze leftover cake in aluminum foil or in a tightly sealed plastic container, frosted or unfrosted, for up to three months. Some will last up to six months, but these are the Bundts and pounds. Whole or half cakes freeze better for longer periods of time than sliced cake.

Another thing to remember when freezing cake is to use heavy-duty aluminum foil. Regular foil is okay, but definitely don't use plastic wrap because it does not lock in moisture. It's easier to wrap a cake if the frosting is hard. So you need to refrigerate uncovered cakes for twenty minutes before wrapping them for the freezer.

Thawing cakes on the counter is fine unless they have a frosting or filling that contains eggs, even cooked eggs. Those should be thawed in the refrigerator. The best advice I have gotten is to keep an unfrosted cake covered until it is three quarters thawed, then uncover the cake and let it finish thawing. This lets the moisture in the cake evaporate and the layers are easier to frost.

◆◆◆◆◆

Love Those Layers

A layer cake is, to me, *the* cake to bake. It is to cake what fireworks are to the Fourth of July and what the Eiffel Tower is to Paris. It is the cake of our birthdays, our weddings, and our anniversaries. It is the cake of tradition, nostalgia, sweet celebration, and easy elegance. A layer cake looks grand and important. People will think you spent hours in the kitchen baking the cake for them. But you won't have, although many cooks still shy away from layer cakes and turn to the seemingly simpler Bundts and sheet cakes. However, with a little practice, and the right recipe, assembling a layer cake becomes effortless, enjoyable, and infinitely rewarding.

Okay, I'll admit I'm so much the cake geek now that I enjoy baking a cake multiple times just to figure out its strengths and flaws. I want to bake it in the sultry humidity of a Nashville summer and then again in a cool January kitchen. But, when I was a teenager I trembled at the thought of a layer cake, and my early cakes were often lopsided and poorly frosted, whereas my mother's cakes were smooth and flawless. Layer cakes don't frighten me anymore, and I am happy to share with you some things I have learned about baking layers, as well as provide you with more than three dozen terrific new recipes for these cakes.

You'll find many tips and tricks and suggestions for baking great layers in this chapter. I'll guide you through the baking process, provide you with new fillings and fun frostings to go with my new layers, and show you how I easily assemble the classic layer cake. As always these cakes are great for toting. Buy a plastic cake saver and write your name on the bottom of it. These are perfect for taking cakes to the office, to a party, to school, to the countless occasions when you want to share layer cakes with others.

And what of the recipes in this chapter? You'll recognize a few favorites from my earlier books—I like to call them classics. And yet even a good thing can take a bit of improvement. So for the banana cake with caramel frosting you will see I have omitted adding sugar to the cake, as well as the banana liqueur. The strawberry cake is a departure in that I no longer call for strawberry-flavored gelatin, instead relying on the flavor of fresh strawberries. And in the chocolate and raspberry cake I now strain the raspberries to remove the seeds and I add miniature chocolate chips. These changes are for the better, in my opinion, so give them a try!

I also share new takes on my favorite combinations, such as an outstanding Fresh Orange Birthday Cake, Classic Yellow Cake with Chocolate Fudge Marshmallow Frosting, Easy Coconut Refrigerator Cake, Kentucky Blackberry Jam Cake, The Best Red Velvet Cake with a cream cheese frosting, Chocolate Chip Layer Cake with Chocolate Cream Cheese Frosting, Sour Cream Chocolate Cake with Chocolate Pan Frosting, and the lovely Lemonade Chiffon Layer Cake with Lemon Cream Cheese Frosting.

New to my recipe box are a Williamsburg Orange Cake, Blueberry Muffin Crumble Cake with a crumbly topping, Hawaiian Wedding Cake, Cinnamon Streusel Layer Cake, Elegant Almond Amaretto Cake, Tiramisu Cake, Triple Decker Chocolate Icebox Cake with Shaved Chocolate Frosting, and many more.

Selecting favorite recipes to mention always seems so subjective to me. Surely as I name a recipe I love the best you will prefer another. That's the wonderful part about taste and opinion. We can differ but also agree that baking cakes—especially layers—is our chance to bring tradition and nostalgia, and celebration and a bit of elegance, back to our kitchens. It's a welcome trend that should never go out of style.

◆◆◆◆◆

A Better Banana Cake with Caramel Frosting

OUR FAMILY HAS BEEN CRAZY ABOUT THIS CAKE ever since I first baked it ten years ago. A Nashville reader sent me the recipe, and it was one of the recipes I shared in the original Cake Mix Doctor story in the local paper, *The Tennessean.* This recipe went on book tour with me, appeared on QVC and *Good Morning America*, and more important, has been the star at so many family birthdays that my ragged copy of *The Cake Mix Doctor* opens to page 72 on its own! But even great recipes need a few tweaks. I now make this cake without brown sugar in the batter, without banana liqueur—just a little vanilla—and with milk or water as the liquid. I still insist on ripe bananas, and I still insist on my mom's caramel frosting to top the cake. What you end up with is a better banana cake!

serves:
12 to 16

prep:
25 minutes

bake:
30 to 32 minutes

cool:
30 minutes

Vegetable oil spray, for misting the pans
Flour, for dusting the pans
1 package (18.25 ounces) plain yellow cake mix
1 to 1½ teaspoons ground cinnamon
2 medium-size ripe bananas, peeled and mashed (1 generous cup)
1 cup milk or water
½ cup vegetable oil
1 teaspoon pure vanilla extract
3 large eggs
Quick Caramel Frosting (page 485)
½ cup chopped toasted pecans (optional; (see page 204)

Recipe Reminders

MADE FOR

PREP NOTES

DON'T FORGET

SPECIAL TOUCHES

1. Place a rack in the center of the oven and preheat the oven to 350°F. Lightly mist two 9-inch round cake pans with vegetable oil spray, then dust them with flour. Shake out the excess flour and set the pans aside.

2. Place the cake mix and cinnamon in a large mixing bowl. Add the mashed bananas, milk, oil, vanilla, and eggs and beat with an electric mixer on low speed until the ingredients are incorporated, 30 seconds. Stop the machine and scrape down the side of the bowl with a rubber spatula. Increase the mixer speed to medium and beat for 2 minutes longer, scraping down the side of the bowl again if needed. The batter should be well blended. Divide the cake batter evenly between the 2 prepared cake pans,

Banana Cake Without the Eggs

My friend Katy Varney is also a big fan of this banana cake and wanted to make it for her nephew who was coming to dinner. But when she gathered the ingredients together she realized she was out of eggs. And with no time to dash to the supermarket, she made the cake without eggs, poured the batter into a brownie pan, and baked it. The results were yummy—a cross between banana cake and bread pudding. Katy's family was thrilled with her resourcefulness, and I was curious. So I tested Katy's recipe and found, indeed, that this cake works without eggs!

To do this, make the Better Banana Cake but omit the eggs. Pour the batter into a greased and floured 13 by 9-inch pan and bake it at 350°F for 38 to 42 minutes. The eggless cake is best served warm in bowls with vanilla ice cream, rum raisin ice cream, or whipped cream. Plato was right—necessity is the mother of invention. Or, as any Cake Mix Doctor would say, inventive mothers cook well sometimes out of necessity!

smoothing the tops with the rubber spatula. Place the cake pans in the oven side by side.

3. Bake the cake layers until they are lightly browned and the tops spring back when lightly pressed with a finger, 30 to 32 minutes. Transfer the cake pans to wire racks and let the cake layers cool for 10 minutes. Run a dinner knife around the edge of each cake layer and give the pans a good shake to loosen the cakes. Invert each layer onto a wire rack, then invert it again onto another rack so that the cakes are right side up. Let the layers cool for 20 minutes longer.

4. After the layers have cooled, make the caramel frosting.

5. While the frosting is warm, assemble the cake. Transfer one layer, right side up, to a serving plate. Spoon about a cup of the warm frosting over the top and spread it out with a long metal spatula, working quickly because the frosting will firm up as it cools. Place the second cake layer, right side up, on top of the first and frost the top and side of the cake with the remaining frosting, making sure to work quickly with smooth, clean strokes. While the frosting is still warm, sprinkle the toasted pecans, if using, on top of the cake so that they cling to the frosting. For easier slicing let the cake cool at least 1 hour.

Keep It Fresh! Store this cake, in a cake saver or loosely covered with plastic wrap, at room temperature for up to three days. Freeze the cake, wrapped in aluminum foil, for up to six months. Let the cake thaw overnight on the counter before serving.

Same Great Cake, Different Wonderful Frosting

Want another way to serve the banana cake? Bake it in layers but frost it with Cream Cheese Frosting (page 471). You will have one of my favorite combinations—spicy cinnamon banana cake and the classic creamy frosting. Yum. Garnish the cake with chopped toasted walnuts or crushed pineapple.

Fresh Strawberry Cake with Strawberry Cream Cheese Frosting

serves:
12 to 16

prep:
30 minutes

bake:
20 to 25 minutes

cool:
25 minutes

If there ever was a classic cake mix recipe, it is this strawberry cake. Countless birthdays, weddings, and anniversaries have been celebrated with this signature cake. There were two triple-layer strawberry cakes in the first *Cake Mix Doctor*—a cake with a buttercream frosting and one with a cream cheese frosting that contained chopped pecans and coconut. Over the years I began combining the two, featuring the cream cheese frosting, usually without the pecans and coconut. And lately I had wanted to tone down the flavor of the strawberry gelatin, a key ingredient in both cakes. So I tested a strawberry cake without the gelatin and with more fresh strawberries. And I made it in three layers with a simple strawberry cream cheese frosting. It's just as moist as the original strawberry cake but lighter and fresher tasting.

For the cake

Vegetable oil spray, for misting the pans
Flour, for dusting the pans
1 package (18.25 ounces) plain white cake mix
1½ cups mashed ripe strawberries, with their juice (about 3 heaping cups of berries rinsed and dried)
½ cup vegetable oil
¼ cup milk
1 teaspoon pure vanilla extract
4 large eggs

Behind Every Successful Cake Are Good Pans

Good pans do help bake great cakes. As I have said before, invest in shiny aluminum pans for baking cake layers. Buy at least three of the same size, preferably nine-inch rounds. You need three pans because many of my recipes call for triple layers. It is a look I like very much for parties and special occasions, although for day-to-day baking you can't beat the casual coziness of the two-layer cake.

Prepping those cake pans is important, and you will get a slight difference in the texture of a cake depending on how you grease and flour the pans. If you only mist and flour the bottom of the pans—not the side—the cake batter will creep up the side and climb to a greater height than if you prep the side of the pans. Take care to run a small, sharp knife around the edge of the cake pan as soon as you remove it from the oven just to release the cake from the pan and make turning it out simpler. This type of pan preparation gives you taller cake layers but also makes for a crumbly exterior. This is fine for light-colored cakes or cakes that will have a dense frosting to cover up the crumbs.

On some layer cakes a crumbly exterior makes frosting a chore. The red velvet cake, for example, needs a smooth side, so you don't drag those red crumbs into your white icing and turn it pink! Frosting all cakes is easier if you prep the bottom and side of the pan with a misting of vegetable oil spray or a light brushing of solid vegetable shortening, then dust it with flour and shake out the excess. When baking chocolate cakes, substitute cocoa for the flour for a more intense flavor.

For the strawberry cream cheese frosting

1 package (8 ounces) cream cheese, at room temperature
4 tablespoons (½ stick) butter, at room temperature
1 tablespoon strawberry puree (see Note)
4½ cups confectioners' sugar, sifted

1. Make the cake: Place a rack in the center of the oven and preheat the oven to 350°F. Lightly mist three 9-inch round cake pans with vegetable oil spray, then dust them with flour. Shake out the excess flour and set the pans aside.

Recipe Reminders

MADE FOR

PREP NOTES

DON'T FORGET

SPECIAL TOUCHES

2. Place the cake mix, mashed strawberries, oil, milk, vanilla, and eggs in a large mixing bowl and beat with an electric mixer on low speed until the ingredients are incorporated, 30 seconds. Stop the machine and scrape down the side of the bowl with a rubber spatula. Increase the mixer speed to medium and beat for 1½ minutes longer, scraping down the side of the bowl again if needed. The strawberries should be well blended into the batter. Divide the cake batter evenly among the 3 prepared cake pans, about 1½ cups of batter per pan, smoothing the tops with the rubber spatula. Place the cake pans in the oven. If your oven is not large enough to hold 3 pans on one rack, place 2 pans on that rack and one in the center of the rack above.

3. Bake the cake layers until they spring back when lightly pressed in the center, 20 to 25 minutes. The cake layer on the higher rack may bake faster so test it for doneness first. Transfer the cake pans to wire racks and let the cake layers cool for 5 minutes. Run a dinner knife around the edge of each cake layer and give the pans a good shake to loosen the cakes. Invert each layer onto a wire rack, then invert it again onto another rack so that the cakes are right side up. Let the layers cool completely, 20 minutes longer.

4. Make the frosting: Place the cream cheese and butter in a medium-size bowl and beat with an electric mixer on medium-high speed until light and fluffy, about 1 minute. Add the strawberry purée and slowly add the confectioners' sugar. Beat on low until the sugar is incorporated, then increase the mixer speed to medium and beat until smooth, 1 to 2 minutes longer. If possible, cover the bowl of frosting and place it in the refrigerator to chill for 30 minutes.

5. To assemble the cake, transfer one layer, right side up, to a serving platter. Spread the top with frosting. Place the second layer of cake, right side up, on the first and frost the top. Repeat this process with the third layer. Use the remaining frosting to frost the side of the cake, working with smooth, clean strokes. Serve the cake at once or refrigerate it for serving later (refrigerating it for 20 minutes will make it easier to slice through the frosting).

Keep It Fresh! Store this cake, in a cake saver or loosely covered with waxed paper, in the refrigerator for up to one week.

Note: To make 1 tablespoon of puree, rinse and pat dry 4 medium-size ripe strawberries. Place them in a sieve and mash them with a spoon into a bowl. Discard any pulp remaining in the sieve.

If You Miss the Strawberry Jell-O

Want a bright pink strawberry cake, just like the ones in the previous *Cake Mix Doctor*? Add a small package (3 ounces) of strawberry gelatin along with the cake mix.

Fruit Frostings May Cause You to Weep

Silly me. I thought I could bake a strawberry cake in April in Tampa and St. Petersburg, using those good local Florida berries. Oh, I didn't just want to bake a fresh strawberry cake, I wanted to cart it around in the car and carry it into TV stations and newspaper offices. I didn't think about the humidity or the moisture the fresh berries add and how the frosting on that cake would run down the side of the plate onto the car, onto everything! So, with that first strawberry cake in mind, I have learned some things about adding fruit to frostings, mostly cream cheese frostings. And I am happy to share what I now know.

When you want to flavor a cream cheese frosting with fresh fruit, use no more than one tablespoon of mashed and well-drained fruit—whether it's strawberries or peaches or fruit preserves. Use full-fat cream cheese because it is less watery than reduced-fat. And chill the frosting thirty minutes before you frost the cake. The cake layers need to be cool. It even helps if the kitchen is cool, and once the cake is assembled and frosted, place the cake in the fridge to let it set before slicing. Always garnish the cake just before serving because fresh fruit gets soggy quickly.

Strawberry Refrigerator Cake

serves:
12 to 16

prep:
50 minutes

bake:
20 to 25 minutes

cool:
30 minutes

I **LOOK AT THIS CAKE AND SEE THE FOURTH OF JULY,** backyard parties, celebrations—all that is right in this world. The cake is all simplicity, with freshness and flavor and a lot of pizzazz. My older daughter says this cake might just be her favorite. She has an April birthday and from now on it will be her birthday cake. Spring is just the right season for strawberry cake as flavorful berries start coming into the market then. Many years ago Pam Rector of Hendersonville, Tennessee, sent me a recipe for a similar cake, a refrigerated strawberry cake recipe that originated in Milledgeville, Georgia. I think I have improved on that cake, and I hope you take this recipe as a starting point and feel free to make the cake with sliced peaches or nectarines or raspberries, whatever ripe and delicious fruit is on hand.

For the cake

Vegetable oil spray, for misting the pans
Flour, for dusting the pans
1 package (18.25 ounces) plain yellow cake mix
4 ounces reduced-fat cream cheese, at room temperature
1 cup water
½ cup vegetable oil
2 teaspoons pure vanilla extract
4 large eggs

For the filling and garnish

2 quarts fresh strawberries, rinsed and drained on paper towels, plus ½ cup, sliced, for garnish
1 cup (8 ounces) sour cream
1 container (8 ounces) frozen whipped topping, thawed
1½ cups confectioners' sugar, sifted

1. Make the cake: Place a rack in the center of the oven and preheat the oven to 325°F. Lightly mist three 9-inch round baking pans with vegetable oil spray, then dust them with flour. Shake out the excess flour and set the pans aside.

2. Place the cake mix, cream cheese, water, oil, vanilla, and eggs in a large mixing bowl and beat with an electric mixer on low speed until the ingredients are incorporated, 30 seconds. Stop the machine and scrape down the side of the bowl with a rubber spatula. Increase the mixer speed to medium and beat until smooth, 2 minutes longer, scraping down the side of the bowl again if needed. Divide the cake batter evenly among the 3 prepared cake pans, about 1¾ cups of batter per pan, smoothing the tops with the rubber spatula. Place the pans in the oven. If your oven is not large enough to hold 3 pans on one rack, place 2 pans on that rack and one in the center of the rack above.

3. Bake the cake layers until they are golden brown and the tops spring back when lightly pressed with a finger, 20 to 25 minutes. The cake layer on the higher rack may bake faster so test it for doneness first.

4. Meanwhile, make the filling: Cut off and discard the caps of the 2 quarts of strawberries. Cut the strawberries into 3 or 4 slices each, place them in a medium-size bowl, and set aside. Place the sour cream, whipped topping, and confectioners' sugar in another medium-size bowl and beat with an electric mixer on low speed for 15 to 20 seconds. Scrape down the side of the bowl

Recipe Reminders

MADE FOR

PREP NOTES

DON'T FORGET

SPECIAL TOUCHES

with a rubber spatula. Increase the mixer speed to medium and beat until fluffy, about 1 minute longer.

5. Transfer the cake pans to wire racks and let the cake layers cool for 15 minutes. Run a dinner knife around the edge of each cake layer and give the pans a good shake to loosen the cakes. Invert each layer onto a wire rack, then invert it again onto another wire rack so that the cakes are right side up. Let the layers cool for 15 minutes longer.

6. To assemble the cake, transfer one layer, right side up, to a serving plate. Spoon a heaping cup of the sour cream filling on that layer and, using a knife, spread it not quite to the edge of the cake. Arrange 1½ cups of sliced strawberries on top of the filling, making sure that you place the berries all the way to the edge. Place the second layer of cake, right side up, on top of the first, spread a heaping cup of filling over that layer, and arrange the remaining strawberries on it as you did with the first layer. Place the third layer of cake, right side up, on top of the second and spread the remaining 1 cup of filling over the top, leaving the side of the cake bare. Place the cake in the refrigerator to chill for up to 4 hours.

7. Just before serving, garnish the top of the cake with the ½ cup of sliced strawberries.

Keep It Fresh! Store this cake, in a cake saver or loosely covered with plastic wrap, in the refrigerator for two days. Freeze only the cake layers, wrapped in aluminum foil, for up to six months. Let the layers thaw overnight on the counter before making the filling and assembling the cake.

Stand Tall

Just like your mom told you to stand up straight so you'd look your best, cakes benefit from standing tall as well. Place a cake on a stand instead of a plate and you'll find even the simplest chocolate cake looks mighty impressive. I learned this trick when appearing on television and bringing an assortment of cakes with me to display. The ones that looked the best were the ones on stands. Place a birthday layer cake on a stand for a celebratory presentation or arrange an assortment of cakes on various stands for a dramatic statement on the dessert buffet. Make sure the stands are of different heights. This moves your eye from cake to cake on the buffet.

Fresh Orange Birthday Cake

A FEW MONTHS AFTER MY FIRST BOOK was published, I went on a book tour. And being a true neophyte I really relied on the expertise of the media escorts in each city I visited. In Dallas I was fortunate to have Kathleen Livingston bake my cakes. I will always remember how she garnished my orange Bundt cake with slices of gorgeous red and orange Cara Cara oranges. I had never seen them before, and they looked like slices of a summer sunset. I got back to Dallas recently, and Kathleen and I talked orange cake again. She thought orange cake was the best birthday choice for kids because they like the flavor, few are allergic to it, and it looks great on a cake stand. I came home ready to create the perfect orange birthday cake—for kids of all ages. Here it is. Enjoy it whether you garnish it with fresh oranges, orange gum drops, or just birthday candles.

serves: 12 to 16

prep: 30 minutes

bake: 18 to 20 minutes

cool: 20 minutes

Vegetable oil spray, for misting the pans
Flour, for dusting the pans
1 large orange
About 1 cup orange juice from a carton
1 package (18.25 ounces) plain yellow cake mix
1 package (3.4 ounces) vanilla instant pudding mix
½ cup vegetable oil
1 teaspoon pure vanilla extract
3 large eggs
Orange Cream Cheese Frosting (page 474)
12 to 15 fresh orange slices, or candy gum drop orange slices, for garnish

Just Want a Two-Layer Cake?

That's easy. Pour the Fresh Orange Birthday Cake batter into two 9-inch round cake pans that have been misted and floured. You'll need to fill them a little fuller than for a three-layer cake and they'll take a little longer to be done; bake the layers until they are golden brown and spring back in the center when lightly pressed with a finger, 25 to 30 minutes. When you assemble the cake, spread the frosting between the two layers more thickly than for a three-layer cake.

A Dozen Dazzling Birthday Party Cakes

1. Place a rack in the center of the oven and preheat the oven to 350°F. Lightly mist three 9-inch round cake pans with vegetable oil spray, then dust them with flour. Shake out the excess flour and set the pans aside.

2. Rinse the orange and pat it dry with paper towels. Grate enough zest to measure 2 to 3 teaspoons. Cut the orange in half and squeeze the juice into a small bowl; you will have about ½ cup of juice. Add enough orange juice from a carton to the fresh orange juice to measure 1⅓ cups.

3. Place the cake mix, pudding mix, oil, vanilla, eggs, and orange juice and orange zest in a large mixing bowl and beat with an electric mixer on low speed until the ingredients are moistened, 30 seconds. Stop the machine and scrape down the side of the bowl with a rubber spatula. Increase the mixer speed to medium and beat the batter until well combined and smooth, about 1½ minutes longer, scraping down the side of the bowl again if needed. Divide the cake batter evenly among the 3 prepared cake pans, about 1¾ cups of batter per pan, smoothing the tops with the rubber spatula. Place the cake pans in the oven. If your oven is not large enough to hold 3 pans on one rack, place 2 pans on that rack and one in the center of the rack above.

4. Bake the cake layers until the tops spring back when lightly pressed with a finger, 18 to 20 minutes. The cake layer on the higher rack may bake faster so test it for doneness first. Transfer the cake pans to wire racks and let the cake layers cool for 5 minutes. Run a long, sharp knife around the edge of each cake layer and give the pans a good shake to loosen the cakes. Invert each layer onto a wire rack, then invert it again onto another wire rack so that the cakes are right side up. Let the layers cool to room temperature, 15 minutes longer.

5. Make the Orange Cream Cheese Frosting.

Recipe Reminders

MADE FOR

____

____

____

____

PREP NOTES

____

____

____

____

DON'T FORGET

____

____

____

____

SPECIAL TOUCHES

____

____

____

____

____

____

____

____

____

6. To assemble the cake, transfer one layer, right side up, to a serving platter. Spread the top with frosting. Place the second layer of cake, right side up, on top of the first and frost the top. Repeat this process with the third layer. Use the remaining frosting to frost the side of the cake, working with smooth, clean strokes. Arrange the fresh orange slices around the base of the cake, or place candy gum drop orange slices on top of the cake. To make slicing easier, place the uncovered cake in the refrigerator until the frosting sets, 20 minutes.

Keep It Fresh! Store this cake, in a cake saver or loosely covered with waxed paper, in the refrigerator for up to one week. Freeze the cake, wrapped in aluminum foil, for up to six months. Let the cake thaw overnight in the refrigerator before serving.

Light the Candles and Make a Wish!

Once a birthday cake is garnished, the candles are ready to be lit. Start with the inside candles and work toward the outside of the cake to prevent burning your hand. Usually it's one candle per year for most children's birthdays and one candle per decade for everyone twenty and up. Remind the birthday honoree to make a secret wish before blowing out the candles. Some cooks whisper a birthday wish to a child as the cake is carried to the table.

Birthday layer cakes slice best with a long, thin knife. Dip the knife into hot water, dry it, then cut the cake. Wipe off the knife between slices for the neatest job. Use a serrated knife on angel food cakes or any cake with a more delicate crumb texture. And don't forget to sing "Happy Birthday"!

Dress Up a Birthday Cake—It's Easy

You don't have to be a professional to turn out a dazzling birthday cake. Some of my favorite cakes have been those that were simply decorated with candy, flowers, fruit, or just candles. Ingredients in your pantry, your refrigerator, or your garden are the best choices and the most accessible, and they're even better suited if they match the flavors of the cake and frosting. For example:

◆ Stock up on colorful sugars and sprinkles to decorate cakes and cupcakes. You can spell out words and names on cakes with larger sprinkles. These adhere best to a freshly frosted cake.

◆ Top chocolate cakes with crushed peppermints.

◆ Sprinkle miniature marshmallows and graham cracker pieces atop a chocolate cake for the s'more lover.

◆ Add jelly beans or colorful gum drops to the top and side of a strawberry or lemon cake.

◆ Crown most any cake with fresh fruit, such as strawberries, cherries, or raspberries.

◆ Top white or angel food cakes with shredded coconut. Tint the coconut a different color by shaking it in a plastic resealable bag with a few drops of food coloring.

◆ Provided they haven't been sprayed with pesticides, garnish the top and around the base of cakes with violets or nasturtiums from your garden.

◆ Dust cocoa powder, cinnamon, or confectioners' sugar over a cake using a fine mesh sieve. Get creative and sprinkle on patterns and designs using stencils.

◆ Even the birthday candles themselves can be decorative. Look for long, slender, colorful candles at gift or cookware shops. They look glamorous on any cake and may be reused.

◆ Chocolate curls are the ultimate edible garnish. To make them, run a sharp vegetable peeler in one long stroke over the top of a bar or square of chocolate. The longer the stroke and the warmer the chocolate, the more elegant the curl. But even the curls that break into shavings look pretty piled in the center or scattered across the top of a chocolate cake.

Williamsburg Orange Cake

serves:
12 to 16

prep:
35 minutes

bake:
20 to 24 minutes

cool:
20 minutes

How to Make Candied Lemon or Orange Zest

Candied citrus zest is easy to make, and is a pretty way to dress up any holiday cake. If you can find organic fruit, all the better. In any case, look for unwaxed oranges and lemons. Organic or not, rinse the fruit well and dry it with paper towels, says my friend Lucille Osborn, who shared this recipe. Cut the zest (the colored part of the peel) into long strands using a zester or run a sharp vegetable peeler around an orange or lemon and

I **HAD HEARD ABOUT THIS CAKE FOR YEARS** and had tried a scratch version of it. I loved how the fresh orange mixed so well with the golden raisins and chopped pecans, flavors typical of Williamsburg and Colonial America. I knew I could turn this medley into a quicker cake without sacrificing flavor. My recipe begins with a vanilla or yellow cake mix. Add half of a package of vanilla pudding just to help suspend the nuts and raisins. Use buttermilk for flavor and moisture and top this with a no-fuss orange buttercream frosting. This is a festive cake, perfect for Thanksgiving on through Christmas. It would even be gorgeous on the New Year's Eve buffet.

For the cake

Vegetable oil spray, for misting the pans
Flour, for dusting the pans
2 medium-size oranges
About 1 cup buttermilk
1 package (18.25 ounces) plain yellow cake mix
Half of a 3.4 ounce package of vanilla instant pudding mix (4 tablespoons)
½ cup vegetable oil
1 teaspoon pure vanilla extract
3 large eggs
½ cup finely chopped pecans
1 cup golden raisins, chopped

When Less (Pudding) Is More

My favorite reason to add instant pudding to a cake mix is for suspension, believe it or not. I know pudding is said to make cake moist, but so do sour cream, oil, buttermilk, mashed banana, and many other add-ins. For some reason pudding mix helps chocolate chips, nuts, raisins, and the like not sink to the bottom of the pan. That's why I've used it in many cakes in this chapter.

A downside to adding instant pudding is that it can cause the layers to shrink back from the side of the pan and decrease in volume as they cool. Martha Bowden, who has tested many recipes for me over the years, came up with the clever trick of using half a package of pudding when the recipe called for an entire package. She seals the remaining half in a plastic bag and places it in her pantry to use in a future cake. The half package of pudding still helps suspend ingredients and the cake bakes up pretty and doesn't shrink as it cools.

For the garnish and orange buttercream frosting

⅓ cup chopped toasted pecans, or 4 or 5 thin strips of orange zest
8 tablespoons (1 stick) butter, at room temperature
4½ cups confectioners' sugar, sifted
⅓ cup orange juice (see Step 2)
1 tablespoon orange zest (see Step 2)

1. Make the cake: Place a rack in the center of the oven and preheat the oven to 325°F. Lightly mist three 9-inch round cake pans with vegetable oil spray, then dust them with flour. Shake out the excess flour and set the pans aside.

then slice the zest into ¼ inch-wide strands. Two medium-size oranges or four lemons will make about 1 cup of strands.

Place 2 cups of granulated sugar and 1¼ cups of water in a medium-size saucepan over medium heat. Stir until the sugar dissolves and the syrup comes to a simmer. Drop the citric zest into the pan and stir until the strands are covered in syrup. Let the mixture barely simmer until the zest is translucent, 1 to 1½ hours. The less you let the zest simmer, the softer in texture it will be, and the longer it simmers the crunchier it will be. Using metal tongs, remove the zest from the syrup and arrange it in a single layer on a metal rack (discard the syrup). Let the zest dry from several hours to overnight; it will be pliable. Twist the candied zest into the shape you desire and coat it with granulated sugar or white sanding (decorating) sugar. Keep the zest in a plastic container for up to one month.

Recipe Reminders

MADE FOR

PREP NOTES

DON'T FORGET

SPECIAL TOUCHES

2. Rinse the oranges and pat them dry with paper towels. Grate enough zest to measure 2 tablespoons. Set aside 1 tablespoon of the zest for the frosting, if desired. Cut one orange in half and squeeze the juice into a small bowl; you will have ⅓ to ½ cup. Set this juice aside for the frosting, if desired. Cut the remaining orange in half, squeeze its juice into a measuring cup. Add enough buttermilk to measure 1⅓ cups of liquid. Pour the orange juice and buttermilk mixture into a large mixing bowl. Add the cake mix, pudding mix, oil, vanilla, eggs, and the remaining 1 tablespoon of orange zest to the bowl and beat with an electric mixer on low speed until the ingredients are incorporated, 1 minute. Stop the machine and scrape down the side of the bowl with a rubber spatula. Increase the mixer speed to medium and beat for 2 minutes longer, scraping down the side of the bowl again if needed. The batter should look well blended. Fold in the ½ cup of chopped pecans and the raisins. Divide the cake batter evenly among the 3 prepared cake pans, about 2 cups batter per pan, smoothing the tops with the rubber spatula. Place the cake pans in the oven. If your oven is not large enough to hold 3 pans on one rack, place 2 pans on that rack and one in the center of the rack above.

3. Bake the cake layers until they are golden brown and the tops spring back when lightly pressed with a finger, 20 to 24 minutes. The cake layer on the higher rack may bake faster so test it for doneness first. Transfer the cake pans to wire racks and let the cake layers cool for 5 minutes. Leave the oven on to toast the pecans. Run a long, sharp knife around the edge of each cake layer and give the pans a good shake to loosen the cakes. Invert each layer onto a wire rack, then invert it again onto another rack so that the cakes are right side up. Let the layers cool to room temperature, 15 minutes longer.

4. Make the garnish and orange buttercream frosting: If garnishing with pecans, spread the nuts out in a small baking pan and place it in the oven. Toast the pecans until they are brown and fragrant, 3 to 4 minutes. Immediately transfer the toasted pecans from the baking pan to a small bowl and set them aside.

5. Place the butter in a medium-size mixing bowl. Beat with an electric mixer on low speed until fluffy, 30 seconds. Stop the machine and add the confectioners' sugar and about ⅓ cup of the reserved orange juice, adding 1 tablespoon of juice at a time. Fold in the reserved 1 tablespoon of orange zest. Beat with the mixer on low speed until the sugar is incorporated, 1 minute. Increase the mixer speed to medium and beat until light and fluffy, 1 minute longer.

6. To assemble the cake, transfer one layer, right side up, to a serving platter. Spread the top with frosting. Place the second layer of cake, right side up, on top of the first and frost the top. Repeat this process with the third layer. Use the remaining frosting to frost the side of the cake, working with smooth, clean strokes. Garnish the top of the cake with the toasted chopped pecans or strips of orange zest. To make slicing easier, place the uncovered cake in the refrigerator until the frosting sets, 20 minutes.

Keep It Fresh! Store this cake, in a cake saver or loosely covered with waxed paper, in the refrigerator for up to one week. Freeze the cake, wrapped in aluminum foil, for up to six months. Let the cake thaw overnight in the refrigerator before serving.

Tips for Baking a Three-Layer Cake

You need to keep the oven light on when baking a three-layer cake because if you've got one layer on the top rack, it will be done more quickly and runs the risk of overbaking. This is especially important in the Williamsburg Orange Cake recipe because the chopped pecans can tend to make the batter dry. That's why I bake this cake at 325°F, which is a lower heat than usual and prevents overbaking. Layers in a 325°F oven will take a little longer to bake—these bake in 20 to 24 minutes—but the moist results are worth it.

This Takes the Cake!

Cakes were meant for sharing with others. Here are ways you can travel with cakes without a lot of fuss or expense.

◆ A 13 by 9-inch metal baking pan with a plastic lid is good for transporting bars, brownies, cakes, and cookies.

◆ Invest in a round plastic cake server—or two. Tupperware cake carriers are not only durable, their lids lock in place; go to www.tupperware.com.

◆ Tote bars, cookies, and cupcakes in shirt boxes after lining the lids with waxed paper.

◆ Oatmeal containers are good for taking cookies to a friend. Decorate the box if you like.

◆ Gallon-size resealable plastic bags hold cookies and brownies.

◆ Cover a square of sturdy cardboard with aluminum foil to make a base for a layer cake. Wrap plastic wrap over the cake and the base to tote.

A Jar of Cake: To ship cakes, bake them in pint-size wide-mouth glass canning jars. The best cake recipes to use for this are simple ones with few add-ins. A Bundt or sheet cake recipe will make five or six jars of cake.

Spray the jars with vegetable oil spray then pour in a scant one cup of cake batter in each jar and set the jars on the oven rack to bake. The cakes will be done after 28 to 30 minutes at 350°F. When the cakes are done, remove the jars from the oven, immediately wipe the rims, and seal the jars with a jar lid and ring. Mail the cakes with tubes of frosting and sprinkles. You can also make banana or zucchini bread the same way.

To make smaller jars of cake, use half-pint jars, fill them with a half cup of batter, and bake them for 18 to 20 minutes.

Blueberry Muffin Crumble Cake

WHO CAN RESIST BLUEBERRY MUFFINS? They are my younger daughter's favorite thing to bake. So with summer blueberries plentiful and sweet, we baked this fun layer cake that tastes just like a giant blueberry muffin. And just like that muffin you've got a crunchy pecan and brown sugar topping and a sugar and milk glaze dripping down the side. And you've got the subtle flavor of lemon, which goes so well with blueberries. Serve this cake warm for brunch at home or take it to the office and slice and serve it with coffee. It's even a treat for dessert with ice cream after a summer barbecue.

serves:
12 to 16

prep:
35 minutes

bake:
24 to 28 minutes

cool:
25 minutes (optional)

1¾ to 2¼ cups fresh blueberries
Vegetable oil spray, for misting the pans
Flour, for dusting the pans
½ cup all-purpose flour
½ cup packed light brown sugar
4 tablespoons (½ stick) cold butter
½ cup finely chopped pecans
1 medium-size lemon
1 package (18.25 ounces) vanilla or yellow cake mix with pudding
1 container (6 ounces; ¾ cup) lemon yogurt
½ cup water
⅓ cup vegetable oil
3 large eggs
1½ cups confectioners' sugar, sifted
3 to 4 tablespoons milk

Recipe Reminders

MADE FOR

PREP NOTES

DON'T FORGET

SPECIAL TOUCHES

1. Rinse the blueberries and drain them on paper towels.

2. Place a rack in the center of the oven and preheat the oven to 350°F. Lightly mist only the sides of two 9-inch round pans with vegetable oil spray, then dust them with flour. Shake out the excess flour.

3. Using a pencil, trace the bottom of a 9-inch round pan onto two pieces of parchment paper. Cut out the two round pieces of paper, place them in the bottom of the two prepared cake pans, and set them aside.

4. Place the flour and brown sugar in a medium-size bowl and toss with your fingers until well mixed. Cut the butter into small cubes and add it to the flour and brown sugar mixture. Using a pastry blender or 2 knives, cut the butter into the mixture until it resembles coarse crumbs. Add the pecans to the mixture and toss to combine. Evenly sprinkle this topping mix onto the parchment paper rounds, about ¾ cup in each cake pan. Set the pans aside.

5. Rinse the lemon and pat it dry with paper towels. Grate 1 teaspoon of lemon zest. Cut the lemon in half and squeeze the juice into a small bowl; you will have about 2 tablespoons. Set 1 tablespoon of juice aside for the glaze.

6. Measure out 1 tablespoon of the cake mix and set it aside. Place the remaining cake mix and the yogurt, water, oil, eggs, and the remaining 1 tablespoon of lemon juice, and the lemon zest, in a large mixing bowl. Beat with an electric mixer on low speed until the ingredients are incorporated, 1 minute. Stop the machine and scrape down the side of the bowl with a rubber spatula. Increase the mixer speed to medium and beat for 2 minutes longer, scraping down the side of the bowl again if needed. The batter should look well blended.

7. Set aside ¼ cup of the drained blueberries for garnish. Place the remaining blueberries in a small bowl and toss them with the reserved 1 tablespoon of cake mix. Fold the blueberries into the cake batter until just evenly combined. Using a large mixing spoon, dollop the cake batter on top of the topping in each cake pan, then carefully spread it evenly to the edges. Place the cake pans in the oven side by side.

8. Bake the cake layers until they are golden brown and the tops spring back when lightly pressed with a finger, 24 to 28 minutes. Transfer the cake pans to wire racks and let the cake layers cool for 5 minutes. Run a long, sharp knife around the edge of each cake layer and give the pans a good shake to loosen the cakes. Invert each layer onto a wire rack so that the topping side is up. Let the layers cool to room temperature, 20 minutes longer, if desired. Peel off and discard the parchment paper circles.

9. For the glaze, whisk the confectioners' sugar and reserved 1 tablespoon of lemon juice in a small bowl. Add 1 tablespoon of milk at a time until the glaze is smooth but still runny enough that it will slowly drip down the side of the cake.

10. To assemble the cake, transfer one layer, topping side up, to a serving platter. Using a spoon, drizzle half of the glaze over the cake and allow it to drip over the edge. Place the second layer on top of the first and drizzle the remaining glaze over it. Garnish the top of the cake with the reserved ¼ cup of blueberries.

Keep It Fresh! Store this cake, in a cake saver or loosely covered with plastic wrap, at room temperature for up to three days. Freeze the cake, wrapped in aluminum foil, for up to six months. Let the cake thaw overnight on the counter before serving.

Gotta Have Blueberry Muffins?

Line 20 to 24 muffin tins with paper liners. Spoon the blueberry batter into each liner until it is three-quarters full. Sprinkle the topping over the batter and place the muffin tins in a 350°F oven. Bake the muffins until they spring back when lightly pressed with a finger, 20 to 25 minutes. Transfer the muffins in their liners to a wire rack to cool for 10 minutes. Drizzle the glaze over the muffins, if desired.

Lemonade Chiffon Layer Cake with Raspberry Filling

serves:
12 to 16

prep:
30 minutes

bake:
25 to 30 minutes

cool:
25 minutes

I **HAVE FOND MEMORIES** of frozen lemonade concentrate. It was the elixir of the beginning of our childhood summers. We'd fill a pitcher with water, then stir in the concentrate until it dissolved—which wasn't too long in the hot sun. Little did we know that lemonade concentrate is a great ingredient to add to cake recipes because in a small amount it adds a big dose of lemon flavor. And that is what you find in this elegant cake—lemon flavor—plus the lightness of a chiffon cake with a ribbon of raspberry filling running through the center. A few extra egg whites beaten and folded into the batter make this cake light on the palate. Serve it at dinner parties after grilled fish, for springtime and summer gatherings, any time a cold glass of lemonade would taste good.

For the cake

Vegetable oil spray, for misting the pans
Flour, for dusting the pans
5 large egg whites
½ teaspoon cream of tartar
1 medium-size lemon
1 package (18.25 ounces) plain yellow cake mix
3 large egg yolks
¾ cup water
½ cup vegetable oil
¼ cup thawed lemonade concentrate (see Note)

For the lemonade buttercream frosting and raspberry filling

8 tablespoons (1 stick) butter, at room temperature
2 tablespoons thawed lemonade concentrate
1 to 2 tablespoons water
3½ to 4 cups confectioners' sugar, sifted
About 1 cup raspberry pie and pastry filling (from one 14-ounce can)

1. Make the cake: Place a rack in the center of the oven and preheat the oven to 325°F. Lightly mist two 9-inch round cake pans with vegetable oil spray, then dust them with flour. Shake out the excess flour and set the pans aside.

2. Place the egg whites and cream of tartar in a medium-size mixing bowl. Beat with an electric mixer on high speed until stiff peaks form, 2 to 3 minutes. Set the bowl aside.

3. Rinse the lemon and pat it dry with paper towels. Grate enough zest to measure 1 teaspoon. Cut the lemon in half and squeeze the juice into a small bowl; you will have 2 to 3 tablespoons.

4. Place the cake mix, egg yolks, ¾ cup of water, oil, ¼ cup of lemonade concentrate, lemon zest, and lemon juice in a large mixing bowl and, using the same beaters used to beat the egg whites (no need to clean them), beat with the electric mixer on low speed until the ingredients are incorporated, 1 minute. Stop the machine and scrape down the side of the bowl with a rubber spatula. Increase the mixer speed to medium and beat for 2 minutes longer, scraping down the side of the bowl again if needed. The batter should look well blended. Turn the beaten egg whites out on top of the cake batter and, using the rubber spatula, fold the whites into the batter until the mixture is light but well combined. Divide the cake batter evenly between the 2 prepared cake pans, smoothing the tops with the rubber spatula. Place the cake pans in the oven side by side.

Recipe Reminders

MADE FOR

PREP NOTES

DON'T FORGET

SPECIAL TOUCHES

Other Fillings for Lemonade Chiffon Layer Cake

You can make the cake without a filling or opt for one of these great fillers. You will need about 1 cup.

1. Strawberry all-fruit preserves or strawberry jam

2. Blueberry all-fruit preserves

3. A quick blueberry sauce: Place 2 cups of rinsed fresh blueberries in a saucepan with 1/4 cup of sugar. Simmer, stirring, until the sauce boils down to 1 cup, about 15 minutes. Let the sauce cool to room temperature, or chill it, before using it to fill the cake.

4. Lemon, lime, or tangerine curd

5. The pineapple and orange filling from the Hawaiian Wedding Cake (page 84)

5. Bake the cake layers until they are golden brown and the tops spring back when lightly pressed with a finger, 25 to 30 minutes. Transfer the cake pans to wire racks and let the cake layers cool for 5 minutes. Run a long, sharp knife around the edge of each cake layer and give the pans a good shake to loosen the cakes. Invert each layer onto a wire rack, then invert it again onto another rack so that the cakes are right side up. Let the layers cool completely, 20 minutes longer.

6. Meanwhile, make the lemon buttercream frosting. Place the butter in a medium-size bowl and beat with an electric mixer on low speed until fluffy, 30 seconds. Stop the machine and add the 2 tablespoons of lemonade concentrate, 1 tablespoon of water, and the confectioners' sugar. Beat with the mixer on low speed until the sugar is incorporated, 1 minute. Increase the mixer speed to medium-high and beat until light and fluffy, 1 minute longer, adding up to 1 tablespoon more of water, if necessary.

7. To assemble the cake, transfer one layer, right side up, to a serving platter. Spread the top with about 1 cup of the frosting. Spread a layer of the raspberry filling carefully on top of the frosting, using about 1 cup of the filling. Place the second layer of cake, right side up, on top of the first. Frost the top of the cake, then the side, working with smooth, clean strokes.

Keep It Fresh! Store this cake, in a cake saver or loosely covered with plastic wrap, at room temperature for up to three days. Freeze the cake, wrapped in aluminum foil, for up to six months. Let the cake thaw overnight on the counter before serving.

Note: The smallest cans of frozen lemonade concentrate are 6 ounces, perfect for this recipe. If you can only find a larger can, return the unused portion to the freezer for making lemonade.

Lemon Lover's Layer Cake with Lemon Cream Cheese Frosting

IF YOU LOVE LEMON you'll love this cake. Without the poppy seeds and white chocolate called for in recipes in my other books, this cake is lemon plain and simple, flavored with lemon yogurt and pudding and fresh lemon juice and zest. The frosting is my lighter cream cheese one with lemon juice and zest. Bake this cake for birthdays and potlucks, and even for dinner parties where you can serve it with a scoop of raspberry sorbet. Or turn this recipe into twenty to twenty-four cupcakes, each garnished with a whole fresh raspberry.

serves:
12 to 16

prep:
25 minutes

bake:
25 to 30 minutes

cool:
30 minutes

For the cake

Vegetable oil spray, for misting the pans
Flour, for dusting the pans
1 medium-size lemon
1 package (18.25 ounces) plain yellow or vanilla cake mix
1 package (3.4 ounces) lemon instant pudding mix
1 container (6 ounces; ¾ cup) low-fat lemon yogurt
¾ cup water
½ cup vegetable oil
4 large eggs

For the lemon cream cheese frosting

4 ounces reduced-fat cream cheese, at room temperature
8 tablespoons (1 stick) butter, at room temperature
About 4 cups confectioners' sugar, sifted

Recipe Reminders

MADE FOR

PREP NOTES

DON'T FORGET

SPECIAL TOUCHES

1. Make the cake: Place a rack in the center of the oven and preheat the oven to 350°F. Lightly mist two 9-inch round cake pans with vegetable oil spray, then dust them with flour. Shake out the excess flour and set the pans aside.

2. Rinse the lemon and pat it dry with paper towels. Grate enough zest to measure 2 teaspoons. Set 1 teaspoon of zest aside for the frosting. Cut the lemon in half and squeeze the juice into a small bowl; you will need 1 tablespoon plus 2 teaspoons. Set 2 teaspoons of lemon juice aside for the frosting.

3. Place the cake mix, pudding mix, yogurt, water, oil, eggs, 1 teaspoon of lemon zest, and 1 tablespoon of lemon juice in a large mixing bowl and beat with an electric mixer on low speed until the ingredients are moistened, 30 seconds. Stop the machine and scrape down the side of the bowl with a rubber spatula. Increase the mixer speed to medium and beat for 1½ minutes longer, scraping down the side of the bowl again if needed. The batter should be thick and well blended. Divide the cake batter evenly between the 2 prepared cake pans, smoothing the tops with the rubber spatula. Place the cake pans in the oven side by side.

4. Bake the cake layers until they are golden brown and the tops spring back when lightly pressed with a finger, 25 to 30 minutes. Transfer the cake pans to wire racks and let the cake layers cool for 10 minutes. Run a dinner knife around the edge of each cake layer and give the pans a good shake to loosen the cakes. Invert each layer onto a wire rack, then invert it again onto another rack so that the cakes are right side up. Let the layers cool completely, 20 minutes longer.

5. Meanwhile, make the lemon cream cheese frosting: Place the cream cheese and butter in a medium-size bowl and beat with an electric mixer on low speed until creamy, 30 seconds. Add 2 cups of the confectioners' sugar and the reserved 1 teaspoon

Love the Lemons

I just don't get how something that is a failure, something that doesn't work, is called a "lemon." The lemon is one of the best tools in the kitchen. It is an ingredient that works in appetizers—like hummus, in salad vinaigrettes, in marinades, squeezed over grilled fish and steak, and especially in baking. Juice a lemon and you've got a tablespoon or two of flavor to perk up cake batter. Zest a lemon and you've got the most intense teaspoon of flavor around—just the right addition for the simplest buttercream frosting.

You'll get more juice from a lemon if it is at room temperature, not chilled from the fridge. So pull lemons out of the refrigerator ahead of time and roll them on the kitchen counter with the palm of your hand to warm them up before juicing. A medium-size lemon will give you about two tablespoons of juice and two teaspoons of grated zest.

My favorite tool for zesting lemons, limes, and oranges is the Microplane. Grate the zest right over the mixing bowl or over waxed paper or a plate should you need to measure it. If you cannot use all the zest, just freeze what's left for future baking. Place it in a small plastic resealable freezer bag and freeze it for up to two months.

of lemon zest and 2 teaspoons of lemon juice, then beat with the mixer on low speed until the mixture is combined, 30 seconds. Add 1½ cups of the remaining confectioners' sugar and beat until smooth and spreadable, 30 seconds. Increase the mixer speed to high and beat, adding the remaining ½ cup of confectioners' sugar if needed to make the frosting thick and fluffy, 1 minute longer.

6. To assemble the cake, transfer one layer, right side up, to a cake plate and spread some of the frosting over the top. Place the second layer of cake, right side up, on top of the first, then

Time-Saving Tips

Cake baking, believe it or not, was made for interruptions. Why do you think parents of small children have been able to pull it off? Even if your life is hectic, if you need a home-baked cake by week's end, you can plan ahead and pull it off. Here's how:

1. A week in advance: Bake the layers, let them cool, wrap them in aluminum foil, and freeze them.

2. Two days out: Make the frosting, cover it, and place it in the refrigerator.

3. A day in advance: Remove the cake layers from the freezer and let them thaw on the counter. Assemble and frost the cake, then place it in a cake saver and place it in the refrigerator until it's time to serve.

4. Day of the party: Relax, slice the cake, and eat!

spread the remaining frosting over the top and side, working with smooth, clean strokes. To make slicing easier, place the uncovered cake in the refrigerator until the frosting sets, 20 minutes.

Keep It Fresh! If your kitchen is warm, store this cake in a cake saver in the refrigerator for up to three days. You can store a covered cake on the counter for 24 hours if the kitchen is cool, then place the cake in the refrigerator. Freeze the cake, in a cake saver, for up to six months. Let the cake thaw overnight in the refrigerator before serving.

Frozen Pink Lemonade Party Cake

My North Carolina readers have told me about a famous pink lemonade cake that is made in the summertime there. It is a yellow layer cake with a layer of frozen ice cream and lemonade concentrate in the center. To make this layer, you combine a quart of softened vanilla ice cream with half of a 6-ounce can of thawed pink lemonade concentrate and six drops of red food coloring. (Set the remaining lemonade concentrate aside for the frosting.) Line a 9-inch round cake pan with plastic wrap, letting the plastic wrap drop over the side of the pan. Spread the ice cream mixture in the cake pan and put it in the freezer for three hours. When you are ready to assemble the cake, place a yellow cake layer on a serving plate and arrange the ice cream layer on top. Use the plastic wrap to lift the ice cream out of the pan. Place a second cake layer on top of the ice cream. For the frosting, combine one cup of heavy cream, two tablespoons of sugar, and the remaining lemonade concentrate and whip them until stiff. Frost the top and side of the cake and return it to the freezer until it's time to slice and serve.

Old-Fashioned Pear and Ginger Cakes

My husband, John, was crazy about the upside-down pear and ginger cake in the first *Cake Mix Doctor* book. But I thought it needed more real pear flavor. So I came up with this rendition, which I think is better. Here the pears are fresh instead of canned and the cake is lighter since it contains no oil, just applesauce. That way you focus on the fresh pear slices and the dreamy brown sugar and butter layer next to them! Bake this cake in two nine-inch round layers but don't layer them. To serve invert the rounds onto serving plates and, while they're still a little warm, cut them into wedges and serve with vanilla ice cream. John loves this pear cake even more!

serves: 12 to 16

prep: 20 minutes

bake: 25 to 27 minutes

cool: 10 minutes

¾ cup packed dark brown sugar
6 tablespoons (¾ stick) butter, melted
4 medium-size, ripe, fresh pears
1 package (18.25 ounces) plain spice cake mix
1 cup unsweetened applesauce
½ cup buttermilk
1 teaspoon ground ginger
½ teaspoon ground cinnamon
3 large eggs
Vanilla ice cream, for serving

1. Place a rack in the center of the oven and preheat the oven to 350°F.

One Big Pear Cake

If you'd like, go ahead and bake this cake in a 13 by 9-inch pan, baking it for about 45 minutes. Don't invert the cake unless you have a rectangular platter large enough to hold it. Cut the cake into squares and invert them onto plates, then serve them with ice cream. I have found this cake is best served the same day it is baked.

Recipe Reminders

MADE FOR

PREP NOTES

DON'T FORGET

SPECIAL TOUCHES

2. Divide the brown sugar between two 9-inch round cake pans, spreading it out evenly. Divide the melted butter between the two pans, covering the top of the brown sugar. Press the brown sugar mixture out so that it covers the entire bottom of each pan. Set the pans aside.

3. Peel the pears, cut them into quarters, and remove the cores from the centers. Cut each quarter pear lengthwise into 3 or 4 slices. Arrange the slices, rounded side up, in rows on top of the brown sugar and butter mixture.

4. Place the cake mix, applesauce, buttermilk, ginger, cinnamon, and eggs in a large mixing bowl and beat with an electric mixer on low speed until the ingredients are incorporated, 30 seconds. Stop the machine and scrape down the side of the bowl with a rubber spatula. Increase the mixer speed to medium and beat for 2 minutes longer, scraping down the side of the bowl again if needed. The batter should look well combined and smooth. Divide the cake batter evenly between the 2 cake pans, pouring the batter over the pears and smoothing it out with the rubber spatula. Place the cake pans in the oven side by side.

5. Bake the cake layers until the tops spring back when lightly pressed with a finger, 25 to 27 minutes. Remove the cake pans from the oven and carefully run a knife around the edge of each cake. Invert the cakes onto serving plates immediately and let them cool for 10 minutes.

6. Cut the cakes into wedges and serve with ice cream.

Keep It Fresh! Store these cakes, in cake savers or loosely covered with plastic wrap, in the refrigerator for up to three days. It does not freeze well.

Apple Butter Spice Cake with Caramel Frosting

SOME OF MY FAVORITE NEW CAKES have come from testing recipes for "A Piece of Cake," my online newsletter. Often these recipes are something I develop out of the blue, but just as often they are to fill a request from a reader. This cake is one of the latter. A reader from San Antonio was looking for a spice cake with a filling of apple butter. I could not get this idea out of my head so I went to work. The apple butter and orange filling is sandwiched between my sour cream spice layers. And the caramel frosting on the top and side makes this a crowd-pleaser.

serves:
12 to 16

prep:
30 minutes

bake:
16 to 18 minutes

cool:
30 minutes

For the cake

Vegetable oil spray, for misting the pans
Flour, for dusting the pans
1 package (18.25 ounces) plain spice cake mix
1 cup sour cream
¾ cup water
½ cup vegetable oil
3 large eggs
1 teaspoon pure vanilla extract

For the filling

1 large egg
1 large orange (see Note)
2 cups apple butter
2 tablespoons (¼ stick) butter
½ cup finely chopped toasted pecans (see page 204)
Quick Caramel Frosting (page 485)

Recipe Reminders

MADE FOR

PREP NOTES

DON'T FORGET

SPECIAL TOUCHES

1. Make the cake: Place a rack in the center of the oven and preheat the oven to 350°F. Lightly mist three 9-inch round cake pans with vegetable oil spray, then dust them with flour. Shake out the excess flour and set the pans aside.

2. Place the cake mix, sour cream, water, oil, 3 eggs, and vanilla in a large mixing bowl and beat with an electric mixer on low speed until the ingredients are incorporated, 30 seconds. Stop the machine and scrape down the side of the bowl with a rubber spatula. Increase the mixer speed to medium and beat for 2 minutes longer, scraping down the side of the bowl again if needed. The batter should look well blended. Divide the cake batter evenly among the 3 prepared cake pans, about 1½ cups of batter per pan, smoothing the tops with the rubber spatula. Place the pans in the oven. If your oven is not large enough to hold 3 pans on the center rack, place 2 pans on that rack and one in the center of the rack above.

3. Bake the cake layers until they are light brown and the tops spring back when lightly pressed with a finger, 16 to 18 minutes. The cake layer on the higher rack may bake faster so test it for doneness first. Transfer the cake pans to wire racks and let the cake layers cool for 10 minutes. Run a dinner knife around the edge of each cake layer and give the pans a good shake to loosen the cakes. Invert each layer onto a wire rack, then invert it again onto another rack so that the cakes are right side up. Let the layers cool completely, 20 minutes longer.

4. Meanwhile, make the filling: Place the egg in a metal bowl and beat until the egg is lemon colored. Rinse the orange and pat it dry with paper towels. Grate enough zest to measure ½ teaspoon. Cut the orange in half and squeeze the juice into a small bowl; you will need ⅓ cup of juice. Add the orange zest and juice to the beaten egg and set this mixture aside.

5. Place the apple butter in a heavy saucepan over medium heat and stir it with a whisk until it is steaming and bubbly. Pour half of the hot apple butter into the egg mixture and whisk briskly to combine. Pour this egg mixture back into the saucepan with the remaining apple butter and whisk briskly over low heat until the mixture bubbles and thickens, 3 to 4 minutes. Remove the pan from the heat, add the butter, stir until it melts, then let cool.

6. To assemble the cake, transfer one layer, right side up, to a serving plate or cake stand, spread half of the filling on top and sprinkle ¼ cup of the pecans over the filling. Place the second cake layer, right side up, on top of the first and spread the remaining filling over it, topping it with the remaining ¼ cup of pecans. Place the third layer of cake on top of the second. Cover the cake with plastic wrap and set it aside.

7. Make the caramel frosting.

8. While the frosting is warm, spoon or pour two thirds of the frosting over the top of the cake, letting it flow down the side. Using a long metal icing spatula, spread out the frosting on top and spread it around the side. Add more frosting as needed to cover the side of the cake, working with smooth, clean strokes. As the frosting cools, it will harden.

Keep It Fresh! Store this cake, in a cake saver or loosely covered with plastic wrap, at room temperature for up to three days. Freeze the cake, wrapped in aluminum foil, for up to six months. Let the cake thaw overnight on the counter before serving.

Note: If the orange does not yield ⅓ cup of juice, use orange juice from a carton to make up the difference.

Can't Find a Spice Cake Mix?

Use a plain vanilla or yellow cake mix and stir in 1 teaspoon of ground cinnamon, ½ teaspoon of ground allspice, and ¼ teaspoon of ground nutmeg.

CINNAMON APPLE SPICE CAKE

serves:
12 to 16

prep:
25 minutes

bake:
25 to 30 minutes

cool:
25 minutes

UNLIKE MOST SHOPPERS I don't stroll down the supermarket aisles just in search of dinner ideas. I also look for new ingredients I might use in baking. And this recipe is a great example for it is based on those cinnamon apple rings that come packed in a jar. I looked at them one day and didn't think roast pork or ham. I thought pureed in a spice cake batter. In this cake the apples create pretty and fragrant, pink and moist layers. If you can't find spiced apple rings substitute 1 cup of cinnamon-flavored applesauce.

Vegetable oil spray, for misting the pans
Flour, for dusting the pans
1 jar (14.5 ounces) spiced apple rings
1 package (18.25 ounces) plain spice cake mix
1 cup buttermilk
½ cup vegetable oil
1 teaspoon pure vanilla extract
3 large eggs
Buttercream Frosting (page 468)
½ cup chopped toasted walnuts (optional; see page 204), for garnish

1. Make the cake: Place a rack in the center of the oven and preheat the oven to 350°F. Lightly mist two 9-inch round cake pans with vegetable oil spray and dust them with flour. Shake out the excess flour and set the pans aside.

2. Drain the apple rings, discarding the juice. Blend the apple rings in a food processor until they are almost smooth, about 6 pulses. You will have almost 1 cup of apples.

3. Place the pureed apple rings, cake mix, buttermilk, oil, vanilla, and eggs in a large mixing bowl and beat with an electric mixer on low speed until the ingredients are incorporated, 30 seconds. Stop the machine and scrape down the side of the bowl with a rubber spatula. Increase the mixer speed to medium-high and beat for 1½ to 2 minutes longer, scraping down the side of the bowl again if needed. The batter should be thickened and nearly smooth. Divide the cake batter evenly between the 2 prepared cake pans, smoothing the tops with the rubber spatula. Place the pans in the oven side by side.

4. Bake the cake layers until they are golden brown and the tops spring back when lightly pressed with a finger, 25 to 30 minutes. Transfer the cake pans to wire racks and let the cake layers cool for 5 minutes. Run a knife around the edge of each cake layer and give the pans a good shake to loosen the cakes. Invert each layer onto a wire rack then invert it again onto another rack so that the layers are right side up. Let the layers cool completely, 20 minutes longer.

5. Meanwhile, make the Buttercream Frosting.

6. To assemble the cake, transfer one layer, right side up, to a serving plate and cover it with 1 cup of the frosting, spreading it out evenly to the edge. Place the second layer, right side up, on top of the first and spread the top and side of the cake with the remaining frosting, working with smooth, clean strokes. Garnish the cake, if desired, by sprinkling the toasted walnuts over the top.

Keep It Fresh! Store this cake, in a cake saver or loosely covered with plastic wrap, at room temperature for up to three days. Freeze the cake, wrapped in aluminum foil, for up to six months. Let the cake thaw overnight on the counter before serving.

Recipe Reminders

MADE FOR

____

____

____

____

PREP NOTES

____

____

____

____

DON'T FORGET

____

____

____

____

SPECIAL TOUCHES

____

____

____

____

____

____

____

____

____

Pineapple Carrot Cake with Cinnamon Cream Cheese Frosting

serves:
12 to 16

prep:
35 to 40 minutes

bake:
30 to 35 minutes

cool:
25 minutes

READER NICOLE BENITEZ of Silver City, New Mexico, sent me this recipe several years ago. She had baked it for a friend who loves carrot cake. I followed Nicole's recipe and thought it needed a little more cinnamon and a splash of vanilla. Then I frosted the cake with my lighter cream cheese frosting, which is rich and creamy but not so heavy as the original. That leaves room for the smorgasbord of goodies in the cake—grated carrots, crushed pineapple, walnuts, coconut, and spices. Bake this cake for friends most any time of the year.

For the cake

Vegetable oil spray, for misting the pans
Flour, for dusting the pans
1 package (18.25 ounces) plain white or yellow cake mix
1 package (3.4 ounces) vanilla instant pudding mix
1 can (8 ounces) crushed pineapple, with juice
½ cup vegetable oil
1 tablespoon pure vanilla extract
1 tablespoon ground cinnamon
½ teaspoon ground ginger
4 large eggs
2 cups grated carrots
½ cup sweetened shredded coconut
½ cup chopped walnuts

For the cinnamon cream cheese frosting

4 ounces reduced-fat cream cheese, at room temperature
8 tablespoons (1 stick) butter, at room temperature
1 teaspoon pure vanilla extract
3 to 3½ cups confectioners' sugar, sifted
½ teaspoon ground cinnamon

1. Make the cake: Place a rack in the center of the oven and preheat the oven to 350°F. Lightly mist two 9-inch round cake pans with vegetable oil spray, and dust them with flour. Shake out the excess flour and set the pans aside.

2. Place the cake mix, pudding mix, crushed pineapple and its juice, oil, 1 tablespoon of vanilla, 1 tablespoon of cinnamon, and the ginger and eggs in a large mixing bowl and beat with an electric mixer on low speed until the ingredients are incorporated, 30 seconds. Stop the machine and scrape down the side of the bowl with a rubber spatula. Increase the mixer speed to medium and beat for 1½ to 2 minutes longer, scraping down the side of the bowl again if needed. The batter should look well blended. Stir in the carrots, coconut, and walnuts until well combined. Divide the cake batter evenly between the 2 prepared cake pans, smoothing the tops with the rubber spatula. Place the pans in the oven side by side.

3. Bake the cake layers until they are golden brown and the tops spring back when lightly pressed with a finger, 30 to 35 minutes. Transfer the cake pans to wire racks and let

Recipe Reminders

MADE FOR

____

____

____

____

PREP NOTES

____

____

____

____

DON'T FORGET

____

____

____

____

SPECIAL TOUCHES

____

____

____

____

____

____

____

____

____

the cake layers cool for 5 minutes. Run a sharp knife around the edge of each cake layer and give the pans a good shake to loosen the cakes. Invert each layer onto a wire rack, then invert it again onto another rack so that the layers are right side up. Let the layers cool completely, 20 minutes longer.

Greasing the Bottoms Only

We're accustomed to greasing both the bottom and side of layer pans for most recipes, but when you grease just the bottom you see a little better rise in the cake and thus more volume. If you want the tallest cake possible, grease and flour only the bottom of the pans. The cake batter works its way up the side of the pans, clinging onto them as it does in an angel food cake. The cake layers are taller. I find you need to run a knife around the edge of the pans immediately after they are removed from the oven so that the cake doesn't stick to the side.

4. Make the cinnamon cream cheese frosting: Place the cream cheese, butter, and 1 teaspoon vanilla extract in a medium-size bowl and beat with an electric mixer on medium-high until fluffy, about 30 seconds. Stop the machine and scrape down the side of the bowl with a rubber spatula. Add 3 cups of the confectioners' sugar and ½ teaspoon of cinnamon, then beat on medium speed until the frosting lightens and is smooth. If the frosting seems too thin, add up to ½ cup more confectioners' sugar.

5. To assemble the cake, transfer one layer, right side up, to a serving plate. Spread the top with about 1 cup of the frosting. Place the second cake layer, right side up, on top of the first and frost the top and side of the cake, working with smooth, clean strokes. To make slicing easier, place the uncovered cake in the refrigerator until the frosting sets, 20 minutes.

Keep It Fresh! Store this cake, in a cake saver or loosely covered with waxed paper, in the refrigerator for up to one week. Freeze the cake, wrapped in aluminum foil, for up to six months. Let the cake thaw overnight in the refrigerator before serving.

Classic Yellow Cake with Chocolate Fudge Marshmallow Frosting

serves:
12 to 16

prep:
25 minutes

bake:
30 to 35 minutes

cool:
25 minutes

W**HEN MY SISTERS AND I WERE YOUNG** our mother would bake a birthday cake of our choosing, and to be honest, our choice was most often yellow cake with chocolate frosting. I've told the story before of how my mom, the consummate scratch cook, just got tired and picked up a cake mix box, never looking back. She continued to cloak that box cake with a chocolate pan frosting that we loved so much we would fight each other to lick the wooden spoon! There is nothing more practical than having such a combination—yellow cake and chocolate frosting—in your repertoire because it makes a grand birthday cake and a great everyday cake, too. The frosting recipe may be even more decadent than what my mom made. It is adapted from a recipe by Martha Pearl Villas and her son James Villas and appeared in one of their cookbooks. I have come to rely on it. The taste is fudgelike and in my house we definitely fight for the spoon!

Vegetable oil spray, for misting the pans
Flour, for dusting the pans
1 package (18.25 ounces) plain yellow or vanilla cake mix
1 package (3.4 ounces) vanilla instant pudding mix
1¼ cups milk
½ cup vegetable oil
3 large eggs
1 teaspoon pure vanilla extract
Chocolate Fudge Marshmallow Frosting (page 479)

Recipe Reminders

MADE FOR

PREP NOTES

DON'T FORGET

SPECIAL TOUCHES

1. Place a rack in the center of the oven and preheat the oven to 350°F. Lightly mist the bottoms only of two 9-inch round cake pans with vegetable oil spray, then dust them with flour. Shake out the excess flour and set the pans aside.

2. Place the cake mix, pudding mix, milk, oil, eggs, and vanilla in a large mixing bowl and beat with an electric mixer on low speed until the ingredients are incorporated, 30 seconds. Stop the machine and scrape down the side of the bowl with a rubber spatula. Increase the mixer speed to medium and beat for 1½ minutes longer, scraping down the side of the bowl again if needed. The batter should look well blended and smooth. Divide the cake batter evenly between the 2 prepared cake pans, smoothing the tops with the rubber spatula. Place the pans in the oven side by side.

Jazz It Up!

Feel free to change my classic yellow cake recipe:

- **Add ½ teaspoon of pure almond extract to the batter.**
- **Substitute orange juice for some of the milk.**
- **Use unsweetened applesauce instead of the oil or for part of it.**
- **Use an egg substitute for the eggs.**
- **Add ¼ teaspoon of maple flavoring to the batter.**
- **Add a mashed ripe banana then decrease the oil to ¼ cup.**

3. Bake the cake layers until they are golden brown and the tops spring back when lightly pressed with a finger, 30 to 35 minutes. Transfer the cake pans to wire racks and let the cake layers cool for 5 minutes. Run a sharp knife around the edge of each cake layer and give the pans a good shake to loosen the cakes. Invert each layer onto a wire rack, then invert it again onto another rack so that the layers are right side up. Let the layers cool completely, 20 minutes longer.

4. After the cakes have cooled, make the Chocolate Fudge Marshmallow Frosting.

5. Immediately frost the cake as the frosting will harden quickly. Transfer one cake layer, right side up, to a serving plate. Spoon a cup of frosting on top and spread it evenly to the edge. Place the second cake layer, right side up, on top of the first and frost the top and side of the cake, working with smooth, clean strokes.

Keep It Fresh! Store this cake, in a cake saver, at room temperature for up to four days or in the refrigerator for up to one week. Freeze the cake, wrapped in aluminum foil, for up to three months. Let the cake thaw overnight in the refrigerator before serving.

Temperature Tests

What is the best temperature for baking the classic yellow cake? 325° or 350°F? I baked this cake at 325°F and then again at 350°F to find if there was a more perfect temperature. My conclusion? No real difference to the average eye. But moving closer and being a perfectionist, I did find the cake baked at the lower temperature had a smaller and more uniform crumb. So suit yourself. Bake the layers either 35 to 40 minutes at 325°F or 30 to 35 minutes at 350°F.

Cream Cheese Pound Cake with Chocolate Toffee Frosting

serves:
12 to 16

prep:
30 minutes

bake:
30 to 35 minutes

cool:
1 hour and 20 minutes

READER LISA CONOVER, who lives in Middletown, Delaware, planted the seed for this wonderful recipe. A professional cake baker, Lisa told me how she places finely minced bits of toffee in her whipped chocolate ganache frosting. What a great idea! It may sound a bit complicated but ganache is simply hot cream poured over chocolate and stirred until the chocolate melts. You chill it and whip it and wind up with a rich and powerful chocolate frosting, with that slight touch of toffee crunch. Pile the ganache onto pound cake layers and you have one serious dessert. Bake this cake for adult birthdays and girls' night out dinners and for someone who has tasted just about everything. It's deliciously over the top!

For the cake

Vegetable oil spray, for misting the pans
Flour, for dusting the pans
1 package (18.25 ounces) plain yellow or vanilla cake mix
4 ounces reduced-fat cream cheese, at room temperature
1 cup water
½ cup vegetable oil
2 teaspoons pure vanilla extract
4 large eggs

For the chocolate toffee bar frosting and garnish

1 cup plus 2 tablespoons heavy (whipping) cream
1 package (12 ounces; 2 cups) semisweet chocolate chips
1½ cups chocolate-covered or plain toffee bits

1. Make the cake: Place a rack in the center of the oven and preheat the oven to 325°F. Lightly mist two 9-inch round cake pans with vegetable oil spray, then dust them with flour. Shake out the excess flour and set the pans aside.

2. Place the cake mix, cream cheese, water, oil, vanilla, and eggs in a large mixing bowl and beat with an electric mixer on low speed until the ingredients are incorporated, 30 seconds. Stop the machine and scrape down the side of the bowl with a rubber spatula. Increase the mixer speed to medium and beat until the batter is smooth, 1½ to 2 minutes longer, scraping down the side of the bowl again if needed. Divide the cake batter evenly between the 2 prepared cake pans, smoothing the tops with the rubber spatula. Place the pans in the oven side by side.

3. Bake the cake layers until they are golden brown and the tops spring back when lightly pressed with a finger, 30 to 35 minutes. Transfer the cake pans to wire racks and let the cake layers cool for 5 minutes. Run a long, sharp knife around the edge of each cake layer and give the pans a good shake to loosen the cakes. Invert each layer onto a wire rack, then invert it again onto

Recipe Reminders

MADE FOR

____
____
____
____

PREP NOTES

____
____
____
____

DON'T FORGET

____
____
____
____

SPECIAL TOUCHES

____
____
____
____
____
____
____
____
____

another rack so that the cakes are right side up. Let the layers cool while you make the frosting.

4. Make the frosting: Place the cream in a small saucepan and bring to a boil over medium heat. Meanwhile, place the chocolate chips in a large stainless steel bowl and set aside. When the cream comes to a boil, pour it over the chocolate chips and stir with a wooden spoon until the chocolate melts, 1 to 2 minutes. When the chocolate mixture cools to room temperature, about 20 minutes, place it in the refrigerator, uncovered, to chill for 1 hour.

5. About 5 minutes before you remove the chilled chocolate from the refrigerator, place a clean set of electric mixer beaters in the freezer to chill. Measure 2 tablespoons of the toffee bits and set them aside for garnish. Place the remaining toffee bits in a food processor. Pulse until the toffee bits are minced but not too finely ground, 20 to 25 times. Set the minced toffee bits aside.

6. Remove the chocolate mixture from the refrigerator and the beaters from the freezer. Beat the chocolate mixture with an electric mixer on high speed until the mixture is light and fluffy, 1 minute. Fold in the reserved minced toffee bits until they are well incorporated.

7. To assemble the cake, transfer one layer, right side up, to a serving plate and top with a generous cup of frosting, spreading it evenly to the edge. Place the second cake layer right side up, on top of the first and generously spread the top and side with the remaining frosting. Garnish the top of the cake with the reserved 2 tablespoons of toffee bits.

Keep It Fresh! Store this cake, in a cake saver, in the refrigerator for up to three days. Freeze the cake, wrapped in aluminum foil, for up to six months. Let the cake thaw in the refrigerator before serving.

From Great to Amazing

It's easy to turn a great chocolate frosting into an amazing one by upgrading the chocolate. Instead of the routine semisweet chocolate chips, use premium bittersweet chocolate chips instead. Remember that one cup of chocolate chips is 6 ounces.

In a Hurry?

Don't whip the chocolate frosting. Spread it onto the cake after it cools to room temperature. Top the cake liberally with toffee bits.

Penny's Mom's Cake with Caramel Frosting

serves:
12 to 16

prep:
25 minutes

bake:
25 to 30 minutes

cool:
25 minutes

AT A COOKING CLASS IN DALLAS not too long ago, I was making an orange cake and, as I was mixing the batter, the class asked me questions and made suggestions—the usual fun back-and-forth conversation that goes along with cooking demos. A woman named Penny sitting near the back raised her hand and wanted to tell me about how her mother, who used to be in the test kitchen of a large cake mix company, doctored up a cake mix. After she had followed the package directions for a yellow or chocolate cake mix, she would add a little mayonnaise, sugar, and almond extract to the batter. I could not wait to get home and try this out, and I will tell you this batter is one of the most delicious I have tasted.

Vegetable oil spray, for misting the pans
Flour, for dusting the pans
1 package (18.25 ounces) plain yellow or vanilla cake mix or cake mix with pudding
1⅓ cups water
⅓ cup vegetable oil
¼ cup light mayonnaise
2 heaping tablespoons granulated sugar
¼ teaspoon pure almond extract
3 large eggs
Quick Caramel Frosting (page 485)

1. Place a rack in the center of the oven and preheat the oven to 350°F. Lightly mist two 9-inch round cake pans with vegetable oil

Chocolate on Your Mind?

Substitute a chocolate cake mix for the yellow, using ½ cup of oil and the same ingredients listed at left. The layers will bake in 23 to 27 minutes.

Recipe Reminders

MADE FOR

PREP NOTES

DON'T FORGET

SPECIAL TOUCHES

spray, then dust them with flour. Shake out the excess flour and set the pans aside.

2. Place the cake mix, water, oil, mayonnaise, granulated sugar, almond extract, and eggs in a large mixing bowl and beat with an electric mixer on low speed until the ingredients are moistened, 30 seconds. Stop the machine and scrape down the side of the bowl with a rubber spatula. Increase the mixer speed to medium and beat until the batter is thick and smooth, 1½ minutes longer. Divide the cake batter evenly between the 2 prepared cake pans, smoothing the tops with the rubber spatula. Place the pans in the oven side by side.

3. Bake the cake layers until they are golden brown and spring back when lightly pressed with a finger, 25 to 30 minutes. Transfer the cake pans to wire racks and let the cake layers cool for 5 minutes. Run a sharp knife around the edge of each cake and give the pans a good shake to loosen the cakes. Invert each layer on a wire rack, then invert it again onto another rack so that the layers are right side up. Let the layers cool completely, 20 minutes longer.

4. After the layers have cooled, make the caramel frosting.

5. While the frosting is warm, assemble the cake. Transfer one cake layer, right side up, to a serving plate. Spoon about a cup of the warm frosting over the top and spread it out with a long metal spatula, working quickly because the frosting will firm up as it cools. Place the second cake layer, right side up, on top of the first and frost the top and side of the cake with the remaining frosting, making sure to work quickly with smooth, clean strokes. Slice the cake and serve.

Keep It Fresh! Store this cake, in a cake saver or loosely covered with plastic wrap, at room temperature for up to three days. Freeze the cake, wrapped in foil, for up to six months. Let the cake thaw overnight on the counter before serving.

Sour Cream Cake with Lemon Filling and Cream Cheese Frosting

AFTER THIS TRIPLE-LAYER sour cream white cake was filled with lemon curd and frosted with cream cheese frosting, it looked so stunning, I thought about calling it the "wedding cake." But if I had, only a handful of folks might have tried the recipe thinking it was too precious or time-consuming to make for everyday gatherings. So, instead I named it as is, and it is up to you to find the right time to bake and serve it to friends.

serves:
12 to 16

prep:
35 minutes

bake:
17 to 19 minutes

cool:
20 minutes

For the cake

Vegetable oil spray, for misting the pans
Flour, for dusting the pans
1 package (18.25 ounces) plain white cake mix
½ cup granulated sugar
1 cup sour cream
¾ cup water
¼ cup vegetable oil
½ teaspoon pure almond extract
4 large egg whites

For the cream cheese frosting and lemon filling

4 ounces reduced-fat cream cheese, at room temperature
4 tablespoons (½ stick) butter, at room temperature
3 cups confectioners' sugar, sifted
1 jar (8 to 12 ounces) lemon curd, at room temperature

Recipe Reminders

MADE FOR

PREP NOTES

DON'T FORGET

SPECIAL TOUCHES

1. Make the cake: Place a rack in the center of the oven and preheat the oven to 350°F. Generously mist three 9-inch round cake pans with vegetable oil spray, then dust them with flour. Shake out the excess flour and set the pans aside.

2. Place the cake mix, granulated sugar, sour cream, water, oil, almond extract, and egg whites in a large mixing bowl and beat with an electric mixer on low speed until the ingredients are incorporated, 30 seconds. Stop the machine and scrape down the side of the bowl with a rubber spatula. Increase the mixer speed to medium and beat for 2 minutes longer, scraping down the side of the bowl again if needed. The batter should look well combined and thickened. Divide the cake batter evenly among the 3 prepared cake pans, about 1½ cups of batter per pan, smoothing the tops with the rubber spatula. Place the pans in the oven. If your oven is not large enough to hold 3 pans on the center rack, place 2 pans on that rack and one in the center of the rack above.

3. Bake the cake layers until they are light brown and the tops spring back when lightly pressed with a finger, 17 to 19 minutes. The cake layer on the higher rack may bake faster so test it for doneness first. Transfer the cake pans to wire racks and let the cake layers cool for 5 minutes. Run a sharp knife around the edge of each cake and give the pans a good shake to loosen the cakes. Invert each layer onto a wire rack, then invert it again onto another rack so that the cakes are right side up. Let the layers cool to room temperature, about 15 minutes longer.

4. Make the frosting: Place the cream cheese and butter in a medium-size bowl. Beat with an electric mixer on low speed until combined, 30 seconds. Stop the machine. Add the confectioners' sugar, a bit at a time, beating with the mixer on low speed until the sugar is well incorporated, 1 minute. Increase the mixer speed to medium and beat the frosting until fluffy, 1 minute longer. Place the frosting in the refrigerator to chill for 20 minutes.

5. To assemble the cake, transfer one layer, right side up, to a cake plate. Spread half (about ⅓ cup) of the lemon curd over the top. Place the second cake layer, right side up, on top of the first and spread the remaining lemon curd over this layer. Place the third layer on top of the second, right side up. Remove the frosting from the refrigerator and frost the top and side of the cake, working with smooth, clean strokes. To make slicing easier, place the uncovered cake in the refrigerator until the frosting sets, 20 minutes.

Keep It Fresh! Store this cake, in a cake saver or loosely covered with waxed paper, in the refrigerator for up to one week. Freeze the cake, wrapped in aluminum foil, for up to six months. Let the cake thaw overnight in the refrigerator before serving.

Want to Make This Cake Even More Lemony?

Turn the cream cheese frosting into a lemon cream cheese frosting by adding a teaspoon of grated lemon zest and a teaspoon of lemon juice (from one lemon).

Easy Coconut Refrigerator Cake

serves:
12 to 16

prep:
35 minutes

bake:
18 to 23 minutes

cool:
20 minutes

I'VE ALWAYS SAID that coconut refrigerator or icebox cakes (the cakes you assemble then stash in the fridge for several days until the frosting has a chance to soak into the cake) are the perfect cake to bake for company because you can make them days in advance. Yet, the coconut cake in my first *Cake Mix Doctor*—Grandma's Coconut Icebox Cake—was often a pain to assemble because the icing slipped down the cake when you tried to spread it. The icing firmed up fine once it chilled. This cake from Sandra Lacey is much easier to prepare, and the secret to its ease is the whipped topping added to the sour cream frosting. The frosting spreads beautifully on the six-layer cake and doesn't slip at all. A tall, picture-perfect cake, this is just the treat for the winter holidays, New Year's Eve, special birthdays, Easter, and even a summer barbecue with family.

For the cake

Vegetable oil spray, for misting the pan
Flour, for dusting the pan
1 package (18.25 ounces) plain white cake mix
1 cup milk
½ cup cream of coconut, plus more cream of coconut (optional) for brushing the baked layers (see Note)
3 large eggs

For the frosting and garnish

2 cups (16 ounces) reduced-fat sour cream
1¾ cups granulated sugar
1 container (8 ounces) frozen whipped topping, thawed
3½ to 4 cups sweetened or unsweetened flaked coconut

1. Make the cake: Place a rack in the center of the oven and preheat the oven to 350°F. Lightly mist three 9-inch round cake pans with vegetable oil spray, then dust them with flour. Shake out the excess flour and set the pans aside.

2. Place the cake mix, milk, ½ cup of cream of coconut, and eggs in a large mixing bowl and beat with an electric mixer on low speed until the ingredients are incorporated, 30 seconds. Stop the machine and scrape down the side of the bowl with a rubber spatula. Increase the mixer speed to medium and beat for 1½ minutes longer, scraping down the side of the bowl again if needed. The batter should look well blended. Divide the cake batter evenly among the 3 prepared pans, about 1½ cups of batter per pan, smoothing the tops with the rubber spatula. Place the pans in the oven. If your oven is not large enough to hold 3 pans on the center rack, place 2 pans on that rack and one in the center of the rack above.

3. Bake the cake layers until they are light brown and the tops spring back when lightly pressed with a finger, 18 to 23 minutes. The cake layer on the higher rack may bake faster so test it for doneness first.

4. While the cakes bake, make the frosting: Place the sour cream and granulated sugar in a large mixing bowl and beat with an electric mixer on low speed for 1½ minutes. Stop the machine and scrape down the side of the bowl with a rubber spatula. Increase the mixer speed to medium and beat until the sugar has

Recipe Reminders

MADE FOR

____

____

____

____

PREP NOTES

____

____

____

____

DON'T FORGET

____

____

____

____

SPECIAL TOUCHES

____

____

____

____

____

____

____

____

____

dissolved, 2 minutes longer. Add the whipped topping and beat on low speed until well blended. Stir in 3 cups of the coconut and beat on low speed until mixed. Place the frosting in the refrigerator to chill for at least 10 minutes.

5. Transfer the cake pans to wire racks and let the cake layers cool for 5 minutes. Run a sharp knife around the edge of each cake layer and give the pans a good shake to loosen the cakes. Invert each layer onto a wire rack, then invert it again onto another rack so that the cakes are right side up. While the cakes cool, if desired, use a small brush, to gently brush the tops of the cakes with the remaining cream of coconut. Let the cakes cool completely, 15 minutes longer. When the cakes are cool, use a large serrated knife to cut each cake in half horizontally to make 6 layers.

6. To assemble the cake, transfer one layer, cut side up, to a serving platter. Spread the top with a heaping ⅔ cup of frosting. Place another cake layer, cut side up, on top of the first layer and frost the top with ⅔ cup frosting. Repeat this process with the remaining cake layers and then frost the top and side of the cake. Sprinkle ½ to 1 cup of coconut on top of the cake for garnish.

Keep It Fresh! Store this cake in a cake saver, in the refrigerator for up to one week. This cake does not freeze well.

Note: You'll find cream of coconut with the ingredients for tropical drinks. It is often sold in 8.5 ounce cans. Be sure and shake the can before opening, and stir the contents as they settle in storage. You can brush some of the remaining cream of coconut onto the cake layers as they cool.

Butter Pecan Cake with Caramel Pecan Frosting

HOUSTON, TEXAS, resident Jill Conyer sent me a butter pecan cake recipe many years ago. She had tasted it at a church supper and asked the cook for the recipe. I moistened up Jill's recipe with sour cream and added a pinch of cinnamon. As for the frosting, it's a modified caramel one with toasted pecans folded in at the last minute. If it's summertime serve this cake with peach ice cream. If you cannot find a butter pecan cake mix, just use a vanilla or yellow mix with pudding.

serves:
12 to 16

prep:
30 minutes

bake:
30 to 35 minutes

cool:
25 minutes

For the cake

1½ cups pecan halves
Vegetable oil spray, for misting the pans
Flour, for dusting the pans
1 package (18 ounces) butter pecan cake mix with pudding
1 cup sour cream or plain yogurt
⅔ cup water
⅓ cup vegetable oil
2 teaspoons pure vanilla extract
Pinch of ground cinnamon (optional)
3 large eggs

For the caramel pecan frosting

5 tablespoons butter
1 cup packed light brown sugar
⅓ cup milk
1 teaspoon pure vanilla extract
2½ cups confectioners' sugar, sifted

Recipe Reminders

MADE FOR

PREP NOTES

DON'T FORGET

SPECIAL TOUCHES

1. Make the cake: Place a rack in the center of the oven and preheat the oven to 350°F. Place the pecans in a baking pan and toast them in the oven while it preheats until they are deep brown in color and aromatic, 10 to 12 minutes.

2. Lightly mist two 9-inch cake pans with vegetable oil spray, then dust them with flour. Shake out the excess flour and set the pans aside.

3. Remove the toasted pecans from the oven and let them cool. Leave the oven on.

4. Place the cake mix, sour cream or yogurt, water, oil, 2 teaspoons of vanilla, cinnamon, if using, and eggs in a large mixing bowl and beat with an electric mixer on low speed until the ingredients are moistened, 30 seconds. Stop the machine and scrape down the side of the bowl with a rubber spatula. Increase the mixer speed to medium and beat until the batter is smooth and thick, 1½ minutes longer, scraping down the side of the bowl again if needed.

5. Chop the toasted pecans into ¼-inch pieces, measure out 1 cup, and fold them into the batter. Set the remaining ½ cup of pecans aside for the frosting. Divide the cake batter evenly between the 2 prepared cake pans, smoothing the tops with the rubber spatula. Place the pans in the oven side by side.

6. Bake the cake layers until they are light brown and the tops spring back when lightly pressed with a finger, 30 to 35 minutes. Transfer the cake pans to wire racks and let the cake layers cool for 5 minutes.

Run a sharp knife around the edge of each cake layer and give the pans a good shake to loosen the cakes. Invert each layer onto a wire rack then invert it again onto another rack so that the cakes are right side up. Let the layers cool completely, 20 minutes longer.

7. When the cakes have cooled, make the caramel pecan frosting: Place the butter and brown sugar in a heavy medium-size saucepan over low heat and stir until the butter melts and the mixture bubbles, 1 to 2 minutes. Add the milk and 1 teaspoon of vanilla and stir until the mixture just comes to a simmer. Remove the pan from the heat and stir in the confectioners' sugar until smooth. Stir in the reserved ½ cup pecans; you'll need to use the frosting at once.

8. To assemble the cake, transfer one layer, right side up, to a cake plate and ladle on about 1 cup of frosting, spreading it to the edge with a thin metal spatula. Place the second layer, right side up, on top of the first and pour the remaining frosting over the top so that it runs down the side. Using the spatula, smooth the top and side of the cake, completely covering it with frosting. The frosting will set as it cools. Slice the cake and serve.

Keep It Fresh! Store this cake, in a cake saver or loosely covered with plastic wrap, at room temperature for up to three days. Freeze the cake, wrapped in aluminum foil, for up to six months. Let the cake thaw overnight on the counter before serving.

Hawaiian Wedding Cake

serves:
12 to 16

prep:
45 minutes

bake:
30 to 35 minutes

cool:
25 minutes

Requests came in to my newsletter for a recipe for a cake like this one. It wasn't a cake with which I was familiar, but it seemed faintly similar to others I had baked. So I baked one version, found it a bit boring, then livened it up with a filling. Adding my lightened version of cream cheese frosting gave the final touch to this cake and its exotic flavors—macadamia nuts, coconut, pineapple, and orange. Often cakes with nuts can be dry but this one has pineapple juice in the batter, and the filling soaks into the cake layers, keeping them moist. The frosting benefits from just a tablespoon of orange juice, which mirrors the orange in the filling and pulls this recipe together. I am not sure that this is an official wedding cake in Hawaii; it's possibly just a glamorous combination of some of the native flavors. Bake it for celebrations, Easter lunch, bridal showers, or as a groom's cake.

For the filling

1 can (8 ounces) crushed pineapple in juice
1 cup orange juice
¾ cup granulated sugar

For the cake

Vegetable oil spray, for misting the pans
Flour, for dusting the pans
1 package (18.25 ounces) yellow, vanilla, or white cake mix with pudding added, or 1 package (18.25 ounces) plain yellow, vanilla, or white cake mix plus 1 package (3.4 ounces) vanilla instant pudding mix
½ cup vegetable oil
2 teaspoons pure vanilla extract
3 large eggs
½ cup finely chopped macadamia nuts (from a 2.25-ounce package)
½ cup sweetened flaked coconut, finely chopped

For the cream cheese frosting and garnish

4 ounces reduced-fat cream cheese, at room temperature
8 tablespoons (1 stick) butter, at room temperature
1 tablespoon orange juice
1 teaspoon pure vanilla extract
3½ to 4 cups confectioners' sugar, sifted
1 cup fresh pineapple or peach slices, or 2 tablespoons chopped macadamia nuts (optional), for garnish

1. Make the filling: Drain the pineapple and set the juice aside for the cake. Place the pineapple, 1 cup of orange juice, and the granulated sugar in a medium-size saucepan over medium heat. Cook, stirring, until the sugar dissolves and the mixture comes to a simmer, then continue to cook it, stirring, until thickened, 10 to 12 minutes. Remove the pan from the heat and let the filling cool completely.

Recipe Reminders

MADE FOR

PREP NOTES

DON'T FORGET

SPECIAL TOUCHES

2. Make the cake: Place a rack in the center of the oven and preheat the oven to 350°F. Lightly mist two 9-inch pans with vegetable oil spray, then dust them with flour. Shake out the excess flour and set the pans aside.

3. Measure the reserved pineapple juice; there should be about ⅓ cup. Add enough water to this juice to make 1⅓ cups of liquid. Place the liquid in a large bowl along with the cake mix, oil, 2 teaspoons of vanilla, and the eggs and beat with an electric mixer on low speed until the ingredients are incorporated, 30 seconds. Stop the machine and scrape down the side of the bowl with a rubber spatula. Increase the mixer speed to medium and beat until the batter is smooth and thickened, 1½ minutes longer, scraping down the side of the bowl again if needed. Stir in the macadamia nuts and the coconut. Divide the cake batter evenly between the 2 prepared cake pans, smoothing the tops with the rubber spatula. Place the pans in the oven side by side.

4. Bake the cake layers until they are golden brown and the tops spring back when lightly pressed with a finger, 30 to 35 minutes. Transfer the cake pans to wire racks and let the cake layers cool for 5 minutes. Run a sharp knife around the edge of each cake layer and give the pans a good shake to loosen the cakes. Invert each layer onto a wire rack, then invert it again onto another rack so that the cakes are right side up. Let the layers cool completely, 20 minutes longer.

5. Meanwhile, make the cream cheese frosting: Place the cream cheese and butter in a medium-size bowl and beat with an electric mixer on high speed until fluffy, 30 seconds. Add

Want a Three-Layer Cake?

To turn the Hawaiian Wedding Cake into a three-layer cake, pour the batter into three 9-inch pans and bake them for about 20 minutes. Double the recipe for the filling, so that you have enough to spread between the three layers. The amount of frosting remains the same.

the 1 tablespoon of orange juice, 1 teaspoon of vanilla, and 3½ cups of the confectioners' sugar. Beat on low speed until the sugar is incorporated, 20 seconds. Add another ¼ to ½ cup of confectioners' sugar if the frosting is too runny. Increase the mixer speed to medium-high and beat until the frosting lightens and is fluffy, 30 seconds longer. Chill the frosting in the refrigerator until it is time to assemble the cake.

6. To assemble the cake, transfer one layer, right side up, to a serving plate. Spoon the filling over the top of this layer and evenly spread it almost to the edge. Spoon about 1 cup of frosting on top of the filling and spread it evenly almost to the edge. Place the second layer, right side up, on top of the first. Spoon another cup of frosting on top of the cake and spread it over it. Frost the side of the cake with the remaining frosting, working with smooth, clean strokes. To make slicing easier, place the uncovered cake in the refrigerator until the frosting sets, 20 minutes. Garnish the cake with the fresh pineapple or peach slices or chopped macadamia nuts, if desired, just before serving.

Keep It Fresh! Store this cake, in a cake saver or loosely covered with waxed paper, in the refrigerator for up to five days. Freeze the cake, wrapped in aluminum foil, for up to six months. Let the cake thaw overnight in the refrigerator before serving.

Get Out Your Sharpest Knife

The secret to incorporating nuts into a cake batter is to chop them finely. If nuts are not chopped finely they are distracting because they fall off the slices and just seem to take your attention off the cake. And, they can dry out a cake, possibly by drawing moisture out of the batter. So, I just make sure nuts (as well as the coconut in the Hawaiian Wedding Cake) are chopped once, and then again for a fine consistency. And I make sure there is adequate liquid in the cake to offset the nuts.

Pumpkin Spice Cake

serves:
12 to 16

prep:
25 minutes

bake:
25 to 30 minutes

cool:
25 minutes

WHEN THE WEATHER TURNS COOL and warm summer days fade into the much anticipated crisp days of fall, change is in the air. Not only in the garden but also in the kitchen where we bake those harvest cakes of spices and autumn fruits and vegetables. In our family, that means apple and pumpkin. This cake is a delicious and easy way to pull together a pumpkin cake, either for dinner at home, a fall birthday, or Halloween. For Halloween parties you might want to tint the frosting with a bit of orange food coloring, or you might want to bake this recipe as twenty to twenty-four cupcakes.

Vegetable oil spray, for misting the pans
Flour, for dusting the pans
1 package (18.25 ounces) plain spice cake mix
1 cup canned pumpkin
½ cup vegetable oil
½ cup water
1 teaspoon ground cinnamon
½ teaspoon ground ginger
3 large eggs
Orange Cream Cheese Frosting (page 474), or Cream Cheese Frosting (page 471)
Candied Orange Zest (page 42) or ½ cup chopped toasted pecans or walnuts (see page 204)

1. Place a rack in the center of the oven and preheat the oven to 350°F. Lightly mist two 9-inch round cake pans with vegetable oil spray, then dust them with flour. Shake out the excess flour and set the pans aside.

2. Place the cake mix, pumpkin, oil, water, cinnamon, ginger, and eggs in a large mixing bowl and beat with an electric mixer on low speed until the ingredients are moistened, 30 seconds. Stop the machine and scrape down the side of the bowl with a rubber spatula. Increase the mixer speed to medium and beat for 2 minutes longer, scraping down the side of the bowl again if needed. The batter should be well blended and smooth. Divide the cake batter evenly between the 2 prepared cake pans, smoothing the tops with the rubber spatula. Place the pans in the oven side by side.

3. Bake the cake layers until the tops spring back when lightly pressed with a finger, 25 to 30 minutes. Transfer the cake pans to wire racks and let the cake layers cool for 5 minutes. Run a sharp knife around the edge of each cake layer and give the pans a good shake to loosen the cakes. Invert each layer onto a wire rack, then invert it again onto another rack so that the cakes are right side up. Let the layers cool completely, 20 minutes longer.

4. Meanwhile, make the frosting of your choice.

5. To assemble the cake, transfer one layer, right side up, to a cake plate and spread about a cup of the frosting over the top. Place the second layer, right side up, on top of the first, then frost the top and side of the cake with the remaining frosting, working with smooth, clean strokes. To make slicing easier, place the uncovered cake in the refrigerator until the frosting sets, 20 minutes. Garnish with the candied zest or toasted nuts just before serving.

Keep It Fresh! Store this cake, in a cake saver or loosely covered with waxed paper, in the refrigerator for up to one week. Freeze the cake, in a cake saver, for up to six months. Let the cake thaw overnight in the refrigerator before serving.

Recipe Reminders

MADE FOR

PREP NOTES

DON'T FORGET

SPECIAL TOUCHES

Kentucky Blackberry Jam Cake

serves:
12 to 16

prep:
30 minutes

bake:
30 to 35 minutes

cool:
20 to 30 minutes

M**ARCY CARRICO** of Raleigh, North Carolina, wrote that her husband's family is from Springfield, Kentucky, and they make jam cake differently from the way we do it in Tennessee: We sandwich blackberry jam between spice cake layers; the people in Kentucky, or at least in the town of Springfield, combine the jam in the cake batter. Marcy asked me to come up with a cake mix version of this regional favorite. I did, and here it is, containing not only blackberry jam but also golden raisins. I've covered the layers in caramel frosting, as all blackberry cakes must be frosted no matter their state of origin! The frosting seals in the flavors, making this cake a good keeper that's moist and spicy.

With or Without Seeds?

Blackberry jam is often sold seedless. Buy this if you prefer no seeds.

Vegetable oil spray, for misting the pans
Flour, for dusting the pans
1 package (18.25 ounces) plain spice cake mix
1 cup blackberry jam
1 cup buttermilk
⅔ cup vegetable oil
½ teaspoon ground cinnamon
3 large eggs
1 cup golden raisins, chopped
2 tablespoons all-purpose flour
1 cup finely chopped pecans
Quick Caramel Frosting (page 485)

1. Place a rack in the center of the oven and preheat the oven to 350°F. Lightly mist two 9-inch round cake pans with vegetable oil spray, then dust them with flour. Shake out the excess flour and set the pans aside.

2. Place the cake mix, blackberry jam, buttermilk, oil, cinnamon, and eggs in a large mixing bowl and beat with an electric mixer on low speed until the ingredients are incorporated, 30 seconds. Stop the machine and scrape down the side of the bowl with a rubber spatula. Increase the mixer speed to medium and beat the batter until smooth, 1½ minutes longer, scraping down the side of the bowl again if needed. Toss the chopped raisins with the flour and add the raisins and pecans to the batter, folding them in until just incorporated. Divide the cake batter evenly between the 2 prepared cake pans, smoothing the tops with the rubber spatula. Place the pans in the oven side by side.

3. Bake the cake layers until the tops spring back when lightly pressed with a finger, 30 to 35 minutes. Transfer the cake pans to wire racks and let the cake layers cool for 5 to 10 minutes. Run a sharp knife around the edge of each cake layer and give the pans a good shake to loosen the cakes. Invert each layer onto a wire rack, then invert it again onto another rack so that the cakes are right side up. Let the layers cool completely, 15 to 20 minutes longer.

4. After the layers have cooled, make the caramel frosting.

5. While the frosting is warm, assemble the cake. Transfer one layer, right side up, to a cake plate and spread about 1 cup of the frosting over the top, working quickly because the frosting will firm up as it cools. Place the second cake layer, right side up, on top of the first and frost the top and side of the cake with the remaining frosting, making sure to work quickly with smooth, clean strokes.

Keep It Fresh! Store this cake, in a cake saver or loosely covered with plastic wrap, at room temperature for up to three days. Freeze the cake, wrapped in aluminum foil, for up to six months. Let the cake thaw overnight on the counter before serving.

Recipe Reminders

MADE FOR

PREP NOTES

DON'T FORGET

SPECIAL TOUCHES

Cinnamon Streusel Layer Cake

serves:
12 to 16

prep:
20 minutes

bake:
30 to 35 minutes

cool:
25 minutes

FOR MANY MONTHS the readers of my online newsletter and website community board were talking about cinnamon cakes, specifically cinnamon bun-type cakes, and more specifically a Cinnabon cake. One recipe that was shared had been clipped from a back issue of *Woman's World* magazine, and I'll admit it sounded tempting. Not only did it call for a layer of cinnamon streusel in the bottom of the cake pan, but some brown sugar and cinnamon were blended into a little of the batter and dropped onto the batter in the pans before baking. The cream cheese frosting looked heavy; I knew my lighter cream cheese frosting would be better on this cake. My curiosity got the best of me and I was soon in the kitchen preheating the oven. After some tweaking and reducing some of the fat, I wound up with one of the most popular recipes in this new collection. It is a hands-down favorite of all ages. I know you will enjoy it, too.

Vegetable oil spray, for misting the pans
¾ cup packed dark or light brown sugar plus 3 tablespoons for the topping
8 tablespoons (1 stick) butter, at room temperature
2 teaspoons ground cinnamon
1 package (18.25 ounces) plain yellow cake mix
1 cup sour cream (see Note)
⅓ cup vegetable oil
¼ cup water
3 large eggs
Cream Cheese Frosting (page 471)

1. Place a rack in the center of the oven and preheat the oven to 350°F. Lightly mist two 9-inch round cake pans with vegetable oil spray. Using a pencil, trace the bottom of one of the cake pans onto two pieces of parchment paper. Cut out the two round pieces of paper and place them in the bottom of the two prepared cake pans.

2. Place ¾ cup of the brown sugar, the butter, and 1 teaspoon cinnamon in a small mixing bowl and beat with an electric mixer on medium-low speed until creamy and smooth, 1 minute. Put half of the streusel mixture in each prepared cake pan. Using a rubber spatula, spread the streusel out to within 2 inches of the edge of the pans. Set the pans aside.

3. Place the cake mix, sour cream, oil, water, and eggs in a large mixing bowl and beat with an electric mixer on low speed until the ingredients are just incorporated, 30 seconds. Stop the machine and scrape down the side of the bowl with a rubber spatula. Increase the mixer speed to medium and beat until smooth, about 1½ minutes longer, scraping down the side of the bowl again if needed. Transfer 1 cup of batter to a smaller bowl and set it aside. Divide the remaining cake batter evenly between the 2 cake pans, spreading the batter over the streusel.

Recipe Reminders

MADE FOR

PREP NOTES

DON'T FORGET

SPECIAL TOUCHES

4. Stir the remaining 3 tablespoons of brown sugar and the remaining teaspoon of cinnamon into the reserved batter until well blended and smooth, about 1 minute. Drop the cinnamon-flavored batter by heaping tablespoonfuls onto the batter in the pans and swirl it to the edge of the pan, being sure not to disturb the streusel layer. Place the pans in the oven side by side.

5. Bake the cake layers until the tops spring back when lightly pressed with a finger, 30 to 35 minutes. Transfer the cake pans to wire racks and let the cake layers cool for 5 minutes. Run a sharp knife around the edge of each cake layer and give the pans a good shake to loosen the cakes. Invert each layer onto a wire rack to cool completely, streusel side up, about 20 minutes longer. Peel off and discard the parchment paper circles.

6. While the cakes cool, make the Cream Cheese Frosting.

7. To assemble the cake, transfer one layer, streusel side up, to a serving platter. Spread the top with about 1 cup of the frosting. Place the second cake layer, streusel side down, on top of the first layer and frost the top and side with the remaining frosting. Place the cake, uncovered, in the refrigerator until the frosting sets, 15 minutes, then slice and serve.

Keep It Fresh! If your kitchen is warm store this cake, in a cake saver or loosely covered with plastic wrap, in the refrigerator for up to 1 week. If your kitchen is cool, you can store this and other cakes with cream cheese frosting on the counter for 24 hours. Freeze the cake, wrapped in aluminum foil, for up to six months. Let the cake thaw overnight on the counter before serving.

Note: You may use regular or reduced-fat sour cream in this cake.

Make Mine Muffins

Turn this recipe into one for muffins by dropping a teaspoon of the cinnamon streusel mixture into 24 paper-lined cupcake pans. Follow directions for making the batter and pour it over the streusel. Bake at 350°F for 25 minutes.

Elegant Almond Amaretto Cake

ONE OF MY FAVORITE "basic" recipes from the first *Cake Mix Doctor* is the Almond Cream Cheese Pound Cake. Here it is in the form of a glamorous layer cake. Amaretto is an almond liqueur, and if you have some on hand, brush it over the baked layers and add a little to the easy frosting.

serves:
12 to 16

prep:
30 minutes

bake:
18 to 22 minutes

cool:
25 minutes

For the cake

Vegetable oil spray, for misting the pans
Flour, for dusting the pans
1 package (18.25 ounces) plain yellow or vanilla cake mix
4 ounces reduced-fat cream cheese, at room temperature
¼ cup granulated sugar
¼ cup all-purpose flour
1 cup water
½ cup vegetable oil
½ teaspoon pure vanilla extract
1 teaspoon pure almond extract
4 large eggs
3 tablespoons amaretto or other almond liqueur (optional; see Note), for brushing the tops of the cake layers

For the frosting and garnish

½ cup sliced almonds (optional)
8 tablespoons (1 stick) butter, at room temperature
4 ounces reduced-fat cream cheese, at room temperature
2 teaspoons amaretto (optional; see Note)
4 to 4½ cups confectioners' sugar, sifted

Recipe Reminders

MADE FOR

PREP NOTES

DON'T FORGET

SPECIAL TOUCHES

1. Make the cake: Place a rack in the center of the oven and preheat the oven to 325°F. Lightly mist three 9-inch round cake pans with vegetable oil spray, then dust them with flour. Shake out the excess flour and set the pans aside.

2. Place the cake mix, 4 ounces of cream cheese, granulated sugar, flour, water, oil, vanilla, almond extract, and eggs in a large mixing bowl and beat with an electric mixer on low speed until the ingredients are incorporated, 30 seconds. Stop the machine and scrape down the side of the bowl with a rubber spatula. Increase the mixer speed to medium and beat for 1½ minutes longer, scraping down the side of the bowl again if needed. The batter should look well blended. Divide the cake batter evenly among the 3 prepared cake pans, about 1¾ cups of batter per pan, smoothing the tops with the rubber spatula. Place the pans in the oven. If your oven is not large enough to hold 3 pans on the center rack, place 2 pans on that rack and one in the center of the rack above.

3. Bake the cake layers until they are golden brown and the tops spring back when lightly pressed with a finger, 18 to 22 minutes. The cake layer on the higher rack may bake faster so test it for doneness first. Transfer the cake pans to wire racks and let the cake layers cool for 5 minutes. If you are using the almonds, leave the oven on for toasting them. Run a sharp knife around the edge of each cake layer and give the pans a good shake to loosen the cakes. Invert each layer onto a wire rack, then invert it again onto another rack so that the cakes are right side up. If desired, brush the warm cakes with the 3 tablespoons of amaretto, using about 1 tablespoon for each layer, and set them aside to cool, 20 minutes longer.

4. Meanwhile, make the garnish, if using, and frosting: Spread the almonds, if using, out in a small baking pan and place it in the oven. Toast the almonds until they are light brown, 3 to 4 minutes. Immediately transfer the toasted almonds from the baking pan to a small bowl and set them aside.

5. Place the butter and 4 ounces of cream cheese in a medium-size bowl. Beat with an electric mixer on medium speed for 1 minute. Add the 2 teaspoons of amaretto, if using, and slowly beat in 4 cups of the confectioners' sugar with the mixer on medium speed. Stop the machine and scrape down the side of the bowl with a rubber spatula. Add the remaining ½ cup of confectioners' sugar if needed to make the frosting thick and fluffy. Increase the mixer speed to high and beat the frosting for about 1 minute longer.

6. To assemble the cake, transfer one cake layer, right side up, to a cake plate. Spread the top with some of the frosting. Place a second cake layer, right side up, on top of the first and frost the top. Repeat this process with the third layer. Use the remaining frosting to frost the side of the cake, working with smooth, clean strokes. Sprinkle the toasted almonds, if desired, on the top of the cake while the frosting is still sticky.

Keep It Fresh! Store this cake, in a cake saver, in the refrigerator for up to one week. Freeze the cake, wrapped in aluminum foil, for up to six months. Let the cake thaw overnight in the refrigerator before serving.

Note: Omit the amaretto if you like. Don't brush it on the cake layers and make the frosting without it. You may, however, add ½ teaspoon pure almond extract to the frosting to make it even more almond flavored.

The Skinny on Reduced-Fat Cream Cheese

Reduced-fat cream cheese works so well as a substitute for the full-fat version that I feel good about this small way of reducing the fat and calories in my cakes. But reduced-fat cream cheese is more watery than regular cream cheese, so when you are making frostings using the lower fat kind take care not to add a lot of liquid. I have found the perfect amount of liquid to add to a cream cheese frosting made with reduced-fat cream cheese—whether it be a liqueur or lemon juice or whatever—is a couple of teaspoons.

Holiday Eggnog Cake with Apricot Filling

serves:
12 to 16

prep:
30 minutes

bake:
18 to 22 minutes

cool:
20 minutes

When eggnog appears in the stores, I know it's time for the holidays. This cake is all about eggnog, and it's delicious served at Thanksgiving, Christmas, or New Year's. There's a great surprise inside, too—a filling of apricot fruit preserves and a little bourbon. Serve the cake with hot coffee or a glass of eggnog. And, if you like, garnish it with candied lemon or orange zest; you'll find the recipe on page 42.

For the cake

Vegetable oil spray, for misting the pans
Flour, for dusting the pans
1 package (18.25 ounces) yellow or vanilla cake mix, plain or with pudding
1¼ cups eggnog
¼ cup vegetable oil
1 teaspoon pure vanilla extract
½ teaspoon ground nutmeg
4 large eggs
3 tablespoons bourbon (optional), for brushing the tops of the cake layers

For the apricot filling

1 jar (10 ounces) apricot all-fruit spread
1 tablespoon bourbon or water

For the spiced cream cheese frosting

4 tablespoons (½ stick) butter, at room temperature
4 ounces reduced-fat cream cheese, at room temperature
3½ cups confectioners' sugar, sifted
Heaping ¼ teaspoon ground nutmeg
¼ teaspoon ground cinnamon

1. Make the cake: Place a rack in the center of the oven and preheat the oven to 350°F. Lightly mist three 9-inch round cake pans with vegetable oil spray, then dust them with flour. Shake out the excess flour and set the pans aside.

2. Place the cake mix, eggnog, oil, vanilla, ½ teaspoon of nutmeg, and the eggs in a large mixing bowl and beat with an electric mixer on low speed until the ingredients are incorporated, 30 seconds. Stop the machine and scrape down the side of the bowl with a rubber spatula. Increase the mixer speed to medium and beat for 2 minutes longer, scraping down the side of the bowl again if needed. The batter should look well blended. Divide the cake batter evenly among the 3 prepared cake pans, about 1½ cups of batter per pan, smoothing the tops with the rubber spatula. Place the pans in the oven. If your oven is not large enough to hold 3 pans on the center rack, place 2 pans on that rack and one in the center of the rack above.

3. Bake the cake layers until they are golden brown and the tops spring back when lightly pressed with a finger, 18 to 22 minutes. The cake layer on the higher rack may bake faster so test it for doneness first. Transfer the cake pans to wire racks and let the cake layers cool for 5 minutes. Run a sharp knife around the edge of each cake layer and give the pans a good shake to loosen the cakes. Invert each layer onto a wire rack, then invert it again onto another rack so that the cakes are right side up. If desired, brush the cakes with the 3 tablespoons of bourbon, using 1 tablespoon for each; set aside to cool, 15 minutes longer.

Recipe Reminders

MADE FOR

____

____

____

____

PREP NOTES

____

____

____

____

DON'T FORGET

____

____

____

____

SPECIAL TOUCHES

____

____

____

____

____

____

____

____

____

4. Meanwhile, make the filling: Place the fruit spread and 1 tablespoon of bourbon or water in a small bowl and stir until well combined.

5. Make the spiced cream cheese frosting: Place the butter and cream cheese in a medium-size bowl and beat with an electric mixer on low speed until well combined, 30 seconds. Stop the machine and scrape down the side of the bowl with a rubber spatula. Add the confectioners' sugar, heaping ¼ teaspoon of nutmeg, and the cinnamon and beat with the mixer on low speed until the ingredients are well incorporated and the frosting has a spreading consistency, 1 to 2 minutes.

6. To assemble the cake, transfer one layer, right side up, to a cake plate. Spread half of the filling to the edge of the first layer, about ½ heaping cup. Place a second cake layer, right side up, on top of the first and spread the remaining filling over it. Place the third layer on top, right side up, and frost the top and side of the cake, working with smooth, clean strokes. To make slicing easier, place the uncovered cake in the refrigerator until the frosting sets, 20 minutes.

Keep It Fresh! Store this cake, in a cake saver or with loosely covered waxed paper, in the refrigerator for up to one week. Freeze the cake, wrapped in aluminum foil, for up to six months. Let the cake thaw overnight in the refrigerator before serving.

Toffee Cake with Brown Butter Cream Cheese Frosting

FOR THE PAST TEN YEARS or so I've been writing an online newsletter, and part of that involves developing the new recipes that readers request. This is a recipe that I came up with after a reader was craving toffee. If you want even more toffee flavor you can fold a half cup of toffee bits into the batter before baking it.

serves:
12 to 16

prep:
20 to 25 minutes

bake:
25 to 28 minutes

cool:
25 minutes

For the cake

Vegetable oil spray, for misting the pans
Flour, for dusting the pans
1 package (18.25 ounces) white cake mix with pudding
¼ cup all-purpose flour
1 cup sour cream
1 cup warm water
1 tablespoon pure vanilla extract
3 large eggs

For the brown butter cream cheese frosting

4 tablespoons (½ stick) butter
1 package (8 ounces) cream cheese, chilled
1 teaspoon pure vanilla extract
4 cups confectioners' sugar, sifted

For the topping

1 cup toffee bits
½ cup finely chopped toasted pecans (optional; see page 204)

Recipe Reminders

MADE FOR

PREP NOTES

DON'T FORGET

SPECIAL TOUCHES

1. Make the cake: Place a rack in the center of the oven and preheat the oven to 350°F. Lightly mist two 9-inch round cake pans with vegetable oil spray, then dust them with flour. Shake out the excess flour and set the pans aside.

2. Place the cake mix, flour, sour cream, water, 1 tablespoon of vanilla, and the eggs in a large mixing bowl and beat with an electric mixer on low speed until the ingredients come together, 30 seconds. Stop the machine and scrape down the side of the bowl with a rubber spatula. Increase the mixer speed to medium and beat until the batter is smooth and thickened, 1½ minutes longer, scraping down the side of the bowl again if needed. Divide the cake batter evenly between the 2 prepared cake pans, smoothing the tops with the rubber spatula. Place the pans in the oven side by side.

3. Bake the cake layers until they are lightly browned and the tops spring back when lightly pressed with a finger, 25 to 28 minutes. Transfer the cake pans to wire racks and let the cake layers cool for 5 minutes. Run a sharp knife around the edge of each cake layer and give the pans a good shake to loosen the cakes. Invert each layer onto a wire rack, then invert it again onto another rack so that the cakes are right side up. Let the layers cool completely, 20 minutes longer.

4. Meanwhile, make the brown butter cream cheese frosting: Place the butter in a small saucepan over medium heat and heat until the butter melts and then browns, about 4 minutes. Place the cream cheese in a large mixing bowl. Pour the hot butter over the cream cheese and add the 1 teaspoon of vanilla. Beat with an electric mixer on low speed until the butter and cream cheese are smooth and combined. Add the confectioners' sugar, a little at a time, beating on low speed until the sugar is incorporated. Once all of the sugar has been added, increase the mixer speed to medium and beat until the frosting is fluffy, 20 seconds.

5. Make the topping: Combine the toffee bits and pecans, if using.

6. To assemble the cake, transfer one layer, right side up, to a serving plate and top it generously with frosting, smoothing it out with a metal spatula. Add a generous, even coating of the topping. Place the second layer, right side up, on top of the first, then frost the top and side of the cake. Sprinkle the remaining topping over the cake. To make slicing easier, place the uncovered cake in the refrigerator until the frosting sets, 20 minutes.

Keep It Fresh! Store this cake, in a cake saver or loosely covered with waxed paper, in the refrigerator for up to one week. Freeze the cake, wrapped in aluminum foil, for up to six months. Let the cake thaw overnight in the refrigerator before serving.

Variation: You can split the cake layers in half horizontally to make a four-layer cake; spread the frosting very thinly between the layers. You can also add ½ cup (4 ounces) of miniature semisweet chocolate chips to the toffee and pecan topping mixture.

Toffee or "Toughy"?

Toffee, the beloved English candy made of sugar and butter, was first spelled "toughy" and "tuffy," no doubt because of the workout it gave your mouth!

The Best Red Velvet Cake

serves:
12 to 16

prep:
30 minutes

bake:
17 to 21 minutes

cool:
20 minutes

A **RED VELVET CAKE ON A POTLUCK TABLE** is like a rock star on tour. People gravitate toward it, swoon over it, fight for a slice. Shocking red with just a hint of chocolate, this cake seems all flash. What is it about the red velvet that warrants so much attention? The moist cake? The rich cream cheese frosting? Guess you have to answer that yourself. This version from a reader in Nashville is one of my favorites. It will be the star of your next party.

For the cake

Solid vegetable oil shortening, for greasing the pans
Flour, for dusting the pans
1 package (18.5 ounces) plain butter recipe golden cake mix
2½ tablespoons unsweetened cocoa powder
1⅓ cups buttermilk
1 bottle (1 ounce) red food coloring
8 tablespoons (1 stick) butter, melted
3 large eggs
1 teaspoon pure vanilla extract
1 teaspoon baking soda
1 tablespoon distilled white vinegar

For the cream cheese frosting

1 package (8 ounces) reduced-fat cream cheese, at room temperature
8 tablespoons (1 stick) butter, at room temperature
1 teaspoon pure vanilla extract
4 cups confectioners' sugar, sifted

1. Make the cake: Place a rack in the center of the oven and preheat the oven to 350°F. Lightly grease three 9-inch round cake pans with solid vegetable shortening, then dust them with flour. Shake out the excess flour and set the pans aside.

2. Place the cake mix, cocoa powder, buttermilk, food coloring, melted butter, eggs, 1 teaspoon of vanilla, and the baking soda and vinegar in a large mixing bowl and beat with an electric mixer on low speed until the ingredients are incorporated, 1 minute. Stop the machine and scrape down the side of the bowl with a rubber spatula. Increase the mixer speed to medium and beat for 2 minutes longer, scraping down the side of the bowl again if needed. The batter should look well blended. Divide the cake batter evenly among the 3 prepared cake pans, about 1½ cups of batter per pan, smoothing the tops with the rubber spatula. Place the pans in the oven. If your oven is not large enough to hold 3 pans on the center rack, place 2 pans on that rack and one in the center of the rack above.

3. Bake the cake layers until they just start to pull away from the side of the pans and the tops spring back when lightly pressed with a finger, 17 to 21 minutes. The cake layer on the higher rack may bake faster so test it for doneness first. Transfer the cake pans to wire racks and let the cake layers cool for 5 minutes. Run a dinner knife around the edge of each cake layer and give the pans a good shake to loosen the cakes. Invert each layer onto a wire rack, then invert it again onto another rack so that the cakes are right side up. Let the layers cool completely, 15 minutes longer.

4. Meanwhile, make the cream cheese frosting: Place the cream cheese and room temperature butter in a large mixing bowl and beat with an electric mixer on high speed until light and fluffy, 1 to 2 minutes. Stop the machine and scrape down the side of the bowl with a rubber spatula. Add the 1 teaspoon vanilla and the confectioners' sugar and beat on medium speed until well combined.

Recipe Reminders

MADE FOR

PREP NOTES

DON'T FORGET

SPECIAL TOUCHES

Increase the mixer speed to high and beat the frosting for 1 minute longer.

5. To assemble the cake, transfer one cake layer, right side up, to a serving platter. Spread the top with some of the frosting. Place a second cake layer, right side up, on top of the first and frost the top. Repeat this process with the third layer. Frost the side of the cake with a thin coat just to seal the crumbs. Use the remaining frosting to go back over this and liberally frost the side, working with smooth, clean strokes. To make slicing easier, place the uncovered cake in the refrigerator until the frosting sets, 20 minutes.

Keep It Fresh! Store this cake, in a cake saver or loosely covered with waxed paper, in the refrigerator for up to one week. Freeze the cake, wrapped in aluminum foil, for up to six months. Let the cake thaw overnight in the refrigerator before serving.

How to Frost a Red Velvet Cake

Until you try it, frosting a red velvet cake might seem like no big deal. But then it happens—the crumbs mix with the cream cheese frosting, and the frosting turns pink from the red food coloring in the cake. The more you try to smooth over the pink frosting, the more the rest of the frosting turns pink. And you wind up with a red and pink velvet cake.

To keep this from happening you can plan ahead. First, grease the pans with solid vegetable shortening and dust them with flour. This forms a crust on the outside of the layers, and the crumbs are much less likely to rub off into the frosting. You can frost the cake with ease.

Second, frost the cake first with a thin skim coat of frosting, then go back and refrost the cake on top of this with a more generous hand. The skim coat seals in the crumbs and you can frost with no worries. To make an even more impenetrable crust, chill the cake for about ten minutes after applying the skim coating of frosting, then continue frosting.

Maryann's Chocolate Layer Cake with Chocolate Syrup Frosting

LITTLE ROCK, ARKANSAS, resident Maryann Wilkerson won one of my online recipe contests with this wonderful chocolate layer cake. It is just the sort of cake you want to take to someone's birthday party, anniversary celebration, or picnic in the backyard. The secret ingredient is chocolate syrup, found in both the cake and the silky, fudgy frosting.

serves:
12 to 16

prep:
35 minutes

bake:
30 to 35 minutes

cool:
25 minutes

Vegetable oil spray, for misting the pans
Flour, for dusting the pans
1 package (18.25 ounces) plain yellow or vanilla cake mix
1 package (3.9 ounces) chocolate instant pudding mix
½ cup unsweetened cocoa powder
1⅓ cups water
1 cup chocolate syrup
⅓ cup vegetable oil
3 large eggs
Chocolate Syrup Frosting (page 482)

1. Place a rack in the center of the oven and preheat the oven to 350°F. Lightly mist two 9-inch round cake pans with vegetable oil spray, then dust them with flour. Shake out the excess flour and set the pans aside.

Craving Cupcakes?

Maryann's recipe is a natural for cupcakes. Bake the cupcakes (20 to 24, filled three quarters full) for 20 to 22 minutes at 350°F.

Recipe Reminders

MADE FOR

PREP NOTES

DON'T FORGET

SPECIAL TOUCHES

2. Place the cake mix, pudding mix, cocoa powder, water, chocolate syrup, oil, and eggs in a large mixing bowl and beat with an electric mixer on low speed until the ingredients are incorporated, 30 seconds to 1 minute. Stop the machine and scrape down the side of the bowl with a rubber spatula. Increase the mixer speed to medium and beat for 1½ to 2 minutes longer, scraping down the side of the bowl again if needed. The batter should look thick and well combined. Divide the cake batter evenly between the 2 prepared cake pans, smoothing the tops with the rubber spatula. Place the pans in the oven side by side.

3. Bake the cake layers until the tops spring back when lightly pressed with a finger, 30 to 35 minutes. Transfer the cake pans to wire racks and let the cake layers cool for 5 minutes. Run a dinner knife around the edge of each cake layer and give the pans a good shake to loosen the cakes. Invert each layer onto a wire rack, then invert it again onto another rack so that the cakes are right side up. Let the layers cool completely, 20 minutes longer.

4. Meanwhile, make the Chocolate Syrup Frosting.

5. To assemble the cake, transfer one layer, right side up, to a cake plate. Spread the top with some of the frosting. Place the second layer, right side up, on top of the first and frost the top and side of the cake, working with smooth, clean strokes.

Keep It Fresh! Store this cake, in a cake saver, at room temperature for up for four days or for up to one week in the refrigerator. Freeze the cake, wrapped in aluminum foil, for up to six months. Let the cake thaw overnight on the counter before serving.

Sour Cream Chocolate Cake with Chocolate Pan Frosting

YOU CANNOT GO WRONG with this cake. It is my stand-by, the cake I fall back on when I have little time and little imagination. Moist and full of chocolate, the cake is strong on its own. And when wrapped in my mom's homemade chocolate frosting, it's unbeatable. No need for garnish, no need for a fancy cake plate, just slice and serve with cold milk.

serves:
12 to 16

prep:
30 minutes

bake:
28 to 32 minutes

cool:
25 minutes

Vegetable oil spray, for misting the pans
Flour, for dusting the pans
1 package (18.25 ounces) chocolate cake mix with pudding
1 cup reduced-fat sour cream
¾ cup water
½ cup vegetable oil
1 teaspoon pure vanilla extract
3 large eggs
Chocolate Pan Frosting (page 476)

1. Place a rack in the center of the oven and preheat the oven to 350°F. Lightly mist two 9-inch round cake pans with vegetable oil spray, then dust them with flour. Shake out the excess flour and set the pans aside.

Bake the Cover Cake

If you'd like to make the cover cake, you can use either a chocolate mix with pudding or a plain one. Divide the Sour Cream Chocolate Cake batter among three pans and bake for 23 to 27 minutes. Fill and frost the cake with the Strawberry Cream Cheese Frosting on page 31 and top it with fresh strawberry slices.

Recipe Reminders

MADE FOR

PREP NOTES

DON'T FORGET

SPECIAL TOUCHES

2. Place the cake mix, sour cream, water, oil, vanilla, and eggs in a large mixing bowl and beat with an electric mixer on low speed until the ingredients are incorporated, 1 minute. Stop the machine and scrape down the side of the bowl with a rubber spatula. Increase the mixer speed to medium and beat for 2 minutes longer, scraping down the side of the bowl again if needed. The batter should look well combined. Divide the cake batter evenly between the 2 prepared cake pans, smoothing the tops with the rubber spatula. Place the pans in the oven side by side.

3. Bake the cake layers until they spring back when lightly pressed with a finger, 28 to 32 minutes. Transfer the cake pans to wire racks and let the cake layers cool for 5 minutes. Run a sharp knife around the edge of each cake layer and give the pans a good shake to loosen the cakes. Invert each layer onto a wire rack, then invert it again onto another rack so that the cakes are right side up. Let the layers cool completely, 20 minutes longer.

4. Meanwhile, make the Chocolate Pan Frosting.

5. To assemble the cake, transfer one cake layer, right side up, to a cake plate. Spread the top with about a cup of the frosting. Place the second layer, right side up, on top of the first and frost the top and side of the cake, working with smooth, clean strokes.

Keep It Fresh! Store this cake, in a cake saver or under a glass dome, in the refrigerator for up to one week. Freeze the cake, in a cake saver, for up to six months. Let the cake thaw overnight in the refrigerator before serving.

Chocolate Chip Layer Cake with Chocolate Cream Cheese Frosting

POUR THE COLD MILK, for here is a dandy of a birthday cake for your family. My kids absolutely adore this cake, and who wouldn't? It is packed with miniature chocolate chips—and I mean packed. I don't like to waste the end of the bag, the can, the you name it, so this cake contains plenty of chips. What you don't fold into the batter you sprinkle on top of the frosted cake. A nice keeper, the cake is moist enough to bake the day ahead of the birthday and store on the kitchen counter in a cool kitchen or covered in the fridge if the kitchen is warm.

serves:
12 to 16

prep:
20 minutes

bake:
33 to 37 minutes

cool:
30 minutes

Vegetable oil spray, for misting the pans
Flour, for dusting the pans
1 package (12 ounces; 2 cups) miniature semisweet chocolate chips
1 package (18.25 ounces) plain yellow cake mix or vanilla cake mix with pudding
1 package (3.4 ounces) vanilla instant pudding mix, if using a plain cake mix
1 cup milk
⅔ cup vegetable oil
1 teaspoon pure vanilla extract
4 large eggs
Chocolate Cream Cheese Frosting (page 473)

Plain Mix or Pudding in the Mix?

With the chocolate chip layer cake you have the choice to use whatever mix is on the store shelf. Choose your favorite yellow or vanilla cake mix. If the mix is plain, add a package—or half a package—of vanilla instant pudding mix. If it contains pudding, don't add any pudding mix.

Recipe Reminders

MADE FOR

PREP NOTES

DON'T FORGET

SPECIAL TOUCHES

1. Place a rack in the center of the oven and preheat the oven to 350°F. Lightly mist two 9-inch round cake pans with vegetable oil spray, then dust them with flour. Shake out the excess flour and set the pans aside.

2. Measure ¼ cup of the chocolate chips and set these aside for garnish.

3. Place the cake mix, pudding mix, if using, milk, oil, vanilla, and eggs in a large mixing bowl and beat with an electric mixer on low speed until the ingredients are incorporated, 30 to 45 seconds. Stop the machine and scrape down the side of the bowl with a rubber spatula. Increase the mixer speed to medium and beat until combined, about 1½ minutes longer. Fold in the remaining 1½ cups of chocolate chips. Divide the cake batter evenly between the 2 prepared cake pans, smoothing the tops with the rubber spatula. Place the pans in the oven side by side.

4. Bake the cake layers until they are golden brown and the tops spring back when lightly pressed with a finger, 33 to 37 minutes. Transfer the cake pans to wire racks and let the cake layers cool for 10 minutes. Run a dinner knife around the edge of each cake layer and give the pans a good shake to loosen the cakes. Invert each layer onto a wire rack, then invert it again onto another rack so that the cakes are right side up. Let the layers cool completely, 20 minutes longer.

5. Meanwhile, prepare the Chocolate Cream Cheese Frosting.

6. To assemble the cake, transfer one layer, right side up, to a serving platter. Spread the top with a generous cup of the frosting. Place the second layer, right side up, on top of the first and frost the top and side of the cake working with smooth, clean strokes. Sprinkle the reserved ¼ cup of chocolate chips over the cake, when the frosting has just been spread so that the chocolate chips will stick to the top of the cake.

Keep It Fresh! Store this cake, in a cake saver or loosely covered with plastic wrap, in the refrigerator for up to one week. If your kitchen is cool, you can store this and other cakes with cream cheese frosting on the counter for 24 hours. Freeze the cake, wrapped in aluminum foil, for up to six months. Let the cake thaw overnight on the counter before serving.

Frosting a Layer Cake: My Favorite Things to Remember

1. It's a lot easier to frost a cake if the layers are cool—let them cool completely on a wire rack. If you are in a hurry, place the layers in the fridge before frosting. And in the summer months, refrigerate the cake again after frosting so it can set, which makes slicing easier and toting a lot less messy.

2. Take care when making frosting to add the liquid a bit at a time so that you don't use too much and wind up either with a runny frosting or a horribly sweet one, because you had to add more sugar to thicken it. Cream cheese frostings don't need any liquid at all other than a bit of vanilla extract or other subtle flavoring. Full-fat cream cheese is less watery than reduced-fat, and it makes a less runny frosting.

3. Level layers make frosting a breeze. Although I appreciate the homey look of a domed cake, it is more difficult to frost. Slice the rounded top off each cake layer with a serrated knife to level it before frosting so that the layers stack evenly.

4. Have the right frosting tools on hand—a rubber spatula to get the frosting from the bowl to the cake and long and short, thin metal spatulas for spreading the frosting in clean strokes.

5. Don't get frustrated—practice does make perfect!

Chocolate Cake with Chocolate Mint Ganache

serves:
12 to 16

prep:
25 minutes

bake:
25 to 30 minutes

cool:
25 minutes

FOR MANY YEARS I HAVE BEEN PART of the herb society in Nashville. When my kids were small I would take them with me to the two large herb gardens the society maintained, and they also helped me manage our own small herb garden in the backyard. Through the years my garden has turned into a mostly perennial one, requiring little maintenance. All I need to do is to plant basil in the late spring and watch so the mint doesn't take over the entire garden. A bossy herb, mint really needs to be planted in a pot and sunk into the garden so it is confined—sort of like a child placed in time-out! But I do love mint in cooking, especially the flavor of fresh mint and chocolate. I first tried infusing my chocolate ganache frosting at a cooking workshop I gave for the herb group. It was fantastic! The flavor of the frosting really dresses up this simple chocolate buttermilk cake. Serve it with a scoop of good vanilla or chocolate mint ice cream.

For the chocolate mint ganache

1 lightly packed cup fresh mint leaves
1 cup heavy (whipping) cream
1⅔ cups chopped semisweet chocolate

For the cake

Vegetable oil spray, for misting the pans
Flour, for dusting the pans
1 package (18.25 ounces) plain chocolate cake mix or chocolate cake mix with pudding
1 tablespoon unsweetened cocoa powder
1⅓ cups buttermilk
½ cup vegetable oil
3 large eggs
1 teaspoon pure vanilla extract

1. Make the chocolate mint ganache: Rinse the mint leaves under cold running water and pat them dry with paper towels. Tear the mint leaves in half with your fingers and put them in a small heavy saucepan with the cream. Bring to a boil over medium heat, then remove the pan from the heat and let rest for 20 minutes to infuse the cream with the mint flavor.

2. Place the chocolate in a large stainless steel or glass bowl and set a strainer over the bowl. Place the pot with the infused cream over medium heat and reheat it gently, just enough to bring up the heat. Pour the cream and mint mixture into the strainer so that the cream runs through to the chocolate and the strainer catches the mint leaves. Discard the mint. Using a wooden spoon, stir the hot cream into the chocolate until the chocolate melts completely, 3 to 4 minutes. Set the ganache aside to cool.

3. Make the cake: Place a rack in the center of the oven and preheat the oven to 350°F. Lightly mist two 9-inch round cake pans with vegetable oil spray, then dust them with flour. Shake out the excess flour and set the pans aside.

Recipe Reminders

MADE FOR

____
____
____
____

PREP NOTES

____
____
____
____

DON'T FORGET

____
____
____
____

SPECIAL TOUCHES

____
____
____
____
____
____
____
____
____

4. Place the cake mix, cocoa powder, buttermilk, oil, eggs, and vanilla in a large mixing bowl and beat with an electric mixer on low speed until the ingredients are incorporated, 30 seconds. Stop the machine and scrape down the side of the bowl with a rubber spatula. Increase the mixer speed to medium and beat for 1½ to 2 minutes longer, scraping down the side of the bowl again if needed. The batter should look well combined. Divide the cake batter evenly between the 2 prepared cake pans, smoothing the tops with the rubber spatula. Place the pans in the oven side by side.

5. Bake the cake layers until the tops spring back when lightly pressed with a finger, 25 to 30 minutes. Transfer the cake pans to wire racks and let the cake layers cool for 5 minutes. Run a sharp knife around the edge of each cake layer and give the pans a good shake to loosen the cakes. Invert each layer onto a wire rack, then invert it again onto another rack so that the cakes are right side up. Let the layers cool completely, 20 minutes longer.

6. Meanwhile, test the thickness of the ganache to see if it is ready for spreading. It needs to be thick enough to cling to a long metal spatula. If it is not, place the bowl in the refrigerator so that the ganache firms up enough to frost.

7. To assemble the cake, when the ganache is spreadable and the layers are cool, transfer one layer, right side up, to a cake plate. Spread the top with about a cup of ganache. Place the second layer, right side up, on top of the first and frost the top and side of the cake, working with smooth, clean strokes.

Keep It Fresh! Store this cake, in a cake saver or under a glass dome, at room temperature for up to one day, then in the refrigerator for up to one week. Freeze the cake, in a cake saver or wrapped in aluminum foil, for up to six months. Let the cake thaw overnight in the refrigerator before serving.

The Chocolate Raspberry Cake

THE STORY GOES that Martha Bowden, my friend and recipe tester, and I had been experimenting with chocolate cake mixes and we tried adding all sorts of fruits to them for flavor and moisture. The idea of chocolate and raspberry really appealed to us, but we thought it would be too reckless, too out of touch, to insist that people go out and buy fresh raspberries and then throw them in a cake batter. Better to save those precious berries for garnishing the top of the cake and let frozen raspberries do the trick in the batter. This cake is the result—easy, flavorful, and having an unexpected "wow" factor. I had to include this favorite classic so I can tell you it is better if you strain out the raspberry seeds before you bake the cake and even more decadent if you fold in one cup of miniature chocolate chips before baking. It is a showstopper if you cover the top of the frosted cake with fresh raspberries and then dust them with confectioners' sugar. We learned to do this at one of my QVC appearances, and this cake became the camera's dream. All eyes will be on it at your house, too.

serves:
12 to 16

prep:
30 minutes

bake:
23 to 27 minutes

cool:
25 minutes

Recipe Reminders

MADE FOR

PREP NOTES

DON'T FORGET

SPECIAL TOUCHES

For the cake

Vegetable oil spray, for misting the pans
Flour, for dusting the pans
1 package (10 ounces) frozen raspberries packed in syrup, thawed (see Note)
1 package (18.25 ounces) chocolate cake mix with pudding
1 cup reduced-fat sour cream
½ cup vegetable oil
3 large eggs
1 cup (6 ounces) miniature semisweet chocolate chips
Chocolate Ganache (page 483)

For the garnish

About 1 cup fresh raspberries (enough to cover the top)
2 teaspoons confectioners' sugar, for dusting
Fresh mint sprig (optional)

1. Make the cake: Place a rack in the center of the oven and preheat the oven to 350°F. Lightly mist three 9-inch round cake pans with vegetable oil spray, then dust them with flour. Shake out the excess flour and set the pans aside.

2. Place the thawed raspberries with their liquid in a fine mesh sieve set over a large mixing bowl. Using a small rubber spatula, press the raspberries through the sieve. Keep pressing until the juice and pulp have been pressed into the bowl and only the seeds remain in the sieve. Discard the seeds.

3. Place the cake mix, sour cream, oil, and eggs in the bowl with the raspberry puree and beat with an electric mixer on low speed until the ingredients are incorporated, 30 seconds. Stop the machine and scrape down the side of the bowl with a rubber spatula. Increase the mixer speed to medium and beat for 1½ to 2 minutes longer, scraping down the side of the bowl again if needed. The batter should look well blended. Fold in the miniature chocolate chips. Divide the cake batter evenly among the 3 prepared cake pans, smoothing the tops with the rubber spatula. Place the pans in the oven. If your oven is not large enough to hold 3 pans on the center rack, place 2 pans on that rack and one in the center of the rack above.

4. Bake the cake layers until the tops spring back when lightly pressed with a finger, 23 to 27 minutes. The cake layer on the higher rack may bake faster so test it for doneness first. Transfer the cake pans to wire racks and let the cake layers cool for 5 minutes. Run a sharp knife around the edge of each cake layer and give the pans a good shake to loosen the cakes. Invert each layer onto a wire rack, then invert it again onto another rack so that the cakes are right side up. Let the layers cool completely, 20 minutes longer.

5. Meanwhile, make the Chocolate Ganache. Let it cool until it is thick and spreadable, 30 minutes.

6. To assemble the cake, transfer one layer, right side up, to a cake plate. Spread the top with some of the ganache. Place a second cake layer, right side up, on top of the first and spread some of the ganache over it. Place the third layer, right side up, on top of the second layer and spread the remaining ganache over the top and side of the cake, working with smooth, clean strokes.

7. Garnish the cake: Cover the top with fresh raspberries. Sift the confectioners' sugar over the cake. Place a mint sprig on top for garnish, if desired. To make slicing easier, place the uncovered cake in the refrigerator until the ganache sets, 20 minutes.

Keep It Fresh! Store this cake, in a cake saver, under a glass dome, or loosely covered with waxed paper, in the refrigerator for up to one week. Freeze the cake, in a cake saver, for up to six months. Let the cake thaw overnight in the refrigerator before serving.

An Easy Substitution

If you cannot find a 10-ounce package of frozen raspberries in syrup, don't fret. I have made this cake with unsweetened frozen raspberries and added ¼ cup of sugar to the batter. Use a very generous cup of unsweetened raspberries instead of the sweetened ones.

Favorite German Chocolate Cake

serves:
12 to 16

prep:
35 minutes

bake:
29 to 33 minutes

cool:
25 minutes

I **USED TO THINK GERMAN CHOCOLATE CAKE** was "guy" cake. You know, it's big and filling and substantial—the thick prime rib of the dessert cart. And sure enough, when I brought German chocolate cake to a book signing, men fell all over it. When I brought German chocolate cake to a TV station, men fell all over it. But along the way, I began to fall for it, too. This version is my favorite because it uses a German chocolate mix, sour cream makes the cake moist, and it contains melted German's chocolate. The frosting is made from scratch by cooking it on top of the stove, as it should be. You can make the frosting even better by toasting the pecans and coconut in the oven ahead of time, but this cake is fantastic without that little touch. It will please both the guys *and* the gals.

For the cake

Vegetable oil spray, for misting the pans
Flour, for dusting the pans
1 bar (4 ounces) German's sweet chocolate
1 package (18.25 ounces) plain German chocolate cake mix
Half of a 3.4 ounce package vanilla instant pudding mix (4 tablespoons)
¾ cup water
½ cup reduced-fat sour cream
¼ cup vegetable oil
4 large eggs

For the frosting

1 can (12 ounces) evaporated milk, or 1½ cups half-and-half
1½ cups granulated sugar
12 tablespoons (1½ sticks) butter
4 large egg yolks, lightly beaten
1½ teaspoons pure vanilla extract
2 cups sweetened flaked coconut
1½ cups chopped pecans

1. Make the cake: Place a rack in the center of the oven and preheat the oven to 325°F. Lightly mist two 9-inch round cake pans with vegetable oil spray, then dust them with flour. Shake out the excess flour and set the pans aside.

2. Chop the German's chocolate into 1-inch pieces and place them in a small microwave-safe glass bowl. Place the bowl in the microwave oven and microwave on high power for 1 to 1½ minutes, stopping the oven and stirring every 30 seconds, until the chocolate is melted. Spoon the chocolate into a large mixing bowl and add the cake mix, pudding mix, water, sour cream, oil, and eggs. Beat with an electric mixer on low speed until the ingredients are incorporated, 30 seconds. Stop the machine and scrape down the side of the bowl with a rubber spatula. Increase the mixer speed

Recipe Reminders

MADE FOR

PREP NOTES

DON'T FORGET

SPECIAL TOUCHES

to medium and beat 1½ minutes longer, scraping down the side of the bowl again if needed. The batter should look smooth and thickened. Divide the cake batter evenly between the 2 prepared cake pans, smoothing the tops with the rubber spatula. Place the pans in the oven side by side. Bake the cake layers until the tops spring back when lightly pressed with a finger, 29 to 33 minutes.

3. Meanwhile make the frosting: Place the evaporated milk, sugar, butter, egg yolks, and vanilla in a large saucepan over medium heat. Cook, stirring constantly, until thickened and golden brown in color, 10 to 12 minutes. Remove from the heat. Stir in the coconut and pecans. Let the frosting cool to room temperature and a spreading consistency, 30 minutes.

4. Transfer the cake pans to wire racks and let the cake layers cool for 5 minutes. Run a sharp knife around the edge of each cake layer and give the pans a good shake to loosen the cakes. Invert each layer onto a wire rack, then invert it again onto another rack so that the cakes are right side up. Let the layers cool completely, 20 minutes longer.

5. To assemble the cake, using a long, serrated knife, carefully slice each cake layer in half horizontally, to make 4 layers (see page 129). Place the bottom half of one layer, cut side up, on a cake plate and spoon about 1 cup of the frosting on top, spreading it evenly to the edge. Place the top half of this layer, right side up, over the frosting. Add another cup of the frosting and spread it to the edge. Place the bottom of the remaining cake layer on top and spread it with another cup of frosting. Place the top half of the second layer, right side up, on top of the frosting and pile the remaining frosting on top of the cake, spreading it out evenly and leaving the side bare. Slice and serve the cake.

Keep It Fresh! Store this cake, in a cake saver, at room temperature for up to three days or one week in the refrigerator. Freeze the cake, wrapped in foil, for up to six months.

Miami Beach Birthday Cake

JANE FRANK, who lives in Mesa, Arizona, wanted to streamline her daughter's favorite birthday cake recipe, so she started using a cake mix. Packed with walnuts, chocolate chips, and graham cracker crumbs, this cake is elegant and easy. Why Miami Beach Birthday Cake? That's where the recipe originated.

serves:
12 to 16

prep:
25 minutes

bake:
23 to 28 minutes

cool:
25 minutes

For the cake

Vegetable oil spray, for misting the pans
Flour, for dusting the pans
⅓ cup semisweet chocolate chips, melted
1 package (18.5 ounces) plain butter recipe golden cake mix
1 cup reduced-fat sour cream
8 tablespoons (1 stick) butter, at room temperature
⅓ cup vegetable oil
¼ cup water
¼ cup granulated sugar
3 large eggs

For the topping

½ cup graham cracker crumbs
½ cup finely chopped walnuts
⅔ cup regular or miniature semisweet chocolate chips
⅓ cup butter, melted

For the frosting

1 cup heavy (whipping) cream
1 package (8 ounces) frozen whipped topping, thawed

Recipe Reminders

MADE FOR

PREP NOTES

DON'T FORGET

SPECIAL TOUCHES

1. Make the cake: Place a rack in the center of the oven and preheat the oven to 350°F. Lightly mist three 9-inch round cake pans with vegetable oil spray, then dust them with flour. Shake out the excess flour and set the pans aside. Place a large mixing bowl and a set of mixer beaters in the refrigerator to chill.

2. Place the chocolate chips in a small microwave-safe bowl and microwave on high power until melted, 30 to 45 seconds, stirring every 15 seconds.

3. Place the cake mix, sour cream, softened butter, oil, water, granulated sugar, melted chocolate, and eggs in a large mixing bowl and beat with an electric mixer on low speed until the ingredients are just combined, 30 seconds. Stop the machine and scrape down the side of the bowl with a rubber spatula. Increase the mixer speed to medium and beat until the batter is well combined, 1½ minutes longer, scraping down the side of the bowl again if needed. Divide the cake batter evenly among the 3 prepared cake pans, 1½ to 1¾ cups of batter per pan, smoothing the tops with the rubber spatula. Set the cake pans aside.

4. Make the topping: Place the graham cracker crumbs, walnuts, chocolate chips, and melted butter in a small mixing bowl and stir with a fork to combine. Using your fingers, distribute the topping evenly over the tops of the cake layers. Place the pans in the oven. If your oven is not large enough to hold 3 pans on the center rack, place 2 pans on that rack and one in the center of the rack above.

5. Bake the cake layers until the tops spring back when lightly pressed with a finger, 23 to 28 minutes. The cake layer on the higher rack may bake faster so test it for doneness first. Transfer the cake pans to wire racks and let the cake layers cool for 10 minutes. Run a sharp knife around the edge of each cake layer and give the pans a good shake to loosen the cakes. Invert each layer onto a wire rack, then invert it again onto another rack so that the cakes are right side up. Let the layers cool completely, 15 minutes longer.

6. Meanwhile, make the frosting: Remove the bowl and beaters from the refrigerator. Pour the cream into the bowl and beat with an electric mixer on high speed until stiff peaks form, 2 to 3 minutes. Fold in the thawed whipped topping just to combine.

7. To assemble the cake, transfer one layer, right side up, to a cake plate. Spread about 1 cup of frosting over the top. Place a second cake layer, right side up, on top of the first and frost it. Place the third layer on top, right side up, and frost the top and side of the cake, working with smooth, clean strokes. Place the cake under a glass dome or in a cake saver in the refrigerator to chill until time to serve.

Keep It Fresh! Store this cake, in a cake saver or under a glass dome, in the refrigerator for up to three days. Freeze only the cake layers, wrapped in aluminum foil, for up to six months. Let the layers thaw overnight on the counter, before making the frosting and assembling the cake.

Chill Out

Keep whipped cream cool by folding in whipped topping. The two make a good team, frosting a pretty cake and keeping their cool.

Smith Island Cake

serves:
12 to 16

prep:
40 minutes

bake:
10 to 12 minutes

cool:
15 to 20 minutes

I **READ ABOUT THIS FAMOUS STACKED CAKE** that comes from Maryland's Smith Island, and I was fainting from hunger, forgetting that you should not read tantalizing recipes before noon. Moist vanilla layers—eight to ten of them—cloaked in fudgelike frosting, with chopped candy bars scattered in between? Just too much! And so I tried my hand at the cake, constructing this dessert masterpiece of eight layers by using a yellow cake mix and baking four rounds, then splitting them. In between the layers I spread my fudge frosting, a little simpler to make than the original, and on top of this I scattered finely chopped Reese's peanut butter cups. Yes, the traditional Chesapeake island cake has a bit more frosting, but mine might just be easier to pull together. And I don't think you'll find I've compromised the flavor one bit.

For the cake

8 Reese's peanut butter cups (12 ounces total)
Vegetable oil spray, for misting the pans
Flour, for dusting the pans
1 package (18.25 ounces) plain yellow cake mix
1½ cups evaporated milk or whole milk
8 tablespoons (1 stick) butter, at room temperature
1 teaspoon pure vanilla extract
4 large eggs

For the frosting

12 tablespoons (1½ sticks) butter
½ cup unsweetened cocoa powder
½ cup plus 3 tablespoons evaporated milk or whole milk
1 teaspoon pure vanilla extract
6 cups confectioners' sugar, sifted

1. Place the peanut butter cups in the freezer.

2. Make the cake: Place a rack in the center of the oven and preheat the oven to 350°F. Lightly mist four 9-inch round cake pans with vegetable oil spray, then dust them with flour. Shake out the excess flour and set the pans aside.

3. Place the cake mix, 1½ cups of milk, 8 tablespoons of butter, 1 teaspoon of vanilla, and the eggs in a large mixing bowl and beat with an electric mixer until well mixed, 30 seconds. Stop the machine and scrape down the side of the bowl with a rubber spatula. Increase the mixer speed to medium and beat until the batter is smooth, 1½ minutes longer, scraping down the side of the bowl again if needed. Divide the cake batter evenly among the 4 prepared cake pans, about 1¾ cups of batter per pan, smoothing the tops with the rubber spatula. Put the pans in the oven, placing 2 pans on the center rack and 2 on the rack above.

Recipe Reminders

MADE FOR

PREP NOTES

DON'T FORGET

SPECIAL TOUCHES

4. Bake the cake layers until they are golden brown and the tops spring back when lightly pressed with a finger, 10 to 12 minutes (the baking time is short here because the batter has been divided among 4 baking pans). Rotate the pans after the layers have baked for 5 minutes. Transfer the cake pans to wire racks and let the cake layers cool for 5 minutes. Run a dinner knife around the edge of each cake layer and give the pans a good shake to loosen the cakes. Invert the each layer onto a wire rack, then invert it again onto another rack so that the cakes are right side up. Let the layers cool completely, 10 to 15 minutes longer.

5. Meanwhile, remove the peanut butter cups from the freezer. Place 3 peanut butter cups in a food processor, pulse the machine to make small chunks, and set these aside for the garnish. Pulse the remaining 5 peanut butter cups to a fine powder and set aside.

6. Make the frosting: Melt the 12 tablespoons of butter in a large saucepan over low heat, 2 to 3 minutes. Stir in the cocoa powder and ½ cup plus 3 tablespoons of milk. Cook 1 minute longer, stirring, until the mixture thickens and just begins to come to a boil. Remove the pan from the heat. Stir in the 1 teaspoon of vanilla and the confectioners' sugar, continuing to stir until the frosting is thickened and smooth and the consistency of hot fudge sauce. To keep the icing from hardening, place the saucepan over low heat while frosting the layers.

7. To assemble the cake, using a long, serrated knife, carefully slice each cake layer in half horizontally to make 8 layers. Place the bottom half of one layer, cut side up, on a cake plate and spoon about ¼ cup of the frosting on top, spreading it evenly to the edge. Sprinkle about 1 tablespoon

It Stacks Up to Cake Love

The residents of Smith Island are proud of their cake. You can sample it on a visit, buy one to take home, or if you can't visit the island, even order a cake online.

Stacked cakes consisting of many thin layers have been popular in the mountains of Tennessee and Kentucky where these layers were baked in cast-iron skillets and often sandwiched with apple butter.

of the powdered peanut butter cups over the frosting. Place the top half of this layer, right side up, over the frosting. Add another ¼ cup of the frosting and spread it to the edge. Then sprinkle another tablespoon of powdered peanut butter cups over it. Repeat with the remaining layers, then frost the top of the cake and sprinkle the reserved chunks of peanut butter cups over it.

Keep It Fresh! Store this cake, in a cake saver or under a glass dome, at room temperature for up to three days or for up to one week in the refrigerator. Freeze the cake, wrapped in aluminum foil or in a cake saver, for up to six months. Let the cake thaw overnight in the refrigerator before serving.

Splitting Layers

This has nothing to do with splitting hairs—slicing a cake layer in half horizontally is a lot easier than it looks. And it is an easy and delicious way to add height and flavor to a cake because a filling or frosting will go between each and every layer. To slice cake layers in half and turn two into four and three into six, use a long, thin serrated knife. Starting on one side, slice halfway through to the center. Turn the layer around to the other side and slice halfway through so that you meet the first cut. If you want layers to match up beautifully when stacked, make small cuts on the side of each layer before splitting it so that you can line the cuts up when the layers are stacked.

To easily slide one layer onto another use a cardboard cake round or the bottom of a springform pan. When stacking split layers, usually it's best to match the bottom with the top of each layer, sandwiching them back together. The exception is when you want the filling or frosting to really sink into the layers as in the coconut refrigerator cake. In this cake you should stack all the layers cut side up.

Chocolate Swirled Cannoli Cake

serves:
12 to 16

prep:
25 minutes

bake:
28 to 32 minutes

cool:
20 to 25 minutes

WHEN HER DAUGHTER asked for a cake that tasted like a cannoli, Ann Readshaw of Huntington Beach, California, came up with a chocolate marbled cake with a cannoli-style frosting. I loved her idea and added a little almond extract to her cake layers. And, I lightened up the ricotta frosting by folding in whipped topping. You could use whipped cream instead of the topping if you like. Since Ann's recipe started with a marble cake mix, and they are often hard to find, I am sharing a way to create a chocolate marble beginning with a yellow mix. Feel free to doctor up this recipe, possibly by adding a little orange zest, pistachios, or any other Italian flavor that says cannoli to you!

For the cake

Vegetable oil spray, for misting the pans
Flour, for dusting the pans
1 package (18.25 ounces) plain yellow or vanilla cake mix
1¼ cups milk
½ cup vegetable oil
4 large eggs
1 teaspoon pure almond extract
½ cup (3 ounces) miniature semisweet chocolate chips
1 tablespoon unsweetened cocoa powder

For the frosting

1 container (15 ounces) part-skim ricotta cheese
¼ cup confectioners' sugar, or more to taste, sifted
1 container (8 ounces) frozen whipped topping, thawed
1 teaspoon pure vanilla extract
¼ teaspoon ground cinnamon
½ cup (3 ounces) miniature semisweet chocolate chips

For the garnish (optional)

Dusting of ground cinnamon
Dusting of unsweetened cocoa powder
Candied orange zest (page 42)

1. Make the cake: Place a rack in the center of the oven and preheat the oven to 350°F. Lightly mist two 9-inch round cake pans with vegetable oil spray, then dust them with flour. Shake out the excess flour and set the pans aside.

2. Place the cake mix, milk, oil, eggs, and almond extract in a large mixing bowl and beat with an electric mixer on low speed until the ingredients come together, 30 seconds. Stop the machine and scrape down the side of the bowl with a rubber spatula. Increase the mixer speed to medium and beat until the batter is smooth and thickened, 1½ minutes longer, scraping down the side of the bowl again if needed. The batter should look smooth and thick.

3. Measure out 1 cup of cake batter and place it in a small bowl. Stir in the ½ cup of chocolate chips and cocoa powder. Divide the remaining cake batter evenly between the 2 prepared cake pans, smoothing the tops with the rubber spatula. Drop the chocolate cake batter by teaspoonfuls over the batter in both pans. Using a dinner knife, swirl the chocolate batter through the plain batter to marble it. Take care not to scrape the bottom of the pans. Place the pans in the oven side by side.

Recipe Reminders

MADE FOR

PREP NOTES

DON'T FORGET

SPECIAL TOUCHES

4. Bake the cake layers until the tops spring back when lightly pressed with a finger, 28 to 32 minutes. Transfer the cake pans to wire racks and let the cake layers cool for 5 to 10 minutes.

5. Meanwhile, make the frosting: Place the ricotta cheese, confectioners' sugar, whipped topping, vanilla, and cinnamon in a large mixing bowl and beat with an electric mixer on low speed until just combined, 15 seconds. Taste for sweetness, adding more confectioners' sugar if necessary. Using a rubber spatula, fold in the ½ cup of chocolate chips. Refrigerate the frosting until it is time to assemble the cake.

6. Run a sharp knife around the edge of each cake layer and give the pans a good shake to loosen the cakes. Invert each layer onto a wire rack, then invert it again onto another rack so that the cakes are right side up. Let the layers cool completely, 15 minutes longer.

7. To assemble the cake, transfer one layer, right side up, to a cake plate. Spread the top with some of the frosting. Place the second layer, right side up, on top of the first and generously frost the top. Working with smooth, clean strokes, spread the remaining frosting over the side of the cake. Garnish the cake with a sprinkling of cinnamon or cocoa powder or with the candied orange zest.

Keep It Fresh! Store this cake, in a cake saver, in the refrigerator for up to one week. Freeze only the cake layers, wrapped in aluminum foil, for up to six months. Let the layers thaw overnight on the counter, before making the frosting and assembling the cake.

Tiramisu Cake

NANCY COPELAND, who lives in Manassas, Virginia, sent me this recipe and said it is her dinner party cake, something she can make in little time and yet people think she has gone to great trouble. Begin with a chocolate cake mix and add the flavors of the classic Italian dessert called tiramisu. Because of the popularity of tiramisu you can find mascarpone cheese in most supermarkets. And either use sweet marsala wine or cream sherry in the frosting and filling.

serves:
12 to 16

prep:
35 minutes

bake:
25 to 30 minutes

cool:
25 minutes

For the cake

Vegetable oil spray, for misting the pans
Flour, for dusting the pans
1 cup water
2 tablespoons instant coffee granules
1 package (18.25 ounces) plain chocolate cake mix
⅔ cup reduced-fat sour cream
3 large eggs

For the frosting

2 cups heavy (whipping) cream
1 tablespoon instant coffee granules
¼ cup granulated sugar

For the filling

8 ounces mascarpone cheese, at room temperature
¼ cup marsala wine or cream sherry
¼ cup granulated sugar

Recipe Reminders

MADE FOR

PREP NOTES

DON'T FORGET

SPECIAL TOUCHES

1. Make the cake: Place a rack in the center of the oven and preheat the oven to 350°F. Lightly mist two 9-inch round cake pans with vegetable oil spray, then dust them with flour. Shake out the excess flour and set the pans aside.

2. Bring the water to a boil and stir in the 2 tablespoons of instant coffee until it dissolves. Set the coffee water aside to cool for 5 minutes.

3. Place the cake mix, sour cream, eggs, and cooled coffee water in a large mixing bowl and beat with an electric mixer on low speed until the ingredients are combined, 30 seconds. Stop the machine and scrape down the side of the bowl with a rubber spatula. Increase the mixer speed to medium and beat until the batter is thick and combined, 1½ minutes longer. Divide the cake batter evenly between the 2 prepared cake pans, smoothing the tops with the rubber spatula. Place the pans in the oven side by side.

4. Bake the cake layers until the tops spring back when lightly pressed with a finger, 25 to 30 minutes.

5. Meanwhile, make the frosting: Place a large mixing bowl and a clean set of electric mixer beaters in the refrigerator to chill. Measure ¼ cup of the cream into a glass measuring cup and place it in a microwave oven on high power until hot, 30 seconds. Stir in the 1 tablespoon of instant coffee until the coffee dissolves. Place the coffee and cream mixture in the refrigerator to cool.

6. Transfer the cake pans to wire racks and let the cake layers cool for 5 minutes. Run a sharp knife around the edge of each cake layer and give the pans a good shake to loosen the cakes. Invert each layer onto a wire rack, then invert it again onto another rack so that the cakes are right side up. Let the layers cool completely, 20 minutes longer.

7. Remove the chilled bowl and beaters from the refrigerator. Pour the remaining 1¾ cups of cream into the bowl and add the ¼ cup of granulated sugar, and the cooled coffee and cream mixture and beat with an electric mixer on high speed until stiff peaks form, 2 minutes. Measure out 1½ cups of this coffee whipped cream, place it in a medium-size bowl, and set it aside. Refrigerate the remaining whipped cream mixture for the frosting.

8. Make the filling: Add the mascarpone cheese, marsala or cream sherry, and ¼ cup of granulated sugar to the bowl with the reserved 1½ cups of coffee whipped cream mixture. Mix well with a wire whisk until smooth.

9. To assemble the cake, using a long, serrated knife, carefully slice each cake layer in half horizontally to make 4 layers. Or, don't slice the layers in half and make a 2-layer cake. Suit yourself (see Note)! Place the bottom half of one layer cut side up on a cake plate and spoon ¾ to 1 cup of the filling on top, spreading it evenly to the edge. Place the top half of this layer, right side up over the filling. Add another ¾ to 1 cup of filling and spread it to the edge. Place the bottom of the remaining cake layer on top and spread it with the remaining ¾ to 1 cup of filling. Place the top half of the second layer, right side up, on top of the filling. Remove the frosting from the refrigerator and spread it on the top and around the side of the cake.

Keep It Fresh! Store this cake, in a cake saver, in the refrigerator for up to four days. Freeze only the layers, wrapped in aluminum foil, for up to six months. Let the layers thaw overnight on the counter before making the frosting and filling and assembling the cake.

Note: If you decide to make this a 2-layer cake, you'll need less filling. Just divide the measurements in half.

How to Garnish Tiramisu

The traditional topping for tiramisu is unsweetened cocoa powder. Along with a dusting of cocoa—either unsweetened or sweetened—you can also garnish this cake with a little cinnamon or shavings of dark chocolate. Any way you garnish it, it is delicious.

Triple Decker Chocolate Icebox Cake with Shaved Chocolate Frosting

serves:
12 to 16

prep:
35 minutes

bake:
18 to 20 minutes

cool:
20 minutes

A **TERRIFIC CAKE** for busy households, I made this cake a day in advance of my daughter's June birthday. It seems her birthday rolls around in the middle of so much happy chaos at our home—people coming and going, schools just out, summer in the air. So it helps to bake ahead and place the cake in the refrigerator knowing that it's going to taste even better a day later. Thus, the beauty of icebox cakes and why they have been popular for so long. And it doesn't hurt that this cake contains shaved Hershey's bars in the frosting, either!

For the cake

Vegetable oil spray, for misting the pans
Flour, for dusting the pans
1 package (18.25 ounces) chocolate cake mix with pudding
1 cup reduced-fat sour cream
¾ cup water
½ cup vegetable oil
3 large eggs
1 teaspoon pure vanilla extract

For the shaved chocolate frosting

12 ounces reduced-fat cream cheese, at room temperature
½ cup granulated sugar
1 cup confectioners' sugar, sifted
1 container (16 ounces) frozen whipped topping, thawed but still cold
4 Hershey's milk chocolate bars (1.55 ounces each), cut into thin shavings (about 1½ cups)

For the garnish

¾ cup toasted slivered almonds (see page 204) and/or 5 or 6 maraschino cherries with stems, drained

1. Make the cake: Place a rack in the center of the oven and preheat the oven to 350°F. Lightly mist three 9-inch round cake pans with vegetable oil spray, then dust them with flour. Shake out the excess flour and set the pans aside.

2. Place the cake mix, sour cream, water, oil, eggs, and vanilla in a large mixing bowl and beat with an electric mixer on low speed until the ingredients are moistened, 30 seconds. Stop the machine and scrape down the side of the bowl with a rubber spatula. Increase the mixer speed to medium and beat for 2 minutes longer, scraping down the side of the bowl again if needed. The batter should look well combined. Divide the cake batter among the 3 prepared cake pans, about 1½ cups of batter per pan, smoothing the tops with the rubber spatula. Place the pans in the oven. If your oven is not large enough to hold 3 pans on the center rack, place 2 pans on that rack and one in the center of the rack above.

3. Bake the cake layers until the tops spring back when lightly pressed with a finger, 18 to 20 minutes. The cake layer on the higher rack may bake faster so test it for doneness first.

Recipe Reminders

MADE FOR

PREP NOTES

DON'T FORGET

SPECIAL TOUCHES

4. Meanwhile, make the shaved chocolate frosting: Place the cream cheese and granulated and confectioners' sugars in a large mixing bowl and beat on medium speed until creamy, 1 to 2 minutes, scraping down the side of the bowl often. Stop the machine and add the whipped topping and chocolate. Beat on low speed until well combined and smooth, about 2 minutes. Set the frosting aside.

5. Transfer the cake pans to wire racks and let the cake layers cool for 5 minutes. Run a sharp knife around the edge of each cake layer and give the pans a good shake to loosen the cakes. Invert each layer onto a wire rack, then invert it again onto another rack so that the cakes are right side up. Let the layers cool completely, 15 minutes longer. (This is a good time to place the almonds in the oven to toast.)

6. When the cake layers have cooled, assemble the cake. Transfer one layer, right side up, to a cake plate. Top it generously with 1½ to 2 cups of frosting, spreading it evenly. Place a second cake layer right side up, on top of the first and frost it generously. Place the third layer on top, right side up, and frost the top and side of the cake generously. Garnish the cake with the toasted almonds and/or maraschino cherries.

Keep It Fresh! Store this cake, in a cake saver or under a glass dome, in the refrigerator for up to one week. Freeze only the layers, wrapped in aluminum foil, for up to six months. Let the layers thaw overnight on the counter, before making the frosting and assembling the cake.

Even Steven—How to Make Even Layers Every Time

Do you ever bake layers and find that one bakes up larger than the other? Well there are ways to prevent that, ways to make sure that your layers, be they two or three, are equal.

1. You can eyeball the amount of batter, which is my favorite method, used day in and day out. Pour some batter into one cake pan. Pour some batter into a second pan. Place them side by side on the counter and see if the contents are equal. If not, make adjustments.

2. You can count your way to perfection. I have found this method works, too. As you pour batter into one pan, count one, two, three, four . . . stopping when think you've reached halfway. Then pour batter into the second pan and see if you can count just as far and in the same cadence. If not, make adjustments, adding more batter to the second pan.

3. For a third and more scientific method, you can "cup it out." This means measuring the same amount of batter into each pan. It will be somewhere just shy of two cups per pan.

4. And for the most precise, the proven method, one you should use if you want perfectly even layers, you should weigh the layers. Place one empty cake pan on a kitchen scale, then add about half of the batter. Place an identical pan on the scale, add the remaining batter. If the measurements are not equal, make adjustments by adding a little batter to one or the other pan. The process is the same for three layers.

Irresistible Icebox Cakes

Turn your favorite cake into an icebox cake. Bake the layers of your choice then fill and frost them with the shaved Chocolate Frosting on page 137 or the whipped cream frosting on page 123.

Chocolate Rum Icebox Cake

serves:
12 to 16

prep:
40 minutes

bake:
28 to 32 minutes

cool:
25 minutes, plus 20 minutes for refrigerating the cake

Here is another refrigerator cake—a chocolate cake sandwiching chocolate-and-rum-flavored whipped cream and then topped with a satiny chocolate glaze that blankets the entire cake, making it irresistible. This cake is dinner or birthday party perfect because it is a do-ahead, chilled and ready when you are. And it feeds a lot!

For the cake

Vegetable oil spray, for misting the pans
Flour, for dusting the pans
1 package (18.25 ounces) chocolate cake mix with pudding
1 cup reduced-fat sour cream
¾ cup water
½ cup vegetable oil
3 large eggs
1 teaspoon pure vanilla extract

For the chocolate rum filling

2 cups heavy (whipping) cream
1 cup confectioners' sugar, sifted
⅓ cup unsweetened cocoa powder
2 teaspoons rum (see Notes), plus 2 teaspoons of rum for brushing the cake layers (optional)

For the chocolate icing

3 squares (1 ounce each) unsweetened chocolate, coarsely chopped
4 tablespoons (½ stick) butter
6 tablespoons milk or heavy (whipping) cream
4 tablespoons light corn syrup
2 teaspoons pure vanilla extract
2½ cups confectioners' sugar, sifted

1. Make the cake: Place a rack in the center of the oven and preheat the oven to 350°F. Lightly mist two 9-inch round cake pans with the vegetable oil spray, then dust them with flour. Shake out the excess flour and set the pans aside. Place a large mixing bowl and a set of mixer beaters in the refrigerator to chill.

2. Place the cake mix, sour cream, water, oil, eggs, and 1 teaspoon of vanilla in a large mixing bowl and beat with an electric mixer on low speed until the ingredients are moistened, 30 seconds. Stop the machine and scrape down the side of the bowl with a rubber spatula. Increase the mixer speed to medium and beat for 2 minutes longer, scraping down the side of the bowl again if needed. The batter should look well combined. Divide the cake batter evenly between the 2 prepared cake pans, smoothing the tops with the rubber spatula. Place the pans in the oven side by side.

3. Bake the cake layers until the tops spring back when lightly pressed with a finger, 28 to 32 minutes.

4. Meanwhile, make the chocolate rum filling: Remove the bowl and beaters from the refrigerator. Pour the 2 cups of cream into the bowl and beat with an electric mixer on high speed until soft peaks form, 1½ to 2 minutes. Stir the confectioners' sugar and cocoa powder together and add them to the beaten cream. Beat on high speed until stiff peaks form, 1 minute longer. Fold in the 2 teaspoons of rum. Place the filling in the refrigerator to chill.

Recipe Reminders

MADE FOR

PREP NOTES

DON'T FORGET

SPECIAL TOUCHES

5. Transfer the cake pans to wire racks and let the cake layers cool for 5 minutes. Run a sharp knife around the edge of each cake layer and give the pans a good shake to loosen the cakes. Invert each layer onto a wire rack, then invert it again onto another rack so that the cakes are right side up. Let the layers cool completely, 20 minutes longer.

6. To assemble the cake, using a long, serrated knife, slice each cake layer in half horizontally to make 4 layers (or leave as 2 layers, see Notes). Brush the cut side of each layer with ½ teaspoon of rum, if desired. Place the bottom half of one layer cut side up on a cake plate and spoon a third of the filling, about 1⅓ cups, on top. Spread the filling evenly nearly to the edge. Place the top half of this layer, right side up, over the filling. Add another third of the filling, spreading it nearly to the edge. Place the bottom of the remaining cake layer on top and spread it with the remaining filling, nearly to the edge. Place the top half of the second layer, right side up, on top of the filling. Cover the cake with a cake saver dome or tent it with aluminum foil and place it in the refrigerator to chill while you make the icing.

7. Make the chocolate icing: Place the chopped chocolate and butter in a medium-size microwave-safe glass bowl in the microwave on high power for 1 minute, then remove the bowl and stir until melted (you may need to return the bowl to the microwave for 15 seconds longer for the chocolate to be fully melted). Stir in the 6 tablespoons of milk or cream, the corn syrup, 2 teaspoons of vanilla, and the 2½ cups of confectioners' sugar. Beat with an electric mixer on medium-low speed until the icing is smooth and satiny, 1 to 2 minutes.

8. Remove the cake from the refrigerator. Pour the icing over the top of the cake and, using a metal spatula, guide it down the side of the cake, smoothing the top first, then the side. Cover the cake and place it back in the refrigerator until time to serve, at least 20 minutes.

Keep It Fresh! Store this cake, in a cake saver or under a glass cake dome, in the refrigerator for up to four days. Freeze only the layers, wrapped in aluminum foil, for up to six months. Let the layers thaw overnight on the counter, before making the filling and icing and assembling the cake.

Notes: You can use either light or dark rum here. Or, you can substitute 1 teaspoon of pure vanilla extract for the rum in the filling.

If you decide to make this a 2-layer cake, you'll need less filling. Just divide the ingredients in half, using 2 tablespoons plus 2 teaspoons cocoa powder.

Cocoa Powder Tips

The cocoa powder used in baking is most often unsweetened. And you can choose either regular cocoa or Dutch-processed. Many people believe that Dutch-processed has a deeper chocolate flavor than regular cocoa, and especially in some frostings, it does. But it is also a darker brown-gray color, and from an aesthetic standpoint this color isn't always the best choice in baking. Remember, we eat with our eyes first! Regular cocoa has a warmer, more earthy shade of brown. If you use Dutch-processed cocoa in the whipped cream filling for the Chocolate Rum Icebox Cake, it will turn the filling gray. Your better choice is regular Hershey's cocoa, which will make a soft tannish-brown filling.

If you use Dutch-processed cocoa when you are making a frosting, it will be a dark brown, something that is a nice contrast against a white or yellow cake. But if you want a warm medium-brown colored chocolate frosting, especially if you are pairing it with a dark chocolate cake, you'd best start with regular cocoa.

Double Chocolate Kahlua Cake

serves:
12 to 16

prep:
25 minutes

bake:
25 to 30 minutes

cool:
25 minutes

CHOCOLATE AND KAHLUA are good together, and in this cake their relationship is exceedingly strong. The coffee flavor of the Kahlúa liqueur plays right along with the dark chocolate batter and creamy chocolate frosting. Since this is a boozy cake, better save it for adult palates. If you want to temper the flavor a bit in the cake batter, reduce the Kahlúa to a half cup and increase the buttermilk to one cup. Serve the sliced cake with a steaming cup of coffee.

For the cake

Vegetable oil spray, for misting the pans
Flour, for dusting the pans
1 package (18.25 ounces) plain chocolate cake mix
2 tablespoons unsweetened cocoa powder
¾ cup Kahlúa (see Note)
¾ cup buttermilk
½ cup vegetable oil
3 large eggs

For the chocolate Kahlúa frosting

⅔ cup unsweetened cocoa powder
6 tablespoons boiling water
2 tablespoons Kahlúa
8 tablespoons (1 stick) butter, at room temperature
4 cups confectioners' sugar, sifted
¼ teaspoon ground cinnamon

1. Make the cake: Place a rack in the center of the oven and preheat the oven to 350°F. Lightly mist two 9-inch round cake pans with vegetable oil spray, then dust them with flour. Shake out the excess flour and set the pans aside.

2. Place the cake mix, 2 tablespoons of cocoa powder, ¾ cup of Kahlúa, and the buttermilk, oil, and eggs in a large mixing bowl and beat with an electric mixer on low speed until the ingredients are incorporated, 30 seconds. Stop the machine and scrape down the side of the bowl with a rubber spatula. Increase the mixer speed to medium and beat for 2 minutes longer, scraping down the side of the bowl again if needed. The batter should look well combined. Divide the cake batter evenly between the 2 prepared cake pans, smoothing the tops. Place the pans in the oven side by side.

3. Bake the cake layers until the tops spring back when lightly pressed with a finger, 25 to 30 minutes. Transfer the cake pans to wire racks and let the cake layers cool for 5 minutes. Run a dinner knife around the edge of each cake layer and give the pans a good shake to loosen the cakes. Invert each layer onto a wire rack, then invert it again onto another rack so that the cakes are right side up. Let the layers cool completely, 20 minutes longer.

4. Meanwhile, make the chocolate Kahlúa frosting: Place the ⅔ cup of cocoa powder in a medium-size heatproof bowl and pour in the boiling water and 2 tablespoons of Kahlúa. Stir with a wooden spoon or rubber spatula until the cocoa comes together into a soft mass. Add the butter and beat with an electric mixer on low speed until the mixture is soft and well combined, 30 seconds. Stop the machine. Add the confectioners' sugar and cinnamon and beat with the mixer on low speed until the sugar is incorporated, 1 minute. Increase the mixer speed to medium and beat until the frosting lightens and is fluffy, 2 minutes longer.

Recipe Reminders

MADE FOR

____

____

____

____

PREP NOTES

____

____

____

____

DON'T FORGET

____

____

____

____

SPECIAL TOUCHES

____

____

____

____

____

____

____

____

____

5. To assemble the cake, transfer one layer, right side up, to a cake plate. Generously and evenly frost the top of the layer. Place the second layer, right side up, on top of the first and generously frost the top, creating decorative swirls with the spatula. Working with smooth, clean strokes, spread the remaining frosting over the side of the cake.

Keep It Fresh! Store this cake, in a cake saver, at room temperature for up to three days or for up to one week in the refrigerator. Freeze the cake, wrapped in aluminum foil or in a cake saver, for up to six months. Let the cake thaw overnight on the counter before serving.

Note: Kahlúa is a very good coffee liqueur.

Five Foolproof Steps to Frosting a Pretty Layer Cake

1. Make sure the layers are cool to the touch before frosting them. Brush off any crumbs, and if one layer is larger or not as perfect looking when it comes out of the pan, make it the bottom layer.

2. Place the bottom layer on a cake plate or stand, with the top side up. Spoon a generous three-quarter cup of frosting on top and spread it evenly across the layer. If the layer is lopsided, you can build it up with some of the frosting.

3. Stack the second layer on top, with the top side up. Spoon a generous three-quarter cup of frosting on top and spread it gently and evenly across the layer.

4. Using about the same amount of frosting, apply a thin layer around the side, repairing any imperfections, trapping any crumbs, and essentially sealing the cake.

5. With the remaining frosting, apply a thicker, more decorative layer of frosting on the top and side. Make swirls on top with the end of a small spatula or spoon. For a smooth side, hold a metal spatula right against the cake with one hand and turn the cake plate with the other.

Make Your Own Wedding Cake

For years readers have asked me how they can bake their own wedding cakes, but this was not my arena, so I often felt uncomfortable doling out advice. For this new book I presented myself with a challenge: I would bake a wedding cake—a modest but elegant three-layer wedding cake that could feed forty-five people. I set aside a weekend for my friend Martha Bowden and me to prepare this wedding cake in my kitchen. We baked the layers on a Saturday and finished the cake on Sunday. In the end we were amazed at what a beautiful cake we created. And we learned a few things in the process.

A wedding cake needs to be moist and sturdy. I chose a white cake because that is the standard. Ours has an unexpected almond flavor, and as always, you'll appreciate the ease and success that comes with starting with a cake mix. The frosting should be both delicious and thick enough to pipe out into decorations. And you need to prepare plenty of it. We opted for a yummy cream cheese frosting, even though we knew it was going to be more difficult to work with than those traditional white bakery frostings made with vegetable shortening. Frosting makes the cake, and we felt flavor had to win over texture.

Groceries and supplies should cost you no more than $40. I've listed some things that you may not have in your battery of equipment. If possible, borrow the cake pans from someone so you don't have to spend money on bakeware you'll never use again. Your real investment, we found, was time. Baking with a friend helps when it comes to things like turning the cake while you frost it and washing the dishes and providing moral support. This cake is proof that you do not need a degree in cake decorating to make a wedding cake. If you are a cake decorating beginner it's easy to stick to simple flourishes like fresh flowers and a band of icing around the bottom of the layers.

Wedding Cake How-To

Before you bake a wedding cake, it's best to read up on what it takes to bake one. Study the charts offered in Wilton books and online that tell you how many servings you will get from the different size pans. These charts also tell you how much frosting you will need to frost the cake. The photographs will inspire you to go above and beyond what I suggest here in this basic wedding cake recipe.

For advanced reading on wedding and other grand cakes look in *The Cake Bible* by Rose Levy Beranbaum. Rose is known for her precision, creativity, and useful tips. The suggestion in the recipe here to use plastic drinking straws as dowels to support the cake layers is something I learned from reading Rose's book. Her method of turning the cake pan upside down on top of the bottom layer is useful for marking the spot that the next layer goes, too.

As always, when in need of baking advice or if you have questions on how to bake a wedding cake, check out the message board at www.cakemixdoctor.com.

A Basic and Beautiful Wedding Cake

BE SURE TO LEAVE YOURSELF enough time to bake this celebratory cake. I've listed the supplies you'll need on the next page. There are a few specialty items you'll probably have to buy or borrow, and having the full list in one place should make figuring it out easier.

serves:
45

prep:
30 minutes

bake:
42 to 53 minutes

cool:
1 hour and 10 minutes

assemble:
3 hours

For the cake

Vegetable shortening, for greasing the pans
2 cups sifted all-purpose flour (see Notes), plus flour for dusting the pans
2 packages (18.25 ounces each) white or vanilla cake mix, plain or with pudding
2 cups granulated sugar
2 cups water
2 cups sour cream
2 whole large eggs
4 large egg whites
4 tablespoons vegetable oil
2 teaspoons pure vanilla extract
2 teaspoons pure almond extract

For the frosting

3 packages (8 ounces each) cream cheese, at room temperature
12 tablespoons (1½ sticks) butter, at room temperature
1 tablespoon pure vanilla extract
14 cups confectioners' sugar, sifted
2 tablespoons meringue powder (see Notes)

Recipe Reminders

MADE FOR

PREP NOTES

DON'T FORGET

SPECIAL TOUCHES

Supplies

One 12-inch round cake pan, at least 2 inches deep
One 8-inch round cake pan, at least 2 inches deep
One 6-inch round cake pan, at least 2 inches deep
Large mixing bowls
Handheld electric mixer or restaurant-size stand mixer
2 large wire racks to cool the 12-inch layer on or 4 smaller racks that you can push together
Space in the fridge for the 12-inch, 8-inch, and 6-inch layers to chill after frosting
Parchment paper
3 cardboard cake rounds: one 12 inches in diameter, one 8 inches, and one 6 inches (see Notes)
Double-sided tape or masking tape
15 to 16 inch round cake plate or cake base
Plastic drinking straws
Pastry bag with #4 or #10 and small star tips
Edible pearl beads (French dragées, size #5)
Candied violets (optional)
Fresh flowers of your choice (see Notes)
Florist's wire, or 1 twist tie

1. Make the cake: Place a rack in the center of the oven and preheat the oven to 325°F. Generously grease and flour the side of each of the cake pans. Shake out the excess flour. Lightly grease the bottoms of the pans. Cut a round of parchment paper to fit the bottom of each cake pan and press these rounds into the bottom of the pans. Set the pans aside.

2. Place the cake mix, flour, and granulated sugar in a large mixing bowl and toss with a large wooden spoon to combine. Set the bowl aside.

3. Place the water, sour cream, whole eggs, egg whites, oil, 2 teaspoons of vanilla, and the almond extract in a very large mixing bowl and beat on low speed with an electric mixer until the egg yolks are incorporated, 15 seconds. Add the cake mix mixture, about 3 cups at a time, beating on low speed until just incorporated, about 15 seconds each time. When all of the dry ingredients have been added, increase the mixer speed to medium and beat until the batter is smooth, 1½ to 2 minutes.

4. Ladle about 6½ cups of cake batter into the prepared 12-inch cake pan, about 3½ cups of batter into the 8-inch pan, and about 2½ cups of batter into the 6-inch pan. The batter will be about 1 inch below the top of the pans. Smooth the tops of the batter with a rubber spatula. Place the pans in the oven. If your oven is not large enough to hold 3 pans on one rack, place 2 pans on the center rack and place the third pan in the center of the highest rack.

5. Bake the cake layers until they just begin to pull away from the side of the pans and the tops are lightly browned. A toothpick inserted in the center of the layers should come out clean. (Although I usually don't advise using a toothpick to test for doneness, these cake layers are dense and thicker than usual.) The 12-inch layer will bake quickest and be done after 42 to 48 minutes and the thicker 8-inch and 6-inch layers will be done after 47 to 53 minutes. Transfer the cake pans to wire racks to cool. Immediately press down gently on the top of each layer for 10 to 15 seconds with your hands or with the bottom of a saucepan that is the same size as the layer (make sure the bottoms of the pans are clean). This will level the layers and make them easier to stack. Let the layers cool in the pans for 10 minutes. Run a knife around the edge of each cake layer and gently shake the pans to loosen the cakes. Invert each layer onto a wire rack, then again onto another rack so that the cakes are right side up.

6. Let the cake layers cool to room temperature, 1 hour longer. Then, wrap them well in plastic wrap and store at room temperature for up to 2 days before frosting. Or, wrap the layers in plastic wrap and then in heavy-duty foil and freeze them for

How to Feed Nearly 100

You can do this by doubling the cake recipe and adding a 16-inch layer to the bottom of the cake. You will also need slightly more frosting; increase it by 1 package of cream cheese, 4 tablespoons of butter, a teaspoon of vanilla, and 4 cups of confectioners' sugar. You'll get at least an additional 52 slices from that 16-inch layer.

How to Use a Pastry Bag

Never fear: I managed to bake cakes for some twenty years before I ever touched a pastry bag to decorate them. When I did, I was in Paris and I was paying for pastry lessons, so you bet I was picking up the pastry bag! But once back to America and life in the suburbs with a family and little children there was no real need to use a pastry bag. If something needed to be piped—a name on a birthday cake or the filling of deviled eggs—I either snipped off the corner of a resealable plastic bag or used the compact pastry bags with fitted tips found on the supermarket baking aisle.

Whether you use the supermarket bags or a more professional pastry bag, follow the steps in this box to do it.

Experiment with tips with small plain holes for thin lines and more elaborate tips for making flowers, fluted borders, and so on. Refill the pastry bag as needed and, when you have completed the job, wash the bag and tips by hand, then dry and store them.

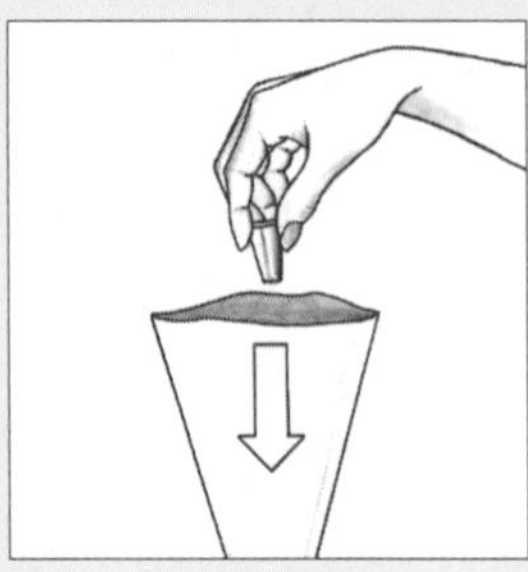

1. *Fit the tip into the end of the bag.*

2. *Place the bag, with the tip at the bottom, in a tall glass or jar.*

3. *Open up the bag and let the edge drape over the side of the glass.*

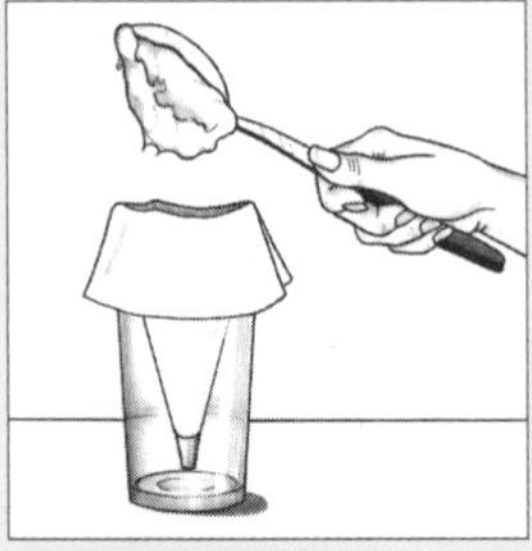

4. *Spoon the frosting into the bag, taking care not to fill it too full.*

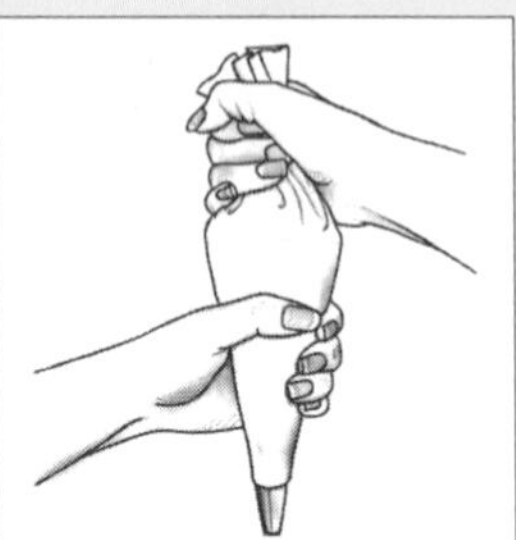

5. *Twist the edge of the bag together, pick up the bag, and push the frosting down to the tip.*

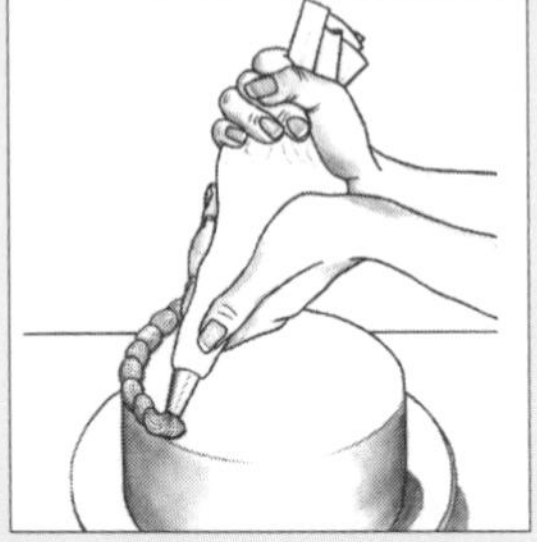

6. *If you are right-handed, pick up the bag with your left hand and use this hand to press on the bag and move frosting toward the tip. If you are left-handed, pick up the bag with your right hand. Hold your free hand down near the tip to balance and steer the bag.*

up to 1 month. In warm weather, make sure the cake layers are cold before frosting them. Place them in the freezer if needed to chill.

7. Make the frosting: Place the cream cheese and butter in a very large mixing bowl and beat with an electric mixer on medium-low speed until creamy, 1 to 1½ minutes. Add the 1 tablespoon of vanilla and 12 cups of the confectioners' sugar, 2 cups at a time, beating on low speed until the sugar is all incorporated. Stop the machine and scrape down the side of the bowl with a rubber spatula. Increase the mixer speed to medium and beat the frosting until it is fluffy, 1 to 2 minutes longer. Place the frosting in the refrigerator to chill for 30 minutes.

8. Frost the cake: Dab 2 tablespoons of frosting onto each cardboard cake round and spread it over the top in a thin layer. Place the 12-inch cake layer on top of the 12-inch round, the 8-inch layer on top of the 8-inch round, and the 6-inch layer on top of the 6-inch round. The dab of icing will keep the layers from sliding. Frost the top and side of the cake layers with a long, thin metal icing spatula. Begin by spreading a thin coat all the way around the side to seal in the crumbs, then go back and apply a thicker coat, using the cake round as a guide for the spatula. Frost the 12-inch and 8-inch layers flat across the top. Frost the 6-inch layer more generously as it will be placed on the top of the cake. Set the three layers, uncovered, in the refrigerator to chill. You should have about 4 cups of frosting remaining. If you are transporting the cake, set aside about 1 cup of this in a plastic container in the refrigerator to use to repair spots in the frosting when you arrive. The remaining frosting will be used to pipe decorations onto the cake.

9. Make the piping frosting: Add the remaining 2 cups of confectioners' sugar and the 2 tablespoons of meringue powder to the remaining frosting and beat with an electric mixer on medium-low speed until incorporated, 30 seconds. Increase the mixer

A Piping Novice?

Frost the cake as directed but when it comes to the piped decorations, use prepared vanilla frosting in the pastry bag. It is easy to pipe and holds up well in warm weather.

speed to medium-high and beat until the frosting mixture stiffens, 30 seconds to 1 minute longer. Place it in the refrigerator to chill for 15 to 20 minutes.

10. Assemble the cake: Place a few pieces of double-sided tape or loops of masking tape in the center of a cake plate or base. The base needs to be 3 to 4 inches larger in diameter than the largest cake layer—15 to 16 inches in diameter. Place the 12-inch cake layer still on its cardboard base on the cake plate or base; the tape will hold it securely. Position the empty 8-inch baking pan upside down on top of the center of the 12-inch cake layer so that it leaves an indentation in the frosting. This marks where you'll place the 8-inch layer. Insert a drinking straw vertically into the center of the 12-inch layer and mark where the top of the cake meets the straw. Remove the straw and cut it and 7 more straws into pieces of this length. To support the next layer, insert one straw back into the center of the cake layer and place the other 6 in an upright spoke pattern around it, halfway between the center and the outline of the 8-inch pan. Carefully place the 8-inch layer with its cardboard base on the 12-inch layer.

Nupi-Tool Know-How

With the right long metal spatula, short metal spatula, and plastic spatula you can frost a beauty of a wedding cake. No need for a pastry bag!

11. Place the 6-inch baking pan upside down on top of the 8-inch layer to mark it. Insert a straw into the center of the 8-inch layer, mark where the top of the cake meets the straw. Remove the straw and cut it and 5 more pieces of straw to this length. Insert one straw in the center of the 8-inch cake layer and insert the remaining 5 pieces of straw in spokes around it. Carefully place the 6-inch layer with its cardboard base on top of the 8-inch layer. Set the cake aside.

12. Remove the piping frosting from the refrigerator. Spoon a generous cup into a pastry bag fitted with a round tip (either #4 for a thin line or #10 for a thicker one). Pipe a line of frosting around the bottom of each cake layer to cover the cardboard rounds. If you need to go back and pipe another line of frosting, either above or below this line, do so. Press the edible pearls

To Cut the Cake

Cutting a wedding cake is a little tricky but not as complicated as it may seem. Because the bottom layer of the cake I've included in this book is wider than the others, we'll start with it.

1. *Make a cut into the bottom layer where it meets the middle layer. Cut around the bottom layer using the middle layer as a guide. You've now separated an outer 2-inch-wide ring of the bottom layer. Cut serving slices from this outer ring. You should get at least 20 slices.*

2. *Carefully remove the top layer from the middle layer and set it aside. Slice it last; you may be able to save it for the bride and groom.*

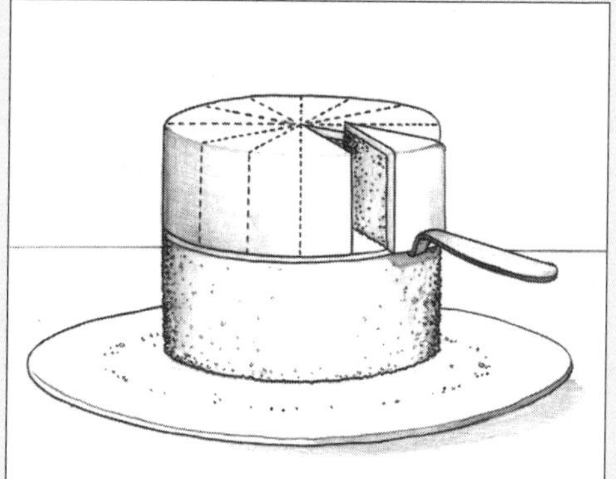

3. *Now, cut the middle layer as you would a round layer cake. Even though it is still sitting on the remaining bottom layer, cut through only the middle layer. You should get at least 12 generous slices from the middle layer.*

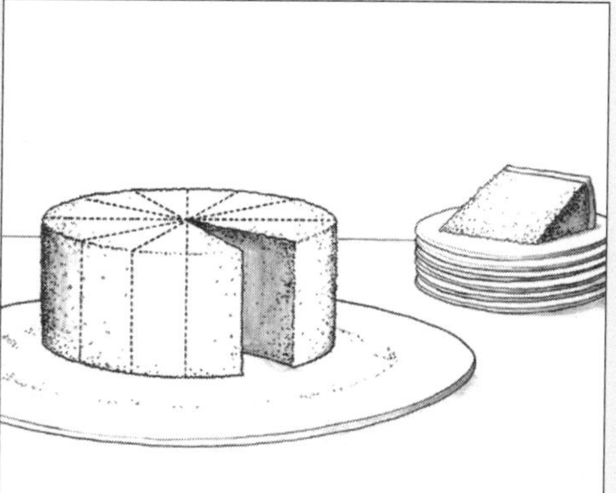

4. *Cut the remaining bottom layer as you would a round layer cake. You should get at least 12 slices more from this portion of the bottom layer.*

gently into each line of frosting, placing them about 1 inch apart. Using a small star tip, pipe a small star between each pearl (or place small candied violets between the pearls). To get the hang of it, practice piping stars onto a plate. The cooler the frosting is, the better formed the stars will be. Feel free to be as decorative as you like with the frosting, adding whatever embellishments you wish. You have plenty of frosting with which to work.

13. For the top, cut three very fresh small roses or some hydrangeas or your choice of edible flowers so they have 1 to 2 inches of stem. Tie them together with florist's wire or a twist tie. Insert the flower bundle into the top of the cake. Feel free to decorate the top with flower leaves (rinsed and patted dry). And decorate the base of the cake with more flowers, if desired.

14. The cake is now finished. Store it in the refrigerator until time to serve.

Notes: It's important to sift the flour before measuring it so you don't add too much to the cake and make it dry. Spoon the sifted flour into dry measuring cups and sweep off the top with a knife or ruler.

Meringue powder and cardboard cake rounds can be found at baking supply stores. The website www.wilton.com is a good source for these and other baking supplies. Candied violets are available from many specialty food stores.

Need a little variation? Opt for a tablespoon of grated lemon or orange zest in the cake batter instead of the almond extract. Brush the cooled layers with amaretto or Kahlúa and let it soak into the cake before frosting. If you want to get really daring, split the cake layers horizontally and fill them with lemon curd or apricot filling (see page 98) before frosting.

Flower Power

Blooms, buds, and petals from fresh flowers make a stunning topper, cascade, or tray garnish for a wedding cake. Make sure the flowers are free from pesticides—preferably organically grown. Match them with the bride's selected colors. My cake decorating favorites are roses of all sizes, orchids, hydrangea, nasturtiums, and daisies. They make a powerful but pretty statement on your cake!

Bundts and Pounds

Layer cakes may be glamorous but it's the Bundt cake that's heartwarming and humble. In my ten years as the Cake Mix Doctor I have baked hundreds (thousands?) of Bundts and pound cakes for bake sales, birthdays, book signings, potlucks, and TV photo opportunities. I know the Bundt looks great on camera, holds well in transit, and doesn't seem to demand the attention it gets.

Why do we love Bundts as well as pound cakes baked in tube pans? Because they are moist. These pans accommodate rich, heavy batters. That's why the tube is in the middle—to let heat come up through the center of the cake and bake it evenly. But the sturdy shape also makes the cakes easy to tote, another reason we love them. We can take them to picnics and parties without worrying about the slip and slide of layer cakes. We can ship them to family and friends across the country and know they will arrive intact. And unlike a flat sheet cake, a Bundt is interesting to the eye. It is architectural. Add a glaze or a dusting of confectioners' sugar and it is dazzling.

The Bundt pan is as much a fixture in today's kitchen as a brownie pan. And the straight-sided tube pan has been around as long as America has been baking angel food and pound cakes. They both have a nostalgic quality to them, and the new decorative Bundt shapes are appealing to young cooks and families. What eight-year-old wouldn't want his birthday cake in the shape of a sand castle? Personally, I love my cathedral

Bundt pan and the Bundt pan shaped like a big cupcake that my daughters gave me for my birthday. But I also love the tube pan that sits alongside the Bundts in the bottom kitchen drawer. It was my mom's pan which she used to bake her chocolate pound cake and sour cream coffee cake and, on really special occasions, her angel food cake. From one pan comes many edible memories.

The recipes in this chapter are a wonderful varied lot and will, I hope, create edible memories for you. Beginning with lemon and fruit and moving into spice and then chocolate and then cakes with alcohol, they are all worth baking. The recipe may suggest they be baked in a Bundt or a tube, but you can bake them in either pan. Keep in mind that the Bundts often bake a little faster, about five minutes, than the tubes using the same recipe.

Throughout this chapter I help you through the process of baking a Bundt cake—from prepping the pan to inverting the cake to glazing it. And I include storage tips with each recipe because it's impossible for most families to finish a cake in one sitting. Leftover cake in the freezer has become my insurance plan. I know I can serve dessert at any hour, any day, since the frozen cake is quickly thawed with the help of the microwave and dressed up with ice cream.

As with the layer cakes, you will recognize some old-time favorites in this chapter—the Darn Good Chocolate Cake, Kathy's Cinnamon Breakfast Cake, Susan's Lemon Cake, and Stacy's Chocolate Chip Cake. They're back, and I have tweaked my original recipes to make them lighter in fat but still have that great signature flavor. I've streamlined the Piña Colada Cake recipe, improved the Zucchini Cake with Penuche Glaze, and have made the Amazing German Chocolate Cake more amazing. I hope you agree.

Others I love include the Lemon Cake with a Blueberry Crown—where fresh blueberries sink to the bottom of the Bundt pan and when inverted form a crown at the top—as well as Cathy's Marbled Spice Cake, Maple Cream Cheese Pound Cake with Caramel Glaze, Jewish Pound Cake, Apricot Cake with Lemon Cream Cheese Filling, and Chocolate Espresso Pound Cake.

I'll stop here. I know as well as you do that this process is subjective and my favorites may not be your favorites. That makes baking cakes and writing about them so much fun. I develop an array of recipes, knowing I've got something for everyone!

Lemon Cake with a Blueberry Crown

I DIDN'T PLAN A LEMON CAKE with a blueberry crown—true confession! I envisioned a lemon cake with blueberries throughout, but after baking and cooling it I found all of the fresh blueberries I had folded into the batter had sunk right to the bottom of the Bundt pan. And when I inverted the pan onto a rack, the cake was lemon on the bottom with what looked like a crown of blueberries resting on top. Drizzled with a light lemony glaze—or just sprinkled with confectioners' sugar—this was simply regal, please pardon the pun.

serves: 12 to 16

prep: 20 minutes

bake: 40 to 45 minutes

cool: 40 minutes

For the cake

Vegetable oil spray, for misting the pan
Flour, for dusting the pan
1 package (18.25 ounces) plain yellow or vanilla cake mix
1½ cups fresh blueberries
1 package (3 ounces) lemon gelatin
⅔ cup hot water
⅔ cup vegetable oil
4 large eggs

For the glaze (optional)

2 medium-size lemons
1 cup confectioners' sugar, sifted

Recipe Reminders

MADE FOR

PREP NOTES

DON'T FORGET

SPECIAL TOUCHES

1. Make the cake: Place a rack in the center of the oven and preheat the oven to 350°F. Lightly mist a 12-cup Bundt pan with vegetable oil spray, then dust it with flour. Shake out the excess flour and set the pan aside.

2. Measure out 2 tablespoons of the cake mix and place it in a small mixing bowl. Rinse and pat the blueberries dry with paper towels. Add the berries to the small bowl and toss them to coat well with the cake mix. Set the blueberries aside.

3. Place the remaining cake mix and the lemon gelatin, hot water, oil, and eggs in a large mixing bowl and beat with an electric mixer on low speed until the ingredients are just incorporated, 30 seconds. Stop the machine and scrape down the side of the bowl with a rubber spatula. Increase the mixer speed to medium and beat until smooth, 2 minutes longer, scraping down the side of the bowl again if needed. Fold the blueberries into the batter. Pour the batter into the prepared Bundt pan, smoothing the top with the rubber spatula, and place the pan in the oven.

4. Bake the cake until it is golden brown and the top springs back when lightly pressed with a finger, 40 to 45 minutes. Transfer the Bundt pan to a wire rack and let the cake cool for 15 minutes. Run a long sharp knife around the edges of the cake, shake the pan gently, and invert the cake onto a wire rack. Let the cake cool completely, about 25 minutes longer.

5. Meanwhile, make the glaze, if using: Rinse and pat the lemons dry with paper towels, then grate enough zest to measure 1 teaspoon. Cut the lemons in half and squeeze the juice into a small bowl; you will need ¼ cup. Add the lemon zest, then whisk in the confectioners' sugar until the glaze is smooth.

6. To glaze the cake, place it on a cake plate and spoon the glaze over the top, allowing it to drip down the sides. Or just dust the cake with confectioners' sugar. Slice and serve the cake.

Keep It Fresh! Store this cake, in a cake saver or covered with plastic wrap, at room temperature for up to three days or for up to one week in the refrigerator. Freeze the unglazed cake, wrapped in aluminum foil, for up to six months. Let the cake thaw overnight on the counter, then glaze it, if desired.

The Story Behind the Bundt Pan

Everyone was gaga over the Bundt pan in the 1960s. If you weren't around then, trust me, the baking world was crazy about Bundt cakes. But the venerable Bundt was created a decade earlier, in 1950. A group of women from the local Hadassah society asked David Dahlquist of Nordic Ware in Minnesota to make a coffee cake pan similar to one they knew in Germany. That pan was called a *bundkuchen* or *bund,* meaning a gathering of people.

Dahlquist made the pan, added a "t" to the end of the word *bund* to make it easier to pronounce, and the rest is history. Americans—and cooks the world over—have loved the Bundt because of its even baking, homey but beautiful appearance, how it serves gatherings of people so well, and because of those grooves along the side that oddly form slicing guides.

The original Bundt holds twelve cups of batter and is therefore a twelve-cup Bundt. It comes in a less expensive lightweight aluminum as well as a more expensive heavier aluminum with a nonstick interior. Don't think the less costly pan doesn't bake as well. It does, and I used it for many of these recipes. If you are baking a light-colored cake in a heavy Bundt with a dark interior you may want to reduce the oven temperature by 25 degrees so that the outside edges aren't overbaked.

There are countless variations on the classic Bundt, fancy pans in the shapes of stars and fleurs-de-lis and cathedrals and Stars of David and flowers, to name a few. Most of these decorative Bundts are ten-cup pans, but don't let that confuse you as they will hold the batter of my recipes. The cakes will bake up taller, however, and you may have to slice off the domed cake before inverting it so that the cake rests level on the plate.

A Lighter Susan's Lemon Cake

serves:
12 to 16

prep:
25 minutes

bake:
38 to 42 minutes

cool:
10 to 15 minutes

MY SISTER SUSAN has become known for her wonderful lemon Bundt cake, which she totes to friends in Atlanta and on weekend getaways. My kids love this cake; we know it as Susan's lemon cake. Susan says credit should really go to Sally Roy, a neighborhood friend, who first shared the recipe with her. So thanks to Susan and to Sally for the many pleasant summer afternoons we have spent enjoying a slice.

Several readers have asked if I would lighten up some Bundts using applesauce instead of oil, and I did that with this cake. The substitution works so well you'll never miss that oil. And while I was lightening things, I reduced the amount of lemon gelatin called for in the original recipe and find you taste more of the real lemon flavor.

Vegetable oil spray, for misting the pan
Flour, for dusting the pan
1 large or 2 small lemons (see Note)
1 package (18.25 ounces) plain yellow or vanilla cake mix
About 3 tablespoons (half of a 3 ounce package) lemon gelatin
⅔ cup unsweetened applesauce
⅔ cup hot water
4 large eggs
¾ cup confectioners' sugar, sifted

1. Place a rack in the center of the oven and preheat the oven to 350°F. Lightly mist a 12-cup Bundt pan with vegetable oil spray, then dust it with flour. Shake out the excess flour and set the pan aside.

2. Rinse and pat the lemon dry with paper towels, then grate 2 teaspoons of lemon zest. Place 1 teaspoon of zest in a large mixing bowl for the cake and set 1 teaspoon aside for the glaze. Cut the lemon in half and squeeze the juice, setting aside 1½ tablespoons of lemon juice for the glaze. Pour any remaining lemon juice into the large mixing bowl with the teaspoon of grated zest.

3. Place the cake mix, lemon gelatin, applesauce, hot water, and eggs in the bowl with the lemon juice and zest and beat with an electric mixer on low speed until the ingredients are incorporated, 1 minute. Stop the machine and scrape down the side of the bowl with a rubber spatula. Increase the mixer speed to medium and beat until the batter is smooth, 2 minutes longer, scraping down the side of the bowl again if needed. The batter should look thick and well blended. Pour the batter into the prepared Bundt pan, smoothing the top with the rubber spatula, and place the pan in the oven.

4. Bake the cake until it is light brown and just starts to pull away from the sides of the pan, (the top will spring back when lightly pressed with a finger) 38 to 42 minutes. Transfer the Bundt pan to a wire rack and let the cake cool for 10 to 15 minutes.

5. Meanwhile, make the glaze: Combine the confectioners' sugar, reserved 1½ tablespoons of lemon juice, and reserved 1 teaspoon of lemon zest in a small bowl and stir until smooth.

6. Run a long, sharp knife around the edges of the cake, shake the pan gently, and invert the cake onto a cake plate. Spoon the glaze evenly over the warm cake so that it drizzles down the side and into the center. Slice the cake and serve it warm or let it cool before slicing.

Recipe Reminders

MADE FOR

____

____

____

____

PREP NOTES

____

____

____

____

DON'T FORGET

____

____

____

____

SPECIAL TOUCHES

____

____

____

____

____

____

____

____

____

How to Bake This Cake in the Clouds

Baking cakes with added sugar or sweetened gelatin is risky at high altitudes because the sugar makes the cake more tender, thus weakening its structure. On the other hand, Bundt pans are quite useful at high heights because they support a cake well. If you are intent on baking this cake in Denver or Albuquerque, add a quarter cup of all-purpose flour and a couple of tablespoons of water to the batter to increase the structure. And as the recipe indicates, not adding the entire package of gelatin is better than adding the whole thing.

Keep It Fresh! Store this cake, covered with plastic wrap or placed under a glass cake dome, at room temperature for up to one week. Freeze the cake, wrapped in aluminum foil, for up to six months. Let the cake thaw overnight on the counter before serving.

Note: The amount of juice you get from a lemon varies, depending on its size, its juiciness, and its temperature. Warm lemons give more juice, so that's why people will pop a cold lemon from the fridge in the microwave for 5 to 7 seconds. You can also warm up a lemon by rolling it between the palm of your hand and the kitchen counter, just to encourage a bit more juice from it. You will get at least 2 tablespoons of juice from a nice large lemon, so what you don't need for the glaze pour into the cake batter or your cup of tea.

This Cake Is Just the Beginning

Nancy Copeland of Manassas, Virginia, is a reader of my newsletter who has all sorts of ideas to transform Susan's Lemon Cake into other delicacies.

◆ Use a lemon cake mix instead of plain yellow or vanilla.

◆ Use lime gelatin and key lime juice instead of lemon juice. Use grated lime zest instead of the lemon zest.

◆ Substitute orange cake mix, orange gelatin, and orange juice and zest.

And Nancy concocts what she calls "boiled syrup"—1 cup of granulated sugar, ⅓ cup of whatever juice you are using in the cake, and ⅔ cup of water. Simmer this until the sugar has dissolved. When the cake is done and cooling in the pan, Nancy pours the warm syrup over the top of the cake. She lets the cake set for 20 minutes, then turns it out onto a serving plate.

Marsha's Lively Lemon Cake

Marsha Gillett of Yukon, Oklahoma, developed this recipe for one of my online recipe contests. She likes to add fruit juices like orange juice to her cake recipes, and she considers herself a "cake aficionado" because she loves cake, bakes cake, and eats cake. Although Marsha serves this cake unadorned, I dusted it with confectioners' sugar before slicing. You'll love the ease of this recipe.

serves:
12 to 16

prep:
15 minutes

bake:
43 to 47 minutes

cool:
35 to 45 minutes

Vegetable oil spray, for misting the pan
Flour, for dusting the pan
1 package (18.25 ounces) plain lemon cake mix
1 package (3.4 ounces) lemon instant pudding mix
¾ cup orange juice (or a combination of orange juice and a tropical juice blend)
¾ cup (6 ounces) lemon yogurt
½ cup vegetable oil
4 large eggs
1 teaspoon grated lemon zest (optional)
1 tablespoon confectioners' sugar

Recipe Reminders

MADE FOR

PREP NOTES

DON'T FORGET

SPECIAL TOUCHES

1. Place a rack in the center of the oven and preheat the oven to 350°F. Lightly mist a 12-cup Bundt pan with vegetable oil spray, then dust it with flour. Shake out the excess flour and set the pan aside.

2. Place the cake mix, pudding mix, orange juice, yogurt, oil, eggs, and lemon zest, if using, in a large mixing bowl. Beat with an electric mixer on low speed until the ingredients are incorporated, 30 seconds. Stop the machine and scrape down the side of the bowl with a rubber spatula. Increase the mixer speed to medium and beat the batter until it is smooth, 2 minutes longer, scraping down the side of the bowl again if needed. Pour the batter into the prepared Bundt pan, smoothing the top with the rubber spatula, and place the pan in the oven.

3. Bake the cake until it is golden brown and the top springs back when lightly pressed with a finger, 43 to 47 minutes. Transfer the Bundt pan to a wire rack and let the cake cool for 10 to 15 minutes. Run a long, sharp knife around the edges of the cake, shake the pan gently, and invert the cake onto a wire rack. Let the cake cool completely, 25 to 30 minutes longer. Sift the confectioners' sugar over the top, then slice and serve the cake.

Keep It Fresh! Store this cake, in a cake saver, at room temperature for up to one week. Freeze the cake, wrapped in aluminum foil, for up to six months. Let the cake thaw overnight on the counter before serving.

Tips for Baking Perfect Bundts and Pounds

The basic cake-baking suggestions apply to Bundts and pound cakes but three need emphasizing for best results:

1. Prep the pan. With tube pans this means mist them with vegetable oil spray and dust them with about two tablespoons of flour. Turn the pan upside down over the sink and tap out the excess flour. You can also mist a Bundt pan and dust it with flour the same way. I don't like vegetable oil sprays that contain propellants (alcohol) because they cause the outside of the cake to darken and toughen as it bakes. And Nordic Ware advises on its website against sprays that have lecithin listed as an ingredient because it leaves a gummy residue on the pan.

Nordic Ware makes highly detailed decorative Bundt pans, like the Star pan, the Festival pan, and the Cathedral pan, modeled after Notre Dame. You don't want the cake to stick in the intricate grooves of these pans. The foolproof way to prep decorative Bundts is to grease them with solid vegetable shortening—that's right, Crisco. Dip a small pastry brush into the container of Crisco and then paint every little nook and cranny of these pans (I often get one of my kids to do this while I am making the cake). Then add two tablespoons of flour, shake it around, and tap out the excess flour over the sink. Not only does this method create a beautiful crust on the outside of the cake, but the cake will invert and come out of the pan cleanly and beautifully every time. I promise!

2. Cool the cake. Let the cake cool for ten to fifteen minutes in the pan placed on a wire rack, then run a sharp knife around the edge of the cake to loosen it from the pan if you are using a heavy pan. Run a plastic knife around the cake edge if using a lighter weight pan with an enamel or nonstick surface that would be scratched by a sharp metal knife. Let the cake cool completely on the rack unless the recipe tells you to invert it onto a serving plate.

3. Choose the pan's best side. Invert the Bundt pan one time on the rack so that it cools with the decorative fluted side up. This is the top of the cake and you just need to slide the cake onto a plate before glazing. On the other hand, the tube pan needs to be inverted once then inverted again onto a rack so that the larger side is up.

Key Lime Pound Cake

serves:
12 to 16

prep:
20 minutes

bake:
47 to 52 minutes

cool:
20 minutes

I **DON'T KNOW ABOUT YOU,** but the words *key lime* make me hungry. I think of a cool and creamy pie resting atop a graham cracker crust. And I think of this simple but satisfying Bundt cake flavored with the same key lime juice. A few years ago Margo Pope, who lives in St. Augustine, Florida, sent me this recipe, which she adapted from a local cookbook. One of the great features of the cake is that it's versatile—you can use a yellow, vanilla, or white cake mix—but make sure you use real key lime juice, found on the juice aisle of most supermarkets. Garnish the cake with lime slices, dollops of whipped cream, and graham cracker crumbs for a festive key lime pie look.

For the cake

Vegetable oil spray, for misting the pan
Flour, for dusting the pan
1 package (18.25 ounces) plain yellow, vanilla, or white cake mix
1 package (3.4 ounces) vanilla instant pudding mix (see Notes)
½ cup key lime juice
½ cup water
½ cup sweetened condensed milk
8 tablespoons (1 stick) butter, at room temperature
1 teaspoon pure vanilla extract
4 large eggs

For the glaze

1 cup confectioners' sugar, sifted
1½ tablespoons key lime juice

For the garnish (optional)

6 to 8 lime slices
1 cup whipped cream (see Notes)
2 tablespoons graham cracker crumbs

1. Make the cake: Place a rack in the center of the oven and preheat the oven to 350°F. Lightly mist a 12-cup Bundt pan with vegetable oil spray, then dust it with flour. Shake out the excess flour and set the pan aside.

2. Place the cake mix, pudding mix, ½ cup of lime juice, water, condensed milk, butter, vanilla, and eggs in a large mixing bowl. Beat with an electric mixer on low speed until the ingredients are incorporated, 30 seconds. Stop the machine and scrape down the side of the bowl with a rubber spatula. Increase the mixer speed to medium and beat the batter until it is smooth and thick, 1½ minutes longer, scraping down the side of the bowl again if needed. Pour the batter into the prepared Bundt pan, smoothing the top with the rubber spatula, and place the pan in the oven.

3. Bake the cake until it is golden brown and the top springs back when lightly pressed with a finger, 47 to 52 minutes. Transfer the Bundt pan to a wire rack and let the cake cool for 10 to 15 minutes. Run a long, sharp knife around the edges of the cake, shake the pan gently, and invert the cake onto a wire rack to cool while you prepare the glaze.

4. Make the glaze: Place the confectioners' sugar and the 1½ tablespoons of lime juice in a small bowl and whisk to combine. Slide the cake onto a serving plate and spoon the glaze over the warm cake.

Recipe Reminders

MADE FOR

PREP NOTES

DON'T FORGET

SPECIAL TOUCHES

A Note About Glazes

Martha Bowden, friend and fearless recipe tester, has a theory about glazes. She thinks warm glazes should go on cooled cakes, so the glaze sinks into the cake and doesn't run down the sides. And room temperature glazes—where ingredients are just stirred together, like the classic confectioners' sugar and milk glaze—can go on warm or cooled cakes. The cooler the cake the less likely the glaze will run down the sides.

5. Garnish the cake with the lime slices, whipped cream, and graham cracker crumbs, if desired. Slice and serve the cake.

Keep It Fresh! Store this cake, in a cake saver or covered with plastic wrap, at room temperature for up to one week. Freeze the cake in a cake saver for up to six months. Let the cake thaw overnight on the counter before serving.

Note: If your Bundt recipes that contain pudding mix bake up nicely but shrink in the pan as they cool, you might want to reduce the amount of pudding mix you add next time. Add half a package instead of the entire package.

You can use whipped cream from a refrigerated aerosol can or whip ½ cup heavy cream sweetened with 1 tablespoon of granulated sugar.

Orange Poppy Seed Pound Cake

THIS FESTIVE BUT EASY-TO-MAKE orange cake is as suitable for fall football tailgates as it is for a winter holiday buffet, springtime graduation brunch, or summer picnic. If you don't have a fresh orange, just omit the zest and use good-quality orange juice from a carton instead.

serves:
12 to 16

prep:
20 minutes

bake:
43 to 48 minutes

cool:
35 to 45 minutes

Vegetable oil spray, for misting the pan
Flour, for dusting the pan
1 large orange (see Notes)
1 package (18.25 ounces) plain yellow or vanilla cake mix, or 1 package (18.5 ounces) plain butter recipe golden cake mix
1 package (3.4 ounces) vanilla instant pudding mix
4 large eggs
1 cup sour cream
¼ cup medium-dry sherry (see Notes)
8 tablespoons (1 stick) butter, melted
2 tablespoons poppy seeds
1 cup confectioners' sugar, sifted

1. Place a rack in the center of the oven and preheat the oven to 350°F. Lightly mist a 12-cup Bundt pan with vegetable oil spray, then dust it with flour. Shake out the excess flour and set the pan aside.

2. Rinse and pat the orange dry with paper towels. Grate enough zest to measure 1 teaspoon. Cut the orange in half and squeeze the juice into a measuring cup. Set aside 2 tablespoons of orange

Recipe Reminders

MADE FOR

PREP NOTES

DON'T FORGET

SPECIAL TOUCHES

juice for the glaze. If there is not ½ cup of juice left, add enough orange juice from a carton to make ½ cup. Place the orange zest and the ½ cup of orange juice in a large mixing bowl.

3. Place the cake mix, pudding mix, eggs, sour cream, sherry, melted butter, and poppy seeds in the bowl with the orange juice and zest. Beat with an electric mixer on low speed until the ingredients are incorporated, 30 seconds. Stop the machine and scrape down the side of the bowl with a rubber spatula. Increase the mixer speed to medium-high and beat until the batter is smooth, 2 minutes longer, scraping down the side of the bowl again if needed. Pour the batter into the prepared Bundt pan, smoothing the top with the rubber spatula, and place the pan in the oven.

4. Bake the cake until it is just starting to pull away from the side of the pan and the top springs back when lightly pressed with a finger, 43 to 48 minutes. Transfer the Bundt pan to a wire rack and let the cake cool for 10 to 15 minutes. Run a long, sharp knife around the edges of the cake, shake the pan gently, and invert the cake onto a wire rack. Let the cake cool completely, 25 to 30 minutes longer.

5. Meanwhile, make the glaze: Place the confectioners' sugar in a small mixing bowl and whisk in the reserved 2 tablespoons of orange juice. Slide the cooled cake onto a cake plate. Pour the glaze over the cake, then slice it and serve.

Keep It Fresh! Store this cake, in a cake saver, at room temperature for up to one week. Freeze the cake in a cake saver for up to six months. Let the cake thaw overnight on the counter before serving.

Notes: You will need ½ cup plus 2 tablespoons of orange juice and 1 teaspoon of orange zest. Choose a juicy orange, such as a Valencia or temple, not a seedless orange like a navel that does not have a lot of juice. If you want to use only fresh orange juice

10 Perfect Do-Ahead Cakes That Freeze Well

Here are some of the best cakes in this chapter to freeze.

in the cake, you may need more than one orange, just so you have enough juice for the cake and the glaze. And yet, you never know how much juice an orange will yield.

If you want to omit the sherry, that's fine, just add more orange juice or water instead.

Freezing Facts

You can freeze almost any cake as long as it doesn't contain whipped cream or some other elaborate creamy frosting. Most pound cakes and Bundts are plain and simple and made for baking ahead, freezing, then thawing. Their dense structure makes them especially good keepers, up to six months in a freezer in the garage (one that isn't opened every day). A cake's shelf life frozen is less—about a month—if stored in the freezer compartment of a kitchen refrigerator.

Apricot Cake with Lemon Cream Cheese Filling

serves:
12 to 16

prep:
25 minutes

bake:
50 to 55 minutes

cool:
45 to 55 minutes

APRICOT NECTAR AND LEMON are a longtime favorite flavor combination of mine, but this cake is a bit different from the usual apricot cake. It comes from reader Lynn Chaumont, a resident of Austin, Texas. She wrote me in distress hoping to find this recipe, which she had lost, only to get back in touch later saying she had found it and wanted to share it with me. I particularly enjoy the creamy coconut filling, a surprise inside, and am sure you will, too. To save time, make the filling in advance and chill it until needed.

For the filling

1 medium-size lemon

1 package (8 ounces) cream cheese, at room temperature

½ cup granulated sugar

1 cup sweetened flaked coconut

For the cake

Vegetable oil spray, for misting the pan

Flour, for dusting the pan

1 package (18.25 ounces) plain yellow or vanilla cake mix

1 cup apricot nectar

4 tablespoons (½ stick) butter, melted

3 large eggs

For the glaze

1½ cups confectioners' sugar, sifted
3 tablespoons apricot nectar

1. Make the filling: Rinse and pat the lemon dry with paper towels. Grate enough zest to measure 1 teaspoon. Cut the lemon in half and squeeze the juice into a medium-size bowl; you will need 2 tablespoons. Add the cream cheese, granulated sugar, lemon zest, and coconut to the mixing bowl. Beat with an electric mixer on low speed until the ingredients are just combined, 1 minute. Set the bowl aside.

2. Make the cake: Place a rack in the center of the oven and preheat the oven to 350°F. Lightly mist a 12-cup Bundt pan with vegetable oil spray, then dust it with flour. Shake out the excess flour and set the pan aside.

3. Place the cake mix, 1 cup of apricot nectar, melted butter, and eggs in a large mixing bowl. Beat with an electric mixer on low speed until the ingredients are incorporated, 30 seconds. Stop the machine and scrape down the side of the bowl with a rubber spatula. Increase the mixer speed to medium and beat for 2 minutes longer, scraping down the side of the bowl again if needed. The batter should look thick and well combined. Pour the batter into the prepared Bundt pan, smoothing the top with the rubber spatula. Spoon the filling on top of the batter, making sure it does not touch the edges of the pan, then place the pan in the oven.

4. Bake the cake until the top springs back when lightly pressed with a finger, 50 to 55 minutes. Transfer the Bundt pan to a wire rack and let the cake cool for 10 to 15 minutes. Run a long, sharp knife around the edges of the cake, shake the pan gently, and invert the cake onto a wire rack. Let the cake cool completely, 25 to 30 minutes longer.

Recipe Reminders

MADE FOR

____

____

____

____

PREP NOTES

____

____

____

____

DON'T FORGET

____

____

____

____

SPECIAL TOUCHES

____

____

____

____

____

____

____

____

____

5. Make the glaze: Place the confectioners' sugar in a small mixing bowl and whisk in the 3 tablespoons of apricot nectar to make a spoonable glaze. Slide the cake onto a cake plate and spoon the glaze over the cake, letting it drip down the sides. Let the glaze set for 10 minutes, then slice and serve the cake.

Keep It Fresh! Store this cake, in a cake saver or under a cake dome, at room temperature for up to one week. Freeze the cake, wrapped in aluminum foil, for up to six months. Let the cake thaw overnight in the refrigerator before serving.

Lemon Love

I cannot bake without lemons on hand. Just to know they are there to pick up the flavor of fruit cakes, add contrast to spice cakes, a bit of attitude to chocolate cakes. Don't just think "lemon cake" with lemons. You'll be surprised what a little lemon zest or juice can do to just about any cake.

Thinking Outside the Bundt

And you thought a Bundt pan was used only for baking? When not baking cakes here are other ways to use your Bundt pan:

- **Fill a lightly oil-misted Bundt with a gelatin mixture and chill it for a fancy mold. To unmold it, fill the sink with warm water and place the Bundt in it briefly until the gelatin shakes loose.**

- **Use it to bake meat loaf and not cake. Mist the Bundt with cooking oil first and the meat loaf will pop right out after it's baked.**

- **Make Rice Krispies Treats and press them into miniature Bundt pans, let them harden, then remove them. Again, mist the Bundts with cooking oil first.**

- **Fill it with water and freeze it for a large ice block on which to pile boiled shrimp. Immerse the Bundt in warm water briefly to loosen the ice.**

- **Fill the Bundt with water then add a handful of cranberries and some sprigs of pine and freeze for a holiday punch mold.**

Carolyn's Mango Cake

Carolyn Seergy's appreciation of mango began when she was growing up in Brooklyn, New York, and would go to the local ice cream shop in the dog days of summer. "They always had some new, exotic flavor to try and it was an adventure to see what the new offerings were. That's where my love of mango and coconut sorbet was formed." Just like that mango sorbet, this cake is perfect for ending summer evenings. Garnish it with toasted coconut.

serves:
12 to 16

prep:
20 minutes

bake:
45 to 50 minutes

cool:
30 to 40 minutes

Vegetable oil spray, for misting the pan
Flour, for dusting the pan
1 package (18.25 ounces) plain yellow or vanilla cake mix
1 package (3 ounces) lemon or mango gelatin
½ cup plus 3 tablespoons mango nectar (see Notes)
½ cup cream of coconut (see Notes)
½ cup vegetable oil
4 large eggs
1 teaspoon pure vanilla extract
¼ cup sweetened flaked coconut
¾ cup confectioners' sugar, sifted

1. Place a rack in the center of the oven and preheat the oven to 350°F. Lightly mist a 12-cup Bundt pan with vegetable oil spray, then dust it with flour. Shake out the excess flour and set the pan aside.

2. Place the cake mix, lemon or mango gelatin, ½ cup of the mango nectar, the cream of coconut, oil, eggs, and vanilla in a large mixing bowl. Beat with an electric mixer on low speed until the ingredients are incorporated, 30 seconds. Stop the machine

Recipe Reminders

MADE FOR

PREP NOTES

DON'T FORGET

SPECIAL TOUCHES

and scrape down the side of the bowl with a rubber spatula. Increase the mixer speed to medium and beat until the batter is thick and smooth, 2 minutes longer, scraping down the side of the bowl again if needed. Pour the batter into the prepared Bundt pan, smoothing the top with the rubber spatula, and place the pan in the oven.

3. Bake the cake until it is golden brown and the top springs back when lightly pressed with a finger, 45 to 50 minutes. Transfer the Bundt pan to a wire rack and let the cake cool 15 to 20 minutes. Leave the oven on.

4. Spread the coconut out in a baking pan and place it in the oven to toast until light brown, watching to see that it does not burn, about 5 minutes. Transfer the toasted coconut to a plate to cool.

5. Run a long, sharp knife around the edges of the cake, shake the pan gently, and invert the cake onto a wire rack. Let the cake cool completely, 15 to 20 minutes longer.

6. Meanwhile, make the glaze: Place the confectioners' sugar and the remaining 3 tablespoons of mango nectar in a small bowl and whisk until smooth. Slide the cake onto a cake plate, then spoon the glaze on top and slice and serve.

Keep It Fresh! Store this cake, in a cake saver, at room temperature for up to one week. Freeze the cake, in a cake saver or wrapped in aluminum foil, for up to six months. Let the cake thaw overnight on the counter before serving.

Notes: Mango nectar can be found in specialty food shops and many supermarkets.

Cream of coconut is sold where you find the ingredients for tropical drinks. It is often sold in 8.5 ounce cans. Be sure to shake the can before opening, and stir the contents before using, as it settles in storage.

Apple Cider Cake with Cider Glaze

This is a lovely Bundt cake, either for serving at home or giving to a friend. It is perfect for baking in the fall and winter as long as you can get good local apple cider. Feel free to glaze the cake or, if you are in a hurry, just dust it with confectioners' sugar.

serves:
12 to 16

prep:
15 minutes

bake:
42 to 48 minutes

cool:
35 to 40 minutes

For the cake

Vegetable oil spray, for misting the pan
Flour, for dusting the pan
1 package (18.25 ounces) plain yellow or vanilla cake mix
1 package (3.4 ounces) vanilla instant pudding mix
4 large eggs
1 cup apple cider
½ cup vegetable oil
¾ teaspoon ground cinnamon
¼ teaspoon ground cloves

For the glaze

1 cup confectioners' sugar, sifted
2 tablespoons apple cider
½ teaspoon grated lemon zest (optional)

1. Make the cake: Place a rack in the center of the oven and preheat the oven to 350°F. Lightly mist a 12-cup Bundt pan with vegetable oil spray, then dust it with flour. Shake out the excess flour and set the pan aside.

Recipe Reminders

MADE FOR

PREP NOTES

DON'T FORGET

SPECIAL TOUCHES

2. Place the cake mix, pudding mix, eggs, the 1 cup of cider, the oil, cinnamon, and cloves in a large mixing bowl and beat on low speed until the ingredients are incorporated, 30 seconds. Stop the machine and scrape down the side of the bowl with a rubber spatula. Increase the mixer speed to medium and beat until the batter is smooth and fluffy, 2 minutes longer, scraping down the side of the bowl again if needed. Pour the batter into the prepared Bundt pan, smoothing the top with the rubber spatula, and place the pan in the oven.

3. Bake the cake until the top springs back when lightly pressed with a finger, 42 to 48 minutes. Transfer the Bundt pan to a wire rack and let the cake cool for 10 to 15 minutes.

4. Meanwhile, make the glaze: Place the confectioners' sugar, 2 tablespoons of cider, and lemon zest, if using, in a small saucepan over low heat. Heat, stirring, until the glaze is smooth.

5. Run a long, sharp knife around the edges of the cake, shake the pan gently, and invert the cake onto a wire rack or cake plate. Pour the glaze over the cake and let the cake cool 25 minutes longer before slicing and serving.

Keep It Fresh! Store this cake, in a cake saver, at room temperature for up to one week. Freeze the cake in a cake saver, for up to six months. Let the cake thaw overnight on the counter before serving.

Ruth's Applesauce Spice Cake

RUTH WACK of Winter Park, Florida, did a little doctoring of my buttermilk spice cake from *The Cake Mix Doctor* to arrive at her signature applesauce spice cake. It is a nice, healthy cake, using ground almonds, applesauce instead of a lot of oil, and an egg substitute instead of eggs. Ruth bakes this in a heavy Bundt pan, which she mists with vegetable oil spray and dusts with a little of the cake mix. I suggest you use any type of applesauce you have on hand—sweetened or unsweetened, even chunky. Ruth folds in one cup of ground almonds, ground in a food processor using the steel blade, but anywhere from a half cup to a whole one gives you the delicate crunch and flavor you need.

serves:
12 to 16

prep:
20 minutes

bake:
40 to 45 minutes

cool:
35 to 40 minutes

Vegetable oil spray, for misting the pan
Flour, for dusting the pan
1 package (18.25 ounces) plain spice cake mix
1½ cups buttermilk
1 cup egg substitute
½ cup applesauce
½ to 1 cup ground almonds (see Note)
⅓ cup granulated sugar
⅓ cup vegetable oil
1 teaspoon ground cinnamon
¼ teaspoon ground nutmeg
Dash of ground cloves (optional)
2 teaspoons confectioners' sugar (optional)

Ruth's Accidental Lemon Spice Cake

Ruth says she was in a hurry one day, about to bake her usual spice cake but she reached for a lemon cake mix instead of spice. She made this recipe with the lemon cake mix, and it was so moist that everyone loved it. So, for a change, substitute the lemon mix for the spice.

Recipe Reminders

MADE FOR

PREP NOTES

DON'T FORGET

SPECIAL TOUCHES

1. Place a rack in the center of the oven and preheat the oven to 350°F. Lightly mist a 12-cup Bundt pan with vegetable oil spray, then dust it with flour. Shake out the excess flour and set the pan aside.

2. Place the cake mix, buttermilk, egg substitute, applesauce, almonds, granulated sugar, oil, cinnamon, nutmeg, and cloves, if using, in a large mixing bowl. Beat with an electric mixer on low speed until the ingredients are incorporated, 30 seconds. Stop the machine and scrape down the side of the bowl with a rubber spatula. Increase the mixer speed to medium and beat the batter for 1½ minutes longer, scraping down the side of the bowl again if needed. The batter should look smooth and thick. Pour the batter into the prepared Bundt pan, smoothing the top with the rubber spatula, and place the pan in the oven.

3. Bake the cake until the top springs back when lightly pressed with a finger, 40 to 45 minutes. Transfer the Bundt pan to a wire rack and let the cake cool for 10 to 15 minutes. Run a long, sharp knife around the edges of the cake, shake the pan gently, and invert the cake onto a wire rack. Let the cake cool completely, about 25 minutes longer. If desired, sift the confectioners' sugar over the cake while it is cooling. Once cool, slice and serve the cake.

Keep It Fresh! Store this cake, in a cake saver or covered with plastic wrap, at room temperature for up to one week. Freeze the cake, wrapped in aluminum foil, for up to six months. Let the cake thaw overnight on the counter before serving.

Note: To grind the almonds, place whole almonds (½ to 1 cup) in a food processor and process until they are finely ground, looking almost like powder, 45 to 60 seconds. Oddly enough, about ½ cup whole almonds will yield ½ cup ground almonds, and so on.

Red Peach Nectar Cake

HAVE YOU EVER SEEN a new ingredient on the store shelf and it looks so good you can't get it out of your mind, sort of like a song you keep singing over and over? It happened to me one day in Williams-Sonoma. I spotted bottles of red peach nectar on a shelf. Red peaches are grown in France, and I thought about this nectar for four days, then returned to buy a bottle. I poured a glass—it was smooth and sweet, just like a fresh peach—then put the rest in this cake. You can use most any fruit nectar—such as peach or apricot or mango—in this cake. Many supermarkets sell fruit nectars, and as for the gelatin, if you cannot find peach gelatin, use lemon instead.

serves:
12 to 16

prep:
25 minutes

bake:
40 to 45 minutes

cool:
45 to 50 minutes

For the cake

Vegetable oil spray, for misting the pan
Flour, for dusting the pan
1 medium-size lemon
1 package (18.25 ounces) plain yellow or vanilla cake mix
1 package (3 ounces) peach or lemon gelatin
1 cup red or plain peach nectar
½ cup vegetable oil
4 large eggs

For the glaze

¾ cup confectioners' sugar, sifted
3 tablespoons red or plain peach nectar

Recipe Reminders

MADE FOR

PREP NOTES

DON'T FORGET

SPECIAL TOUCHES

5 Easy Glazes

No recipe to top that cake? No worries.

1. Dust confectioners' sugar over a cake while it is still warm. The sugar will form its own glaze.

2. Microwave white chocolate chips until melted, then stir in enough cream or milk to make a glaze that can be poured from a large spoon.

3. Drizzle chocolate ice cream syrup over a cooled cake.

4. Spoon on good bottled caramel sauce.

5. Make an impromptu drizzle—lemon juice, orange juice, or milk with enough confectioners' sugar to make it spoonable. A good ratio is 1 to 2 tablespoons of liquid to 1 cup sugar.

1. Make the cake: Place a rack in the center of the oven and preheat the oven to 350°F. Lightly mist a 12-cup Bundt pan with vegetable oil spray, then dust it with flour. Shake out the excess flour and set the pan aside.

2. Rinse and pat the lemon dry with paper towels. Grate enough zest to measure 1 teaspoon. Place this in a large mixing bowl. Set the lemon aside.

3. Place the cake mix, peach or lemon gelatin, 1 cup of peach nectar, the oil, and eggs in the bowl with the lemon zest. Beat with an electric mixer on low speed until the ingredients are incorporated, 30 seconds. Stop the machine and scrape down the side of the bowl with a rubber spatula. Increase the mixer speed to medium and beat the batter until it is smooth and thick, 1½ minutes longer, scraping down the side of the bowl again if needed. Pour the batter into the prepared Bundt pan, smoothing the top with the rubber spatula, and place the pan in the oven.

4. Bake the cake until it is light brown and the top springs back when lightly pressed with a finger, 40 to 45 minutes. Transfer the Bundt pan to a wire rack and let the cake cool for 10 to 15 minutes. Run a long, sharp knife around the edges of the cake, shake the pan gently, and invert the cake onto a wire rack. Let the cake cool completely, about 25 minutes longer.

5. Make the glaze: Place the confectioners' sugar in a small bowl. Add the 3 tablespoons of peach nectar. Cut the reserved lemon in half and squeeze 1 teaspoon of juice into the bowl. Whisk until the glaze is smooth. Slide the cake onto a serving plate and spoon the glaze over it. Let the glaze set for 10 minutes, then slice and serve the cake.

Keep It Fresh! Store this cake, in a cake saver or covered with plastic wrap, at room temperature for up to one week. Freeze the cake, wrapped in aluminum foil, for up to six months. Let the cake thaw overnight on the counter before serving.

Cathy's Marbled Spice Cake

serves:
12 to 16

prep:
20 minutes

bake:
40 to 45 minutes

cool:
35 to 45 minutes

For the past ten years I have been the lucky recipient of readers' great recipes. Cathy Tolbert, who lives in Onancock, Virginia, a town situated on the Chesapeake Bay, is one such reader. She sent me this spiced pound cake recipe after first reading *The Cake Mix Doctor*. Her grandmother used to make a marbled spice cake from scratch, but without the recipe and only a memory of how that cake tasted, Cathy developed a similar recipe beginning with a cake mix. Her family raves about the result, so do I, and so will you!

Vegetable oil spray, for misting the pan
Flour, for dusting the pan
1 package (18.25 ounces) plain yellow cake mix, or 1 package (18.5 ounces) plain butter recipe golden cake mix
¾ cup vegetable oil
1 cup sour cream
¼ cup granulated sugar
½ teaspoon pure almond extract
4 large eggs
2 tablespoons molasses
1 teaspoon ground cinnamon
½ teaspoon ground nutmeg
¼ teaspoon ground cloves
1 tablespoon confectioners' sugar

Want a Marbled Gingerbread Coffee Cake?

Add ¼ teaspoon of ground ginger instead of the cloves. And for an easy molasses glaze to top the cake, whisk together ⅓ cup of molasses and ¼ cup of confectioners' sugar. Spoon the glaze over the cooled cake.

1. Place a rack in the center of the oven and preheat the oven to 350°F. Lightly mist a 12-cup Bundt pan with vegetable oil spray, then dust it with flour. Shake out the excess flour and set the pan aside.

2. Place the cake mix, oil, sour cream, granulated sugar, almond extract, and eggs in a large mixing bowl. Beat with an electric mixer on low speed until the ingredients are incorporated, 30 seconds. Stop the machine and scrape down the side of the bowl with a rubber spatula. Increase the mixer speed to medium and beat the batter for 1½ minutes longer, scraping down the side of the bowl again if needed. The batter should look smooth and thick.

3. Measure out 1½ cups of the batter and place it in a small bowl. Add the molasses, cinnamon, nutmeg, and cloves and stir until combined. Set this spice batter aside.

4. Pour the plain batter into the prepared Bundt pan. Pour the spice batter in a ring on top of it, keeping it away from the edges. Swirl the spice batter into the plain batter using a long spoon or chopstick. Place the pan in the oven.

5. Bake the cake until the top springs back when lightly pressed with a finger, 40 to 45 minutes. Transfer the Bundt pan to a wire rack and let the cake cool for 10 to 15 minutes. Run a long, sharp knife around the edges of the cake, shake the pan gently, and invert the cake onto a wire rack. Let the cake cool completely, 25 to 30 minutes longer.

6. Slide the cake onto a cake plate and sift the confectioners' sugar over the top, then slice and serve the cake.

Keep It Fresh! Store this cake, in a cake saver or loosely covered with plastic wrap, at room temperature for up to one week. Freeze the cake, wrapped in aluminum foil, for up to six months. Let the cake thaw overnight on the counter before serving.

Recipe Reminders

MADE FOR

____

____

____

____

PREP NOTES

____

____

____

____

DON'T FORGET

____

____

____

____

SPECIAL TOUCHES

____

____

____

____

____

____

____

____

____

A New Zucchini Cake with Penuche Icing

serves:
12 to 16

prep:
25 minutes

bake:
45 to 50 minutes

cool:
35 to 45 minutes, plus 1 hour for the glaze to set

FOR ALL OF YOU WHO LOVED the zucchini cake from the first book but were frustrated because the cake fell as it cooled, here is a new improved recipe that won't fall and has better flavor and the irresistible penuche icing. I began with a spice cake mix this go-round. Because shredded zucchini is a wet ingredient, I cut back on the sour cream, eggs, and pudding from the original recipe. This made for a lighter cake, and one I know you will enjoy. Be sure to measure the zucchini by gently and lightly packing it in the measuring cup. And be sure to spoon the icing on while warm.

Vegetable oil spray, for misting the pan
Flour, for dusting the pan
1 package (18.25 ounces) plain spice cake mix
Half of a 3.4 ounce package of vanilla instant pudding mix, about 4 tablespoons
½ cup reduced-fat sour cream or plain yogurt
½ cup water
¼ cup vegetable oil
3 large eggs
1 teaspoon ground cinnamon
2 cups lightly packed shredded zucchini (about 8 ounces)
⅓ cup chopped walnuts (optional), for garnish
Penuche Icing (page 486)

Got Fruit or Vegetables in the Cake? Cut Back on the Oil

Any time you add shredded veggies, like zucchini or carrots, or pureed veggies like pumpkin and butternut squash, or pureed fruits like mashed bananas and applesauce to a cake recipe, you can easily cut back on some of the oil. The veggies and fruit provide moisture and will keep the cake moist for days. They can, as in the case of bananas, also add flavor. Or, they may not provide any flavor at all, as with pumpkin, but add a lot of healthy fiber. If I am making an adjustment like this to a recipe, as a rule I substitute half the oil called for with an equal amount of fruit or vegetables. If this succeeds, I might try it again and substitute even more fruit or veggies for the oil or omit the oil altogether.

1. Place a rack in the center of the oven and preheat the oven to 350°F. Lightly mist a 12-cup Bundt pan with vegetable oil spray, then dust it with flour. Shake out the excess flour and set the pan aside.

2. Place the cake mix, pudding mix, sour cream, water, oil, eggs, and cinnamon in a large mixing bowl. Beat with an electric mixer on low speed until the ingredients are incorporated, 30 seconds. Stop the machine and scrape down the side of the bowl with a rubber spatula. Increase the mixer speed to medium and beat the batter for 1½ minutes longer, scraping down the side of the bowl again if needed. The batter should look smooth and thick. Fold in the shredded zucchini. Pour the batter into the prepared Bundt pan, smoothing the top with the rubber spatula, and place the pan in the oven.

Recipe Reminders

MADE FOR

PREP NOTES

DON'T FORGET

SPECIAL TOUCHES

3. Bake the cake until the top springs back when lightly pressed with a finger, 45 to 50 minutes. Transfer the Bundt pan to a wire rack and let the cake cool for 10 to 15 minutes. Leave the oven on.

4. Place the chopped walnuts, if using, in a small baking pan and toast them in the oven until deep brown and fragrant, 3 to 5 minutes. Transfer the toasted walnuts to a small plate to cool.

5. Run a long, sharp knife around the edges of the cake, shake the pan gently, and invert the cake onto a wire rack. Let the cake cool completely, 25 to 30 minutes longer.

6. Meanwhile, make the Penuche Icing.

7. Slide the cake onto a cake plate. Spoon the icing over the cooled cake. If desired, press the chopped toasted walnuts into the glaze while it is still warm. Let the icing set for 1 hour, then slice and serve the cake.

Keep It Fresh! Store this cake, in a cake saver or loosely covered with plastic wrap, at room temperature for up to one week. Freeze the cake, wrapped in aluminum foil, for up to six months. Let the cake thaw overnight on the counter before serving.

Kathy's Cinnamon Breakfast Cake

YOU KNOW A CAKE IS A CLASSIC when your cookbook automatically falls open to its page or that page is sticky and smeared with cake ingredients or you hear people coast to coast rave about it. The coffee cake recipe here, given to me years ago by a friend and former neighbor Kathy Sellers, is deliciously guilty of all three and is thus a classic. I would like to say I have changed Kathy's recipe for the better through these years, but honestly it stands on its own.

serves:
12 to 16

prep:
15 minutes

bake:
55 to 60 minutes

cool:
35 to 45 minutes

For the filling and cake

Vegetable oil spray, for misting the pan
Flour, for dusting the pan
½ cup finely chopped pecans or walnuts
⅓ cup packed light brown sugar
2 teaspoons ground cinnamon
1 package (18.5 ounces) plain butter recipe golden cake mix, or 1 package (18.25 ounces) plain yellow or vanilla cake mix
1 package (3.4 ounces) vanilla instant pudding mix
¾ cup vegetable oil (see Note)
¾ cup water
4 large eggs
1 teaspoon pure vanilla extract

For the glaze

1 cup confectioners' sugar, sifted
2 tablespoons milk
½ teaspoon pure vanilla extract

Recipe Reminders

MADE FOR

PREP NOTES

DON'T FORGET

SPECIAL TOUCHES

1. Place a rack in the center of the oven and preheat the oven to 350°F. Lightly mist a 12-cup Bundt pan with vegetable oil spray, then dust it with flour. Shake out the excess flour. Sprinkle the pecans or walnuts in the bottom of the pan and set the pan aside.

2. Make the filling: Place the brown sugar and cinnamon in a small bowl and stir until combined. Set the filling aside.

3. Make the cake: Place the cake mix, pudding mix, oil, water, eggs, and 1 teaspoon of vanilla in a large mixing bowl. Beat with an electric mixer on low speed until the ingredients are incorporated, 30 seconds. Stop the machine and scrape down the side of the bowl with a rubber spatula. Increase the mixer speed to medium and beat the batter for 1½ minutes longer, scraping down the side of the bowl again if needed. The batter should look smooth and thick. Pour one third of the batter into the prepared Bundt pan. Scatter half of the filling evenly over the batter. Pour another third of the batter evenly over the filling. Scatter the remaining filling over the batter. Pour the remaining batter evenly over the top, smoothing it out with the rubber spatula. Place the pan in the oven.

4. Bake the cake until it is golden brown and the top springs back when lightly pressed with a finger, 55 to 60 minutes. Transfer the Bundt pan to a wire rack and let the cake cool for 10 to 15 minutes. Run a long, sharp knife around the edges of the cake, shake the pan gently, and invert the cake onto a wire rack. Let the cake cool completely, 25 to 30 minutes longer.

5. Meanwhile, make the glaze: Place the confectioners' sugar, milk, and ½ teaspoon of vanilla in a small bowl and stir until smooth. Slide the cake onto a serving plate and spoon the glaze over the top so that it drizzles down the sides, then slice and serve.

To Sift or Not to Sift . . .

Sifting confectioners' sugar often seems like a time-consuming step. And often you can avoid it. If the package of sugar is freshly opened, I usually don't sift. If the confectioners' sugar has been stored a while or came from a box, as opposed to a plastic bag, it might contain lumps, and therefore needs sifting. Go ahead and take the time to do this so you won't have those unsightly lumps in your glaze. I take care when storing the sugar to avoid the lumps. I buy it in plastic bags, and then tape them shut or place the opened bag in another plastic resealable bag for storage.

A word on measuring confectioners' sugar: If the recipe reads "1 cup confectioners' sugar, sifted" that means to measure the sugar first and then sift it if needed. But if the recipe reads "1 cup sifted confectioners' sugar" you need to sift first and then measure. I usually write recipes that call for measuring first because if I can measure and possibly not sift I am a happier cook!

Keep It Fresh! Store this cake, in a cake saver or covered with plastic wrap, at room temperature for up to one week. Freeze the cake, wrapped in aluminum foil, for up to six months. Let the cake thaw overnight on the counter before serving.

Note: If you want to reduce the oil in this recipe, use only ½ cup (instead of ¾ cup) and increase the water to 1 cup.

Cinnamon Sour Cream Coffee Cake

serves:
12 to 16

prep:
15 minutes

bake:
52 to 55 minutes

cool:
35 to 45 minutes

ONE OF OUR FAMILY'S FAVORITE RECIPES when I was young was a made-from-scratch sour cream coffee cake filled with cinnamon, sugar, and pecans. But it was too rich and buttery. I thought I'd try my hand at creating such a coffee cake beginning with a cake mix. The plan was to create a from-scratch tasting cake that would be less heavy. This is such a recipe. It doesn't pain you to enjoy it! Bake it for weekend trips away and for brunch or for giving to a friend—these are times when a cake helps create memories.

Vegetable oil spray, for misting the pan
Flour, for dusting the pan
1 package (18.5 ounces) plain butter recipe golden cake mix
¼ cup all-purpose flour
½ cup packed light brown sugar
2 teaspoons ground cinnamon
½ cup finely chopped pecans (optional)
1 cup sour cream (see Note)
4 large eggs
⅓ cup vegetable oil
¼ cup water
1 teaspoon pure vanilla extract

1. Place a rack in the center of the oven and preheat the oven to 350°F. Lightly mist a 10-inch tube pan with vegetable oil spray, then dust it with flour. Shake out the excess flour and set the pan aside.

2. Place the cake mix and flour in a large mixing bowl and stir to combine. Measure out 2 tablespoons of this mixture and place it in a small bowl. Add the brown sugar, cinnamon, and pecans, if using, to the small bowl and stir to combine. Set the filling mixture aside.

3. Add the sour cream, eggs, oil, water, and vanilla to the large mixing bowl with the cake mix and flour. Beat with an electric mixer on low speed until the ingredients are incorporated, 30 seconds. Stop the machine, and scrape down the side of the bowl with a rubber spatula. Increase the mixer speed to medium and beat until the mixture is well combined and is smooth and fluffy, 1½ to 2 minutes longer, scraping down the side of the bowl again if needed. Spoon half of the batter into the prepared tube pan. Scatter all but 2 tablespoons of the brown sugar and cinnamon filling on top of the batter. Spoon the remaining batter into the pan and carefully spread it out so as not to disturb the layer of filling. Sprinkle the remaining filling on top of the batter and place the pan in the oven.

4. Bake the cake until lightly browned and the top springs back when lightly pressed with a finger, 52 to 55 minutes. Transfer the tube pan to a wire rack and let the cake cool for 10 to 15 minutes. Run a long, sharp knife around the edges of the pan. Shake the pan gently and invert the cake once, then again so that the cake rests right side up on the cooling rack. Let the cake cool for 25 to 30 minutes longer, then slice and serve.

Keep It Fresh! Store this cake, in a cake saver or covered with plastic wrap, at room temperature for up to one week. Freeze the cake, wrapped in aluminum foil, for up to six months. Let the cake thaw overnight on the counter before serving.

Note: You can use either regular or reduced-fat sour cream in this cake.

Recipe Reminders

MADE FOR

____

____

____

____

PREP NOTES

____

____

____

____

DON'T FORGET

____

____

____

____

SPECIAL TOUCHES

____

____

____

____

____

____

____

____

____

Maple Cream Cheese Pound Cake with Caramel Glaze

serves:
12 to 16

prep:
25 minutes

bake:
42 to 47 minutes

cool:
45 to 55 minutes

ONE OF MY FAVORITE RECIPES from the first *Cake Mix Doctor* book was the almond cream cheese pound cake, and through the years I found myself tweaking the recipe a bit every time I baked it. At first I substituted reduced-fat cream cheese for full fat, then I added maple flavoring instead of almond. Finally, I created a caramel glaze for the top. If you press toasted pecans into the warm glaze as it cools, you have a dazzling cake, perfect in the fall and to serve for brunch all year long.

For the cake

Vegetable oil spray, for misting the pan
Flour, for dusting the pan
1 package (18.5 ounces) plain butter recipe golden cake mix
1 package (8 ounces) reduced-fat cream cheese, at room temperature
½ cup granulated sugar
½ cup water
½ cup vegetable oil
4 large eggs
1 teaspoon pure vanilla extract
1 teaspoon maple flavoring
¼ cup finely chopped pecans (optional), for the garnish

For the glaze

3 tablespoons butter
3 tablespoons packed light brown sugar
3 tablespoons granulated sugar
3 tablespoons heavy (whipping) cream
½ teaspoon pure vanilla extract

1. Make the cake: Place a rack in the center of the oven and preheat the oven to 350°F. Lightly mist a 12-cup Bundt pan with vegetable oil spray, then dust it with flour. Shake out the excess flour and set the pan aside.

2. Place the cake mix, cream cheese, ½ cup of granulated sugar, water, oil, eggs, 1 teaspoon of vanilla, and the maple flavoring in a large mixing bowl. Beat with an electric mixer on low speed until the ingredients are incorporated, 30 seconds. Stop the machine and scrape down the side of the bowl with a rubber spatula. Increase the mixer speed to medium and beat the batter for 1½ to 2 minutes longer, scraping down the side of the bowl again if needed. The batter should look smooth and thick. Pour the batter into the prepared Bundt pan, smoothing the top with the rubber spatula, and place the pan in the oven.

3. Bake the cake until the top springs back when lightly pressed with a finger, 42 to 47 minutes. Transfer the Bundt pan to a wire rack and let the cake cool for 10 to 15 minutes. Leave the oven on.

4. Place the chopped pecans, if using, in a small baking pan and toast them in the oven until they are deep brown and fragrant, 3 to 5 minutes. Transfer the toasted pecans to a small plate to cool.

5. Run a long, sharp knife around the edges of the cake, shake the pan gently, and invert the cake onto a wire rack. Let the cake cool completely, 25 to 30 minutes longer.

Recipe Reminders

MADE FOR

____
____
____
____

PREP NOTES

____
____
____
____

DON'T FORGET

____
____
____
____

SPECIAL TOUCHES

____
____
____
____
____
____
____
____
____

6. Meanwhile, make the glaze: Place the butter, brown sugar, 3 tablespoons of granulated sugar, and the cream in a medium-size saucepan over medium heat. Let the mixture come to a boil, stirring, then let it boil for 1 minute, stirring constantly. Remove the pan from the heat.

7. Slide the cake onto a cake plate and pour the glaze over it so that it drizzles down the sides. Press the toasted pecans, if using, into the glaze while the glaze is warm. Let the glaze set for 10 minutes, then slice and serve the cake.

Keep It Fresh! Store this cake, in a cake saver, at room temperature for up to one week. Freeze the cake, wrapped in aluminum foil, for up to six months. Let the cake thaw overnight on the counter before serving.

These Cakes Were Made for Shipping

Firm pound cakes with no frostings are the best for shipping out of town to friends and family. Bake them in a tube pan or Bundt pan, let them cool completely, then wrap them in aluminum foil and place them in a large resealable plastic bag. Freeze the cake for two to three days before sending it off.

Nancy Copeland of Manassas, Virginia, packs her frozen cakes in boxes that are about the size of the cake. Place crumpled packing paper in the bottom of the box, then add the frozen cake still wrapped in foil and the plastic bag. Surround the cake with packing peanuts or crumpled paper so it won't shift. Seal the box with clear packing tape and address it. Nancy places the box back in the freezer if she is not going straight to the post office. The trick is to mail a cake that is frozen.

"When my son was in San Francisco I sent him two or three cakes a year with great success. My officemate's son was sent to Kuwait and I felt the need to send him something. I made a Darn Good Chocolate Cake and shipped it. It took six days but it arrived intact and fresh."

Almond Pound Cake

HERE'S ANOTHER FUN WAY to doctor up a cake mix and turn it into a pound cake. Not only is it rich and buttery but it bakes up tall in the pan thanks to the added flour and eggs. It is flavored with both vanilla and almond, which mellow nicely as the cake rests on the counter. My mother always said a pound cake tastes better on day two or three. Serve it with fresh fruit of the season, such as sweetened peaches or strawberries.

serves:
12 to 16

prep:
20 minutes

bake:
52 to 58 minutes

cool:
35 to 45 minutes

Vegetable oil spray, for misting the pan
Flour, for dusting the pan
1 cup (2 sticks) butter, at room temperature
1 cup granulated sugar
6 large eggs
1½ teaspoons pure almond extract
½ teaspoon pure vanilla extract
½ cup all-purpose flour
1 package (18.5 ounces) plain butter recipe golden cake mix
1 cup milk (see Note)

1. Place a rack in the center of the oven and preheat the oven to 350°F. Lightly mist a 10-inch tube pan or 12-cup Bundt with vegetable oil spray, then dust it with flour. Shake out the excess flour and set the pan aside.

Recipe Reminders

MADE FOR

PREP NOTES

DON'T FORGET

SPECIAL TOUCHES

2. Place the butter and sugar in a large mixing bowl and beat with an electric mixer on medium-low speed until blended and creamy, 1 minute. Stop the machine and scrape down the side of the bowl with a rubber spatula. Add 1 egg at a time, beating on low speed until each egg is blended into the batter. Stop the machine and add the almond and vanilla extracts and flour. Beat 30 seconds on medium-low speed. Stop the machine and scrape down the side of the bowl again. Add the cake mix and milk alternately in thirds, blending on low speed after each addition. Let the mixer run for another 30 seconds on medium speed to blend the batter well until it is smooth and thick. Pour the batter into the prepared tube pan, smoothing the top with the rubber spatula, and place the pan in the oven.

3. Bake the cake until it is just starting to pull away from the sides of the pan and the top springs back when lightly pressed with a finger, 52 to 58 minutes. Transfer the tube pan to a wire rack and let the cake cool for 10 to 15 minutes. Run a long, sharp knife around the edges of the cake and shake the pan gently. Invert the cake onto a wire rack, then invert it again onto another rack so the cake is right side up. Let the cake cool for 25 to 30 minutes longer, then slice and serve.

Keep It Fresh! Store this cake, in a cake saver or covered with plastic wrap, at room temperature for up to one week. Freeze the cake, wrapped in aluminum foil, for up to six months. Let the cake thaw overnight on the counter before serving.

Note: You may use any milk you have in your refrigerator in this recipe. If you use whole or evaporated milk you will have a richer cake.

Baking a Reduced-Sugar Cake

If you want to serve a cake that's not so super sugary, choose a Bundt cake. Bundts don't have a frosting, and it is the frosting that contains so much sugar.

There are some reduced-sugar cake mixes on the market, made with the artificial sweetener Splenda. I tried them and was not overly excited at the results—the texture was mushy and the flavor was not natural enough. But if you must bake with one of these mixes, you might want to turn it into a more substantial pound cake using the following recipe. It's easy to make and the cake is moist. Slice it and serve it with fresh peaches or strawberries.

Reduced-Sugar Pound Cake

To an 18.25-ounce package of reduced-sugar yellow or chocolate cake mix add:

4 large eggs
1/2 cup vegetable oil
1 1/4 cups milk
1 tablespoon pure vanilla extract
1 teaspoon pure almond extract (optional)

Combine the cake mix, eggs, oil, milk, vanilla, and almond extract, if using, in a large bowl, beating them on low for 30 seconds, then on medium-high for 1½ minutes. Pour the batter into a vegetable-oil-misted and floured 12-cup Bundt pan and bake at 350°F for 40 to 45 minutes. Let the pan cool for 10 minutes on a rack, then invert the cake onto a wire rack and let it cool completely, 30 minutes longer. Slice the cake and serve it with fresh fruit.

Cute as a Cupcake

Bake this recipe as cupcakes, filling 20 to 24 cupcake liners about three-quarters of the way with batter. These cute reduced-sugar cupcakes bake in 20 to 25 minutes at 350°F.

Butter Pecan Bundt Cake with Butterscotch Glaze

serves:
12 to 16

prep:
25 minutes

bake:
60 to 65 minutes

cool:
50 to 60 minutes

I **FIRST SHARED THIS CAKE** in one of my newsletters; it was contributed by Debra Grizzle, who lives in Royston, Georgia. The cake is made for those folks who are fans of butterscotch—it's both in the pudding and in the glaze. Incredibly moist, the pound cake is perfect for those of you who love moist cake. It begins with a cake mix with pudding, to which you add a package of pudding mix. The glaze is nice and creamy but I found that the butterscotch chips don't always melt at the same time. If this happens to you and you've got a few stubborn chips that just won't melt all the way, strain the glaze through a sieve.

For the cake

Vegetable oil spray, for misting the pan
Flour, for dusting the pan
1 package (18 ounces) butter pecan cake mix with pudding
1 package (3.4 ounces) butterscotch instant pudding mix
4 large eggs
1 cup reduced-fat sour cream
½ cup vegetable oil
½ cup water
½ cup finely chopped pecans

For the butterscotch glaze

¼ cup milk
4 tablespoons (½ stick) butter
¼ cup confectioners' sugar, sifted
1 cup butterscotch chips

1. Make the cake: Place a rack in the center of the oven and preheat the oven to 350°F. Lightly mist a 12-cup Bundt pan with vegetable oil spray, then dust it with flour. Shake out the excess flour and set the pan aside.

2. Place the cake mix, pudding mix, eggs, sour cream, oil, and water in a large mixing bowl. Beat with an electric mixer on low speed until the ingredients are incorporated, 30 seconds. Stop the machine and scrape down the side of the bowl with a rubber spatula. Increase the mixer speed to medium and continue beating until the batter is thick and well combined, 2 minutes longer, scraping down the side of the bowl again if needed. Fold in the pecans. Pour the batter into the prepared Bundt pan, smoothing the top with the rubber spatula, and place the pan in the oven.

3. Bake the cake until golden brown and the top springs back when lightly pressed with a finger, 60 to 65 minutes. Transfer the Bundt pan to a wire rack and let the cake cool for 10 to 15 minutes. Run a long, sharp knife around the edges of the cake, shake the pan gently, then invert the cake onto a wire rack. Let the cake cool completely, 25 to 30 minutes longer.

4. Make the glaze: Place the milk and butter in a small saucepan over medium heat and let come to a boil, stirring. Remove the pan from the heat and whisk in the confectioners' sugar and butterscotch chips. Whisk until the chips have melted. If all of the chips do not melt, pour the glaze through a fine-mesh sieve before spooning it over the cooled cake.

5. Slide the cake onto a serving plate and spoon the glaze over. Let the glaze set for 15 minutes, then slice and serve the cake.

Recipe Reminders

MADE FOR

____

____

____

____

PREP NOTES

____

____

____

____

DON'T FORGET

____

____

____

____

SPECIAL TOUCHES

____

____

____

____

____

____

____

____

____

Keep It Fresh! Store this cake, in a cake saver, at room temperature for up to four days or in the refrigerator for up to one week. Freeze the cake in the cake saver for up to six months. Let the cake thaw overnight on the counter before serving.

I'm Nuts About You

Nuts add flavor and texture to cakes, and they are especially welcome in the big boy recipes of this chapter. And, if you have a few extra minutes, toasting those nuts really brings out their flavor. Begin with a 350°F oven. Spread the nuts evenly in a single layer in a baking pan before toasting. Place the pan in the oven and watch the nuts closely to make sure they don't burn. Stir the nuts once or twice with a metal spatula or long wooden spoon while they are toasting. Remove the nuts just when you smell the sweet, toasty aroma and before their color deepens too much. Take care not to overtoast chopped nuts; they take less time to toast than whole nuts.

Almonds: Whole almonds will toast in about 10 minutes; slivered almonds take 2 to 3 minutes. They are done when they turn light brown.

Hazelnuts: Hazelnuts take 20 minutes to toast. Rub off the skins with a clean kitchen towel while the nuts are warm.

Macadamia nuts: Whole macadamia nuts will be golden brown in 7 to 8 minutes. Chopped nuts take 3 to 4 minutes.

Pecans: Pecan halves will be deep brown in 4 to 5 minutes. Chopped pecans take 2 to 3 minutes to toast.

Walnuts: Walnut halves will be golden brown in 7 to 8 minutes. Chopped walnuts take 3 to 4 minutes to toast.

Pumpkin Spice Cake with White Chocolate Glaze

A CUP OF CANNED PUMPKIN is an easy addition to just about any Bundt cake, and it is a natural for the spice flavors in this cake that are so appealing in the fall. This is an incredibly simple cake, and you can make it your own by adjusting the spices to your liking, placing chopped pecans in the bottom of the pan, or possibly by folding in miniature chocolate chips. I add only a cup of pumpkin because adding any more makes a gummy cake. Save the rest of the can for another recipe by placing it in a glass dish in the refrigerator where it will keep for up to a week.

serves:
12 to 16

prep:
25 minutes

bake:
45 to 50 minutes

cool:
50 to 60 minutes

Vegetable oil spray, for misting the pan
Flour, for dusting the pan
½ cup finely chopped pecans (optional)
1 package (18.25 ounces) plain spice cake mix
1 cup canned pumpkin
⅔ cup milk
⅓ cup vegetable oil
4 large eggs
1 teaspoon ground cinnamon
White Chocolate Glaze (page 488)

When You're in the Mood for Dark Chocolate

It's easy for chocolate-lovers to adapt this pumpkin spice cake. Add 1½ cups of miniature semisweet chocolate chips to the batter before baking. Then, pour Martha's Chocolate Icing (page 480) over the top after the cake cools.

Recipe Reminders

MADE FOR

PREP NOTES

DON'T FORGET

SPECIAL TOUCHES

1. Place a rack in the center of the oven and preheat the oven to 350°F. Lightly mist a 12-cup Bundt pan with vegetable oil spray, then dust it with flour. Shake out the excess flour. Scatter the pecans, if using, in the bottom of the pan. Set the pan aside.

2. Place the cake mix, pumpkin, milk, oil, eggs, and cinnamon in a large mixing bowl. Beat with an electric mixer on low speed until the ingredients are incorporated, 30 seconds. Stop the machine and scrape down the side of the bowl with a rubber spatula. Increase the mixer speed to medium and beat the batter for 1½ minutes longer, scraping down the side of the bowl again if needed. The batter should look smooth and thick. Pour the batter into the prepared Bundt pan, smoothing the top with the rubber spatula, and place the pan in the oven.

3. Bake the cake until the top springs back when lightly pressed with a finger, 45 to 50 minutes. Transfer the Bundt pan to a wire rack and let the cake cool for 10 to 15 minutes. Run a long, sharp knife around the edges of the cake, shake the pan gently, and invert the cake onto a wire rack. Let the cake cool completely, 25 to 30 minutes longer.

4. Meanwhile, make the White Chocolate Glaze. When the cake has cooled, slide the cake onto a serving plate and spoon the warm glaze over the top. Let the glaze set for 15 minutes, then slice and serve the cake.

Keep It Fresh! Store this cake, in a cake saver, at room temperature for up to one week. Freeze the cake, wrapped in aluminum foil, for up to six months. Let the cake thaw overnight on the counter before serving.

Chocolate Flan Cake

CAROLYN KIMBLE, who lives in Pearland, Texas, told me about a flan cake her neighbor baked because she enjoyed flan so much. She prepared a cake mix following the package directions, then poured an egg and milk mixture over that, which would sink and create a flan in the bottom of the pan. Well, I experimented with Carolyn's recipe and found it worked and produced the most amazing looking final result, but I felt the flavor needed some enlivening. So, I changed the cake to chocolate and one time added mashed bananas, and another time canned pumpkin, to the batter—both were delicious additions. And to perfect the texture and flavor of the flan I used just the yolks of the eggs instead of whole eggs. Inverted onto a cake plate, this is one gorgeous cake.

serves:
12 to 16

prep:
20 minutes

bake:
52 to 57 minutes

cool:
20 to 25 minutes

Vegetable oil spray, for misting the pan
Flour, for dusting the pan
⅓ cup caramel or dulce de leche ice cream topping or sauce
1 can (14 ounces) sweetened condensed milk
1 can (12 ounces) evaporated milk
4 large egg yolks
2 teaspoons pure vanilla extract
½ teaspoon pure almond extract
1 package (18.25 ounces) plain chocolate cake mix
1 cup canned pumpkin, or ¾ cup mashed bananas (from 2 ripe bananas)
¾ cup water
⅓ cup vegetable oil
3 large eggs
½ teaspoon ground cinnamon

Flan Do

Really get creative with this basic recipe by using, for example, a butter recipe golden cake mix. Or add a tablespoon of rum to the flan mixture instead of the vanilla and almond.

Recipe Reminders

MADE FOR

PREP NOTES

DON'T FORGET

SPECIAL TOUCHES

1. Place a rack in the center of the oven and preheat the oven to 325°F. Lightly mist a 12-cup Bundt pan with vegetable oil spray, then dust it with flour. Shake out the excess flour. Pour the caramel or *dulce de leche* topping in the bottom of the pan and set the pan aside.

2. Place the sweetened condensed milk, evaporated milk, 4 egg yolks, and vanilla and almond extracts in a medium-size mixing bowl (or in a blender). Beat with an electric mixer on medium speed or blend until the egg yolks are well combined and the flan mixture is smooth, 1 minute. Set the flan mixture aside.

3. Place the cake mix, canned pumpkin or mashed bananas, water, oil, whole eggs, and cinnamon in a large mixing bowl. Beat (using the same beaters; no need to wash them) with an electric mixer on low speed until the ingredients are incorporated, 30 seconds. Stop the machine and scrape down the side of the bowl with a rubber spatula. Increase the mixer speed to medium and beat the batter for 1½ minutes longer, scraping down the side of the bowl again if needed. The batter should look smooth and thick. Transfer the batter to the prepared Bundt pan, pouring it on top of the caramel topping. Slowly pour the reserved flan mixture over the cake batter. Do not mix the two together. Carefully place the Bundt pan in the oven.

4. Bake the cake until the top springs back when lightly pressed with a finger, 52 to 57 minutes. Transfer the Bundt pan to a wire rack and let the cake cool for 10 minutes. Run a long, sharp knife around the edges of the cake and invert it onto a cake plate to cool for 10 to 15 minutes before slicing and serving. The flan mixture will have sunk to the bottom of the Bundt pan and will be a golden glaze on top of the cake after you invert it.

Keep It Fresh! Store this cake, in a cake saver or under a glass cake dome, in the refrigerator for up to four days. It does not freeze well.

Fudge Brownie Pound Cake

IF YOUR MOUTH ISN'T WATERING from the title of this recipe it will be when you see fudgy chunks of unbaked brownies folded into the cake batter. The brownie pieces form a gooey chocolate crown and slightly marble the batter as the cake bakes. It was an idea that came to me as I was retesting the chocolate chip cookie dough cupcakes. Begin with a roll of refrigerated brownie dough and either a yellow or butter recipe golden cake mix. A milk chocolate glaze tops the baked cake, and you can press chopped pecans into the glaze as it cools, if you like. Or, if you're in a hurry, forgo the glaze and dust the top of the cake with confectioners' sugar. Most of the other ingredients should be right on your pantry shelf.

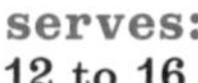

serves:
12 to 16

prep:
25 minutes (see Note)

bake:
55 to 60 minutes

cool:
45 to 60 minutes

For the cake

1 roll (16.5 ounces) refrigerated brownie dough
Vegetable oil spray, for misting the pan
Flour, for dusting the pan
1 package (18.25 ounces) plain yellow, vanilla, or 1 package (18.5 ounces) plain butter recipe golden cake mix
1 package (3.4 ounces) vanilla instant pudding mix
1¼ cups milk
½ cup vegetable oil
4 large eggs
2 teaspoons pure vanilla extract

For the milk chocolate glaze

1 cup (6 ounces) milk chocolate chips
4 tablespoons (½ stick) butter
2 tablespoons light corn syrup

Recipe Reminders

MADE FOR

PREP NOTES

DON'T FORGET

SPECIAL TOUCHES

1. Make the cake: Place the roll of brownies in the freezer for at least 1 hour before using.

2. Place a rack in the center of the oven and preheat the oven to 325°F. Lightly mist a 10-inch tube pan with vegetable oil spray, then dust it with flour. Shake out the excess flour and set the pan aside.

3. Place the cake mix, pudding mix, milk, oil, eggs, and vanilla in a large mixing bowl. Beat with an electric mixer on low speed until the ingredients are incorporated, 30 seconds. Stop the machine and scrape down the side of the bowl with a rubber spatula. Increase the mixer speed to medium and beat for 2 minutes longer, scraping down the side of the bowl again if needed. The batter should look well combined. Set the bowl of batter aside.

4. Remove the roll of brownie dough from the freezer. Unwrap and slice the roll into fourths lengthwise. Then slice each strip into about 14 pieces. Work quickly because the dough will thaw quickly. There should be about 56 half-inch pieces. Fold the pieces of dough into the cake batter until they are well distributed. Pour the batter into the prepared tube pan, smoothing the top with the rubber spatula, and place the pan in the oven.

5. Bake the cake until it is just starting to pull away from the sides of the pan and the top springs back when lightly pressed with a finger, 55 to 60 minutes. Transfer the tube pan to a wire rack and let the cake cool for 10 to 15 minutes. Run a long, sharp knife around the edges of the pan and shake the pan gently. Invert the cake onto a wire rack, then invert it again onto another rack so that the cake is right side up. Let the cake cool completely, 25 to 30 minutes longer.

6. Meanwhile, make the glaze: Place the chocolate chips, butter, and corn syrup in a large microwave-safe glass bowl and place it in the microwave oven on high power for 1 to 1½ minutes. Remove the bowl from the oven and stir the glaze with a wire whisk until the butter and chocolate have melted and the glaze is smooth and spreadable. Slide the cake onto a serving plate, pour the glaze over the top of the cooled cake. Let the glaze set for 10 to 15 minutes, then slice and serve the cake.

Keep It Fresh! Store this cake, in a cake saver, at room temperature for up to four days or for up to one week in the refrigerator. Freeze the cake, wrapped in aluminum foil, for up to six months. Let the cake thaw overnight on the counter before serving.

Note: The roll of brownie dough needs to be placed in the freezer for 1 hour before being added to the cake batter.

Top-Secret Glaze Tip

You heard it from me: If you want a glistening glaze of chocolate make sure to add 1 to 2 tablespoons light corn syrup to the pot. The corn syrup gives the chocolate a shine and helps the glaze flow seductively down the sides of the cake.

Chocolate Chip Cappuccino Coffee Cake

serves:
12 to 16

prep:
20 minutes

bake:
45 to 50 minutes

cool:
35 to 45 minutes

A **TRUE COFFEE CAKE,** this easy Bundt is not only delicious served with coffee, but coffee is an ingredient. Katie Sloan of Charlotte, North Carolina, passed along the recipe some years ago. She says not only does it fill her home with wonderful aromas but, whenever she brings it to a potluck, she comes home with an empty plate. And it's no wonder—it looks beautiful and is easy to tote. Perfect for a morning meeting or Sunday brunch. To make this coffee cake less intense, substitute water for the coffee. But would it still be a coffee cake? You be the judge.

For the chocolate chip streusel

1 lightly packed cup light brown sugar
¾ cup finely chopped pecans
½ cup (3 ounces) miniature semisweet chocolate chips
2 tablespoons plus 1 teaspoon all-purpose flour
2 teaspoons ground cinnamon
2 teaspoons unsweetened cocoa powder
3 tablespoons butter, melted

For the cake

Vegetable oil spray, for misting the pan
Flour, for dusting the pan
1 package (18.25 ounces) plain yellow or vanilla cake mix
1 package (3.4 ounces) vanilla instant pudding mix
1 cup sour cream
½ cup strong brewed coffee or water
4 large eggs
1 teaspoon pure vanilla extract

For the topping

1 tablespoon confectioners' sugar
1 teaspoon unsweetened cocoa powder

1. Place a rack in the center of the oven and preheat the oven to 350°F.

2. Make the streusel: Place the brown sugar, pecans, chocolate chips, flour, cinnamon, 2 teaspoons of cocoa powder, and the melted butter in a large mixing bowl and stir to combine. Set the streusel aside.

3. Make the cake: Lightly mist a 12-cup Bundt pan with vegetable oil spray, then dust it with flour. Shake out the excess flour and set the pan aside.

4. Place the cake mix, pudding mix, sour cream, coffee or water, eggs, and vanilla in a large mixing bowl and beat with an electric mixer on low speed until the ingredients just come together, 30 seconds. Stop the machine and scrape down the side of the bowl with a rubber spatula. Increase the mixer speed to medium and beat until the batter is thick and smooth, 1½ minutes longer, scraping down the side of the bowl again if needed. Pour two thirds of the batter into the prepared Bundt

Recipe Reminders

MADE FOR

____

____

____

____

PREP NOTES

____

____

____

____

DON'T FORGET

____

____

____

____

SPECIAL TOUCHES

____

____

____

____

____

____

____

____

____

pan and sprinkle half of the streusel mixture on top of the batter. Pour the remaining third of the batter on top of the streusel and, using a rubber spatula, spread the batter to reach the side of the pan. Sprinkle the remaining streusel on top. Place the pan in the oven.

5. Bake the cake until the top springs back when lightly pressed with a finger, 45 to 50 minutes. Transfer the Bundt pan to a wire rack and let the cake cool for 10 to 15 minutes. Run a long, sharp knife around the edges of the cake, shake the pan gently, and invert the cake onto a serving plate so that the streusel stays on the bottom of the cake. Let the cake cool completely, 25 to 30 minutes longer.

6. Make the topping: Place the confectioners' sugar and 1 teaspoon of cocoa powder in a small bowl and stir to combine. Sift the confectioners' sugar mixture on top of the cake, then slice and serve.

Keep It Fresh! Store this cake, in a cake saver or loosely covered with plastic wrap, at room temperature for up to five days. Freeze the cake, wrapped in aluminum foil, for up to six months. Let the cake thaw overnight on the counter before serving.

Topping for Chocolate Lovers

If you want a more elaborate topping, make a quick chocolate glaze. Melt 1 cup of semisweet chocolate chips in the microwave on high power, 45 to 50 seconds, stirring it halfway through. Then stir in 2 to 3 tablespoons of confectioners' sugar and 1 teaspoon of vanilla extract, and then a few tablespoons of milk, cream, or sour cream, 1 tablespoon at a time, to thin out the mixture. Spoon this over the top of the cake and spread it down the side. If glazing, store the cake in the refrigerator.

A Lighter Stacy's Chocolate Chip Cake

EVER SINCE NASHVILLE COOK Stacy Ross passed along the recipe for this cake ten years ago it has been a favorite of our crowd. But through the years I have sought to lighten it up, mostly in response to your e-mails asking how to make this great cake with less oil. And, since the original recipe used semisweet chocolate chips, often those chips would sink. Switching to miniature chips, I have found, solves that problem—those little chips suspend beautifully in the batter. You can vary this cake even further, omitting the grated chocolate on days when you don't have a bar of German's chocolate on hand; it will still be a great cake. One last note; as yellow cake mixes seem to have become more yellow in color through the years, I now prefer a butter recipe golden mix in this recipe. It does not contain the same amount of yellow coloring and is the better backdrop to all of the delicious chocolate chips inside.

serves:
12 to 16

prep:
20 minutes

bake:
50 to 55 minutes
(see Notes)

cool:
35 to 45 minutes

Vegetable oil spray, for misting the pan
Flour, for dusting the pan
1 bar (4 ounces) German's sweet chocolate
1 package (18.5 ounces) plain butter recipe golden cake mix
1 package (3.4 ounces) vanilla instant pudding mix
1½ cups milk (see Notes)
½ cup vegetable oil
4 large eggs
1 teaspoon pure vanilla extract
1 cup (6 ounces) miniature semisweet chocolate chips

Recipe Reminders

MADE FOR

PREP NOTES

DON'T FORGET

SPECIAL TOUCHES

1. Place a rack in the center of the oven and preheat the oven to 350°F. Lightly mist a 12-cup Bundt pan (see Notes) with vegetable oil spray, then dust it with flour. Shake out the excess flour and set the pan aside.

2. Break the German's chocolate bar into four pieces. Finely grate the bar using a food processor or a hand grater (if you are using a food processor, insert the steel blade and drop the chocolate pieces into the processor one at a time). Set the grated chocolate aside.

A Checkerboard Chocolate Chip Cake? No Problem

Divide the cake batter in half before folding in the chocolate chips. Add ½ cup of chocolate syrup to one half of the batter, stirring well, and fold the chocolate chips into the second half. Place a big tablespoon of the chocolate batter in a greased and floured Bundt pan at 12:00, 3:00, 6:00, and 9:00 o'clock, as if the bottom of the pan were a clock. Now place one big tablespoon of the chocolate chip batter halfway between each of the tablespoons of chocolate batter—at 1:30, 4:30, 7:30, and 10:30. Now make a second layer, placing a big tablespoon of chocolate batter on top of each of the tablespoons of chocolate chip batter, then filling in the spaces between with tablespoons of the chocolate batter placed on top of the tablespoons of chocolate chip batter. For the third and last layer place tablespoons of the chocolate batter on top of the chocolate chip, and chocolate chip on top of the chocolate. You will have created a checkerboard effect. The cake will not bake up in a precise checkerboard, but you will have a wonderfully marbled cake after it is done, beautiful when sliced.

3. Place the cake mix, pudding mix, milk, oil, eggs, and vanilla in a large mixing bowl. Beat with an electric mixer on low speed until the ingredients are incorporated, 30 seconds. Stop the machine, fold in the grated German's chocolate, and scrape down the side of the bowl with a rubber spatula. Increase the mixer speed to medium and beat for 2 minutes longer, scraping down the side of the bowl again if needed. Fold in the chocolate chips. Pour the batter into the prepared Bundt pan, smoothing the top with the rubber spatula, and place the pan in the oven.

4. Bake the cake until it is golden brown and the top springs back when lightly pressed with a finger, 50 to 55 minutes. Transfer the Bundt pan to a wire rack and let the cake cool for 10 to 15 minutes. Run a long, sharp knife around the edges of the cake, shake the pan gently, and invert the cake onto a wire rack. Let the cake cool completely, 25 to 30 minutes longer, then slice and serve.

Keep It Fresh! Store this cake, wrapped in aluminum foil or covered with plastic wrap, at room temperature for up to one week. Freeze the cake, wrapped in aluminum foil, for up to six months. Let the cake thaw overnight on the counter before serving.

Notes: You can bake this cake in a tube pan at 350°F for 55 to 60 minutes.

As for the milk, use whatever milk is in your refrigerator. And if you want to make a slightly richer cake, use ⅔ cup vegetable oil and 1⅓ cups milk.

A Great Chocolate Chip Cupcake

For a recent birthday my daughters bought me the Nordic Ware "Great Cupcake Pan," which bakes a cake in the shape of a very large cupcake. They christened the pan with Stacy's chocolate chip cake. It was a huge hit, frosted with my Fluffy Chocolate Frosting (page 478) and then garnished with colorful confetti sprinkles. If you own one of those pans, just use the chocolate chip batter and bake the cake at 325°F for 65 to 70 minutes.

Chocolate Chip Zucchini Cake

serves:
12 to 16

prep:
20 minutes

bake:
45 to 50 minutes

cool:
35 to 40 minutes

A **NO-NONSENSE BUNDT,** this cake is perfect for baking in the summertime when fresh zucchini is in the marketplace and you need a fun, fast cake to take to a potluck supper or picnic. It assembles quickly, bakes in less than an hour, and it needs no glaze or adornment, just a dusting of confectioners' sugar, if you wish. Shredded zucchini makes this a very moist cake, and the chocolate of the German cake mix is complemented by the folded in chocolate chips.

Vegetable oil spray, for misting the pan
Flour, for dusting the pan
1 package (18.25 ounces) plain German chocolate cake mix
1 package (3.4 ounces) vanilla instant pudding mix
⅔ cup milk
½ cup vegetable oil
3 large eggs
1 teaspoon pure vanilla extract
½ teaspoon ground cinnamon
2 cups gently packed shredded zucchini (8 ounces)
1 cup (6 ounces) miniature semisweet chocolate chips

1. Place a rack in the center of the oven and preheat the oven to 350°F. Lightly mist a 12-cup Bundt pan with vegetable oil spray, then dust it with flour. Shake out the excess flour and set the pan aside.

2. Place the cake mix, pudding mix, milk, oil, eggs, vanilla, and cinnamon in a large mixing bowl. Beat with an electric mixer on low speed until the ingredients are incorporated, 30 seconds. Stop the machine and scrape down the side of the bowl with a rubber spatula. Increase the mixer speed to medium and beat the batter for 1½ minutes longer, scraping down the side of the bowl again if needed. The batter should look smooth and thick. Fold in the shredded zucchini and chocolate chips. Pour the batter into the prepared Bundt pan, smoothing the top with the rubber spatula, and place the pan in the oven.

3. Bake the cake until the top springs back when lightly pressed with a finger, 45 to 50 minutes. Transfer the Bundt pan to a wire rack and let the cake cool for 15 minutes. Run a long, sharp knife around the edges of the cake, shake the pan gently, and invert the cake onto a wire rack. Let the cake cool completely, 20 to 25 minutes longer, then slice and serve.

Keep It Fresh! Store this cake, in a cake saver, at room temperature for up to one week. Freeze the cake, wrapped in aluminum foil, for up to six months. Let the cake thaw overnight on the counter before serving.

Note: For a simple garnish, stir together 2 teaspoons of confectioners' sugar and ¼ teaspoon of cinnamon and dust the spiced sugar mixture over the cooled cake.

Recipe Reminders

MADE FOR

____

____

____

____

PREP NOTES

____

____

____

____

DON'T FORGET

____

____

____

____

SPECIAL TOUCHES

____

____

____

____

____

____

____

____

____

Jewish Pound Cake

serves:
12 to 16

prep:
20 minutes

bake:
47 to 53 minutes

cool:
35 to 45 minutes

THIS MARVELOUS RECIPE has been shared in my online newsletter and it bears repeating. The best answer I have as to why I think it is called "Jewish" pound cake is that it's somewhat similar in flavor to the traditional *babkas* filled with chocolate and cinnamon that are popular with Jewish cooks. I got this recipe from my friend Martha Bowden who got it from her friend Anita Forlines, who got the recipe from a friend in Arkansas. It's a snap to prepare, you can change it in all sorts of ways to suit your taste—omit the coconut, use walnuts instead of pecans, put pecans on the bottom of the Bundt pan, or fold them in the batter just before baking.

Vegetable oil spray, for misting the pan
Flour, for dusting the pan
1 cup finely chopped pecans or walnuts
1 package (18.25 ounces) plain yellow or vanilla cake mix
1 package (3.4 ounces) vanilla instant pudding mix
¾ cup granulated sugar
1 tablespoon unsweetened cocoa powder
1 teaspoon ground cinnamon
1 cup sour cream
⅔ cup vegetable oil
4 large eggs
1 teaspoon pure vanilla extract
½ cup sweetened flaked coconut (optional)
1 tablespoon confectioners' sugar (optional)

1. Place a rack in the center of the oven and preheat the oven to 350°F. Lightly mist a 12-cup Bundt pan with vegetable oil spray, then dust it with flour. Shake out the excess flour and place the nuts in the bottom of the pan, if you'd like them at the top of the finished cake. Set the pan aside.

2. Place the cake mix, pudding mix, granulated sugar, cocoa powder, cinnamon, sour cream, oil, eggs, and vanilla in a large mixing bowl and beat with an electric mixer on low speed until the ingredients are incorporated, 30 seconds. Stop the machine and scrape down the side of the bowl with a rubber spatula. Increase the mixer speed to medium-high and beat for 2 minutes longer, scraping the side of the bowl down again if needed. If desired, fold in the coconut, and add the nuts here. Pour the batter into the prepared Bundt pan, smoothing the top with the rubber spatula, and place the pan in the oven.

3. Bake the cake until it is golden brown and the top springs back when lightly pressed with a finger, 47 to 53 minutes. Transfer the Bundt pan to a wire rack and let the cake cool for 10 to 15 minutes. Run a long, sharp knife around the edges of the cake, shake the pan gently, and invert the cake onto a wire rack. Let the cake cool completely, 25 to 30 minutes longer. Sift the confectioners' sugar over the cake, if desired, then slice and serve.

Keep It Fresh! Store this cake, in a cake saver or loosely covered with plastic wrap, at room temperature for up to five days. Freeze the cake, wrapped in aluminum foil, for up to six months. Let the cake thaw overnight on the counter before serving.

Recipe Reminders

MADE FOR

PREP NOTES

DON'T FORGET

SPECIAL TOUCHES

Aimee's Almond Chocolate Chip Cake

serves:
12 to 16

prep:
15 minutes

bake:
45 to 50 minutes

cool:
35 to 45 minutes

NASHVILLE RESIDENT Aimee Lurey is a good cook who had told me about her favorite chocolate cake—a dense no-oil cake with loads of chocolate. I baked it and loved the heavy, fudgy dense texture as well as the abundance of chocolate chips! Whereas Aimee bakes her cake with two eggs, I prefer four to make a bigger cake. And, I have *also* baked it using an egg substitute, so if you are trying to cut back on fat and cholesterol, this is a cake to try. The almond flavor improves with sitting, so bake the cake a day ahead of when you plan to serve it to the chocolate lovers on your list.

Vegetable oil spray, for misting the pan
Flour, for dusting the pan
1 package (18.25 ounces) plain chocolate cake mix
1 package (3.9 ounces) chocolate instant pudding mix
1 package (12 ounces; 2 cups) semisweet chocolate chips
4 large eggs (see Note)
1¾ cups milk or water
2 teaspoons pure almond extract
1 tablespoon confectioners' sugar or 2 tablespoons sliced almonds, for garnish

1. Place a rack in the center of the oven and preheat the oven to 350°F. Lightly mist a 12-cup Bundt pan with vegetable oil spray, then dust it with flour. Shake out the excess flour and set the pan aside.

2. Place the cake mix, pudding mix, chocolate chips, eggs, milk, and almond extract in a large mixing bowl. Beat with an electric mixer on low speed until the ingredients are incorporated, 30 seconds. Stop the machine and scrape down the side of the bowl with a rubber spatula. Increase the mixer speed to medium and beat for 1½ minutes longer, scraping down the side of the bowl again if needed. Pour the batter into the prepared Bundt pan, smoothing the top with the rubber spatula, and place the pan in the oven.

3. Bake the cake until the top springs back when lightly pressed with a finger, 45 to 50 minutes. Transfer the Bundt pan to a wire rack and let the cake cool for 10 to 15 minutes. Run a long, sharp knife around the edges of the cake, shake the pan gently, and invert the cake onto a wire rack. Let the cake cool completely, 25 to 30 minutes longer. Sift the confectioners' sugar over the cake or top it with the sliced almonds. Slice and serve.

Keep It Fresh! Store this cake, in a cake saver or loosely covered with plastic wrap, at room temperature for up to one week. Freeze the cake, wrapped in aluminum foil, for up to six months. Let the cake thaw overnight on the counter before serving.

Note: You can use 1 cup of egg substitute to take the place of the 4 eggs. The egg substitute I used was Egg Beaters. Egg substitutes are easy to use—just read the label and see how much you need to measure for each egg the recipe requires.

Recipe Reminders

MADE FOR

PREP NOTES

DON'T FORGET

SPECIAL TOUCHES

More Amazing German Chocolate Cake

serves:
12 to 16

prep:
10 minutes

bake:
42 to 47 minutes

cool:
35 to 40 minutes

THIS CRAZY BUT DELICIOUS CAKE has become my exception to the rule—the rule being that I never use store-bought frosting and always make my own from scratch. In this cake, however, the tub of frosting goes in the cake batter. I know it is shocking and I didn't believe it either when I first heard about this cake while on a Raleigh, North Carolina, radio show. But then I baked it and agreed it was amazing. However, one flaw of the original recipe was that when it cooled the cake often shrunk back and sunk in the pan. I was out to solve this dilemma when I retested the recipe for this book. And I came up with a solution—add a little flour to the batter. This makes the batter more substantial and with the added structure the cake doesn't sink. You have the same great flavor, moist texture, lightning fast prep time, plus a taller cake. And so I dub this cake "more amazing."

Vegetable oil spray, for misting the pan
Flour, for dusting the pan
1 package (18.25 ounces) plain German chocolate cake mix
1 container (14.5 ounces) coconut pecan frosting (see Note)
1 cup water
⅓ cup all-purpose flour
⅓ cup vegetable oil
3 large eggs
1 tablespoon confectioners' sugar (optional)

1. Place a rack in the center of the oven and preheat the oven to 350°F. Lightly mist a 12-cup Bundt pan with vegetable oil spray, then dust it with flour. Shake out the excess flour and set the pan aside.

2. Place the cake mix, frosting, water, flour, oil, and eggs in a large mixing bowl. Beat with an electric mixer on low speed until the ingredients are incorporated, 30 seconds. Stop the machine and scrape down the side of the bowl with a rubber spatula. Increase the mixer speed to medium and beat the batter for 1½ minutes longer, scraping down the side of the bowl again if needed. The batter should look smooth and thick. Pour the batter into the prepared Bundt pan, smoothing the top with the rubber spatula, and place the pan in the oven.

3. Bake the cake until the top springs back when lightly pressed with a finger, 42 to 47 minutes. Transfer the Bundt pan to a wire rack and let the cake cool for 15 minutes. Run a long, sharp knife around the edges of the cake, shake the pan gently, and invert the cake onto a wire rack. Let the cake cool completely, 20 to 25 minutes longer. Sift the confectioners' sugar over the cake, if desired, then slice and serve.

Keep It Fresh! Store this cake, in a cake saver or loosely covered with plastic wrap, at room temperature for up to five days. Freeze the cake, wrapped in aluminum foil, for up to six months. Let the cake thaw overnight on the counter before serving.

Note: Purists might need some help as to how to find frosting in the supermarket. It is sold right next to the cake mix! Those containers are shrinking, however; there is a little less frosting in them than when I first published this recipe in *Chocolate from the Cake Mix Doctor*. Even if the containers continue to get smaller this recipe should still work.

Recipe Reminders

MADE FOR

____

____

____

____

PREP NOTES

____

____

____

____

DON'T FORGET

____

____

____

____

SPECIAL TOUCHES

____

____

____

____

____

____

____

____

____

German Chocolate Darn Good Cake

serves:
12 to 16

prep:
15 minutes

bake:
55 to 58 minutes

cool:
35 to 45 minutes

YOU CAN'T BEAT the Darn Good Chocolate Cake recipe when it comes to a rich, moist, and simple cake that travels well. I wondered if I could change the recipe to include the German chocolate cake flavors our family loves. And it worked beautifully! Place the pecans and coconut in the bottom of the pan, then pour in the sour cream batter that is based on a German chocolate cake mix. Be sure to include chocolate chips—either semisweet or milk chocolate. This cake stays moist for days.

Vegetable oil spray, for misting the pan
Flour, for dusting the pan
¼ cup chopped pecans
¼ cup sweetened flaked coconut
1 package (18.25 ounces) plain German chocolate cake mix
1 package (3.4 ounces) vanilla instant pudding mix
1 cup reduced-fat sour cream
⅔ cup water
½ cup vegetable oil
4 large eggs
2 teaspoons pure vanilla extract
1½ cups (9 ounces) semisweet chocolate or milk chocolate chips

1. Place a rack in the center of the oven and preheat the oven to 350°F. Lightly mist a 12-cup Bundt pan with vegetable oil spray, then dust it with flour. Shake out the excess flour. Sprinkle the pecans and coconut in the bottom of the pan and set the pan aside.

2. Place the cake mix, pudding mix, sour cream, water, oil, eggs, and vanilla in a large mixing bowl. Beat with an electric mixer on low speed until the ingredients are incorporated, 30 seconds. Stop the machine and scrape down the side of the bowl with a rubber spatula. Increase the mixer speed to medium and beat for 2 minutes longer, scraping down the side of the bowl again if needed. The batter should look thick and well combined. Fold in the chocolate chips, making sure they are well distributed. Pour the batter into the prepared Bundt pan, smoothing the top with the rubber spatula, and place the pan in the oven.

3. Bake the cake until it just starts to pull away from the sides of the pan and the top springs back when lightly pressed with a finger, 55 to 58 minutes. Transfer the Bundt pan to a wire rack and let the cake cool for 10 to 15 minutes. Run a long, sharp knife around the edges of the cake, shake the pan gently, and invert the cake onto the wire rack. Let the cake cool completely, 25 to 30 minutes longer before slicing and serving. Or invert the cake onto a serving platter to slice and serve while still warm.

Keep It Fresh! Store this cake, in a cake saver or covered with plastic wrap, at room temperature for up to five days. Freeze the cake, wrapped in aluminum foil, for up to six months. Let the cake thaw overnight on the counter before serving.

Recipe Reminders

MADE FOR

____

____

____

____

PREP NOTES

____

____

____

____

DON'T FORGET

____

____

____

____

SPECIAL TOUCHES

____

____

____

____

____

____

____

____

____

Classic Darn Good Chocolate Cake

serves:
12 to 16

prep:
10 minutes

bake:
55 to 60 minutes

cool:
at least 15 to 20 minutes

I'M OFTEN ASKED which of the cakes I have baked is my favorite. And although this makes me uncomfortable, as if someone has asked who is the favorite child, I do have an answer. I favor this cake because it has some history with my family, it's so utterly decadent served warm, and it's versatile. My late aunt, Louise Grissim, loved to bake this cake. She gave the recipe to my mother, and I have chuckled with family members that I had to clean up the name a bit before publishing it because Louise used to call it something else. This is the cake I serve on birthdays when I am in a rush because I know all the ingredients will be on hand. This is the cake I stash in the freezer for unexpected company because if you zap it in the microwave it thaws and those chocolate chips melt once again, as if it was fresh and warm from the oven. And lastly, in what is starting to sound like an ode to this cake, this is a recipe that is easily adapted. I bake it with reduced-fat sour cream or plain yogurt now. I have added a teaspoon of almond extract successfully. I have baked the cake as cupcakes and frosted them with Martha's Chocolate Icing (page 480) or Fluffy Chocolate Frosting (page 478). But most of the time this cake goes to the table unadorned, garnished with birthday candles and served with good ice cream. It's always ready for a party.

Vegetable oil spray, for misting the pan
Flour, for dusting the pan
1 package (18.25 ounces) plain chocolate cake mix
1 package (3.9 ounces) chocolate instant pudding mix
4 large eggs
1 cup reduced-fat sour cream or plain or vanilla yogurt
⅔ cup water
½ cup vegetable oil
1 teaspoon pure vanilla extract
1½ cups (9 ounces) semisweet chocolate chips

1. Place a rack in the center of the oven and preheat the oven to 350°F. Lightly mist a 12-cup Bundt pan with vegetable oil spray, then dust it with flour. Shake out the excess flour and set the pan aside.

2. Place the cake mix, pudding mix, eggs, sour cream or yogurt, water, oil, and vanilla in a large mixing bowl. Beat with an electric mixer on low speed until the ingredients are incorporated, 30 seconds. Stop the machine and scrape down the side of the bowl with a rubber spatula. Increase the mixer speed to medium and beat the batter for 1½ minutes longer, scraping down the side of the bowl again if needed. The batter should look smooth and thick. Fold in the chocolate chips. Pour the batter into the prepared Bundt pan, smoothing the top with the rubber spatula, and place the pan in the oven.

3. Bake the cake until the top springs back when lightly pressed with a finger, 55 to 60 minutes. Transfer the Bundt pan to a wire rack and let the cake cool for 15 to 20 minutes. Run a long, sharp knife around the edges of the cake, shake the pan gently, and invert the cake to a wire rack. To let the cake cool completely, allow 25 to 30 minutes.

Recipe Reminders

MADE FOR

____

____

____

____

PREP NOTES

____

____

____

____

DON'T FORGET

____

____

____

____

SPECIAL TOUCHES

____

____

____

____

____

____

____

____

____

Keep It Fresh! Store this cake, in a cake saver or covered with plastic wrap, at room temperature for up to one week. Freeze the cake, wrapped in aluminum foil, for up to six months. Let the cake thaw overnight on the counter before serving.

It's All in the Chocolate Chips

So what makes this cake so "darn good"? The ingredients aren't complicated. I'd have to say two things—the cake is incredibly moist (credit the oil and sour cream) and it's incredibly chocolaty. Credit those chocolate chips. You can even add more than the recipe suggests; go ahead and add two cups of chips if you like (that's a whole 12-ounce package). For everyday baking I buy the Nestlé's semisweet chips. But if I am making this cake for company I'll pay a little more and buy the Ghirardelli bittersweet chips. The Whole Foods 365 brand of semisweet chips are also great, and for really nice occasions, I use the Callebaut chocolate chips that I buy at a specialty food store. What's nice about a 12-ounce bag is that once I measure out a cup and a half, what's left (3 ounces) makes good nibbling for the cook!

White Chocolate Macadamia Darn Good Chocolate Cake

A DANDY BAKE SALE OFFERING, this cake appeals to everyone who loves white chocolate and macadamia nut cookies. Several readers had encouraged me to make a blond version of the Darn Good cake. I tried it with a yellow cake mix and it worked just great, but it wasn't blond enough. So I moved to a white cake mix, added vanilla pudding mix, and folded in macadamia nuts and white chocolate chips. This cake is sure to be a favorite in your repertoire!

serves:
12 to 16

prep:
15 minutes

bake:
55 to 58 minutes

cool:
45 to 55 minutes

For the cake

Vegetable oil spray, for misting the pan
Flour, for dusting the pan
1 package (18.25 ounces) plain white or vanilla or 1 package (18.5 ounces) plain butter recipe golden cake mix
1 package (3.4 ounces) vanilla instant pudding mix
4 large eggs
1 cup reduced-fat sour cream or vanilla yogurt
⅔ cup water
½ cup vegetable oil
1 teaspoon pure vanilla extract
1½ cups (about an 8 ounce-bag) white chocolate chips and chopped macadamias

For the glaze

¾ cup (4 ounces) white chocolate chips or chopped white chocolate
2 tablespoons milk or heavy (whipping) cream

Chocolate Chips and Macadamias, Oh My!

Hershey's sells bags of white baking chips with macadamias added, and this makes preparation a breeze. If you can't find a white chocolate chip and macadamia nut mix, make your own by chopping ¾ cup of unsalted macadamia nuts and mixing them with ¾ cup of white chocolate chips.

Recipe Reminders

MADE FOR

PREP NOTES

DON'T FORGET

SPECIAL TOUCHES

1. Make the cake: Place a rack in the center of the oven and preheat the oven to 350°F. Lightly mist a 12-cup Bundt pan with vegetable oil spray, then dust it with flour. Shake out the excess flour and set the pan aside.

2. Place the cake mix, pudding mix, eggs, sour cream or yogurt, water, oil, and vanilla in a large mixing bowl. Beat with an electric mixer on low speed until the ingredients are incorporated, 30 seconds. Stop the machine and scrape down the side of the bowl with a rubber spatula. Increase the mixer speed to medium and beat the batter for 1½ minutes longer, scraping down the side of the bowl again if needed. The batter should look smooth and thick. Fold in the white chocolate chips and macadamia nuts. Transfer the batter to the prepared Bundt pan, smoothing the top with the rubber spatula.

3. Bake the cake until the top springs back when lightly pressed with a finger, 55 to 58 minutes. Transfer the Bundt pan to a wire rack and let the cake cool for 10 to 15 minutes. Run a long, sharp knife around the edges of the cake, shake the pan gently, and invert the cake onto a wire rack. Let the cake cool completely, 25 to 30 minutes longer.

4. Make the glaze: Place the white chocolate chips or pieces in a small microwave-safe glass bowl in the microwave oven on high power for 1 minute. Remove the bowl and stir the white chocolate until it melts. Stir in the milk or cream to make the chocolate more spreadable. Spoon the warm glaze over the cooled cake. Let the glaze set for 10 minutes before slicing and serving the cake.

Keep It Fresh! Store this cake, in a cake saver or covered with plastic wrap, at room temperature for up to five days. Freeze the cake, wrapped in aluminum foil, for up to six months. Let the cake thaw overnight on the counter before serving.

Double Coconut Macadamia Cake

I DON'T KNOW WHAT IS MORE FUN—this cake or the story behind it. Kate Motoyama of San Bruno, California, was raised in Honolulu. She recalls that her mom and friends were some of the best cooks around. Over the years they competed as to who could make the best teriyaki chicken, guava jam, and yes, coconut macadamia cake. They anonymously dropped off food at one another's houses just so the others could taste for themselves. With no "cake ladies" as neighbors now, Kate has to bake her own cakes, and this one is a lively combination of Hawaiian flavors.

serves:
12 to 16

prep:
40 minutes

bake:
52 to 57 minutes

cool:
50 to 60 minutes

½ cup chopped unsalted macadamia nuts
6 large eggs
2 cups sweetened flaked coconut
½ cup granulated sugar
¼ cup all-purpose flour, plus flour for dusting the pan
2½ teaspoons pure vanilla extract
Vegetable oil spray, for misting the pan
1 package (18.25 ounces) plain yellow or 1 package (18.5 ounces) plain butter recipe golden cake mix
1 package (3.4 ounces) vanilla instant pudding mix
½ cup vegetable oil
1 can (13.5 ounces) unsweetened coconut milk, about 1¾ cups
1 teaspoon coconut flavoring
4 tablespoons (½ stick) butter, melted
¼ cup sweetened condensed milk

Recipe Reminders

MADE FOR

PREP NOTES

DON'T FORGET

SPECIAL TOUCHES

1. Place a rack in the center of the oven and preheat the oven to 350°F. Place the macadamia nuts in a small baking pan to toast them in the oven while it preheats, 4 to 5 minutes.

2. Remove the macadamia nuts from the oven and let them cool. Set aside ¼ cup of the macadamias for the topping. Leave the oven on.

3. To make the filling, beat 2 of the eggs in a medium-size bowl and add the remaining ¼ cup of toasted macadamias. Then add 1½ cups of the flaked coconut, ¼ cup of the granulated sugar, the flour, and 1 teaspoon of the vanilla and stir with a fork until the eggs are well combined. Set the filling aside.

4. Lightly mist a 12-cup Bundt pan with vegetable oil spray, then dust it with flour. Shake out the excess flour and set the pan aside.

5. Place the cake mix, pudding mix, oil, coconut milk, coconut flavoring, the remaining 4 eggs, and ½ teaspoon of the vanilla in a large mixing bowl. Blend with an electric mixer on low speed until the ingredients are combined, 30 seconds. Stop the machine and scrape down the side of the bowl with a rubber spatula. Increase the mixer speed to medium and beat the batter for 2 minutes longer, scraping down the side of the bowl again if necessary. The batter should look smooth and thick. Pour half of the batter into the prepared Bundt pan. Spoon the filling over the top, making sure to keep it in a ring and away from the sides of the pan. Carefully spoon the remaining batter over the filling, and spread it out evenly with a rubber spatula. Place the pan in the oven.

6. Bake the cake until the top springs back when lightly pressed with a finger, 52 to 57 minutes. Transfer the Bundt pan to a wire rack and let the cake cool for 10 to 15 minutes. Run a long, sharp knife around the edges of the cake, shake the pan gently, and invert the cake onto a wire rack to cool completely, 25 to 30 minutes.

7. Meanwhile, preheat the broiler.

8. Prepare the topping: Place the remaining ½ cup of flaked coconut, the reserved ¼ cup of toasted macadamias, the remaining ¼ cup of granulated sugar, the remaining 1 teaspoon of vanilla, and the butter and condensed milk in a medium-size bowl and stir with a wooden spoon to combine.

9. Line a baking sheet with aluminum foil and slide the cooled cake onto the foil. Spoon the topping on top of the cake, not allowing any to fall down the sides of the cake. Place the baking sheet under the broiler, on the second rack from the top, and broil the topping until it drizzles down the cake and the nuts toast, 1 to 2 minutes. Remove the cake from the broiler, let it cool 15 minutes, then slice and serve.

Keep It Fresh! Store this cake, in a cake saver, at room temperature for one day or for up to one week in the refrigerator. Freeze the cake, wrapped in aluminum foil, for up to three months. Let the cake thaw overnight in the refrigerator for 4 to 6 hours before serving.

Make the Most of Macadamias

Macadamia nuts are delicious but costly so preserve their precious flavor and crunch by storing them in the freezer, not the pantry. You can toast them straight from the freezer.

Chocolate Espresso Pound Cake

serves:
12 to 16

prep:
15 minutes

bake:
48 to 54 minutes

cool:
40 minutes

Sally Kerr in Toronto calls herself the "Coffee Cake Queen," referring to her keen ability for making great coffee cakes. She passed along this recipe for turning a chocolate cake mix into so much more by adding espresso powder, flour, and a handful of other ingredients. She enjoyed a recipe I had shared in *The Dinner Doctor*, called The Best Pound Cake, and couldn't help but doctor it up. It's always a compliment when someone tweaks my recipes!

Vegetable oil spray, for misting the pan
Flour, for dusting the pan
1 package (18.25 ounces) plain chocolate cake mix
¾ cup granulated sugar
¾ cup all-purpose flour
¼ cup unsweetened cocoa powder
4 tablespoons (½ stick) butter, at room temperature
1 cup sour cream
1 cup evaporated milk (see Notes)
½ cup vegetable oil
5 large eggs
1 to 2 tablespoons espresso powder or regular instant coffee granules (see Notes)
2 teaspoons pure vanilla extract
½ recipe of Martha's Chocolate Icing (page 480), or 1 tablespoon confectioners' sugar

1. Place a rack in the center of the oven and preheat the oven to 350°F. Lightly mist a 10-inch tube pan with vegetable oil spray, then dust it with flour. Shake out the excess flour and set the pan aside.

2. Place the cake mix, sugar, flour, cocoa powder, butter, sour cream, milk, oil, eggs, espresso powder, and vanilla in a large mixing bowl. Beat with an electric mixer on low speed until the ingredients are combined, 30 seconds. Stop the machine and scrape down the side of the bowl with a rubber spatula. Increase the mixer speed to medium and beat the batter for 1½ minutes longer, scraping down the side of the bowl again if needed. The batter should look smooth and thick. Pour the batter into the prepared tube pan, smoothing the top with the rubber spatula, and place the pan in the oven.

3. Bake the cake until the top springs back when lightly pressed with a finger, 48 to 54 minutes. Transfer the tube pan to a wire rack and let the cake cool for 15 minutes. Run a long, sharp knife around the edges of the cake, shake the pan gently, and invert the cake onto a wire rack, then invert it again onto another wire rack so that the cake is right side up. Let the cake cool completely, about 25 minutes longer.

4. To glaze the cake, prepare half a recipe of Martha's Chocolate Icing and pour it over the top of the cooled cake. Or, sift the confectioners' sugar over the top of the cake. Slice the cake and serve.

Keep It Fresh! Store this cake, in a cake saver or loosely covered with plastic wrap, at room temperature for up to one week. Freeze the cake, wrapped in aluminum foil, for up to six months. Let the cake thaw overnight on the counter before serving.

Notes: Buy a 12-ounce can of evaporated milk and use the remainder in the icing, if desired.

Espresso powder is sold in many supermarkets and in specialty food shops.

Recipe Reminders

MADE FOR

____

____

____

____

PREP NOTES

____

____

____

____

DON'T FORGET

____

____

____

____

SPECIAL TOUCHES

____

____

____

____

____

____

____

____

____

Apricot Amaretto Cake

serves:
12 to 16

prep:
15 minutes

bake:
45 to 48 minutes

cool:
35 to 40 minutes

APRICOTS AND THE ALMOND LIQUEUR known as amaretto are perfect partners in this easy Bundt recipe. You just puree the canned fruit and fold it in with a cake mix, sour cream, eggs, pudding mix, and some amaretto. The glaze couldn't be easier—warmed apricot preserves and more amaretto.

For the cake

Vegetable oil spray, for misting the pan
Flour, for dusting the pan
1 can (15.25 ounces) apricot halves, packed in juice
1 package (18.5 ounces) plain butter recipe golden cake mix
1 package (3.4 ounces) vanilla instant pudding mix
4 large eggs
1 cup sour cream
¾ cup amaretto

For the glaze

½ cup apricot preserves (see Note)
1 tablespoon amaretto or other almond liqueur

1. Make the cake: Place a rack in the center of the oven and preheat the oven to 350°F. Lightly mist a 12-cup Bundt pan with vegetable oil spray, then dust it with flour. Shake out the excess flour and set the pan aside.

2. Drain the apricots and discard the juice. Place the apricots in a food processor and process until they are pureed, 20 to 30 seconds. Using a rubber spatula, transfer the apricots to a large mixing bowl.

3. Place the cake mix, pudding mix, eggs, sour cream, and ¾ cup of amaretto in the bowl with the pureed apricots. Beat with an electric mixer on low speed until the ingredients are combined, 30 seconds. Stop the machine and scrape down the side of the bowl with a rubber spatula. Increase the mixer speed to medium and beat the batter for 1½ minutes longer, scraping down the side of the bowl again if needed. The batter should look smooth and thick. Pour the batter into the prepared Bundt pan, smoothing the top with the rubber spatula, and place the pan in the oven.

4. Bake the cake until the top springs back when lightly pressed with a finger, 45 to 48 minutes. Transfer the Bundt pan to a wire rack and let the cake cool for 10 to 15 minutes. Run a long, sharp knife around the edges of the cake, shake the pan gently, and invert the cake onto a wire rack. Let the cake cool completely, about 25 minutes longer.

5. Meanwhile, make the glaze: Place the apricot preserves in a microwave-safe glass dish in the microwave oven. Heat on high power until hot and soupy, 30 seconds. Strain the preserves through a wire sieve, pressing with a spoon to extract the juice from the fruit. Add the 1 tablespoon of amaretto to the strained apricot preserves and stir to combine. Spoon this glaze over the cake while the glaze is still warm. Slice the cake and serve.

Keep It Fresh! Store this cake, in a cake saver, at room temperature for up to three days or for up to one week in the refrigerator. Freeze the cake, wrapped in waxed paper and placed in a resealable plastic bag, for up to six months. Let the cake thaw overnight on the counter before serving.

Note: If you don't have apricot preserves you can still glaze this cake. Stir 1 to 1½ tablespoons of amaretto into 1 cup of confectioners' sugar until smooth, then spoon the glaze over the cake.

Recipe Reminders

MADE FOR

PREP NOTES

DON'T FORGET

SPECIAL TOUCHES

Baileys Irish Bundt Cake

serves:
12 to 16

prep:
20 minutes

bake:
48 to 52 minutes

cool:
25 to 30 minutes

Kathryn Board sent me this recipe a few years ago. She made it for a St. Patrick's Day party and the men at the party loved it. "When a man likes a cake, you know you've got something yummy." So true. Men often would rather have a slice of pie than cake. But this cake is irresistible with the Baileys Irish Cream liqueur and the pecans that toast as they bake. It's perfect for March 17.

For the cake

Vegetable oil spray, for misting the pan
Flour, for dusting the pan
1 cup finely chopped pecans
1 package (18.25 ounces) plain yellow or vanilla cake mix
1 package (3.4 ounces) vanilla instant pudding mix
4 large eggs
¾ cup Baileys Irish Cream liqueur
½ cup vegetable oil
¼ cup water

For the glaze

8 tablespoons (1 stick) butter
1 cup granulated sugar
¼ cup Baileys Irish Cream liqueur
Vanilla ice cream, for serving

1. Make the cake: Place a rack in the center of the oven and preheat the oven to 350°F. Lightly mist a 12-cup Bundt pan with vegetable oil spray, then dust it with flour. Shake out the excess flour. Sprinkle the chopped pecans evenly over the bottom of the pan and set the pan aside.

2. Place the cake mix, pudding mix, eggs, ¾ cup of liqueur, oil, and water in a large bowl. Beat with an electric mixer on low speed until the ingredients are combined, 30 seconds. Stop the machine and scrape down the side of the bowl with a rubber spatula. Increase the mixer speed to medium and beat the batter for 1½ minutes longer, scraping down the side of the bowl again if needed. The batter should look smooth and thick. Pour the batter over the nuts in the prepared Bundt pan, smoothing the top with the rubber spatula, and place the pan in the oven.

3. Bake the cake until the top springs back when lightly pressed with a finger, 48 to 52 minutes. Transfer the Bundt pan to a wire rack and let the cake cool for 10 to 15 minutes.

4. Meanwhile, make the glaze: Place the butter, sugar, and ¼ cup of water in a medium-size saucepan. Bring to a boil over medium-high heat, stirring, and let the mixture boil for 4 to 5 minutes, stirring constantly. Remove the saucepan from the heat and stir in the ¼ cup of liqueur.

5. Run a long, sharp knife around the edges of the cake, shake the pan gently, and invert the cake onto a serving plate with raised sides. Using a long wooden skewer, poke 16 holes in the top of the cake. Spoon the glaze slowly over the top of the cake. Allow the cake to absorb the glaze, scooping up what collects on the plate and spooning it back over the top of the cake. Repeat this process until all of the glaze has been absorbed; it will take about 15 minutes. Slice the cake and serve it with vanilla ice cream.

Keep It Fresh! Store this cake, in a cake saver, at room temperature for up to three days or for up to one week in the refrigerator. Freeze the cake, wrapped in aluminum foil, for up to six months. Let the cake thaw overnight on the counter before serving.

Recipe Reminders

MADE FOR

PREP NOTES

DON'T FORGET

SPECIAL TOUCHES

Banana Buttered Rum Cake

serves:
12 to 16

prep:
30 minutes

bake:
50 to 55 minutes

cool:
35 to 45 minutes

THE COMBINATION OF BANANA AND RUM is a favorite of mine, and it dates back to the first time I had that classic New Orleans dessert Bananas Foster. Prepared tableside, not in New Orleans, but at Brennan's restaurant in Atlanta, the sautéed bananas were doused with sugar and rum. Up until then bananas at our house were sliced onto cereal or mashed and folded into banana bread! Here I've turned the bananas into a rum-flavored cake. And a brown sugar, butter, and rum glaze soaks down into every crumb. Serve this with vanilla ice cream at dinner parties, slice it as adult coffee cake, or wrap it up with a big ribbon and take it to the next bake sale. No doubt, it will be a favorite of yours, too.

For the cake

Vegetable oil spray, for misting the pan
Flour, for dusting the pan
½ cup finely chopped walnuts
3 medium-size ripe bananas, or 2 large ripe bananas
1 package (18.5 ounces) plain butter recipe golden cake mix
1 package (3.4 ounces) vanilla instant pudding mix
½ cup light or dark rum
½ cup water
¼ cup vegetable oil
1 teaspoon pure vanilla extract
4 large eggs

For the glaze

8 tablespoons (1 stick) butter
1 cup packed dark brown sugar
¼ cup light or dark rum
¼ cup water

1. Make the cake: Place a rack in the center of the oven and preheat the oven to 325°F. Lightly mist a 12-cup Bundt pan with vegetable oil spray, then dust it with flour. Shake out the excess flour. Sprinkle the chopped walnuts evenly over the bottom of the pan and set the pan aside.

2. Peel the bananas and place them in a large mixing bowl. Beat the bananas with an electric mixer on low speed until mashed. Add the cake mix, pudding mix, ½ cup of rum, ½ cup of water, and the oil, vanilla, and eggs to the bananas. Beat on low speed until the ingredients are combined, 1 minute. Stop the machine and scrape down the side of the bowl with a rubber spatula. Increase the mixer speed to medium and beat for 2 minutes longer, scraping down the side of the bowl again if needed. The batter should look thick and well combined. Pour the batter over the walnuts in the prepared Bundt pan, smoothing the top with the rubber spatula. Place the pan in the oven.

3. Bake the cake until it is just starting to pull away from the sides of the pan and the top springs back when lightly pressed with a finger, 50 to 55 minutes. Transfer the Bundt pan to a wire rack and let the cake cool for 10 to 15 minutes.

4. While the cake is cooling, make the glaze: Melt the butter in a medium-size saucepan over medium heat. Add the brown sugar, ¼ cup of rum, and ¼ cup of water to the butter. Stir constantly over medium heat until the mixture boils, 3 to 4 minutes. Let the glaze boil and continue stirring until the glaze thickens, 3 minutes longer. Remove the saucepan from the heat and set the glaze aside to cool for 10 minutes.

Recipe Reminders

MADE FOR

____
____
____
____

PREP NOTES

____
____
____
____

DON'T FORGET

____
____
____
____

SPECIAL TOUCHES

____
____
____
____
____
____
____
____
____

5. Run a long, sharp knife around the edges of the cake, shake the pan gently, and invert the cake onto a wire rack. Let the cake cool 10 minutes longer, then place it on a cake plate with raised sides.

6. Using a long wooden skewer, poke 12 to 16 holes in the top of the cake and slowly spoon the warm glaze over the warm cake. Keep spooning until most of the glaze is absorbed (see Note). Let the cake cool to room temperature, 15 to 20 minutes, then slice it and serve.

Keep It Fresh! Store this cake, wrapped in aluminum foil, covered with plastic wrap, or in a cake saver, at room temperature for up to five days. Freeze the cake, wrapped in aluminum foil, for up to six months. Let the cake thaw overnight on the counter before serving.

Note: This makes a generous amount of glaze and the glaze contributes to the moist and flavorful cake. But if you like, spoon only half of the glaze over the cake and save the other half to reheat gently and spoon over the cake slices when serving them with ice cream.

Gotta Glaze!

Be patient as you spoon the warm glaze over the cake, allowing each spoonful to soak down into the holes you've poked on top before adding more. The glaze keeps the cake moist for days.

Pumpkin Cranberry Christmas Cake

ONE OF MY VIVID CHILDHOOD Christmas memories is seeing rows of wrapped fruitcakes waiting on the dining room table. My mom would spend weeks baking fruitcakes then soaking them in bourbon before wrapping them in red cellophane with a big green bow. To be honest, the packaging was more interesting than the cake, for as a child I was not a big fruitcake fan. And even today I like it only when it is very moist and the dried fruit inside is interesting. When I baked this cake last Christmas all those memories came rushing back, except this time they were better! Here were the dried fruit and spices and bourbon I remembered, but this cake was more moist because of the addition of pumpkin and the bourbon that the raisins and cranberries soaked up. I put on the kettle for a cup of tea, then sat down with a slice and really savored it. Bake this for holiday brunches and parties and for gift giving.

serves:
12 to 16

prep:
30 minutes

bake:
50 to 55 minutes

cool:
40 to 45 minutes

Recipe Reminders

MADE FOR

PREP NOTES

DON'T FORGET

SPECIAL TOUCHES

For the cake

Vegetable oil spray, for misting the pan
Flour, for dusting the pan
¾ cup finely chopped pecans
½ cup golden raisins
½ cup dried sweetened cranberries
1 package (18.25 ounces) plain yellow or vanilla cake mix (see Note)
¼ cup packed light brown sugar
2 teaspoons ground cinnamon
½ teaspoon ground nutmeg
½ teaspoon ground allspice
1 can (15 ounces) pumpkin, about 2 cups
⅔ cup vegetable oil
⅓ cup bourbon or water
4 large eggs

For the glaze

4 tablespoons (½ stick) butter
½ cup packed light brown sugar
¼ cup bourbon or apple juice

1. Make the cake: Place a rack in the center of the oven and preheat the oven to 325°F. Place the pecans in a baking pan and toast them in the oven while it preheats until they are fragrant and deep brown, 4 to 5 minutes.

2. Lightly mist a 12-cup Bundt pan with vegetable oil spray, then dust it with flour. Shake out the excess flour and set the pan aside.

3. Remove the toasted pecans from the oven and let them cool, then set aside ½ cup of pecans for the cake batter and ¼ cup for the topping. Leave the oven on.

4. Place the raisins and cranberries on a cutting board and chop them in thirds (see sidebar, facing page).

Raise a Rack Up

Many cooling racks have little feet on them to raise the rack off the kitchen counter an inch or two. You need this airflow underneath the cooling cake to speed up the process. If your wire rack does not have feet, you can place two wooden spoons lying facedown underneath, one at each end. Or, there are other items from your kitchen drawer that would also work—upside-down measuring cups, little jars of sugar sprinkles, and so on.

5. Place the cake mix, ¼ cup of brown sugar, cinnamon, nutmeg, allspice, pumpkin, oil, ⅓ cup of bourbon or water, and the eggs in a large mixing bowl. Beat with an electric mixer on low speed until the ingredients are combined, 30 seconds. Stop the machine and scrape down the side of the bowl with a rubber spatula. Increase the mixer speed to medium and beat for 1½ minutes longer, scraping down the side of the bowl again if needed. The batter should look smooth and thick. Fold in the reserved ½ cup of toasted pecans. Then, fold the raisins and cranberries into the batter and pour the batter into the prepared Bundt pan, smoothing the top with the rubber spatula. Place the pan in the oven.

6. Bake the cake until the top springs back when lightly pressed with a finger, 50 to 55 minutes. Transfer the Bundt pan to a wire rack and let the cake cool for 15 minutes. Run a long, sharp knife around the edges of the cake, shake the pan gently, and invert the cake onto a wire rack. Let the cake cool completely, 25 to 30 minutes longer.

7. Meanwhile, make the glaze: Place the butter, ½ cup of brown sugar, and ¼ cup of bourbon or apple juice in a small pan over

Get Out Your Chopping Knife and Board

Throughout this book I suggest you finely chop pecans or walnuts. There is a plain and simple reason for this. A smaller piece of nut blends into the crumb of the cake better than a large chunk. When you slice cake and have large pieces of nuts and fruit inside, these fall out onto the plate or make slicing difficult. The same goes for dried fruit. Whole raisins and cranberries are too large for folding into the batter. You need to pile them on a cutting board and chop them in thirds using the best, heaviest knife you own. I say "thirds" but am really guessing and I don't expect you to cut each one individually into thirds. Pile them in a heap and then "have at it" with the knife, cutting them into smaller pieces. To stop dried fruit from sticking to your knife, mist the knife with vegetable oil spray first.

medium-high heat. Bring just to a boil, stirring constantly, then reduce the heat and let the mixture simmer until slightly thickened, 2 minutes, stirring. Set the glaze aside.

8. Slide the cake onto a serving plate. Using a long wooden skewer, poke 12 to 16 holes in the top of the cake. Spoon the glaze over the top of the cake and garnish it with the reserved ¼ cup of toasted pecans. Slice and serve the cake or wrap it and serve the next day.

Keep It Fresh! Store this cake, in a cake saver or in a tin lined with cheesecloth, at room temperature for up to five days or for up to ten days in the refrigerator.

Note: In a hurry? Substitute a spice cake mix for the yellow and omit the spices. And, forgo the glaze. Dust confectioners' sugar on the top before slicing.

Spice of Life

Feel free to add a pinch of ginger or cardamom to the batter, or any of your favorite holiday spices. And, on the other hand, if spices are not your thing, forgo the nutmeg and allspice and just increase the ground cinnamon to 1 tablespoon.

Pina Colada Cake

A FAVORITE RECIPE OF MINE from *The Cake Mix Doctor*, this cake was the subject of a story by newspaper food columnist Linda Cicero. She doctored—and improved—my original recipe by streamlining it. When testing recipes for this book, I looked at her recipe and adapted the cake even more. A cake with an attitude, this is my new favorite dinner party cake.

serves:
12 to 16

prep:
35 minutes

bake:
43 to 48 minutes

cool:
30 to 45 minutes

1 can (8 ounces) crushed pineapple packed in juice
1 can (8.5 ounces) cream of coconut (see Note)
½ cup plus 2 tablespoons light or dark rum
Vegetable oil spray, for misting the pan
Flour, for dusting the pan
1 package (18.25 ounces) plain yellow, vanilla, or 1 package (18.5 ounces) plain butter recipe golden cake mix
1 package (3.4 ounces) vanilla instant pudding mix
⅓ cup vegetable oil
4 large eggs
1 cup unsweetened flaked coconut
1 cup heavy (whipping) cream
⅓ cup confectioners' sugar, sifted

Recipe Reminders

MADE FOR

PREP NOTES

DON'T FORGET

SPECIAL TOUCHES

1. Drain the pineapple, reserving the juice. Measure out 3 tablespoons of the juice and place it in a small bowl for the glaze. Place the pineapple and the remaining juice in a large mixing bowl and set it aside. Stir the cream of coconut in its can, measure out ½ cup, and place this in the small bowl with the 3 tablespoons of pineapple juice. Pour the remaining cream of coconut into the large bowl with the pineapple. Stir 2 tablespoons of the rum into the small bowl with the pineapple juice and cream of coconut and set the glaze aside.

2. Place a rack in the center of the oven and preheat the oven to 350°F. Lightly mist a 12-cup Bundt pan with vegetable oil spray, then dust it with flour. Shake out the excess flour and set the pan aside.

3. Place the cake mix, pudding mix, oil, eggs, and the remaining ½ cup of rum in the large bowl with the pineapple and cream of coconut. Beat with an electric mixer on low speed until the ingredients are combined, 30 seconds. Stop the machine and scrape down the side of the bowl with a rubber spatula. Increase the mixer speed to medium and beat for 1½ minutes longer, scraping down the side of the bowl again if needed. The batter should look smooth and thick. Pour the batter into the prepared Bundt pan, smoothing the top with the rubber spatula, and place the pan in the oven.

4. Bake the cake until the top springs back when lightly pressed with a finger, 43 to 48 minutes. Transfer the Bundt pan to a wire rack and let the cake cool for 10 to 15 minutes. Leave the oven on.

5. Place ¼ cup of the flaked coconut in a baking pan and place it in the oven to toast until lightly browned, 3 to 4 minutes. Remove the coconut and set it aside to cool for the garnish.

6. Run a long, sharp knife around the edges of the cake, shake the pan gently, and invert the cake onto a serving plate. Using a wooden skewer, poke 12 to 16 holes in the top of the cake. Slowly spoon the glaze over the warm cake. Let the cake cool to room temperature, 20 minutes.

7. Meanwhile, make the topping: Place a medium-size mixing bowl and electric mixer beaters in the freezer for 5 minutes. Remove the bowl and beaters from the freezer and pour the cream into the chilled bowl. Stir in the confectioners' sugar. Beat on high speed until stiff peaks form, 2 to 3 minutes. Fold in the remaining ¾ cup of coconut. Pile the topping onto the top of the cake and sprinkle it with the reserved toasted coconut. Slice and serve the cake.

Keep It Fresh! Store this cake, in a cake saver, without the whipped cream topping for up to three days. Freeze the cake, wrapped in aluminum foil, for up to six months. Let the cake thaw overnight on the counter before adding the topping and serving.

Note: Cream of coconut is sold where you find the ingredients for tropical drinks. Be sure to shake the can before opening, and stir the contents before using, as it settles in storage.

Craving More Coconut Flavor?

Use coconut-flavored instant pudding mix instead of vanilla or add 1 teaspoon of coconut flavoring to the cake batter.

Margarita Cake

serves:
12 to 16

prep:
25 minutes

bake:
42 to 47 minutes

cool:
45 to 50 minutes

THIS CAKE WAS ALL THE BUZZ on the Cake Mix Doctor community board as readers were weighing in on its merits and giving others advice on what ingredients to use. I had to give it a try! And lo and behold—it actually tastes like a margarita with the lime juice, triple sec, and tequila. To give it that margarita in a glass look, I garnished the top of the cake with thin lime slices and the coarsest decorating sugar I could find.

For the cake

Vegetable oil spray, for misting the pan
Flour, for dusting the pan
1 package (18.25 ounces) plain yellow, vanilla, or lemon cake mix
Half of a package (3.4 ounces) vanilla instant pudding mix (4 tablespoons)
¼ cup granulated sugar
⅔ cup water
½ cup vegetable oil
⅓ cup fresh lime or key lime juice
¼ cup tequila
2 tablespoons triple sec
1 teaspoon grated lime zest
4 large eggs

For the glaze and garnish

1¼ cups confectioners' sugar, sifted
1 tablespoon tequila
1 tablespoon triple sec
1 tablespoon fresh lime juice or key lime juice
1 lime, cut into thin slices
1 to 2 teaspoons coarse sugar (see Note)

1. Make the cake: Place a rack in the center of the oven and preheat the oven to 350°F. Lightly mist a 12-cup Bundt pan with vegetable oil spray, then dust it with flour. Shake out the excess flour and set the pan aside.

2. Place the cake mix, pudding mix, granulated sugar, water, oil, ⅓ cup of lime juice, ¼ cup of tequila, 2 tablespoons of triple sec, and the lime zest and eggs in a large mixing bowl. Beat with an electric mixer on low speed until the ingredients are combined, 30 seconds. Stop the machine and scrape down the side of the bowl with a rubber spatula. Increase the mixer speed to medium and beat for 1½ minutes longer, scraping down the side of the bowl again if needed. The batter should look smooth and thick. Pour the batter into the prepared Bundt pan, smoothing the top with the rubber spatula, and place the pan in the oven.

3. Bake the cake until the top springs back when lightly pressed with a finger, 42 to 47 minutes. Transfer the Bundt pan to a wire rack and let the cake cool for 10 to 15 minutes. Run a long, sharp knife around the edges of the cake, shake the pan gently, and invert the cake onto a wire rack. Let the cake cool completely, about 25 minutes longer.

4. Meanwhile, make the glaze: Place the confectioners' sugar, 1 tablespoon of tequila, 1 tablespoon of triple sec, and 1 tablespoon of lime juice in a small bowl and whisk until smooth.

Recipe Reminders

MADE FOR

PREP NOTES

DON'T FORGET

SPECIAL TOUCHES

5. Slide the cake onto a serving plate. Using a long wooden skewer, poke 12 to 16 holes in the top of the cake. Spoon the glaze over the top of the cake, letting it drip down the sides. Garnish the cake with the lime slices and a sprinkling of coarse sugar. Let the glaze set for 10 minutes, then slice and serve the cake.

Keep It Fresh! Store this cake, in a cake saver, at room temperature for up to five days. Freeze the cake, wrapped in waxed paper and aluminum foil or in a cake saver, for up to six months. Let the cake thaw overnight on the counter before serving.

Note: Coarse sugar is this cake's version of the coarse salt that sticks to the rim of a glass filled with a margarita. It is often called sanding sugar and you can buy it at stores that sell cake and cookie decorating supplies. To make sure that the sugar sticks to the cake, sprinkle it on while the glaze is still wet.

Chocolate Rum Raisin Cake

THE FLAVORS OF RUM AND RAISINS are natural partners. And when combined with chocolate, they make a German chocolate cake mix taste mighty festive. Bake this during the holidays and turn it into smaller pans to bake for gifts. If you are not pressed for time, make this cake a day ahead, and the rum flavor will intensify.

serves:
12 to 16

prep:
25 minutes

bake:
45 to 50 minutes

cool:
at least 10 to 15 minutes

For the cake

1 cup dark rum
½ cup golden raisins
Vegetable oil spray, for misting the pan
Flour, for dusting the pan
1 package (18.25 ounces) plain German chocolate cake mix
½ cup milk
½ cup vegetable oil
2 tablespoons all-purpose flour
4 large eggs

For the glaze

4 tablespoons (½ stick) butter
2 tablespoons dark rum
1 tablespoon light corn syrup
½ cup confectioners' sugar, sifted
1 tablespoon unsweetened cocoa powder

1. Make the cake: Place a rack in the center of the oven and preheat the oven to 350°F. Place the 1 cup of rum in a small bowl and stir in the raisins. Let the raisins steep for 15 minutes.

Recipe Reminders

MADE FOR

PREP NOTES

DON'T FORGET

SPECIAL TOUCHES

2. Lightly mist a 12-cup Bundt pan with vegetable oil spray, then dust it with flour. Shake out the excess flour and set the pan aside.

3. Place the cake mix, milk, oil, flour, and eggs in a large mixing bowl. Drain the rum the raisins steeped in into the bowl and set aside the raisins. Beat with an electric mixer on low speed until the ingredients just come together, 30 seconds. Stop the machine and scrape down the side of the bowl with a rubber spatula. Increase the mixer speed to medium and beat until the batter is smooth and thick, 1½ minutes longer. Using the rubber spatula, fold in the raisins. Pour the batter into the prepared Bundt pan, smoothing the top with the rubber spatula, and place the pan in the oven.

4. Bake the cake until the top springs back when lightly pressed with a finger, 45 to 50 minutes. Transfer the Bundt pan to a wire rack and let the cake cool for 10 to 15 minutes.

5. Make the glaze: Place the butter in a small saucepan over medium heat and stir until it melts. Stir in the 2 tablespoons of rum and the corn syrup. Combine the confectioners' sugar and the cocoa powder and whisk this into the warm butter mixture until the sugar dissolves. Set the glaze aside briefly.

6. Run a long, sharp knife around the edges of the cake, shake the pan gently, and invert the cake onto a serving plate. Using a wooden skewer, poke 12 to 16 holes in the top of the cake. Spoon the warm glaze over the cake, allowing the cake to absorb the glaze before adding more. Slice and serve the cake warm or let it rest for 25 to 30 minutes, then slice and serve.

Keep It Fresh! Store this cake, in a cake saver, at room temperature for up to five days. Freeze the cake, in a cake saver or wrapped in aluminum foil, for up to six months. Let the cake thaw overnight on the counter before serving.

Sheet Cakes

I remember the summer when we were moving from one house to another and most of our belongings were stored in boxes in the garage. Thinking I was organized and clever and would be so ready come moving day, I had cleaned out the kitchen cabinets ahead of the move. But a birthday rolled around, and then a potluck supper, and then a block party. I couldn't find my 13 by 9–inch metal baking pan to at least make a pan of brownies. So I went out and bought another.

Life may be partly preparing for the days ahead but it's also celebrating the present. And the 13 by 9–inch pan is all about the day-to-day. It's the pan you most likely stash in the bottom drawer and use at least once a week. It might be warped and worn. It might be cared for, complete with a snap-on plastic lid. It might be one of many because maybe you, like me, can't live without it.

Tailgate parties, Thanksgiving dinners, holiday brunch, New Year's morning, spring picnics, graduation cookouts, church potluck suppers, and birthday cakes at school—these are all occasions when I have pulled out the 13 by 9–inch pan and made what I call a sheet cake. Now technically in restaurant speak a sheet cake is a cake baked in the more shallow sheet pan, what we home bakers call a large jelly roll pan. In this chapter sheet cakes are baked in a 13 by 9–inch pan, which for better heat distribution should be metal and not glass.

While testing the recipes—both old and new—for this chapter I found that what you bake in that pan is full of endless possibilities.

There are cakes you poke holes in, pour a glaze over, and serve warm right from the pan, such as the Hot Lemon Poke Cake and Hot Prune Cake with Buttermilk Glaze. There are cakes you bake, top with a glaze, and run under the broiler right in the pan, such as the Broiled Peanut Butter Crunch Cake.

There are traditional sheet cakes you bake, let cool, and then frost, such as the Old-Fashioned Chocolate Sheet Cake, Mandarin Orange Cake with Sherry Cream Cheese Frosting, Hummingbird Cake with Cream Cheese Frosting, and Birthday Cake for a Crowd. There are refrigerator cakes—Lemon Curd Icebox Cake, Overnight Chocolate Caramel Cake, Moist and Creamy Coconut Sheet Cake, and the lovely Caramel Tres Leches Cake.

And there are unexpected treats in this chapter—peach and pineapple upside-down cakes, cheesecakes, and a Warm Chocolate Pudding Cake. In addition, there are coffee cakes for toting and serving to friends. I especially love the Orange Cranberry Coffee Cake and Nancy's Cinnamon Swirl Coffee Cake.

Have I made you sufficiently hungry? I hope so because I'm about to dash to the kitchen and have another square of coffee cake. I'll cut a piece from the pan on the counter. Did I mention that sheet cakes are easy on clean-up because it's just one pan? And did I tell you that all of these recipes can be baked in two 9-inch square pans instead of the 13 by 9–inch pan? The smaller pans take less time to bake—seven to eight minutes less—but what makes them nice is that your family can eat one cake and share the second cake with friends or freeze it for a future meal.

Little prep, little assembly, little clean-up, but big flavor—just what I love about sheet cakes.

◆◆◆◆◆

Hot Lemon Poke Cake

This cake is so good, so basic, so appealing to all ages, it needs to be in your "bring-to-a-potluck" recipe file—that is if you want to serve the cake at room temperature. It's even more delicious when served warm after glazing, accompanied by a scoop of vanilla ice cream. We're partial to lemon cake around our house. And this one is even more special because it's a little bit lemon and, with the addition of orange juice, a little bit orange. No orange juice? Just add water.

serves:
16 to 20

prep:
15 minutes

bake:
32 to 37 minutes

For the cake

Vegetable oil spray, for misting the pan
Flour, for dusting the pan
1 package (18.25 ounces) plain yellow cake mix
1 package (3 ounces) lemon gelatin
1 cup orange juice or water
½ cup vegetable oil
4 large eggs

For the glaze

1 large lemon
1 heaping cup confectioners' sugar, sifted

1. Make the cake: Place a rack in the center of the oven and preheat the oven to 350°F. Lightly mist a 13 by 9–inch metal cake pan with vegetable oil spray, then dust it with flour. Shake out the excess flour and set the pan aside.

Want an Orange Poke Cake?

Substitute 1 package (3 ounces) of orange gelatin for the lemon gelatin in the cake and use fresh orange juice and orange zest instead of the lemon in the glaze.

Recipe Reminders

MADE FOR

PREP NOTES

DON'T FORGET

SPECIAL TOUCHES

How to Bake for a Crowd

Sheet cakes can handle feeding a lot of people since you can get as many as twenty servings from each 13 by 9-inch pan. I find the best way to make dessert for a crowd is to bake ahead of time and freeze the results. Borrow pans from friends if needed so you have enough. Or, use the disposable aluminum pans sold at the supermarket.

◆ Metal pans bake evenly and can go right into the freezer. Bake your cake of choice and let it cool in the pan on a wire rack. This will take about thirty minutes.

◆ Frost the cake, then refrigerate it, uncovered, to let the frosting set, about twenty minutes.

◆ Wrap the pan in heavy-duty aluminum foil. If you have an acidic frosting, such as chocolate or lemon, cover the chilled frosting first with waxed paper or cover the pan with a snap-on plastic lid and then wrap the pan with foil. Place the pan in the freezer.

◆ The cakes can store in the freezer for up to six months. The recommended storage time really depends on the type of cake. The more dense and sturdy the cake, the better and longer it will keep frozen.

◆ Remove the pans from the freezer to the kitchen counter to let the cakes thaw. When partially thawed, remove the aluminum foil and precut the servings with a long sharp knife. You will make a neater cut if the cake is still a little frozen. Place the foil back over the pan so that the cake is partially covered, and let the cake continue to thaw completely.

2. Place the cake mix, lemon gelatin, orange juice, oil, and eggs in a large mixing bowl and beat with an electric mixer on low speed until the ingredients are incorporated, 30 seconds. Stop the machine and scrape down the side of the bowl with a rubber spatula. Increase the mixer speed to medium and beat until the mixture lightens and is smooth, about 1½ minutes longer, scraping down the side of the bowl again if needed. Pour the batter into the prepared cake pan, smoothing the top with the rubber spatula, and place the pan in the oven.

3. Bake the cake until it just starts to pull away from the sides of the pan and the top springs back when lightly pressed with a finger, 32 to 37 minutes. If the cake becomes too brown as it bakes, lightly tent it with aluminum foil.

4. While the cake bakes, make the glaze: Rinse the lemon and pat it dry with paper towels. Grate enough zest to measure 2 teaspoons. Cut the lemon in half and squeeze about 3 tablespoons of lemon juice into a small microwave-safe glass bowl. Place the bowl in a microwave oven and microwave on high power for 20 to 30 seconds to warm. Whisk in the confectioners' sugar until smooth.

5. Remove the cake from the oven. Using a wooden skewer or chopstick, poke holes in the hot cake. Slowly spoon the glaze over the top of the cake so it has a chance to sink down into the holes. Slice the cake and serve it warm.

Keep It Fresh! Store this cake, covered with plastic wrap or aluminum foil, at room temperature for up to four days. Or cut the cake into pieces and freeze them in a plastic container with a tight-fitting lid for up to three months. Let the cake thaw overnight on the counter before serving.

Lemon Streusel Cake

serves:
16 to 20

prep:
30 minutes

bake:
30 to 35 minutes

cool:
20 minutes

Readers of my newsletter have often sent me in search of recipes, and this was one requested several years ago. It turned out to be a popular recipe, baked coast to coast, and no one was sure of its origin. I have found this cake to be a crowd-pleaser. Take it to a party—it travels well in the pan in which it was baked or it can be cut into pieces and arranged on a platter. It's very lemony, which I love. For a less intense lemon flavor, use a yellow or vanilla cake mix.

For the cake and streusel topping

½ cup finely chopped pecans
Vegetable oil spray, for misting the pan
Flour, for dusting the pan
1 package (18.25 ounces) plain lemon or yellow cake mix
1 package (3.4 ounces) lemon instant pudding mix
8 tablespoons (1 stick) butter, cold
¾ cup milk
2 large eggs

For the lemon cream cheese topping

1 small lemon
1 package (8 ounces) reduced-fat cream cheese, at room temperature
¼ cup granulated sugar

For the glaze

1 cup confectioners' sugar, sifted
1 to 2 tablespoons milk

1. Make the cake and streusel topping: Place a rack in the center of the oven and preheat the oven to 350°F. Place the pecans in a baking pan and toast them in the oven while it preheats until they are lightly browned, 3 to 4 minutes.

2. Lightly mist a 13 by 9–inch metal cake pan with vegetable oil spray, then dust it with flour. Shake out the excess flour and set the pan aside.

3. Remove the toasted pecans from the oven, let them cool, then set them aside for the streusel topping. Leave the oven on.

4. Place the cake mix and pudding mix in a medium-size bowl. Stir with a wire whisk or spoon until well combined. Cut the butter into small chunks and place them in the bowl with the cake mixture. Using a pastry blender or two dinner knives, blend in the butter until crumbly. Measure out 1 cup of the cake mix mixture for the streusel topping and place it in a small bowl. Stir in the toasted pecans and set this bowl aside.

5. Add the ¾ cup of milk and the eggs to the medium-size bowl with the cake mixture and beat with an electric mixer on low speed until the ingredients are incorporated, 30 seconds. Stop the machine and scrape down the side of the bowl with a rubber spatula. Increase the mixer speed to medium and beat for 1½ to 2 minutes longer, scraping down the side of the bowl again if needed. The batter will be thick. Pour the batter into the prepared cake pan and spread it evenly to the sides of the pan with the rubber spatula. Set the pan aside.

Recipe Reminders

MADE FOR

PREP NOTES

DON'T FORGET

SPECIAL TOUCHES

6. Make the lemon cream cheese topping: Rinse and pat the lemon dry with paper towels. Grate enough zest to measure 1 teaspoon and place it in a medium-size bowl. Cut the lemon in half and squeeze 1 tablespoon of lemon juice. Add the cream cheese and granulated sugar and beat with an electric mixer on medium speed until the topping is well combined and fluffy, 1 to 1½ minutes.

7. Using a teaspoon, dollop small amounts of the lemon cream cheese topping on top of the cake batter. Using the rubber spatula, spread the dollops together so you form a thin layer of the topping evenly over the batter.

8. Sprinkle the reserved streusel topping over the cream cheese topping. Place the cake pan in the oven. Bake the cake until it just starts to pull away from the sides of the pan and the top springs back when lightly pressed with a finger, 30 to 35 minutes. Transfer the cake pan to a wire rack and let the cake cool to room temperature, 20 minutes.

9. Make the glaze: Place the confectioners' sugar and 1 tablespoon of milk in a small bowl. Stir with a wire whisk, adding up to 1 more tablespoon of milk, until the glaze is smooth. Drizzle the glaze over the cooled cake and serve.

Keep It Fresh! Store this cake, covered with plastic wrap or aluminum foil, at room temperature for up to four days or for up to one week in the refrigerator. Freeze the cake in the pan, covered with aluminum foil, for up to three months. Let the cake thaw overnight on the counter before serving.

Lemon Curd Icebox Cake

I'VE SHARED THIS RECIPE in my newsletter, and it bears repeating here because few cakes are as delicious or simple. You begin with a lemon or yellow cake mix and add the usual ingredients plus lemon curd, an intense and creamy condiment found on supermarket shelves with the jams and jellies. Serve this on summer nights with a spoonful of fresh raspberries alongside. It needs to be stored in the refrigerator, or what used to be called the icebox, hence the name. Thanks to the Desperation Dinner gals—Beverly Mills and Alicia Ross—for originally publishing this recipe in their newspaper column.

serves:
16 to 20

prep:
15 minutes

bake:
30 to 35 minutes

cool:
1 hour and
25 minutes

For the cake

Vegetable oil spray, for misting the pan
Flour, for dusting the pan
1 package (18.25 ounces) plain lemon or yellow cake mix
1⅓ cups water
⅓ cup lemon curd (from a 10-ounce jar)
⅓ cup vegetable oil
3 large eggs

For the topping

1 cup heavy (whipping) cream, chilled (see Note)
1 tablespoon confectioners' sugar
⅔ cup lemon curd, or the remainder from the 10-ounce jar (see above)

Recipe Reminders

MADE FOR

PREP NOTES

DON'T FORGET

SPECIAL TOUCHES

1. Make the cake: Place a rack in the center of the oven and preheat the oven to 350°F. Lightly mist a 13 by 9–inch metal cake pan with vegetable oil spray, then dust it with flour. Shake out the excess flour and set the pan aside.

2. Place the cake mix, water, ⅓ cup of lemon curd, oil, and eggs in a large mixing bowl and beat with an electric mixer on low speed until the ingredients are incorporated, 30 seconds. Stop the machine and scrape down the side of the bowl with a rubber spatula. Increase the mixer speed to medium and beat until the batter is thick and well combined, 1½ minutes longer, scraping down the side of the bowl again if needed. Pour the batter into the prepared cake pan, smoothing the top with the rubber spatula, and place the pan in the oven.

3. Bake the cake until the top has turned golden brown and springs back when lightly pressed with a finger, 30 to 35 minutes. Transfer the cake pan to a wire rack and let the cake cool to room temperature, 25 minutes.

4. Make the topping: Place a clean large mixing bowl and electric mixer beaters in the refrigerator to chill.

5. When the cake has cooled, remove the bowl and beaters from the refrigerator. Beat the cream on high speed until stiff peaks form, 2 minutes. Fold in the confectioners' sugar and the ⅔ cup of lemon curd. Spoon the topping on top of the cooled cake and spread it out evenly with a rubber spatula. Cover the cake pan with plastic wrap or the plastic top of the pan and place the cake in the refrigerator to chill for at least 1 hour before slicing and serving the cake.

Keep It Fresh! Store this cake, covered with plastic wrap or the plastic lid of the cake pan, in the refrigerator for up to five days. Freeze the unfrosted cake in the pan, covered with aluminum foil, for up to three months. Let the cake thaw overnight on the counter, then spread the top evenly with the topping and serve.

Note: If you are in a big hurry, substitute 8 ounces of thawed frozen whipped topping for the whipped cream and confectioners' sugar.

A Patriotic Lemon Flag Cake

Bake the Lemon Curd Icebox Cake as suggested. After letting it cool in the pan for fifteen minutes, you can turn the cake out of the pan onto a long platter, or you can leave it in the pan and let it cool completely, twenty minutes. Either way, frost the cooled cake with the topping and chill. Then, no more than one hour before serving, here's how to turn it into a flag cake.

You'll need:

- *1 frosted Lemon Curd Icebox Cake (page 265)*
- *2 pints fresh strawberries, rinsed, patted dry, hulled, and sliced lengthwise*
- *1 pint fresh blueberries, rinsed and patted dry*

Make sure the cake is frosted evenly. Arrange 50 blueberries in the top left hand corner of the cake to resemble the 50 stars by making 6 rows of 8 blueberries and squeezing 2 more blueberries in. Then, arrange the strawberries in horizontal rows for the red stripes, leaving a space of the cream topping in between each of the rows. If there are leftover strawberries, serve them on the side. Slice the cake and serve.

Pink Lemonade Party Cake

serves:
16 to 20

prep:
20 minutes

bake:
30 to 35 minutes

cool:
2 hours and 15 minutes

SAY **"PINK LEMONADE PARTY CAKE"** out loud and you have to smile. It makes me think of those backyard birthday parties we used to host when our kids were small. We'd invite our family, a few neighbors, a few of our girls' friends, turn on the sprinkler and let the girls run around in bathing suits, or have an egg hunt or a scavenger hunt, and then wind up with cake and ice cream. This cake begins with frozen pink lemonade concentrate. Jerrie Chilcote of Nashville shared this recipe. Bake it and serve it right from the pan, with fresh strawberries on the side.

For the cake

Vegetable oil spray, for misting the pan
Flour, for dusting the pan
1 package (18.25 ounces) lemon cake mix, plain or with pudding
1¼ cups water
⅓ cup vegetable oil
3 large eggs

For the glaze and topping

1 can (6 ounces) frozen pink lemonade concentrate, thawed (see Note)
¾ cup confectioners' sugar, sifted
Sweetened Whipped Cream (see page 489)

1. Make the cake: Place a rack in the center of the oven and preheat the oven to 350°F. Lightly mist a 13 by 9–inch metal cake pan with vegetable oil spray, then dust it with flour. Shake out the excess flour and set the pan aside.

2. Place the cake mix, water, oil, and eggs in a large mixing bowl and beat with an electric mixer on low speed until the ingredients are incorporated, 30 seconds. Stop the machine and scrape down the side of the bowl with a rubber spatula. Increase the mixer speed to medium and beat until the batter lightens, 2 minutes longer, scraping down the side of the bowl again if needed. Pour the batter into the prepared cake pan, smoothing the top with the rubber spatula, and place the pan in the oven.

3. Bake the cake until the top springs back when lightly pressed with a finger, 30 to 35 minutes. Transfer the cake pan to a wire rack and let the cake cool for 15 minutes.

4. Make the glaze: Place the lemonade concentrate and confectioners' sugar in a small bowl and whisk until smooth. Poke a long-tined fork into the top of the warm cake every ½ inch, wiping the fork occasionally to remove crumbs. Drizzle the lemonade glaze over the top of the cake.

5. Cover the cake pan with plastic wrap and place the cake in the refrigerator to chill for 2 hours. Remove the pan from the refrigerator and spread the Sweetened Whipped Cream over the top. Slice the cake, and serve.

Keep It Fresh! Store this cake, covered with plastic wrap, in the refrigerator for up to five days. Freeze the unfrosted cake in the pan, covered with aluminum foil, for up to three months. Let the cake thaw on the counter before spreading the Sweetened Whipped Cream over the top and serving.

Note: It is sometimes hard to find a 6-ounce can of pink lemonade concentrate. You can buy a 12-ounce can, thaw it, and just use ¾ cup.

Recipe Reminders

MADE FOR

PREP NOTES

DON'T FORGET

SPECIAL TOUCHES

Mandarin Orange Cake with Sherry Cream Cheese Frosting

serves:
16 to 20

prep:
20 minutes

bake:
30 to 35 minutes

cool:
20 minutes

ONE OF MY FAVORITE WAYS to doctor up a cake mix is to add fruit. After all, this combination turns out the famous strawberry cake, and the banana cake, and applesauce cake, and believe it or not, a pretty incredible mandarin orange cake. I always have a can of mandarin oranges in the pantry, making this cake doable at the drop of a hat. The oranges and the oil make it incredibly moist, and to boost the flavor I add a tablespoon of sherry, but you could just as easily use vanilla. Thanks to all the readers who have sent me their versions of mandarin orange cakes through the years. This recipe is a product of them all, with my added touches.

For the cake

Vegetable oil spray, for misting the pan
Flour, for dusting the pan
1 can (15 ounces) mandarin oranges packed in juice
1 package (18.25 ounces) plain yellow or vanilla cake mix
½ cup vegetable oil
3 large eggs
1 tablespoon medium-dry sherry or pure vanilla extract

How to Make the Best Cream Cheese Frosting

Cream cheese frosting is great for many reasons—it's as creamy as its name suggests, it's not as sweet as buttercream frosting, and it's a snap to prepare. After making it hundreds of times while testing recipes for my books, I've come to some conclusions that should help you in the kitchen.

1. Reduced-fat cream cheese seems to be moister than regular cream cheese. But if I am making a plain cream cheese frosting I will use either one—whichever is in the refrigerator. However, if I am adding fruit to the frosting, as in strawberry cream cheese or pineapple cream cheese frosting, I'll use regular cream cheese so the frosting will firm up nicely.

2. Depending on the cake and my mood, I often add a half stick of butter to a package of cream cheese or a half package of cream cheese to a stick of butter, to lighten up the frosting. By making this simple adjustment you can create a frosting that is either more cream cheese–like in texture or more buttery and fluffy.

3. Always place your cream cheese and butter on the counter so they can come to room temperature before you beat them. Allow your liquids to come to room temperature, too.

4. If you have no choice, place the unwrapped cream cheese on a plate in the microwave on high power until soft, 20 to 30 seconds.

5. After frosting a cake with cream cheese frosting, whether it is a sheet cake or a layer cake, place the cake in the refrigerator to chill so the frosting has time to set; it will take about 20 minutes. Then you can cover the pan or the cake with aluminum foil or place it in a cake saver and take it with you. This makes slicing easier, too.

For the sherry cream cheese frosting

8 tablespoons (1 stick) butter, at room temperature
4 ounces cream cheese, at room temperature
2 tablespoons medium-dry sherry
3½ cups confectioners' sugar, sifted

1. Make the cake: Place a rack in the center of the oven and preheat the oven to 350°F. Lightly mist a 13 by 9–inch metal cake

Recipe Reminders

MADE FOR

PREP NOTES

DON'T FORGET

SPECIAL TOUCHES

pan with vegetable oil spray, then dust it with flour. Shake out the excess flour and set the pan aside.

2. Drain the mandarin oranges and reserve ½ cup of the juice. Place the mandarin oranges, the ½ cup of juice, cake mix, oil, eggs, and 1 tablespoon of sherry in a large mixing bowl and beat with an electric mixer on low speed until the ingredients are incorporated, 30 seconds. Stop the machine and scrape down the side of the bowl with a rubber spatula. Increase the mixer speed to medium and beat until the mixture lightens and the oranges are nearly smooth, about 1½ minutes longer, scraping down the side of the bowl again if needed. Pour the batter into the prepared cake pan, smoothing the top with the rubber spatula, and place the pan in the oven.

3. Bake the cake until it is golden brown and the top springs back when lightly pressed with a finger, 30 to 35 minutes. Transfer the cake pan to a wire rack and let the cake cool for about 20 minutes.

4. While the cake cools, make the sherry cream cheese frosting. Place the butter and cream cheese in a large mixing bowl and beat with an electric mixer on low speed until creamy, 30 seconds. Add the 2 tablespoons of sherry and the confectioners' sugar and beat on low speed until the sugar is incorporated, then increase the mixer speed to medium and beat until the frosting is smooth, creamy, and lightened, 2 to 3 minutes longer. Spread the frosting evenly over the top of the cooled cake and serve.

Keep It Fresh! Store this cake, covered with plastic wrap or aluminum foil, at room temperature for one day or for up to one week in the refrigerator. Freeze the cake in the pan, covered with aluminum foil, for up to three months. Let the cake thaw overnight on the counter before serving.

Orange Cranberry Coffee Cake

I PICTURE MY BRAIN covered with little yellow Post-it Notes. So when it comes to developing a new recipe such as this, I just refer to those notes. There's one on which I've commented on the flavor of fresh orange zest and another on how well whole-berry cranberry sauce holds together while baking. The result here is a coffee cake using those compatible ingredients and an easy method. It reminds me of a cranberry relish I used to make for Thanksgiving, but it is a lot more delicious with a hot cup of tea and should be baked year round.

serves:
16 to 20

prep:
20 minutes

bake:
55 to 60 minutes

cool:
30 minutes

For the cake

Vegetable oil spray, for misting the pan
Flour, for dusting the pan
1 package (18.5 ounces) plain butter recipe golden cake mix
½ cup granulated sugar
1 cup sour cream
¾ cup vegetable oil
4 large eggs
1 teaspoon grated orange zest
½ teaspoon pure almond extract
1 can (16 ounces) whole berry cranberry sauce

For the glaze

1 cup confectioners' sugar, sifted
2 tablespoons fresh orange juice
½ teaspoon grated orange zest

Recipe Reminders

MADE FOR

PREP NOTES

DON'T FORGET

SPECIAL TOUCHES

1. Make the cake: Place a rack in the center of the oven and preheat the oven to 325°F. Lightly mist a 13 by 9–inch metal cake pan with vegetable oil spray, then dust it with flour. Shake out the excess flour and set the pan aside.

2. Place the cake mix, granulated sugar, sour cream, oil, eggs, 1 teaspoon orange zest, and almond extract in a large mixing bowl and beat with an electric mixer on low speed until the ingredients are incorporated, 30 seconds. Stop the machine and scrape down the side of the bowl with a rubber spatula. Increase the mixer speed to medium and beat until the mixture lightens and is smooth, about 1½ minutes longer, scraping down the side of the bowl again if needed. Pour half of the cake batter into the prepared cake pan, smoothing the top with the rubber spatula. Dollop half of the cranberry sauce on top of the cake batter by the tablespoon. Pour the remaining cake batter on top of the cranberry sauce, smoothing the top with the rubber spatula. Dollop the remaining cranberry sauce evenly on top of the cake batter. Place the pan in the oven.

3. Bake the cake until it is golden brown and the top springs back when lightly pressed with a finger, 55 to 60 minutes. Transfer the cake pan to a wire rack and let the cake cool for about 20 minutes.

4. Make the glaze: Place the confectioners' sugar, orange juice, and ½ teaspoon of orange zest in a small bowl. Whisk until smooth. Drizzle the glaze over the top of the cake. Let the glaze set for 10 minutes, then cut the cake into serving pieces.

Keep It Fresh! Store this cake, covered with plastic wrap, at room temperature for up to three days or for up to one week in the refrigerator. Freeze the cake in the pan, wrapped in waxed paper or plastic wrap and then covered with aluminum foil, for up to three months. Let the cake thaw overnight on the counter before serving.

Chunky Applesauce Cake with Caramel Glaze

ONE OF MY FAVORITE INGREDIENTS to use in baking is applesauce. It easily replaces some of the oil and makes a very moist cake. In this cake, applesauce is the star, contributing flavor, moistness, and texture. The cake is perfect for fall, to bake and serve for dessert after you've grilled pork tenderloins. For a crunchy bottom, sprinkle a half cup of finely chopped pecans in the empty pan (instead of on top of the cake as a garnish). Add a cup of shredded carrots to the batter for a carrot and applesauce cake. The caramel glaze is my favorite topper but if you prefer a creamy frosting go with Cream Cheese Frosting (page 471).

serves:
16 to 20

prep:
15 minutes

bake:
45 to 50 minutes

cool:
25 minutes

Vegetable oil spray, for misting the pan
Flour, for dusting the pan
1 package (18.25 ounces) plain spice cake mix
2 cups chunky sweetened applesauce
½ cup vegetable oil
½ cup buttermilk or water
3 large eggs
¼ teaspoon ground nutmeg
2 batches of Caramel Glaze (page 487)
½ cup chopped toasted walnuts or pecans (optional; page 204), for garnish

Recipe Reminders

MADE FOR

PREP NOTES

DON'T FORGET

SPECIAL TOUCHES

1. Place a rack in the center of the oven and preheat the oven to 350°F. Lightly mist a 13 by 9–inch metal cake pan with vegetable oil spray, then dust it with flour. Shake out the excess flour and set the pan aside.

2. Place the cake mix, applesauce, oil, buttermilk, eggs, and nutmeg in a large mixing bowl and beat with an electric mixer on low speed until the ingredients are incorporated, 30 seconds. Stop the machine and scrape down the side of the bowl with a rubber spatula. Increase the mixer speed to medium and beat until the mixture lightens and is smooth, about 1½ minutes longer, scraping down the side of the bowl again if needed. Pour the batter into the prepared cake pan, smoothing the top with the rubber spatula, and place the pan in the oven.

3. Bake the cake until it is light brown and the top springs back when lightly pressed with a finger, 45 to 50 minutes. Transfer the cake pan to a wire rack and let the cake sit until nearly cool, about 20 minutes.

4. Make the Caramel Glaze.

5. Pour the warm glaze over the cake. If desired, scatter the nuts over the top of the cake. Let the glaze set for 5 minutes before slicing the cake.

Keep It Fresh! Store this cake, covered with aluminum foil or in a cake saver, at room temperature for up to three days or for up to one week in the refrigerator. Freeze the cake in the pan, covered with aluminum foil, for up to three months. Let the cake thaw overnight on the counter before serving.

Sour Cream and Cinnamon Raisin Cake

WHO CAN RESIST sour cream coffee cake? I love the plain simple goodness of this cake, how it stays moist on the counter for a few days, and how people think I've gone to far more trouble than is really the case! Have fun substituting dried cranberries for the raisins in the filling and varying the glaze a bit to jazz it up. For a pretty crosshatch pattern, I drizzle the glaze in one direction, then turn the pan and drizzle it in the other.

serves:
16 to 20

prep:
20 minutes

bake:
50 to 55 minutes

cool:
30 minutes

For the cake

Vegetable oil spray, for misting the pan
Flour, for dusting the pan
1 package (18.5 ounces) plain butter recipe golden cake mix
⅓ cup granulated sugar
1 cup sour cream
¾ cup vegetable oil
4 large eggs
1 teaspoon pure vanilla extract
1 teaspoon grated lemon zest
½ cup finely chopped pecans
½ cup raisins (see Note)
4 teaspoons ground cinnamon

For the glaze

1 cup confectioners' sugar, sifted
1 tablespoon milk
2 to 3 teaspoons fresh lemon juice

1. Make the cake: Place a rack in the center of the oven and preheat the oven to 325°F. Lightly mist a 13 by 9–inch metal cake pan with vegetable oil spray, then dust it with flour. Shake out the excess flour and set the pan aside.

2. Place the cake mix, granulated sugar, sour cream, oil, eggs, vanilla, and lemon zest in a large mixing bowl and beat with an electric mixer on low speed until the ingredients are incorporated, 30 seconds. Stop the machine and scrape down the side of the bowl with a rubber spatula. Increase the mixer speed to medium and beat until the mixture lightens and is smooth, about 1½ minutes longer, scraping down the side of the bowl again if needed. Pour half of the cake batter into the prepared cake pan, smoothing the top with a rubber spatula.

3. Place the pecans, raisins, and cinnamon in a small bowl and stir to combine. Spoon this mixture on top of the batter in the cake pan, distributing it evenly. Pour the remaining batter on top of the nut mixture, smoothing the top with a rubber spatula. It does not matter if the nut and raisin mixture is visible from the top of the pan. Place the pan in the oven.

4. Bake the cake until it is golden brown and the top springs back when lightly pressed with a finger, 50 to 55 minutes. Transfer the cake pan to a wire rack and let the cake cool, about 20 minutes.

5. Make the glaze: Place the confectioners' sugar, milk, and 2 teaspoons of lemon juice in a small bowl. Whisk, adding up to 1 more teaspoon of lemon juice, until the glaze is smooth. Drizzle the glaze over the top of the cake. Let the glaze set for 10 minutes, then cut the cake into serving pieces.

Keep It Fresh! Store this cake, covered with plastic wrap or aluminum foil, at room temperature for up to three days or for up to one week in the refrigerator. Freeze the cake in the pan, covered with aluminum foil, for up to three months. Let the cake thaw overnight on the counter before serving.

Note: Look for baking raisins, packaged raisins that have been softened in water so that when you add them to baked goods they turn out soft and chewy. If you can't find any raisins labeled "baking raisins" you can simulate their texture by adding a little water to your raisins and then placing them in the microwave oven on high power until they plump up and soften, 20 seconds.

Recipe Reminders

MADE FOR

____

____

____

____

PREP NOTES

____

____

____

____

DON'T FORGET

____

____

____

____

SPECIAL TOUCHES

____

____

____

____

____

____

____

____

____

Hummingbird Cake with Cream Cheese Frosting

serves:
16 to 20

prep:
25 minutes

bake:
35 to 40 minutes

cool:
30 minutes

Plan Ahead to Bake Banana Cakes

As with all banana cakes, the riper the banana the better the flavor of the cake. So let those bananas get really dark and ripe before making this cake. To speed up the bananas' ripening, place them in a closed paper bag. The length of time depends on how much ripening needs to happen—anywhere from overnight to a day or two.

For ten years everyone has been humming over my Hummingbird Cake, a moist and rich banana and pineapple offering popular in the South. I haven't met anyone who isn't fond of this cake. But, since layer cakes topped with cream cheese frostings are messy to tote in warm weather, here's a variation made as a sheet cake. Bake it in a 13 by 9–inch pan, then frost it and put it in the refrigerator until you are ready to travel or entertain guests. (If you'd rather make a layer cake, pour the batter into two 9-inch round pans and bake it for 30 to 35 minutes.)

½ cup chopped pecans
Vegetable oil spray, for misting the pan
Flour, for dusting the pan
1 package (18.25 ounces) plain yellow or vanilla cake mix
1 can (8 ounces) crushed pineapple packed in juice, undrained
1 cup mashed bananas (from 2 to 3 very ripe bananas)
½ cup water
½ cup vegetable oil
3 large eggs
1 teaspoon pure vanilla extract
1 teaspoon ground cinnamon
Cream Cheese Frosting (make the amount for a sheet cake; page 471)

1. Place a rack in the center of the oven and preheat the oven to 350°F. Place the pecans in a small baking pan and toast them in the oven while it preheats until they are deep brown and fragrant, 3 to 5 minutes.

2. Lightly mist a 13 by 9–inch metal cake pan with vegetable oil spray, then dust it with flour. Shake out the excess flour and set the pan aside.

3. Remove the toasted pecans from the oven, let them cool, then set them aside for the garnish. Leave the oven on.

4. Place the cake mix, pineapple with its juice, mashed bananas, water, oil, eggs, vanilla, and cinnamon in a large mixing bowl and beat with an electric mixer on low speed until incorporated, 30 seconds. Stop the machine and scrape down the side of the bowl with a rubber spatula. Increase the mixer speed to medium and beat until the mixture lightens and is smooth, about 1½ minutes longer, scraping down the side of the bowl again if needed. Pour the batter into the prepared cake pan, smoothing the top with the rubber spatula, and place in the oven.

5. Bake the cake until it is golden brown and the top springs back when lightly pressed with a finger, 35 to 40 minutes. Transfer the cake pan to a wire rack and let the cake cool completely, about 30 minutes.

6. Meanwhile, make the Cream Cheese Frosting. When the cake has cooled, spread the frosting over the top and scatter the toasted pecans over the frosting. Cut the cake into serving pieces.

Keep It Fresh! Store this cake, covered with plastic wrap or aluminum foil, at room temperature for one day or for up to one week in the refrigerator. Freeze the cake in the pan, covered with aluminum foil, for up to three months. Let the cake thaw overnight on the counter before serving.

Recipe Reminders

MADE FOR

____

____

____

____

PREP NOTES

____

____

____

____

DON'T FORGET

____

____

____

____

SPECIAL TOUCHES

____

____

____

____

____

____

____

____

____

Banana Chocolate Chip Cake

serves:
16 to 20

prep:
20 minutes

bake:
43 to 48 minutes

cool:
20 minutes

SUSAN POWELL of Buford, Georgia, wrote asking me to help her make a particular kind of banana cake. It seems her mother had clipped a recipe many years ago for a Bundt cake that began with a banana cake mix batter to which you folded in chocolate chips and pecans. Unable to find a banana mix, Susan wanted to know if I had ideas on how to make the cake without it. I used a yellow cake mix and added fresh bananas. And I baked this easy cake in a 13 by 9–inch pan, which makes it just right for dusting with confectioners' sugar and toting to the office, to a meeting, or to the lake. You can also bake this batter in a Bundt pan, but allow 50 to 55 minutes baking time.

Vegetable oil spray, for misting the pan
Flour, for dusting the pan
1 cup mashed bananas (from 2 to 3 very ripe bananas)
1 package (18.25 ounces) plain yellow or vanilla cake mix
¼ cup granulated sugar
¾ cup vegetable oil
½ cup sour cream
4 large eggs
2 teaspoons pure vanilla extract
1 cup (6 ounces) miniature semisweet chocolate chips
¾ cup finely chopped pecans
2 teaspoons confectioners' sugar, for dusting

1. Place a rack in the center of the oven and preheat the oven to 350°F. Lightly mist a 13 by 9–inch metal cake pan with vegetable oil spray, then dust it with flour. Shake out the excess flour and set the pan aside.

2. Place the mashed bananas, cake mix, granulated sugar, oil, sour cream, eggs, and vanilla in a large mixing bowl and beat with an electric mixer on low speed until the ingredients are incorporated, 30 seconds. Stop the machine and scrape down the side of the bowl with a rubber spatula. Increase the mixer speed to medium and beat until the mixture lightens and is smooth, about 1½ minutes longer, scraping down the side of the bowl again if needed. Fold in the chocolate chips. Pour the batter into the prepared cake pan, smoothing the top with the rubber spatula. Scatter the pecans evenly over the top and place the pan in the oven.

3. Bake the cake until it is deeply golden brown and the top springs back when lightly pressed with a finger, 43 to 48 minutes. Remove the cake from the oven and immediately sift the confectioners' sugar over the top so that it melts and forms a glaze. Let the cake cool for 20 minutes, then slice it and serve while still a little warm.

Keep It Fresh! Store this cake, covered with plastic wrap or aluminum foil, at room temperature for up to three days or for up to one week in the refrigerator. Freeze the cake in the pan, covered with aluminum foil, for up to three months. Let the cake thaw overnight on the counter before serving.

Recipe Reminders

MADE FOR

PREP NOTES

DON'T FORGET

SPECIAL TOUCHES

Pineapple Dump Cake

serves:
16 to 20

prep:
10 minutes

bake:
40 to 45 minutes

PLACE THIS CAKE in the oven before you toss dinner together and it will be hot and bubbly as soon as the dinner dishes have been cleared from the table. This is a dandy dessert to tote to potluck suppers, too, as it feeds so many. Leftovers can be stored in the refrigerator and reheated in a warm oven. Although I usually say to bake sheet cakes in metal pans, this cake is so packed with acidic fruit that it needs to be baked in a glass pan. Sometimes acidic fruits cause aluminum pans to pit and discolor.

Vegetable oil spray, for misting the pan
Flour, for dusting the pan
2 cans (20 ounces each) crushed pineapple, one drained and one undrained
1 package (18.25 ounces) plain white or yellow cake mix
8 tablespoons (1 stick) butter, cut into ½-inch pieces
½ teaspoon ground cinnamon
1 cup chopped pecans or almonds
Vanilla ice cream or whipped cream, for serving

Add "Ta-Da" to Dump Cake

Vary the dump cake spices by adding nutmeg instead of cinnamon. For a grown-up twist, serve this with rum raisin ice cream.

1. Place a rack in the center of the oven and preheat the oven to 350°F. Lightly mist a 13 by 9–inch glass baking pan with vegetable oil spray, then dust it with flour. Shake out the excess flour and set the pan aside.

2. Spread the pineapple on the bottom of the prepared cake pan. Sprinkle the cake mix evenly over the pineapple. Dot the cake mix evenly with the butter and sprinkle the cinnamon and the pecans or almonds over it. Place the pan in the oven.

3. Bake the cake until it is golden and the fruit begins to bubble around the edges, 40 to 45 minutes. Remove the pan from the oven and scoop the warm cake into bowls along with ice cream or whipped cream.

Keep It Fresh! Store this cake, covered with plastic wrap, at room temperature for up to three days or for up to one week in the refrigerator. To reheat it, cover the cake lightly with aluminum foil and place it in a 350°F oven for 20 minutes. The cake does not freeze well.

Recipe Reminders

MADE FOR

PREP NOTES

DON'T FORGET

SPECIAL TOUCHES

Pineapple Upside-Down Cake

serves:
16 to 20

prep:
20 minutes

bake:
43 to 48 minutes

cool:
12 to 17 minutes

CHARLOTTE TWARO, who lives in Garfield Heights, Ohio, sent me this recipe several years back. She said it was her signature cake and that she takes it to family reunions and picnics. It is so good that she seldom comes home with leftovers. Easy to tote regardless of the season, a pineapple upside-down cake is low-maintenance. It doesn't need refrigeration or reheating. It doesn't need garnish—the top says it all. And it doesn't expect a lot of oohing and aahing, but the irony is that this simple but spectacular cake gets it.

1 can (20 ounces) pineapple chunks packed in juice
8 tablespoons (1 stick) butter, melted
1 packed cup light brown sugar
½ cup finely chopped pecans or walnuts
1 jar (6 ounces) maraschino cherries, drained (see Note)
1 package (18.25 ounces) yellow or vanilla cake mix with pudding
⅓ cup vegetable oil
3 large eggs
1 teaspoon pure vanilla extract

1. Place a rack in the center of the oven and preheat the oven to 350°F.

2. Open the can of pineapple chunks and pour them into a sieve set over a small bowl to catch the juice. Set aside the pineapple and the juice separately.

3. Place the melted butter and brown sugar in a 13 by 9–inch metal cake pan. Stir them together and spread the mixture evenly over the bottom of the pan. Sprinkle the chopped pecans or walnuts over the butter and sugar mixture. Then, arrange the reserved pineapple chunks and the maraschino cherries on top.

4. Measure ¾ cup of the reserved pineapple juice and place it and the cake mix, oil, eggs, and vanilla in a large mixing bowl. Beat with an electric mixer on low speed until the ingredients are incorporated, 30 seconds. Stop the machine and scrape down the side of the bowl with a rubber spatula. Increase the mixer speed to medium-low and beat until the batter is smooth, 1½ minutes longer, scraping down the side of the bowl again if needed. Pour the batter evenly over the pineapple and cherries and place the pan in the oven.

5. Bake the cake until it is golden brown and the top springs back when lightly pressed with a finger, 43 to 48 minutes. Transfer the cake pan to a wire rack and let the cake cool for 2 to 3 minutes. Run a dinner knife around the edges of the cake and give the pan a good shake to loosen the cake. Invert the cake onto a rectangular serving platter so that it is right side up and serve at once or let it cool for 15 minutes before covering it to tote.

Keep It Fresh! Store this cake, covered with plastic wrap or aluminum foil, at room temperature for up to three days or for up to one week in the refrigerator. Freeze the cake in the pan, covered with aluminum foil, for up to three months. Let the cake thaw on the kitchen counter for 3 to 4 hours or overnight, then lightly cover it with aluminum foil and reheat it in a 350°F oven until warmed through, 20 minutes, before inverting and serving it.

Note: If you have a 10 or 12 ounce jar of maraschino cherries, use half.

Recipe Reminders

MADE FOR

PREP NOTES

DON'T FORGET

SPECIAL TOUCHES

Brandied Peach Upside-Down Cake

serves:
16 to 20

prep:
1 hour

bake:
40 to 45 minutes

cool:
25 minutes

NOT YOUR TYPICAL upside-down cake, this one begins with fresh peaches that are soaked in brandy and spices, then placed on top of a vanilla cake batter, baked, and flipped upside-down before serving. Feel free to increase the amount of nutmeg and ginger in the spiced peach mixture. But, when you have great summer-time peaches you might want to keep the spices minimal so the real peach flavor can come through. As with all coffee cakes and upside-down cakes, this is best served warm.

For the brandied peaches

6 medium-size peaches, rinsed
3 tablespoons brandy or orange juice
¼ teaspoon ground nutmeg
¼ teaspoon ground ginger
1 to 2 teaspoons fresh lemon juice

For the cake

Vegetable oil spray, for misting the pan
Flour, for dusting the pan
Parchment paper, for lining the pan
6 tablespoons (¾ stick) butter
1 cup packed light brown sugar
1 package (18.25 ounces) plain yellow cake mix
½ cup vegetable oil
4 large eggs
4 ounces reduced-fat cream cheese, at room temperature
1¼ cups heavy (whipping) cream, or 1 batch Sweetened Whipped Cream (2 cups; page 489), for garnish

1. Prepare the peaches: Peel, pit, and slice the peaches about ¼-inch thick into a medium-size bowl and sprinkle the brandy, nutmeg, ginger, and lemon juice over them. Gently toss the peaches so that they are well coated. Set the peaches aside for 30 minutes, tossing them 2 to 3 times.

2. Make the cake: Place a rack in the center of the oven and preheat the oven to 350°F. Lightly mist a 13 by 9–inch metal cake pan with vegetable oil spray, then dust it with flour. Shake out the excess flour. Trace the bottom of the pan onto a piece of parchment paper and cut along the trace marks. Place the piece of parchment paper in the bottom of the pan and set the pan aside.

3. Melt the butter in a medium-size saucepan over medium heat. Stir in the brown sugar, continuing to stir constantly until the mixture comes to a low boil. Remove the saucepan from the heat and pour the warm brown sugar mixture over the parchment paper in the cake pan, spreading it evenly to the sides of the pan.

4. After the peaches have stood for 30 minutes, drain the liquid from them through a sieve set over a small bowl. Set the bowl aside, allowing the peaches to continue draining for 5 minutes.

Recipe Reminders

MADE FOR

PREP NOTES

DON'T FORGET

SPECIAL TOUCHES

5. While the peaches are draining, place the cake mix, oil, eggs, and cream cheese in a large mixing bowl. Pour the liquid from the strained peach slices into a measuring cup and add enough water to make 1 cup of liquid. Pour the liquid into the bowl with the cake mix and beat with an electric mixer on low speed until the ingredients are incorporated, 1 minute. Stop the machine and scrape down the side of the bowl with a rubber spatula. Increase the mixer speed to medium and beat for 2 minutes longer, scraping down the side of the bowl again if needed. The batter should look well blended. Set the bowl with the batter aside.

6. Arrange the drained peach slices in the pan on top of the brown sugar mixture, using about 10 peach slices per row. There will be about 6 rows. Next, pour the cake batter over the rows of peaches, spreading it evenly to the edges of the pan. Place the pan in the oven.

7. Bake the cake until it is golden brown and the top springs back when lightly pressed with a finger, 40 to 45 minutes. Transfer the cake pan to a wire rack and let the cake cool for 10 minutes. Run a long, sharp knife around the edges of the cake and give the pan a good shake to loosen the cake. Invert the cake onto a serving platter so that it is right side up. Peel off and discard the parchment paper and let the cake cool for 15 minutes. Slice servings onto dessert plates and pour 1 tablespoon of heavy cream or spoon a dollop of Sweetened Whipped Cream on top of each serving.

Keep It Fresh! Store this cake, covered with plastic wrap or aluminum foil, at room temperature for up to three days or for up to one week in the refrigerator. Freeze the cake in the pan, covered with aluminum foil, for up to three months. Let the cake thaw in the refrigerator overnight before serving.

Brown Sugar and Rhubarb Upside-Down Cake

Because I grew up in the South, rhubarb wasn't something I was accustomed to finding in pies and cakes. So it was a revelation when I finally tasted rhubarb in a pie some twenty years later. It was fantastic—tangy and sharp and just the right complement to brown sugar. If you have fresh rhubarb at your fingertips in the springtime by all means use it in this recipe, but even if you don't, you can find rhubarb in the freezer section of the supermarket. Just remember, you need to drain thawed frozen rhubarb well. For a fun change of pace substitute two cups of sliced strawberries for half of the rhubarb.

serves:
16 to 20

prep:
20 minutes

bake:
43 to 48 minutes

cool:
12 to 18 minutes

1 package (16 ounces; 4 cups) frozen chopped rhubarb
6 tablespoons (¾ stick) butter, melted
1 cup packed light brown sugar
1 teaspoon ground cinnamon
1 package (18.5 ounces) plain butter recipe golden cake mix
1 cup sour cream
3 large eggs
½ cup vegetable oil
⅓ cup water
2 teaspoons pure vanilla extract

1. Thaw the frozen rhubarb in its plastic bag according to the directions on the package. When it has thawed, cut a small hole

Recipe Reminders

MADE FOR

PREP NOTES

DON'T FORGET

SPECIAL TOUCHES

in one corner of the bag and squeeze it to drain out the water. Open the bag and spread the rhubarb out on paper towels to let it drain well. Set the drained rhubarb aside.

2. Place a rack in the center of the oven and preheat the oven to 350°F.

3. Place the melted butter, brown sugar, and cinnamon in a small bowl and stir to combine. Spoon this into a 13 by 9–inch metal cake pan, spreading it in a thin layer over the bottom of the pan. Drop the rhubarb pieces on top of the brown sugar mixture and set the pan aside.

4. Place the cake mix, sour cream, eggs, oil, water, and vanilla in a large mixing bowl and beat with an electric mixer on low speed until the ingredients are incorporated, 30 seconds. Stop the machine and scrape down the side of the bowl with a rubber spatula. Increase the mixer speed to medium-low and beat until the batter is smooth, 1½ minutes longer, scraping down the side of the bowl again if needed. Pour the batter evenly over the rhubarb and place the pan in the oven.

5. Bake the cake until it is golden brown and the top springs back when lightly pressed with a finger, 43 to 48 minutes. Transfer the cake pan to a wire rack and let the cake cool for 2 to 3 minutes. Run a dinner knife around the edges of the cake and give the pan a good shake to loosen the cake. Invert the cake onto a rectangular serving platter so that it is right side up. Let the cake cool for 10 to 15 minutes longer, then serve.

Keep It Fresh! Store this cake, covered with plastic wrap or aluminum foil, at room temperature for up to three days or for up to one week in the refrigerator. Freeze the cake in the pan, covered with aluminum foil, for up to three months. Let the cake thaw overnight in the fridge.

Carrot and Raisin Spice Cake

IN A BIT MORE TIME than it takes to measure two cups of shredded carrots, you can add a spice cake mix, oil, applesauce, and eggs and have a carrot cake baking in the oven. Let the cake cool, dust it with confectioners' sugar, and cut it into squares for an old-fashioned treat. Or top the cake with a cream cheese frosting. Then you could scatter toasted walnuts on top—or maybe pecans or coconut. The choices are endless and up to you!

serves:
16 to 20

prep:
15 minutes

bake:
35 to 40 minutes

cool:
20 to 40 minutes

Vegetable oil spray, for misting the pan
Flour, for dusting the pan
1 package (18.25 ounces) plain spice cake mix
¾ cup vegetable oil
½ cup sweetened applesauce
½ cup water
4 large eggs
2 packed cups shredded carrots
1 cup baking raisins, or 1 cup chopped raisins (see Note)
Cream Cheese Frosting (make the amount for a sheet cake; page 471), or 2 teaspoons confectioners' sugar, sifted

1. Place a rack in the center of the oven and preheat the oven to 350°F. Lightly mist a 13 by 9–inch metal cake pan with vegetable oil spray, then dust it with flour. Shake out the excess flour and set the pan aside.

2. Place the cake mix, oil, applesauce, water, and eggs in a large mixing bowl and beat with an electric mixer on low speed until

Recipe Reminders

MADE FOR

PREP NOTES

DON'T FORGET

SPECIAL TOUCHES

the ingredients are incorporated, 30 seconds. Stop the machine and scrape down the side of the bowl with a rubber spatula. Increase the mixer speed to medium and beat until the batter lightens and is smooth, about 1½ minutes, scraping down the side of the bowl again if needed. Set the batter aside.

3. Place the shredded carrots in a food processor and process in 8 to 10 on-off pulses until the carrots are cut into smaller pieces. Fold the carrots into the batter along with the raisins. Pour the batter into the prepared cake pan, smoothing the top with a rubber spatula, and place the pan in the oven.

4. Bake the cake until it is light brown and the top springs back when lightly pressed with a finger, 35 to 40 minutes. Transfer the cake pan to a wire rack and let the cake sit until nearly cool, about 20 minutes.

5. Make the Cream Cheese Frosting.

6. Spread the frosting smoothly over the top of the cake. To make slicing easier, place the cake in the refrigerator to chill until the frosting sets, 20 minutes. Or let the cake cool completely, 20 minutes longer, and dust it with confectioners' sugar.

Keep It Fresh! Store this cake, covered with plastic wrap or aluminum foil, at room temperature for one day if it is frosted or for up to four days if unfrosted. Or store a frosted or unfrosted cake in the refrigerator for up to one week. Freeze the cake in the pan, covered with aluminum foil, for up to three months. Let the cake thaw overnight on the counter before serving.

Note: Baking raisins are softer than regular raisins and contribute to the cake's moist texture. If you are using regular raisins soften them in a little water in the microwave oven and drain them before adding them to the batter. Or you can chop regular raisins in half before adding them to the batter.

Gingerbread Spice Cake with Lemon Cream Cheese Frosting

WHILE DEVELOPING RECIPES for this book, I'd planned to include a pan of moist gingerbread—the type you'd see in your grandmother's kitchen. And I envisioned it topped with a creamy lemon frosting. To come up with a recipe for that cake took a little experimentation, but it was a delicious exercise, and the result is sure to please your crowd. Yes, it contains both a gingerbread mix and a spice cake mix. And yes, you can have seconds!

serves:
16 to 20

prep:
25 minutes

bake:
40 to 45 minutes

cool:
30 minutes

For the cake

Vegetable oil spray, for misting the pan
Flour, for dusting the pan
1 package (18.25 ounces) plain spice cake mix
1 package (14.5 ounces) gingerbread mix
2 cups buttermilk
1 cup sweetened applesauce
½ cup vegetable oil
⅓ cup molasses
4 large eggs
1 teaspoon ground ginger

For the lemon cream cheese frosting

4 tablespoons (½ stick) butter, at room temperature
4 ounces reduced-fat cream cheese, at room temperature
3 cups confectioners' sugar, sifted
1 heaping teaspoon grated lemon zest (from 1 lemon)

Recipe Reminders

MADE FOR

PREP NOTES

DON'T FORGET

SPECIAL TOUCHES

1. Make the cake: Place a rack in the center of the oven and preheat the oven to 350°F. Lightly mist a 13 by 9–inch metal cake pan with vegetable oil spray, then dust it with flour. Shake out the excess flour and set the pan aside.

2. Place the spice cake mix, gingerbread mix, buttermilk, applesauce, oil, molasses, eggs, and ginger in a large mixing bowl and beat with an electric mixer on low speed until the ingredients are incorporated, 30 seconds. Stop the machine and scrape down the side of the bowl with a rubber spatula. Increase the mixer speed to medium and beat until the mixture lightens and is smooth, about 1½ minutes longer, scraping down the side of the bowl again if needed. Pour the batter into the prepared cake pan, smoothing the top with the rubber spatula, and place the pan in the oven.

3. Bake the cake until the top springs back when lightly pressed with a finger, 40 to 45 minutes. Transfer the cake pan to a wire rack and let the cake sit until nearly cool, about 20 minutes.

4. Make the frosting: Place the butter and cream cheese in a large mixing bowl. Beat with an electric mixer on low speed until creamy, 20 seconds. Add the confectioners' sugar and lemon zest and beat on low speed until combined, 1 minute. Increase the mixer speed to medium-high and beat until the frosting is creamy and light, 1 minute longer. Spread the frosting evenly on top of the cooled cake. To make slicing easier, let the cake rest for 10 minutes before slicing or place it in the refrigerator for 10 minutes.

Keep It Fresh! Store this cake, covered with plastic wrap or aluminum foil, at room temperature for up to three days or for up to one week in the refrigerator. Freeze the cake in the pan, covered with aluminum foil, for up to three months. Let the cake thaw overnight on the counter before serving.

Pumpkin Cranberry Cake

BAKE THIS FESTIVE CAKE when you can find cranberries—fresh or frozen. Jennifer Degler of Lexington, Kentucky, sent this recipe to me a while back. She promised that the cake smells so good baking that "you'll want to lay down and scream!" So I baked the cake, and yes, I will say it smelled of cinnamon and everything that is good and right with this world. Admittedly, I didn't lay down and scream, but the cake was still mighty good!

serves:
16 to 20

prep:
25 minutes

bake:
45 to 50 minutes

cool:
10 minutes

For the streusel topping

½ cup packed light brown sugar
5 tablespoons butter, melted
½ teaspoon ground cinnamon

For the cake

Vegetable oil spray, for misting the pan
Flour, for dusting the pan
2 cups cranberries, fresh or thawed frozen
1 package (18.25 ounces) plain yellow cake mix
1 package (8 ounces) reduced-fat cream cheese, softened
½ cup vegetable oil
½ cup granulated sugar
¼ cup milk
¼ cup water
3 large eggs
1 cup canned pumpkin
2 teaspoons pumpkin pie spice
1 teaspoon ground cinnamon

Recipe Reminders

MADE FOR

PREP NOTES

DON'T FORGET

SPECIAL TOUCHES

1. Make the streusel topping: Place the brown sugar, melted butter, and ½ teaspoon of cinnamon in a small mixing bowl and mix with a fork. Set the streusel topping aside.

2. Make the cake: Place a rack in the center of the oven and preheat the oven to 350°F. Lightly mist a 13 by 9–inch metal cake pan with vegetable oil spray, then dust it with flour. Shake out the excess flour and set the pan aside.

3. If using frozen cranberries, drain them well in a colander. Coarsely chop the cranberries and pat them dry with paper towels. Set the cranberries aside.

4. Place the cake mix, cream cheese, oil, granulated sugar, milk, water, eggs, pumpkin, pumpkin pie spice, and 1 teaspoon of cinnamon in a large mixing bowl and beat with an electric mixer on low speed until the ingredients are incorporated, 30 seconds. Stop the machine and scrape down the side of the bowl with a rubber spatula. Increase the mixer speed to medium and beat until the mixture is smooth, 1½ minutes longer, scraping down the side of the bowl again if needed. Stir in 1 cup of the chopped cranberries.

5. Pour the batter into the prepared cake pan, smooth the top with the rubber spatula, and sprinkle the remaining chopped cranberries on top. Scatter the streusel topping over the cake.

6. Bake the cake until it is golden brown and the top springs back when lightly pressed with a finger, 45 to 50 minutes. Let the cake cool for 10 minutes, then slice it and serve warm.

Keep It Fresh! Store this cake, covered with plastic wrap or aluminum foil, at room temperature for up to four days or for up to one week in the refrigerator. Freeze the cake in the pan, covered with aluminum foil, for up to three months. Let the cake thaw overnight on the counter before serving.

Take This Cake! 10 Festive Cakes to Take with You

You've got to love a cake in a 13 by 9-inch pan because it is always ready to go wherever you're going. These cakes are made for taking.

Craving Cranberries Year Round

Why do we think cranberries have to be limited to cool-weather baking? Just because cranberry season is during the colder months, and often the season is short, doesn't mean you won't crave them come spring. I finally found a store that sells frozen cranberries, which you thaw and use in recipes just like you would if they were fresh. You do need to drain the cranberries well and pat them dry with paper towels before using. This year I'm going to fill resealable plastic bags with fresh cranberries and freeze my own.

Hot Prune Cake with Buttermilk Glaze

serves:
16 to 20

prep:
25 minutes

bake:
42 to 47 minutes

cool:
20 minutes

SIMILAR TO THE PRUNE CAKE in *The Cake Mix Doctor*, this is a sheet cake topped with a rich, old-fashioned glaze from my mother's recipe file. A fresher take on that prune cake, this is made with a spice cake mix and calls for just half a recipe of that legendary glaze.

For the cake

Vegetable oil spray, for misting the pan
Flour, for dusting the pan
1 package (18.25 ounces) plain spice cake mix
Half of a 3.4 ounce package of vanilla instant pudding mix (4 tablespoons)
1 cup water
½ cup sour cream
½ cup vegetable oil
3 large eggs
½ teaspoon ground cinnamon
1½ cups chopped pitted prunes, from 2 cups whole pitted prunes

For the buttermilk glaze

½ cup granulated sugar
¼ cup buttermilk
3 tablespoons butter
2 teaspoons light corn syrup
¼ teaspoon baking soda
¼ teaspoon pure vanilla extract

1. Make the cake: Place a rack in the center of the oven and preheat the oven to 350°F. Lightly mist a 13 by 9–inch metal cake pan with vegetable oil spray, then dust it with flour. Shake out the excess flour and set the pan aside.

2. Place the cake mix, pudding mix, water, sour cream, oil, eggs, and cinnamon in a large mixing bowl and beat with an electric mixer on low speed until the ingredients are incorporated, 30 seconds. Stop the machine and scrape down the side of the bowl with a rubber spatula. Increase the mixer speed to medium and beat for 1½ minutes longer, scraping down the side of the bowl again if needed. The batter should look thick and well blended. Fold in the chopped prunes. Pour the batter into the prepared pan, smoothing the top with the rubber spatula, and place the pan in the oven.

3. Bake the cake until it is golden brown and the top springs back when lightly pressed with a finger, 42 to 47 minutes. Transfer the cake pan to a wire rack to cool for 10 minutes while you make the buttermilk glaze.

4. Make the glaze: Place the granulated sugar, buttermilk, butter, corn syrup, baking soda, and vanilla in a small saucepan over medium heat. Bring to a boil, stirring constantly. The glaze will foam up and thicken as the sugar dissolves and the butter melts, 3 minutes.

5. Poke holes all over the top of the cake with a toothpick or wooden skewer and pour the glaze over the top, spreading it out with a spoon to reach the edges. Let the cake cool for 10 minutes longer before cutting it into squares and serving.

Keep It Fresh! Store this cake, covered with plastic wrap or aluminum foil, at room temperature for up to two days or for up to one week in the refrigerator. Freeze the cake in the pan, covered with aluminum foil, for up to six months. Let the cake thaw overnight on the counter before serving.

Recipe Reminders

MADE FOR

PREP NOTES

DON'T FORGET

SPECIAL TOUCHES

Nancy's Cinnamon Swirl Coffee Cake

serves:
16 to 20

prep:
15 minutes

bake:
40 to 45 minutes

cool:
20 minutes

IN ORDER TO PUT THIS COOKBOOK together, I stashed away ideas and recipes for eight years, and often my method of filing was haphazard at best. I stuck things in a favorite cookbook, in a file in my office, on the computer—various places. This recipe I actually filed. It surprised me when I found it, for my late mother had scribbled it on the back of a bridge score sheet. Her friend Nancy Bradshaw of Nashville had obviously made this coffee cake for a bridge game they played together. And then the memories of a conversation came back to me. My mom and I were standing in the kitchen and she was telling me about this great coffee cake and how I ought to put it my next cookbook. Well, I baked it, my house filled with the wonderful aroma of cinnamon, and my kids said it was the best coffee cake they had ever eaten. Similar to the Honey Bun Cake in the first book, this recipe is a bit simpler, without the glaze. The beauty is that you can make it in two 9-inch square pans: Eat one cake and freeze the second. But for large gatherings bake it in a 13 by 9–inch pan for 50 to 55 minutes.

For the cake

Vegetable oil spray, for misting the pan
Flour, for dusting the pan
1 package (18.5 ounces) plain butter recipe golden cake mix
1 cup sour cream
¾ cup vegetable oil
¼ cup granulated sugar
4 large eggs
1 tablespoon pure vanilla extract

For the topping

½ cup packed light brown sugar
¼ cup finely chopped pecans (optional)
1 tablespoon ground cinnamon

1. Make the cakes: Place a rack in the center of the oven and preheat the oven to 325°F. Lightly mist two 9-inch (or one 13 by 9–inch) metal cake pans with vegetable oil spray, then dust them with flour. Shake out the excess flour and set the pans aside.

2. Place the cake mix, sour cream, oil, granulated sugar, eggs, and vanilla in a large mixing bowl and beat with an electric mixer on low speed until the ingredients are incorporated, 30 seconds. Stop the machine and scrape down the side of the bowl with a rubber spatula. Increase the mixer speed to medium and beat until the mixture lightens and is smooth, 2 minutes longer, scraping down the side of the bowl again if needed. Pour half the cake batter into the 2 prepared cake pans, dividing it evenly between them. Smooth the tops with the rubber spatula.

3. Make the topping: Combine the brown sugar, pecans, if using, and cinnamon in a small bowl. Spoon half of the topping over the batter in the cake pans. Pour the remaining cake batter over the topping in the two cake pans, dividing it evenly between them. Spoon the rest of the topping over the cake batter.

Recipe Reminders

MADE FOR

PREP NOTES

DON'T FORGET

SPECIAL TOUCHES

Gotta Have a Glaze?

Whisk 1 cup of confectioners' sugar with 1 to 2 tablespoons of milk and drizzle this glaze over the cooled cinnamon coffee cakes.

4. Place the pans in the oven side by side. Bake the cakes until they are golden brown and the tops spring back when lightly pressed with a finger, 40 to 45 minutes. Transfer the cake pans to wire racks and let the cakes sit until nearly cool, 20 minutes. Slice and serve the cakes while still a bit warm.

Keep It Fresh! Store these cakes, covered with aluminum foil, at room temperature for up to four days or for up to one week in the refrigerator. Freeze the cakes in the pans, covered with aluminum foil, for up to three months. Let the cakes thaw overnight on the counter before serving.

How to Soften Brown Sugar

Nothing is more frustrating than finding hard brown sugar in the bag or box. You know the routine: You dip the measuring spoon or cup into the bag and it hits the sugar like a rock. I have found that buying brown sugar in resealable plastic bags keeps it soft and fresher longer than in boxes. And if you have leftover brown sugar in a box you should transfer it to a resealable plastic bag for storage to keep it soft and fresh. But that's shoulda, woulda, coulda. How to soften brown sugar that wasn't sealed up and stored airtight?

Place no more than one cup of brown sugar at a time in a microwave-safe glass bowl. Cover the brown sugar with two pieces of wet paper towel. Cover the bowl tightly with plastic wrap. Now place it in the microwave oven on high power for 1½ to 2 minutes. Carefully unwrap the bowl, remove the paper towels, and fluff the brown sugar with a fork. Let the sugar cool, then use it in your cake batter.

Birthday Cake for a Crowd

Here it is, the sheet cake everyone needs when hosting a birthday party for a gaggle of kids or hungry adults! Or if you promise, quite bigheartedly, to tote the birthday cake with you. This is the type of birthday cake we love at our house. It's not covered with decorations—maybe a handful of sugar sprinkles and some birthday candles. But it is big on flavor and memories. The yellow pound cake stays moist for days, and the pan frosting is the most decadent and nostalgic frosting I know.

serves:
16 to 20

prep:
25 minutes

bake:
35 to 40 minutes

cool:
30 minutes

Vegetable oil spray, for misting the pan
Flour, for dusting the pan
1 package (18.25 ounces) plain yellow or vanilla cake mix
1 package (3.4 ounces) vanilla instant pudding mix
1¼ cups milk
½ cup vegetable oil
3 large eggs
1 teaspoon pure vanilla extract
Chocolate Pan Frosting (make the amount for a sheet cake; page 476)
Multicolor sugar sprinkles, birthday candles, and other decorations

Recipe Reminders

MADE FOR

PREP NOTES

DON'T FORGET

SPECIAL TOUCHES

1. Place a rack in the center of the oven and preheat the oven to 350°F. Lightly mist a 13 by 9–inch metal cake pan with vegetable oil spray, then dust it with flour. Shake out the excess flour and set the pan aside.

2. Place the cake mix, pudding mix, milk, oil, eggs, and vanilla extract in a large mixing bowl and beat with an electric mixer on low speed until the ingredients are incorporated, 30 seconds. Stop the machine and scrape down the side of the bowl with a rubber spatula. Increase the mixer speed to medium and beat for 1½ minutes longer, scraping down the side of the bowl again if needed. The batter should look well blended and smooth. Pour the batter into the prepared cake pan, smoothing the top with the rubber spatula, and place the pan in the oven.

3. Bake the cake until it is golden brown and the top springs back when lightly pressed with a finger, 35 to 40 minutes. Transfer the cake pan to a wire rack and let the cake cool completely, 25 minutes.

4. While the cake cools, make the Chocolate Pan Frosting.

5. Pour the warm frosting over the cooled cake and spread it with a long metal spatula so that it is smooth. If you wish, immediately add sugar sprinkles so that they stick to the frosting. Let the frosting set for 5 minutes before slicing the cake.

Keep It Fresh! Store this cake, covered with aluminum foil, at room temperature for up to four days or for up to one week in the refrigerator. Freeze the cake in the pan, covered with aluminum foil, for up to three months. Let the cake thaw overnight on the counter before serving.

Dress Up Your Sheet Cake

The 13 by 9-inch pan may be the best-loved pan in the kitchen, and there's no doubting its usefulness, sturdiness, and ability to travel to and fro to parties. But it can be a bit boring to look at, especially when the cake stays in the pan. Here are some simple ways you can dress up a sheet cake.

1. Invert. Don't leave the cake in the pan—invert it! Run a knife around the edges as the cake cools and, after fifteen to twenty minutes, give the pan a good shake to loosen it. Turn the pan over to invert the cake onto a rectangular platter to finish cooling. Then, frost, garnish, and serve.

2. Frost. If you invert the cake, frost the top and sides. If you leave the cake in the pan, frost just the top. You won't need as much frosting for sheet cakes as you will for layers.

3. Top. If the cake is a coffee cake or some other cake that is not designed to be frosted, you can add a streusel topping or even just miniature chocolate chips and chopped nuts before baking. Add blueberries to a lemon cake or press peach slices into plain yellow cake. These add eye appeal and texture.

4. Dust. Now, if the cake is really simple —as in no frosting, no streusel or crumble, no nothing—you can at least sift confectioners' sugar or cocoa powder over the top of a cooled cake before serving. If you're feeling fancy, sift it through a stencil to create a pattern on top. If you want the sugar or cocoa powder to show you must do this over a cooled cake. However, sifting the confectioners' sugar over a warm cake, right from the oven, makes the sugar melt and creates an easy glaze that is a nice touch for spice cakes. One to two teaspoons of confectioners' sugar is enough.

5. Garnish. The rule for garnishes has been that they should have something in common with the food they are dressing up. So, lime slices are fine on a lime cake, lemon slices with lemon cake, and strawberries with strawberry cake, and so on. But the delicious exceptions to this rule are those garnishes that can go on anything—mint leaves (although best with chocolate and alongside fruit) and toasted nuts such as pecans and almonds (best with chocolate, carrot cake, and caramel).

Broiled Peanut Butter Crunch Cake

serves:
16 to 20

prep:
15 minutes

bake:
32 to 37 minutes

cool:
15 to 20 minutes

When Irvine, California, resident Nelson Wong posted on my website that he was looking for a peanut butter cake he remembered as a boy, Hazel Phillips passed on this marvelous and easy sheet cake recipe. Warning: topped with a very crunchy peanut butter glaze that bubbles up under the broiler, this is for serious peanut butter lovers only.

For the cake

Vegetable oil spray, for misting the pan
Flour, for dusting the pan
1 package (18.25 ounces) plain yellow cake mix
1⅓ cups water
⅓ cup crunchy or smooth peanut butter
⅓ cup vegetable oil
3 large eggs

For the topping

⅔ cup packed light brown sugar
¼ cup heavy (whipping) cream or evaporated milk
¼ cup crunchy peanut butter
4 tablespoons (½ stick) butter, at room temperature
1 cup chopped dry roasted peanuts

1. Make the cake: Place a rack in the center of the oven and preheat the oven to 350°F. Lightly mist a 13 by 9–inch pan with vegetable oil spray, then dust it with flour. Shake out the excess flour and set the pan aside.

2. Place the cake mix, water, ⅓ cup of peanut butter, oil, and eggs in a large mixing bowl and beat with an electric mixer on low speed until the ingredients are incorporated, 30 seconds. Stop the machine and scrape down the side of the bowl with a rubber spatula. Increase the mixer speed to medium and beat for 2 minutes longer, scraping down the side of the bowl again if needed. The batter should be well combined. Pour the batter into the prepared cake pan, smoothing the top with the rubber spatula, and place the pan in the oven.

3. Bake the cake until the top springs back when lightly pressed with a finger, 32 to 37 minutes. Transfer the cake pan to a wire rack and let the cake cool while you assemble the topping.

4. Make the topping: Place the brown sugar, cream, ¼ cup of peanut butter, and butter in a medium-size mixing bowl. Beat with an electric mixer on low speed until just combined, 30 seconds. Spread the topping over the hot cake with a long metal spatula. Scatter the peanuts over the top.

5. Move the oven rack to the second position from the top and preheat the broiler to medium.

6. Place the cake under the broiler until the topping is bubbly and browned, 45 seconds to 1 minute. Do not let it overcook. Transfer the cake pan from the oven to a wire rack to cool. Let the cake rest for 10 minutes, then slice and serve.

Keep It Fresh! Store this cake, covered with plastic wrap, at room temperature for up to three days or for up to one week in the refrigerator. Freeze the cake in the pan, covered with aluminum foil, for up to three months. Let the cake thaw overnight on the counter before serving.

Recipe Reminders

MADE FOR

____

____

____

____

PREP NOTES

____

____

____

____

DON'T FORGET

____

____

____

____

SPECIAL TOUCHES

____

____

____

____

____

____

____

____

____

Mindy's Jack Cake with Tennessee Drizzle

serves:
16 to 20

prep:
25 minutes

bake:
35 to 40 minutes

cool:
30 minutes

My **COOKING FRIEND** Mindy Merrell knows how to turn out great food for crowds. She threw a Christmas party one year, and I couldn't stop eating the cake she had made with Jack Daniel's whiskey. Dense and moist, the cake contained pecans and chocolate chips and was drizzled with a glaze that was like a hard sauce. Bake this and see what I mean . . . it's irresistible!

For the cake

Vegetable oil spray, for misting the pan
Flour, for dusting the pan
1 package (18.25 ounces) yellow or vanilla cake mix with pudding
12 tablespoons (1½ sticks) butter, melted
¾ cup milk
½ cup Jack Daniel's Tennessee whiskey
3 large eggs
1 cup chopped pecans
1 cup (6 ounces) miniature semisweet chocolate chips

For the drizzle

4 tablespoons (½ stick) butter, melted
2 tablespoons Jack Daniel's Tennessee whiskey
1 tablespoon milk
2 cups confectioners' sugar, sifted

1. Make the cake: Place a rack in the center of the oven and preheat the oven to 325°F. Lightly mist a 13 by 9–inch metal cake pan with vegetable oil spray, then dust it with flour. Shake out the excess flour and set the pan aside.

2. Place the cake mix, 12 tablespoons of butter, ¾ cup of milk, ½ cup of whiskey, and the eggs in a large mixing bowl and beat with an electric mixer on low speed until the ingredients are incorporated, 30 seconds. Stop the machine and scrape down the side of the bowl with a rubber spatula. Increase the mixer speed to medium and beat for 1½ minutes longer, scraping down the side of the bowl again if needed. The batter should look well blended. Pour the batter into the prepared cake pan. Scatter the chopped pecans and chocolate chips over the cake batter. Place the cake pan in the oven.

3. Bake the cake until it is golden brown and the top springs back when lightly pressed with a finger, 35 to 40 minutes.

4. Meanwhile, make the drizzle: Place the 4 tablespoons of melted butter, 2 tablespoons of whiskey, 1 tablespoon of milk, and the confectioners' sugar in a medium-size mixing bowl and whisk until the drizzle is smooth and well blended.

5. Transfer the cake pan to a wire rack and let the cake cool for 20 minutes. Once the cake has cooled, pour the drizzle over the top of the cake. Let the cake rest for 10 minutes, then slice it and serve.

Keep It Fresh! Store this cake, covered with plastic wrap or aluminum foil, at room temperature for up to three days or for up to one week in the refrigerator. Freeze the cake in the pan, covered with aluminum foil, for up to three months. Let the cake thaw overnight on the counter before serving.

Recipe Reminders

MADE FOR

____

____

____

____

PREP NOTES

____

____

____

____

DON'T FORGET

____

____

____

____

SPECIAL TOUCHES

____

____

____

____

____

____

____

____

____

Lemon-Lime Cake with Pineapple Icing

serves:
16 to 20

prep:
25 minutes

bake:
38 to 42 minutes

cool:
30 minutes

THE FIRST CAKE MIX BOOK had its share of fun and crazy recipes, and here is one for this book. You've got to laugh at and love those recipes that have been out there as long as cake mixes have been on the shelves. This one relies on 7UP and a lemon cake mix. Sounds a little whacky, I know, but just wait until you taste it. I have lightened the original icing, however, using less sugar so that the flavor of the crushed pineapple comes through.

For the cake

Vegetable oil spray, for misting the pan
Flour, for dusting the pan
1 package (18.25 ounces) plain lemon cake mix
Half of a 3.4 ounce package vanilla instant pudding mix (4 tablespoons)
1 can (12 ounces) 7UP (see Note)
⅔ cup vegetable oil
4 large eggs

For the pineapple icing and garnish

4 tablespoons (½ stick) butter
½ cup granulated sugar
1 tablespoon all-purpose flour
1 can (8 ounces) crushed pineapple, drained
1 large egg
½ teaspoon pure vanilla extract
⅓ cup sweetened flaked coconut (optional)

1. Make the cake: Place a rack in the center of the oven and preheat the oven to 350°F. Lightly mist a 13 by 9–inch metal cake pan with vegetable oil spray, then dust it with flour. Shake out the excess flour and set the pan aside.

2. Place the cake mix, pudding mix, 7UP, oil, and 4 eggs in a large mixing bowl and beat with an electric mixer on low speed until the ingredients are incorporated, 30 seconds. Stop the machine and scrape down the side of the bowl with a rubber spatula. Increase the mixer speed to medium and beat until the mixture lightens and is smooth, about 1½ minutes longer, scraping down the side of the bowl again if needed. Pour the batter into the prepared cake pan, smoothing the top with the rubber spatula, and place the pan in the oven.

3. Bake the cake until it is golden brown and the top springs back when lightly pressed with a finger, 38 to 42 minutes. Transfer the cake pan to a wire rack and let the cake sit until nearly cool, about 20 minutes.

4. Make the pineapple icing: Melt the butter in a small, heavy saucepan over medium-low heat. Remove the pan from the heat and stir in the sugar until incorporated. Stir in the flour until incorporated. Stir in the pineapple until well mixed.

5. Crack the egg into a small bowl and whisk it with a fork until lemon colored. Spoon several tablespoons of the warm pineapple mixture into the egg and beat to combine and to warm the egg. Transfer the egg mixture to the pan with the pineapple mixture. Place the pan over medium heat and cook, stirring constantly, until the icing thickens, 4 to 5 minutes. Spoon the warm icing over the cake and garnish it by sprinkling the coconut on top. Let the cake sit for 10 minutes before slicing and serving.

Keep It Fresh! Store this cake, covered with plastic

Recipe Reminders

MADE FOR

____

____

____

____

PREP NOTES

____

____

____

____

DON'T FORGET

____

____

____

____

SPECIAL TOUCHES

____

____

____

____

____

____

____

____

____

Tired of Your Cakes Shrinking as They Cool?

I don't know if I can promise you a miracle cure for cakes that shrink as they cool. But I do know that instant pudding mix can cause cakes to pull back from the pan and lose volume while they are cooling. So with certain cakes I use just half a package in my batter. Seal up the remaining half, place it in a small plastic bag, and save it until the next baking day.

wrap or aluminum foil, in the refrigerator for up to one week. This cake does not freeze well.

Note: You can use another lemon-lime soda in this cake instead of the 7UP. And you can substitute a diet soda as well. The original recipe called for a 10-ounce bottle of 7UP, which is tough to find, but you can use anywhere from 10 to 12 ounces of the soda.

The Cake Mix Doctor Dating Game—Flavors I Love Together

Chocolate isn't just chocolate anymore: It has a background of support from cinnamon or coffee. And vanilla isn't just vanilla. It might be caramel or maple and possibly contain fruit. How do I put flavors together when I develop recipes? I look for tastes that just beg for each other. Have you ever tasted a bite of carrot cake, for example, and thought it needed cinnamon ice cream? Those are the sorts of flavor matchups I like to make, a little like a culinary dating game. Here are some of my favorite combos:

◆ Chocolate—introduce it to apricots, coffee, peppermint, almonds, or cinnamon.

◆ Lemon—match it with pineapple, raspberries, almonds, or strawberries.

◆ Coconut—try other tropical flavor mates like pineapple, mango, and rum.

◆ Caramel—it cries out for toasted nuts like pecans or almonds, chocolate, and peaches or bananas.

Moist and Creamy Coconut Cake

C*AKE MIX DOCTOR* READER Carolyn Baner of New Jersey shared her coconut cake recipe with me a while back. As the cake sits in the fridge, the glaze and topping soak into the cake, but only if you have any leftovers left sitting in the fridge! This refreshing surprise is the perfect cake to tote to a summer picnic because you can make it ahead. Whereas my previous coconut cake called for frozen unsweetened coconut, I have learned this is a difficult ingredient to find across the country. So now I suggest you make the cake with sweetened flaked coconut.

serves:
16 to 20

prep:
25 minutes

bake:
40 to 45 minutes

cool:
55 minutes

For the cake

Vegetable oil spray, for misting the pan
Flour, for dusting the pan
1 package (18.25 ounces) plain yellow or vanilla cake mix
1 package (3.4 ounces) vanilla instant pudding mix
1 cup water
⅓ cup vegetable oil
4 large eggs

For the glaze and topping

2 cups sweetened flaked coconut (see Coconut Tips, on this page)
1¼ cups milk
⅓ cup granulated sugar
8 ounces frozen whipped topping, thawed

Coconut Tips

I make store-bought flaked coconut look freshly grated by pulsing it in a food processor. You can make the Moist and Creamy Coconut Cake even more "coconutty" by using coconut milk instead of water and adding 1 to 2 teaspoons of coconut flavoring to the cake batter.

1. Make the cake: Place a rack in the center of the oven and preheat

Recipe Reminders

MADE FOR

PREP NOTES

DON'T FORGET

SPECIAL TOUCHES

the oven to 350°F. Lightly mist a 13 by 9–inch glass or metal cake pan with vegetable oil spray, then dust it with flour. Shake out the excess flour and set the pan aside.

2. Place the cake mix, pudding mix, water, oil, and eggs in a large mixing bowl and beat with an electric mixer on low speed until the ingredients are incorporated, 30 seconds. Stop the machine and scrape down the side of the bowl with a rubber spatula. Increase the mixer speed to medium and beat for 1½ minutes longer, scraping down the side of the bowl again. The batter should look well blended. Pour the batter into the prepared cake pan, smoothing the top with the rubber spatula, and place the pan in the oven.

3. Bake the cake until it is golden brown and the top springs back when lightly pressed with a finger, 40 to 45 minutes. Transfer the cake pan to a wire rack and let the cake cool for 15 minutes. Poke holes in the cake using a fork.

4. Make the glaze and topping: While the cake cools, grate the coconut by placing it in a food processor and pulsing it for 10 to 15 seconds. Set the grated coconut aside.

5. Heat the milk and sugar in a small saucepan over medium to high heat, stirring constantly. Continue to stir just until the milk begins to steam. Remove the pan from the heat and add ½ cup of the grated coconut. Slowly spoon the warm glaze over the cake, allowing it to soak into the cake. Let the cake cool to room temperature, 20 minutes, before frosting.

6. Place ½ cup of the grated coconut in a large bowl and stir in the whipped topping. Spread the coconut topping over the top of the cooled cake. Scatter the remaining 1 cup of coconut over the top. Cover the cake and refrigerate it for 20 minutes before serving.

Keep It Fresh! Store this cake, covered with plastic wrap, in the refrigerator for up to five days.

Caramel Tres Leches Cake

I'VE HAD THE GOOD FORTUNE to have traveled to Texas many times on book tours. I love the friendliness of the people there, and I always come away having learned about a new (for me) ingredient. I remember the first time I heard about the *tres leches* cake from the students in my cooking class. This is a Nicaraguan cake that is soaked in a syrup made from three milks (the *tres leches* of its name). By the end of the class I had a pretty good idea how to make one.

Before I left for the airport I was wandering the aisles of the wonderful Central Market, shopping for some items to take home in my suitcase (pre 9/11 as you can tell) and I found *dulce de leche*, a caramelized version of sweetened condensed milk. I made a *tres leches* cake when I returned to Nashville and have since shared my recipes for it in my books.

Here is that recipe, a wonderful twist on the classic cake. Make it when good peaches are at hand, for they are delicious sliced and served on top. *Dulce de leche* is now easily found in many supermarkets along with the canned milks.

serves:
16 to 20

prep:
30 minutes

bake:
32 to 35 minutes

chill:
4 hours

Recipe Reminders

MADE FOR

PREP NOTES

DON'T FORGET

SPECIAL TOUCHES

For the cake

Vegetable oil spray, for misting the pan
Flour, for dusting the pan
1 package (18.25 ounces) vanilla or yellow cake mix with pudding
1¼ cups milk
½ cup vegetable oil
4 large eggs

For the milk syrup

1 can (12 ounces) evaporated milk
1 can (13.4 ounces) dulce de leche, about 1½ cups (see Note)
1 cup heavy (whipping) cream
1 tablespoon rum
1 teaspoon pure vanilla extract

For the garnish

1 cup chopped salted pecans, toasted (optional; see page 204)
2 cups sliced peeled ripe peaches or nectarines (optional)
Sweetened Whipped Cream (optional; page 489)

1. Make the cake: Place a rack in the center of the oven and preheat the oven to 350°F. Lightly mist a 13 by 9–inch glass baking pan with vegetable oil spray, then dust it with flour. Shake out the excess flour and set the pan aside.

2. Place the cake mix, milk, oil, and eggs in a large mixing bowl and beat with an electric mixer on low speed until the ingredients are incorporated, 30 seconds. Stop the machine and scrape down the side of the bowl with a rubber spatula. Increase the mixer speed to medium and beat for 1½ minutes longer, scraping down the side of the bowl again if needed. The batter should look well blended. Pour the batter into the prepared cake pan, smoothing the top with the rubber spatula, and place the pan in the oven.

3. Bake the cake until it is golden brown and the top springs back when lightly pressed with a finger, 32 to 35 minutes. Transfer the cake pan to a wire rack and let the cake cool for 2 hours.

4. When cake has thoroughly cooled, pierce it all over the top with the tines of a fork or a wooden skewer. The holes should completely cover the top.

5. Make the milk syrup: Whisk together the evaporated milk, *dulce de leche*, cream, rum, and vanilla in a medium-size bowl. Using a large spoon or ladle, spoon the milk syrup over the cake and let it soak before spooning on more. Continue spooning the syrup over the cake until all of it has been used. Cover the cake with plastic wrap and refrigerate it for 2 hours before serving.

6. Garnish the cake with the toasted pecans or sliced peaches, or both. Slice the cake and serve it with a dollop of sweetened whipped cream or just as is.

Keep It Fresh! Store this cake, covered with plastic wrap, in the refrigerator for up to five days. The cake does not freeze well.

Note: If you cannot find *dulce de leche*, substitute a 14-ounce can of sweetened condensed milk.

Ready, Set, Whipped Cream

Why stabilize whipped cream? The cream will hold up better for longer and not separate if you are serving it to a crowd. Here are two ways to stabilize whipped cream.

◆ Gently combine whipped cream with an equal amount of thawed whipped topping.

◆ Soften 1 teaspoon of unflavored gelatin in a tablespoon of cold water and heat in a microwave oven for 8 to 10 seconds on high power, then stir until the gelatin dissolves. Add the gelatin mixture to 1 cup of heavy cream and refrigerate it for 1 hour. Then, beat on high power with an electric mixer until stiff peaks form, sweetening the cream to taste with confectioners' sugar. You'll have about 2 cups of whipped cream. Refrigerate the whipped cream until needed.

German Chocolate Cake with Cheesecake Pockets

serves:
16 to 20

prep:
25 minutes

bake:
44 to 48 minutes

cool:
20 to 30 minutes

I **CHALLENGE YOU TO EAT JUST ONE** serving of this incredibly tempting cake. Its gooey pockets of cream cheese mixed with coconut and pecans bakes into the batter giving you a deliciously moist surprise bite after bite.

For the cake

Vegetable oil spray, for misting the pan
Flour, for dusting the pan
1 package (18.25 ounces) plain German chocolate cake mix
1⅓ cups buttermilk or water
½ cup vegetable oil
3 large eggs
1 teaspoon pure vanilla extract

For the cheesecake mixture

1 package (8 ounces) regular or reduced-fat cream cheese, at room temperature
8 tablespoons (1 stick) butter, at room temperature
3 cups confectioners' sugar, sifted
1 cup sweetened flaked coconut
½ cup finely chopped pecans

For the garnish

¼ cup finely chopped pecans, or 2 teaspoons confectioners' sugar

1. Make the cake: Place a rack in the center of the oven and preheat the oven to 350°F. Lightly mist a 13 by 9–inch metal cake pan with vegetable oil spray, then dust it with flour. Shake out the excess flour and set the pan aside.

2. Place the cake mix, buttermilk, oil, eggs, and vanilla in a large mixing bowl and beat with an electric mixer on low speed until the ingredients are incorporated, 30 seconds. Stop the machine and scrape down the side of the bowl with a rubber spatula. Increase the mixer speed to medium and beat until the mixture lightens and is smooth, about 1½ minutes longer. Pour the batter into the prepared cake pan, smoothing the top with the rubber spatula.

3. Make the cheesecake mixture: Place the cream cheese and butter in another large mixing bowl. Beat with an electric mixer on low speed until creamy, 30 to 45 seconds. Add the confectioners' sugar and beat on low speed until the mixture comes together, then increase the speed to medium and beat until fluffy, 30 seconds. Stir in the coconut and ½ cup of pecans. Drop the cheesecake mixture by tablespoonfuls on top of the German chocolate batter, nearly covering the top. If using, sprinkle ¼ cup pecans over the top for garnish.

4. Place the pan in the oven and bake the cake until the top feels firm but the cheesecake pockets jiggle a little when you gently shake it, 44 to 48 minutes. Transfer the cake pan to a wire rack and let the cake cool for 20 minutes.

5. Dust the top of the cake with confectioners' sugar if using. Cut the cake into serving pieces and serve warm or let cool to room temperature, 10 minutes longer.

Keep It Fresh! Store this cake, covered with plastic wrap or aluminum foil, in the refrigerator for up to one week. The cake does not freeze well.

Recipe Reminders

MADE FOR

PREP NOTES

DON'T FORGET

SPECIAL TOUCHES

Fast Fixing Chocolate Chip Cake

serves:
16 to 20

prep:
30 minutes

bake:
38 to 42 minutes

cool:
25 minutes

GLORIA NELSON, who lives in Roswell, Georgia, recalls first making this easy chocolate sheet cake in the 1970s. She calls it a fast fixing cake because you combine the ingredients in the pan, then stir them together and bake. It is an easy cake to take to school bake sales, potluck suppers, or on weekend trips, or it can be tucked into your freezer.

For the cake

Vegetable oil spray, for misting the pan
1 package (18.25 ounces) plain devil's food cake mix
1 package (3.9 ounces) chocolate instant pudding mix
1¼ cups water
½ cup vegetable oil
3 large eggs
1 teaspoon pure vanilla extract
1 cup (6 ounces) semisweet chocolate chips

For the chocolate frosting

8 tablespoons (1 stick) butter
3 tablespoons unsweetened cocoa powder
4 tablespoons milk
1 teaspoon pure vanilla extract
3 cups confectioners' sugar, sifted

1. Make the cake: Place a rack in the center of the oven and preheat the oven to 350°F. Lightly mist a 13 by 9–inch metal cake pan with vegetable oil spray.

2. Place the cake mix, pudding mix, water, oil, eggs, and 1 teaspoon of vanilla in the prepared cake pan. Stir the mixture with a fork until the ingredients, especially the eggs, are well blended, 1 minute. Fold in the chocolate chips until they are well distributed. Place the pan in the oven.

3. Bake the cake until the top springs back when lightly pressed with a finger, 38 to 42 minutes. Transfer the cake pan to a wire rack and let the cake cool for 10 minutes.

4. Meanwhile, make the frosting: Place the butter, cocoa powder, milk, and 1 teaspoon of vanilla in a medium-size saucepan over medium heat and cook, stirring, until the butter has melted and the mixture comes to a boil, 2 minutes. Remove the pan from the heat and stir in the confectioners' sugar until the frosting is smooth. Pour the frosting over the top of the cooling cake, spreading the frosting to the sides of the pan with a long metal spatula. Let the frosting set for 15 minutes, then slice and serve the cake.

Keep It Fresh! Store this cake, covered with plastic wrap or in a cake saver, for up for three days at room temperature or for up to one week in the refrigerator. Freeze the cake in the pan, covered with aluminum foil, for up to two months. Let the cake thaw overnight on the counter before serving.

Recipe Reminders

MADE FOR

____

____

____

____

PREP NOTES

____

____

____

____

DON'T FORGET

____

____

____

____

SPECIAL TOUCHES

____

____

____

____

____

____

____

____

____

Chocolate Bayou City Cake

serves:
16 to 20

prep:
15 minutes

bake:
40 to 45 minutes

cool:
10 minutes

JILL CONYER SAYS Houston, Texas, is known as the "Bayou City" because bayous snake their way around the town. Those bayous are "dark and sticky—just like this cake." I left this cake in the pan, spread the glaze on it, and sliced it while still warm. The pears in the fruit cocktail melt into the batter, making the cake moist and fun. It's like a soft and gooey brownie!

For the cake

Vegetable oil spray, for misting the pan
Flour, for dusting the pan
1 package (18.25 ounces) plain devil's food cake mix
1 package (3.9 ounces) chocolate instant pudding mix
1 can (15¼ ounces) fruit cocktail, undrained
4 large eggs
¼ cup vegetable oil
½ cup packed light brown sugar
½ cup coarsely chopped pecans

For the glaze

8 tablespoons (1 stick) butter
½ cup granulated sugar
2 tablespoons unsweetened cocoa powder
½ cup milk
1 cup coarsely chopped pecans (optional)

1. Make the cake: Place a rack in the center of the oven and preheat the oven to 325°F. Lightly mist a 13 by 9–inch metal cake pan with vegetable oil spray, then dust it with flour. Shake out the excess flour and set the pan aside.

2. Place the cake mix, pudding mix, fruit cocktail and its liquid, eggs, and oil in a large mixing bowl and beat with an electric mixer on low speed until the ingredients are incorporated, 30 seconds. Stop the machine and scrape down the side of the bowl with a rubber spatula. Increase the mixer speed to medium and beat for 1½ minutes longer, scraping down the side of the bowl again if needed. The batter should be thickened and nearly smooth. Pour the batter into the prepared cake pan, smoothing the top with the rubber spatula.

3. Combine the light brown sugar and ½ cup of chopped pecans in a small bowl. Sprinkle this mixture on top of the cake. Place the pan in the oven.

4. Bake the cake until the top springs back when lightly pressed with a finger, 40 to 45 minutes.

5. While the cake is baking, make the glaze: Place the butter, granulated sugar, cocoa powder, and milk in a small saucepan over medium heat. Bring to a boil, stirring constantly, and let simmer until the sugar dissolves, 2 minutes. Remove the pan from the heat and stir in the 1 cup of chopped pecans, if using. Keep the glaze warm.

6. Transfer the cake pan to a wire rack and let the cake cool for 10 minutes. Spoon the glaze over the warm cake, spreading it evenly to the sides of the pan, if desired. Slice and serve the cake warm or at room temperature.

Keep It Fresh! Store this cake, covered with plastic wrap, at room temperature for two days or for up to one week in the refrigerator. Freeze the cake in the pan, covered with aluminum foil, for up to one month. Let the cake thaw overnight on the counter before serving.

Recipe Reminders

MADE FOR

PREP NOTES

DON'T FORGET

SPECIAL TOUCHES

A New Chocolate-Covered Cherry Cake

serves:
16 to 20

prep:
20 minutes

bake:
30 to 35 minutes

cool:
20 minutes

A NEW AND IMPROVED chocolate-covered cherry cake, this one is just as moist as the one featured in the first *Cake Mix Doctor*—so don't worry! But it does have the addition of chocolate chips in the cake batter, making the chocolate flavor even richer. And I do suggest that you add the cherry pie filling to the batter at the end so that some of the cherries remain whole and give the cake more texture. Adding a little light corn syrup makes the glaze nice to work with. The cake bakes up well as a sheet cake or as cupcakes. (If you want to make cupcakes, bake them about twenty minutes.)

Vegetable oil spray, for misting the pan
Flour, for dusting the pan
1 package (18.25 ounces) chocolate cake mix with pudding
3 large eggs
2 teaspoons pure almond extract
1 cup (6 ounces) semisweet chocolate chips
1 can (21 ounces) cherry pie filling
Martha's Chocolate Icing (page 480)

1. Place a rack in the center of the oven and preheat the oven to 350°F. Lightly mist a 13 by 9–inch metal cake pan with vegetable oil spray, then dust it with flour. Shake out the excess flour and set the pan aside.

2. Place the cake mix, eggs, and almond extract in a large mixing bowl and beat with an electric mixer on medium speed until the ingredients are incorporated, 1 minute. Stop the machine and scrape down the side of the bowl with a rubber spatula. Add the chocolate chips and beat on low speed for 30 seconds, scraping down the side of the bowl again if needed. Add the cherry pie filling and beat on medium speed until just blended, 20 to 30 seconds. The batter will be thick. Pour the batter into the prepared cake pan, smoothing the top with the rubber spatula, and place the pan in the oven.

3. Bake the cake until it just starts to pull away from the sides of the pan and the top springs back when lightly pressed with a finger, 30 to 35 minutes. Transfer the cake to a wire rack, and let the cake cool slightly while you prepare Martha's Chocolate Icing, making sure to prepare enough to cover a sheet cake.

4. Spread the frosting over the warm cake and let the cake cool completely, 20 minutes, before serving.

Keep It Fresh! Store this cake, covered with aluminum foil, at room temperature for up to five days or for up to one week in the refrigerator. Freeze the cake in the pan, covered with aluminum foil, for up to six months. Let the cake thaw overnight on the counter before serving.

Recipe Reminders

MADE FOR

____

____

____

____

PREP NOTES

____

____

____

____

DON'T FORGET

____

____

____

____

SPECIAL TOUCHES

____

____

____

____

____

____

____

____

____

Chocolate Peanut Butter Marble Cake

serves:
16 to 20

prep:
30 minutes

bake:
30 to 35 minutes

cool:
25 to 30 minutes

Peanut butter and jelly might be soul mates but so, too, are peanut butter and chocolate. In fact, there is something truly compatible about this combination, whether it be in a candy bar or in this fun sheet cake. The peanut butter part is the cake, and the chocolate part is both in the swirl and in the frosting. Cut a slice, pour a glass of milk, and enjoy the good times!

Vegetable oil spray, for misting the pan
Flour, for dusting the pan
1 package (18.25 ounces) plain yellow or vanilla cake mix
⅓ cup smooth peanut butter
½ cup vegetable oil
3 large eggs
1 teaspoon pure vanilla extract
1⅓ cups water
¼ cup unsweetened cocoa powder
2 tablespoons confectioners' sugar
2 tablespoons (¼ stick) butter, melted
2 tablespoons warm water
Chocolate Pan Frosting (make the amount for a sheet cake; page 476)

1. Place a rack in the center of the oven and preheat the oven to 350°F. Lightly mist a 13 by 9–inch metal cake pan with vegetable oil spray, then dust it with flour. Shake out the excess flour and set the pan aside.

2. Place the cake mix, peanut butter, oil, eggs, vanilla, and 1⅓ cups of water in a large mixing bowl and beat with an electric mixer on low speed until blended, 30 seconds. Stop the machine and scrape down the side of the bowl with a rubber spatula. Increase the mixer speed to medium and beat for 2 minutes longer, scraping down the side of the bowl again if needed. The batter should be well blended.

3. Measure out 1½ cups of the cake batter and place it in a medium-size bowl. Set the bowl aside. Pour the remaining batter into the prepared cake pan, smoothing the top with the rubber spatula.

4. Make the chocolate marble by stirring the cocoa powder, confectioners' sugar, butter, and 2 tablespoons of warm water into the reserved 1½ cups of cake batter until well combined. Spoon tablespoon-size dollops of this mixture on top of the peanut butter batter. Swirl with a knife to marble the cake, but be careful not to touch the bottom of the pan. Place the pan in the oven.

5. Bake the cake until the top springs back when lightly pressed with a finger, 30 to 35 minutes. Transfer the cake pan to a wire rack and let the cake cool while you make the Chocolate Pan Frosting, 10 to 15 minutes.

6. Pour the warm frosting over the cake, spreading it with a spatula so that it reaches the edges of the cake. Work quickly because this frosting goes on best while still warm. Let the frosting set for 15 minutes, then slice and serve the cake.

Keep It Fresh! Store this cake, covered with plastic wrap or aluminum foil, at room temperature for up to three days or for up to one week in the refrigerator. Freeze the cake in the pan, covered with aluminum foil, for up to three months. Let the cake thaw overnight on the counter before serving.

Recipe Reminders

MADE FOR

PREP NOTES

DON'T FORGET

SPECIAL TOUCHES

Old-Fashioned Chocolate Sheet Cake

serves:
16 to 20

prep:
20 minutes

bake:
30 to 35 minutes

cool:
25 to 35 minutes

WHEN IN DOUBT, bake this cake. When you can't decide what to bake for the family picnic, the office potluck, or the neighborhood block party, bake this cake. It was the cake my mother made quite often, using a cake mix to save time and then pouring her famous chocolate pan frosting over the top. Vary it by adding marshmallows or toasted pecans, as you like. This is such a good basic cake, it's much like that classic little black dress.

Vegetable oil spray, for misting the pan
Flour, for dusting the pan
1 package (18.25 ounces) plain chocolate cake mix or chocolate cake mix with pudding
1 tablespoon unsweetened cocoa powder
1⅓ cups buttermilk
½ cup vegetable oil
3 large eggs
1 tablespoon pure vanilla extract
Chocolate Pan Frosting (make the amount for a sheet cake; page 476)

1. Place a rack in the center of the oven and preheat the oven to 350°F. Lightly mist a 13 by 9–inch metal cake pan with vegetable oil spray, then dust it with flour. Shake out the excess flour and set the pan aside.

2. Place the cake mix, cocoa powder, buttermilk, oil, eggs, and vanilla in a large mixing bowl and beat with an electric mixer on low speed until the ingredients are incorporated, 30 seconds. Stop the machine and scrape down the side of the bowl with a rubber spatula. Increase the mixer speed to medium and beat until the mixture lightens and is smooth, about 1½ minutes longer, scraping down the side of the bowl again if needed. Pour the batter into the prepared cake pan, smoothing the top with the rubber spatula, and place the pan in the oven.

3. Bake the cake until the top springs back when lightly pressed with a finger, 30 to 35 minutes. Transfer the cake pan to a wire rack and let the cake cool while you make the Chocolate Pan Frosting, 10 to 15 minutes.

4. Pour the warm frosting over the cake, spreading it with a spatula so that it reaches the edges of the cake. Let the frosting set for 15 to 20 minutes before slicing and serving the cake.

Keep It Fresh! Store this cake, covered with plastic wrap or aluminum foil, at room temperature for up to three days or for up to one week in the refrigerator. Freeze the cake in the pan, covered with aluminum foil, for up to three months. Let the cake thaw overnight on the counter before serving.

Mississippi Mud Cake

Bake the Old-Fashioned Chocolate Sheet Cake as directed. When you remove the cake pan from the oven immediately scatter 2 cups of miniature marshmallows over the top of the cake. Let the marshmallows melt while you make the frosting. Pour the warm Chocolate Pan Frosting over the marshmallows and gently smooth the top. Let the frosting set for 30 minutes before slicing and serving the cake.

Recipe Reminders

MADE FOR

PREP NOTES

DON'T FORGET

SPECIAL TOUCHES

Rocky Road Cake

Bake the Mississippi Mud Cake but, after adding the marshmallows, sprinkle ½ cup of chopped dry-roasted peanuts on top. Pour the warm Chocolate Pan Frosting over the marshmallows and peanuts and gently smooth the top. Let the frosting set for 30 minutes before slicing and serving the cake.

Texas (or Georgia) Sheet Cake

Bake the Old-Fashioned Chocolate Sheet Cake as directed. After pouring the frosting over the cake, immediately sprinkle the top with ½ cup of chopped toasted pecans.

How to Turn a White Cake Mix into a Chocolate Cake Mix

Life is all about substitutions, isn't it? The older you get the wiser you become and you learn how to make do, combining what is in the pantry so you don't have to make a trip to the store. If you want chocolate cake but only have a white or yellow cake mix on the shelf, here are ways you can turn that cake into chocolate.

- **Add ¼ cup of unsweetened cocoa powder.**
- **Add one small package (3.9 ounces) chocolate instant pudding mix.**
- **Fold 1 cup of miniature semisweet chocolate chips or grated semisweet chocolate into the batter.**
- **Spoon the batter into the pan, but before baking, drizzle chocolate syrup over the top to create marbled swirls as it bakes.**

Warm Chocolate Pudding Cake

THIS CAKE IS UNBELIEVABLY DELICIOUS; as it bakes, pudding forms in the bottom of the pan. Spoon it warm into bowls and serve it with mint chocolate chip, vanilla, or coffee ice cream. To reheat servings, spoon them into serving bowls, drizzle a little heavy cream (two teaspoons per serving) on top, and put them in the microwave until heated through, thirty to forty seconds. The cake lends itself to all sorts of variations—a drizzle of amaretto or rum by chance?

serves:
16 to 20

prep:
15 minutes

bake:
35 to 40 minutes

For the cake

1 package (18.25 ounces) plain chocolate cake mix
¾ cup buttermilk
½ cup vegetable oil
3 large eggs
1 teaspoon pure vanilla extract

For the topping

½ cup packed light brown sugar
¼ cup unsweetened cocoa powder
¼ cup miniature semisweet chocolate chips
1 teaspoon instant coffee granules
2¼ cups boiling water

Recipe Reminders

MADE FOR

PREP NOTES

DON'T FORGET

SPECIAL TOUCHES

1. Make the cake: Place a rack in the center of the oven and preheat the oven to 325°F.

2. Place the cake mix, buttermilk, oil, eggs, and vanilla in a large mixing bowl and beat with an electric mixer on low speed until the ingredients are incorporated, 30 seconds. Stop the machine and scrape down the side of the bowl with a rubber spatula. Increase the mixer speed to medium-low and beat until the batter is smooth, 1½ minutes longer, scraping down the side of the bowl again if needed. Pour the batter into a 13 by 9–inch glass baking pan.

3. Make the topping: Mix the brown sugar, cocoa powder, chocolate chips, and coffee granules in a small bowl and sprinkle the topping evenly over the batter in the baking pan. Pour the boiling water over the batter and carefully place the pan in the oven.

4. Bake the cake until the edges are firm but the center still jiggles when you shake the pan, 35 to 40 minutes. Remove the cake pan from the oven and spoon the warm pudding cake into bowls. Serve with ice cream.

Keep It Fresh! Store this cake, covered with plastic wrap, at room temperature for up to three days or for up to one week in the refrigerator. Freeze the cake in the pan, covered with aluminum foil, for up to three months. Let the cake thaw overnight on the counter before serving.

Overnight Chocolate Caramel Cake

A **CHOCOLATE CAKE** topped with a creamy caramel sauce, real whipped cream, and toffee bits, this cake is similar to the Better Than . . . Cake, but it's an even more memorable version. It's a behemoth of a dessert that is at its best baked a day in advance of a party so the flavors have time to soak into the cake. But if you don't have time for it to sit overnight, don't fret because the cake is delicious the moment you garnish the top with toffee! Want to make it even better? Make your own caramel sauce. And toffee lovers might want to substitute a yellow or vanilla cake mix for the chocolate and add some chopped toasted pecans to the toffee bits on top.

serves:
16 to 20

prep:
40 minutes

bake:
30 to 35 minutes

chill:
overnight

Vegetable oil spray, for misting the pan
Flour, for dusting the pan
1 package (18.25 ounces) chocolate cake mix with pudding
1 cup water
½ cup vegetable oil
½ cup sour cream
3 large eggs
1 can (14 ounces) sweetened condensed milk
1 bottle (12.25 ounces) caramel topping
Sweetened Whipped Cream (page 489)
1⅓ cups chocolate-covered toffee bits

Recipe Reminders

MADE FOR

PREP NOTES

DON'T FORGET

SPECIAL TOUCHES

1. Place a rack in the center of the oven and preheat the oven to 350°F. Lightly mist a 13 by 9–inch metal cake pan with vegetable oil spray, then dust it with flour. Shake out the excess flour and set the pan aside.

2. Place the cake mix, water, oil, sour cream, and eggs in a large mixing bowl and beat with an electric mixer on low speed until the ingredients are incorporated, 30 seconds. Stop the machine and scrape down the side of the bowl with a rubber spatula. Increase the mixer speed to medium and beat for 1½ minutes longer, scraping down the side of the bowl again if needed. The batter should look well combined. Pour the batter into the prepared cake pan, smoothing the top with the rubber spatula, and place the pan in the oven.

3. Bake the cake until the top springs back when lightly pressed with a finger, 30 to 35 minutes. Transfer the cake pan to a wire rack and let the cake cool for 10 minutes.

4. Use a fork to poke holes in the cake, pour the condensed milk over it. Let the condensed milk soak in for a few minutes. Pour the caramel topping over the cake and let it soak in. Let the cake cool completely, 20 minutes longer. Cover the cake pan with plastic wrap and place the cake in the refrigerator to chill while you prepare the Sweetened Whipped Cream.

5. Remove the cake from the refrigerator. Spread the Sweetened Whipped Cream over the top of the cake. Scatter the chocolate-covered toffee bits over the cream, re-cover the cake, and refrigerate it overnight.

Keep It Fresh! Store this cake, covered with plastic wrap, in the refrigerator for up to three days. The cake does not freeze well.

Cookies and Cream Cheesecake

I HAVE SHARED many cheesecake recipes in my books and here's another great one. This recipe is one of my children's favorite flavor combinations with plenty of crushed chocolate sandwich cookies in the crust as well as the topping.

serves: 16 to 20

prep: 30 minutes

bake: 55 to 60 minutes

chill: at least 2 hours

For the crust

1 package (18.25 ounces) yellow or vanilla cake mix with pudding
1 large egg
6 tablespoons (¾ stick) butter, melted
1 heaping cup crushed chocolate sandwich cookies (8 Oreos)

For the filling

2 packages (8 ounces each) cream cheese, at room temperature
½ cup granulated sugar
1 can (12 ounces; 1½ cups) evaporated milk
1½ teaspoons pure vanilla extract

For the topping

2 cups heavy (whipping) cream
½ cup confectioners' sugar, sifted
½ teaspoon pure vanilla extract
2 tablespoons unsweetened cocoa powder
1½ cups crushed chocolate sandwich cookies (12 Oreos)

Recipe Reminders

MADE FOR

PREP NOTES

DON'T FORGET

SPECIAL TOUCHES

1. Place a rack in the center of the oven and preheat the oven to 325°F.

2. Make the crust, set aside 1 cup of cake mix for the filling. Place the remaining cake mix and the egg and butter in a medium-size mixing bowl and beat with an electric mixer on low speed until the ingredients are incorporated, 2 minutes. Scrape down the side of the bowl with a rubber spatula. Add the 1 cup of crushed chocolate sandwich cookies and beat until just combined. Spread the crust over the bottom of a 13 by 9–inch glass baking pan, evenly pressing the mixture over the bottom and about 1 inch up the sides of the pan (see Note). Set the baking pan aside.

3. Make the filling: Wash and dry the medium-size bowl and the beaters to remove the cookie crumbs. Place the cream cheese and granulated sugar in the bowl and beat with an electric mixer on medium speed until creamy, 1 to 1½ minutes, scraping down the side of the bowl if needed. Slowly add the evaporated milk, 1½ teaspoons of vanilla, and the reserved cake mix while beating on low speed. Scrape down the side of the bowl again with the rubber spatula if needed. Beat on medium speed until the mixture is well combined and smooth, about 1 minute. Pour the filling into the crust, spreading it evenly with the rubber spatula. Gently place the pan in the oven.

4. Bake the cheesecake until it looks shiny and lightly browned and the center barely jiggles when you shake the baking pan, 55 to 60 minutes. Transfer the baking pan to a wire rack and let the cheesecake cool to room temperature, about 1 hour. Then lightly cover the pan with plastic wrap and place the cheesecake in the refrigerator to chill for at least 1 hour, or preferably 24 hours, for the flavors to meld.

5. Make the topping: Place a large metal bowl and electric mixer beaters in the freezer to chill.

6. Remove the bowl and beaters from the freezer, pour the cream into the chilled bowl, and beat with an electric mixer on high speed until the cream thickens, 1½ minutes. Stop the machine and add the confectioners' sugar, ½ teaspoon of vanilla, and cocoa powder. Beat the cream on high speed until stiff peaks form, 1 to 2 minutes longer. Stop the machine and scrape down the side of the bowl with a rubber spatula. Fold in the 1½ cups of crushed chocolate sandwich cookies, if desired (you can also sprinkle them on top of the cheesecake after you add the topping).

7. Spread the topping over the cheesecake and cut it into squares to serve.

Keep It Fresh! Store this cake, covered first with plastic wrap and then with aluminum foil, in the refrigerator for up to five days. The cake does not freeze well.

Note: You can also bake this cake in a 10-inch springform pan. It will take about an hour to bake.

Key Lime Cheesecake

serves:
16 to 20

prep:
25 minutes

bake:
55 to 60 minutes

chill:
at least 2 hours

Here is another winning do-ahead cheesecake that's a snap to prepare. It's a lot easier to find key lime juice in supermarkets these days, and the juice has the most wonderful tropical flavor that will surely take you to the warm weather climates every time you take a bite of this cheesecake. Serve this to crowds after grilling fish or cooking burgers on the grill.

For the crust

Heaping ½ cup coarsely chopped pecans

1 package (18.25 ounces) yellow or vanilla cake mix with pudding

1 teaspoon ground cinnamon

1 large egg

6 tablespoons (¾ stick) butter, melted

For the filling

2 packages (8 ounces each) cream cheese, at room temperature

1 can (14 ounces) sweetened condensed milk

3 large eggs, at room temperature

½ cup key lime juice, at room temperature

1 small lime (optional; see Note)

For the topping

⅓ cup finely chopped pecans

1 cup Sweetened Whipped Cream (page 489), or frozen whipped topping, thawed

1. Place a rack in the center of the oven and preheat the oven to 325°F.

2. Make the crust: Place the ½ cup of pecans in a food processor and pulse until the nuts are finely chopped, about 20 seconds. Scrape down the side of the bowl with a rubber spatula. Add the cake mix and cinnamon and pulse until well combined, 20 to 30 seconds. Add 1 egg and the melted butter while the food processor is pulsing and blend until well combined, 15 seconds longer.

3. Spread the crust over the bottom of a 13 by 9–inch glass baking pan, evenly pressing the mixture over the bottom and about 1 inch up the sides of the pan. Set the baking pan aside.

4. Make the filling: Place the cream cheese and condensed milk in a large mixing bowl. Beat with an electric mixer on low speed until just combined, 30 seconds. Increase the mixer speed to medium and beat 1 minute longer to thoroughly cream the mixture. Stop the machine and add the 3 eggs and the key lime juice.

5. Rinse the small lime, if using, and dry it with paper towels. Grate enough zest to measure ½ teaspoon and add it to the mixing bowl with the filling. Cut the lime in half and squeeze 1 to 2 tablespoons of juice. Add this to the mixing bowl with the cream cheese mixture. Beat on medium speed for 1 minute. Scrape down the side of the bowl with the rubber spatula. Pour the filling into the crust, spreading it evenly with a rubber spatula. Gently place the pan in the oven.

6. Bake the cheesecake until it looks shiny and the center barely jiggles when you shake the baking pan, 55 to 60 minutes. Transfer the baking pan to a wire rack and let the cheesecake cool to room temperature, about 1 hour. Then lightly cover the pan with plastic wrap and place the cheesecake in the refrigerator to chill for at least 1 hour, or preferably 24 hours, for the flavors to meld.

Recipe Reminders

MADE FOR

____

____

____

____

PREP NOTES

____

____

____

____

DON'T FORGET

____

____

____

____

SPECIAL TOUCHES

____

____

____

____

____

____

____

____

____

7. Preheat the oven to 350°F.

8. Make the topping: Place the ⅓ cup of chopped pecans in a small baking pan and toast them in the oven until they are lightly browned, 3 to 4 minutes. Remove the pan from the oven and let the nuts cool.

9. Prepare the Sweetened Whipped Cream if using.

10. Spread the whipped cream or frozen whipped topping over the cheesecake and sprinkle the toasted pecans on top.

Keep It Fresh! Store this cake, covered first with plastic wrap and then with aluminum foil, in the refrigerator for up to five days. The cake does not freeze well.

Note: Use a small Persian lime, which is larger than a key lime. This is an optional ingredient, but adding the fresh lime juice and zest gives this cheesecake a more pronounced flavor. You will get at least ½ teaspoon of zest and 1 to 2 tablespoons of juice from one Persian lime.

Cupcakes and Muffins

It's no surprise that I love cupcakes. I wrote an entire book about them, from simple to sensational. And in this chapter I share more favorite recipes plus some for muffins, and a few surprises. Cupcakes are easy to adore. Maybe it's because each is an individual cake that we can take ownership of. We spot one on the platter and reach for it. It's ours. Cupcakes can be nostalgic and delicate on the one hand or bold and sassy on the other.

Cupcakes are also easy to bake. The only extra supplies you need are a cupcake pan and paper liners. In fact, you can turn your favorite cake recipe into cupcakes just by filling the paper liners about three-quarters full and baking the batter from twenty to twenty-five minutes. A typical recipe will yield twenty to twenty-four cupcakes. And they're delicious frosted in any fashion —with a thick and creamy buttercream, a spoonful of glaze, or simply a dusting of confectioners' sugar.

You'll see in this chapter that I've got a wonderful lemon cupcake, a strawberry cupcake, and a dazzling red velvet one, plus a white cupcake that's perfect for weddings and birthdays and a caramel cupcake recipe custom-made for bake sales. But I've also got recipes for chocolate lovers like me. I especially love the Chocolate Buttermilk Cupcakes with Chocolate Fudge Marshmallow Frosting, the Cream-Filled Chocolate Cupcakes (my take on the Hostess cupcake), and the remake of my cookie dough cupcake from the cupcake book.

Muffins, on the other hand, are a cupcake without attitude. And, without a liner and frosting. However, the lines have been blurred between muffins and cupcakes as muffins now come packed with chocolate chips and fruit and fun toppings. But essentially, muffins have a crisp exterior and are intended to be eaten for breakfast or a snack. You can serve the Sock-It-to-Me Muffins, a take-off on the famous Bundt cake, for breakfast or brunch. The Chocolate Chip Muffins are a favorite at our house any time of the day. And the Apple Spice Muffins are perfect for fall brunches and tailgate parties.

The two surprise recipes? A cinnamon roll made using a cake mix and Whoopie Pies, a soft chocolate cream sandwich recipe that many readers have both requested and shared through the years. I am pleased to be able to include these two recipes in this book.

As always, read through my recipes and adapt them to your tastes. I want you to be the best cupcake baker, so feel free to mix and match the frostings. Let my ideas begin your cupcake baking fun.

◆◆◆◆◆

A Better Chocolate Chip Cookie Dough Cupcake

THE COOKIE DOUGH CUPCAKE has to be one of our family favorites from *Cupcakes from the Cake Mix Doctor*. But I noticed that sometimes the dough would rise up out of the baked cupcakes. Martha Bowden figured a solution to this—setting aside some of the batter before filling the cupcake pans and spooning a teaspoon of the reserved batter onto the filled cupcakes just before baking. This seals in the cookie dough and makes a prettier cupcake. Don't worry, the same great taste is still here.

makes:
22 to 24 cupcakes (2½ inches in diameter)

prep:
15 minutes

bake:
23 to 27 minutes

cool:
20 minutes

24 paper liners for cupcake pans (2½ inch size)
1 package (18.25 ounces) plain yellow cake mix
1 package (3.4 ounces) vanilla instant pudding mix
1 cup milk
1 cup vegetable oil
4 large eggs
1 teaspoon pure vanilla extract
1 package (1 pound) frozen chocolate chip cookie dough (see Note)
Fluffy Chocolate Frosting (page 478)

1. Place a rack in the center of the oven and preheat the oven to 350°F. Line 24 cupcake cups with paper liners and set the pans aside.

2. Place the cake mix, pudding mix, milk, oil, eggs, and vanilla in a large mixing bowl and beat with an electric mixer on low speed until the ingredients are incorporated, 30 seconds. Stop

Recipe Reminders

MADE FOR

PREP NOTES

DON'T FORGET

SPECIAL TOUCHES

the machine and scrape down the side of the bowl with a rubber spatula. Increase the mixer speed to medium and beat for 1½ to 2 minutes longer, scraping down the side of the bowl again if needed. The batter should look well blended.

3. Set aside ¾ to 1 cup of the cupcake batter before filling the cupcake pans. Using the rest of the batter, spoon or scoop a heaping ¼ cup of batter into each lined cupcake cup, filling it two thirds of the way full. (You will get between 22 and 24 cupcakes; remove the empty liners, if any.)

4. Cut the pieces of frozen cookie dough in half to make 24 pieces. Place a piece of frozen cookie dough on top of each cupcake and push it down into the batter. Top each piece of cookie dough with about 1 teaspoon of the reserved cupcake batter.

5. Place the pans in the oven and bake the cupcakes until they are golden and the tops spring back when lightly pressed with a finger, 23 to 27 minutes. Remove the pans from the oven and place them on wire racks to cool for 5 minutes. Run a dinner knife around the edge of the cupcake cups, lift the cupcakes up from the bottom of the pans using the end of the knife, and pick the cupcakes out of the pans carefully with your fingertips. Place the cupcakes on a wire rack to cool for 15 minutes longer before frosting.

6. Meanwhile, make the Fluffy Chocolate Frosting.

7. Spoon a heaping tablespoon of frosting on top of each cupcake and swirl it with a short metal spatula or spoon to spread it out, taking care to cover the top completely. The cupcakes are then ready to serve.

Keep It Fresh! Store these cupcakes, in a cake saver or under a glass dome, at room temperature for up to three days or for up to one week in the refrigerator. Freeze the cupcakes, in a cake saver or wrapped in aluminum foil, for up to three months. Let the cupcakes thaw overnight in the refrigerator before serving.

Note: If you can't find frozen chocolate chip cookie dough you can substitute an 18-inch log of refrigerated cookie dough.

My Favorite Cupcake Baking Tips

If you want to make great cupcakes and muffins, keep these things in mind.

1. Cupcake batter is a little more forgiving than muffin batter, which needs to be beaten gently. I beat cupcake batter using an electric mixer and muffin batter by hand with a wooden spoon.

2. Use paper liners in cupcake pans for easy clean up.

3. Choose cupcake pans that are as deep as your paper liners. A pan that is not as deep will cause the cupcakes or muffins to bake up and over the side, creating a big top—nice on a muffin but not so easy to frost on a cupcake.

4. Mist the top of the cupcake pan lightly with vegetable oil spray so the cupcakes or muffins don't stick to it.

5. Use a scoop to portion just the right amount of batter into each cupcake liner. A standard ice cream scoop holds about ⅓ cup of batter, enough for a 2½-inch cupcake. A smaller scoop will fill a mini pan with 1½ to 2 tablespoons of batter. Using a scoop with a spring-action lever that sweeps across the scoop's bottom and removes the batter makes cupcake assembly a mess-free breeze. Fill cupcake liners about two thirds to three quarters full, depending on the recipe.

6. If you can find a short metal spatula, you can use it to run around the edges of the cupcakes after baking, making removal easy. And a small spatula makes frosting the little cupcakes a real pleasure.

Peanut Butter Cookie Dough Cupcakes

makes:
22 to 24 cupcakes (2½ inches in diameter)

prep:
15 minutes

bake:
18 to 23 minutes

cool:
20 minutes

I LOVED THE IDEA of pairing cookie dough and cupcakes so much that I wanted to create a peanut butter version. You can find peanut butter cookie dough in the refrigerated section of the supermarket. Bake the cupcakes until the cake portion is done and the cookie dough is still a little soft and wonderful. With a homemade chocolate icing spooned on top, life doesn't get much better than this. Pour the milk!

24 paper liners for cupcake pans (2½-inch size)
1 package (18.25 ounces) plain yellow cake mix
3 tablespoons vanilla instant pudding mix
1 cup reduced-fat sour cream
¾ cup milk
½ cup vegetable oil
3 large eggs
1 teaspoon pure vanilla extract
1 package (16.5 ounces) refrigerated peanut butter cookie dough, chilled
Martha's Milk Chocolate Icing (page 481)
Unsalted roasted peanuts, for garnish (optional)

1. Place a rack in the center of the oven and preheat the oven to 350°F. Line 24 cupcake cups with paper liners and set the pans aside.

10 Fast Cupcake Toppers

When I'm in a hurry but still want to be creative, here are toppings I sprinkle on frosted cupcakes.

1. Chocolate curls
2. Toasted pecans or almonds
3. Miniature marshmallows
4. Grated lemon or orange zest
5. Edible flowers
6. Maraschino cherries
7. Fresh strawberries or raspberries
8. Gum drops or another favorite candy
9. Sugar sprinkles
10. A dusting of confectioners' sugar

2. Place the cake mix, pudding mix, sour cream, milk, oil, eggs, and vanilla in a large mixing bowl and beat with an electric mixer on low speed until the ingredients are incorporated, 30 seconds. Stop the machine and scrape down the side of the bowl with a rubber spatula. Increase the mixer speed to medium and beat for 1½ to 2 minutes longer, scraping down the side of the bowl again if needed. The batter should look well blended.

3. Set aside about ¾ cup of the cupcake batter before filling the cupcake pans. Using the rest of the batter, spoon or scoop a

Recipe Reminders

MADE FOR

PREP NOTES

DON'T FORGET

SPECIAL TOUCHES

heaping ¼ cup of batter into each lined cupcake cup, filling it two thirds of the way full. (You will get between 22 and 24 cupcakes; remove the empty liners, if any.)

4. Unwrap the cookie dough and slice the log lengthwise into four pieces. Then cut each piece into 6 even chunks. Place a chunk of cookie dough on top of each cupcake and push it down into the batter. Top each piece of cookie dough with about 1 teaspoon of the reserved cupcake batter.

5. Place the pans in the oven and bake the cupcakes until they are golden and the tops spring back when lightly pressed with a finger, 18 to 23 minutes. Remove the pans from the oven and place them on wire racks to cool for 5 minutes. Run a dinner knife around the edge of the cupcake cups, lift the cupcakes up from the bottom of the pans using the end of the knife, and pick the cupcakes out of the pans carefully with your fingertips. Place the cupcakes on a wire rack to cool for 15 minutes longer before frosting.

6. Meanwhile, make Martha's Milk Chocolate Icing.

7. Spoon a heaping tablespoon of icing on top of each cupcake and spread it out with a short metal spatula or spoon. Garnish with 2 or 3 peanut halves, if desired. Place the cupcakes on a rack so the icing can set, 10 minutes.

Keep It Fresh! Store these cupcakes, in a cake saver or under a glass dome, at room temperature for up to three days or for up to one week in the refrigerator. Freeze the cupcakes, in a cake saver or wrapped in aluminum foil, for up to three months. Let the cupcakes thaw overnight in the refrigerator before serving.

How to Make Cupcake Bites

Most every snack food in the pantry has been reinvented as "bites." So it was inevitable that cupcakes, too, would become the next "bite." Look at Laura's Fudgy Rum Balls (page 459) and you'll see that the idea for mixing baked crumbled cake with other add-ins and then serving them as cookies or bites has been around for a while. But now cooks are mixing the baked cake with frosting so you have in one bite the whole cupcake experience. More a fad than a trend, but still fun, here is how you can create cupcake bites. One cake recipe makes about three dozen cupcake bites.

1. Bake the cake of your choice in a 13 inch by 9-inch pan or two 9-inch round cake pans following my recipe or the directions on the package.

2. Let the cake cool in the pan for 20 minutes.

3. While the cake is still a little warm to the touch, crumble it into a large mixing bowl and beat it with an electric mixer on low speed until you have fine crumbs.

4. Fold in 1½ to 2 cups of homemade frosting—cream cheese or buttercream frostings work the best. Cover the bowl with plastic wrap and place it in the refrigerator to chill for two hours.

5. Remove the bowl from the refrigerator and, using your hands or a small scoop, form the mixture into 1 to 1½ inch balls. Arrange the balls of cake on baking sheets lined with waxed paper. Place the baking sheets in the freezer, uncovered, and let the balls freeze completely, 5 to 6 hours.

6. Remove the baking sheets from the freezer and dip the balls into a melted white or dark chocolate confectionary coating (found at craft and cake decorating stores). Using toothpicks, carefully place the balls back on the waxed paper to let the coating harden. Sprinkle the cupcake bites with sugar sprinkles or confetti sprinkles while the coating is still a little soft.

7. Or, don't bother with freezing and dipping in chocolate. Chill the cupcake bites for one hour after you've shaped them. Then, dredge them in confectioners' sugar and serve.

Have fun with the flavor combinations—pair chocolate cake with peppermint cream cheese frosting and coat the cupcake bites in dark chocolate; dust balls of lemon cake and lemon buttercream with confectioners' sugar; use white chocolate to coat cupcake bites of strawberry cake and frosting.

Cream-Filled Chocolate Cupcakes

makes:
24 cupcakes (2½ inches in diameter)

prep:
20 minutes

bake:
16 to 20 minutes

cool:
20 minutes

After completing *Cupcakes from the Cake Mix Doctor*, I had frosted and filled countless cupcakes with just about every combination of wonderful ingredients, but alas, I had not created a version of the classic Hostess-style cupcake. So I set out to create my own version of the popular cream-filled cupcake with chocolate icing and a white squiggle down the middle. You will need an icing bag and plain tip to squirt the filling into the center of the baked cupcakes. I must say this version is far better than the cupcake in the package! See for yourself.

For the cupcakes

24 paper liners for cupcake pans (2½-inch size)
1 package (18.25 ounces) chocolate cake mix with pudding
1 cup sour cream
¾ cup water
½ cup vegetable oil
3 large eggs
1 teaspoon pure vanilla extract

For the filling

4 ounces frozen whipped topping, thawed but still cold
½ cup (4 ounces) sour cream, cold
½ cup confectioners' sugar, sifted
½ teaspoon pure vanilla extract

For the frosting

Chocolate Pan Frosting (make the amount for cupcakes; page 476)
1 tube (4.25 ounces) white decorating icing

1. Make the cupcakes: Place a rack in the center of the oven and preheat the oven to 350°F. Line 24 cupcake cups with paper liners and set the pans aside.

2. Place the cake mix, sour cream, water, oil, eggs, and 1 teaspoon of vanilla in a large mixing bowl and beat with an electric mixer on low speed until the ingredients are incorporated, 1 minute. Stop the machine and scrape down the side of the bowl with a rubber spatula. Increase the mixer speed to medium and beat for 1½ to 2 minutes longer, scraping down the side of the bowl again if needed. The batter should look well combined. Spoon or scoop the batter into the lined cupcake cups, filling each about two thirds of the way full.

3. Place the pans in the oven and bake the cupcakes until the tops spring back when lightly pressed with a finger, 16 to 20 minutes. Remove the pans from the oven and place them on wire racks to cool for 5 minutes. Run a dinner knife around the edge of the cupcake cups, lift the cupcakes up from the bottom of the pans using the end of the knife, and pick the cupcakes out of the pans carefully with your fingertips. Place the cupcakes on a wire rack to cool for 15 minutes longer before filling.

4. Make the filling: Place the whipped topping, sour cream, confectioners' sugar, and ½ teaspoon of vanilla in a mixing bowl and

Recipe Reminders

MADE FOR

____
____
____
____

PREP NOTES

____
____
____
____

DON'T FORGET

____
____
____
____

SPECIAL TOUCHES

____
____
____
____
____
____
____
____
____

Mix and Match Frostings

Don't just take my word for what cupcakes go with what frosting—doctor the Doctor! Here are just a few ways you can create new cupcake and frosting matches.

Caramel frosting: Top spice cupcakes, vanilla cupcakes, chocolate chip cupcakes, or orange cupcakes

Chocolate frosting: Top peanut butter cupcakes, banana cupcakes, cinnamon cupcakes, or vanilla cupcakes

Cream cheese frosting: Top lemon cupcakes, spice cupcakes, red velvet cupcakes, or chocolate cupcakes

beat with an electric mixer on medium speed until smooth and well blended, about 1 minute. Place the bowl in the refrigerator until the cupcakes are completely cooled.

5. Using an icing bag and a plain tip with a large hole, fill the bag with filling. Push the tip through the top of each cupcake and squeeze in about 2 tablespoons of filling. Place the cupcakes in the refrigerator to chill.

6. Make the Chocolate Pan Frosting.

7. Spoon about a tablespoon of frosting on top of each cupcake and spread it out with a short metal spatula or spoon to coat. Place the cupcakes on a rack so the frosting can set, 10 minutes.

8. Using the white icing and a decorating tip, squeeze a squiggly line on top of each cupcake.

Keep It Fresh! Store these cupcakes, in a cake saver or wrapped in plastic, in the refrigerator for up to three days.

Chocolate Marbled Cupcakes

THE FIRST TIME I marbled a cupcake I must have been twelve and squirted chocolate syrup right into the yellow cake batter before baking. The chocolate swirled around and down into the batter and made the most beautiful marbleized effect. I was hooked. Through the years I've included recipes for swirling batters together, but there is something so simple and yet so delicious about swirling in chocolate that I've got to share it here. A step up from my early cupcakes, in this one you melt semisweet chocolate and then fold it into a little of the yellow cake batter. The chocolate mixture is then swirled into the main cupcake batter before baking. This way, the chocolate flows beautifully through the cake. These cupcakes are delicate and rich.

makes:
22 to 24 cupcakes (2½ inches in diameter)

prep:
15 minutes

bake:
23 to 28 minutes

cool:
20 minutes

24 paper liners for cupcake pans (2½-inch size)
½ cup (3 ounces) semisweet chocolate chips, or 4 ounces semisweet chocolate, chopped
2 tablespoons milk or water
1 package (18.5 ounces) plain butter recipe golden cake mix
1 package (8 ounces) reduced-fat cream cheese, at room temperature
½ cup vegetable oil
½ cup water
2 tablespoons granulated sugar
4 large eggs
2 teaspoons pure vanilla extract
Martha's Chocolate Icing (make the amount for cupcakes; page 480), optional

Recipe Reminders

MADE FOR

PREP NOTES

DON'T FORGET

SPECIAL TOUCHES

1. Place a rack in the center of the oven and preheat the oven to 350°F. Line 24 cupcake cups with paper liners and set the pans aside.

2. Place the chocolate and the milk or water in a medium-size microwave-safe glass bowl and microwave on high power for 40 to 45 seconds. Remove the bowl from the microwave and stir to melt the chocolate. If you need to return the bowl to the microwave to complete the melting, do so 5 seconds at a time, stirring in between. Set the melted chocolate mixture aside.

3. Place the cake mix, cream cheese, oil, water, granulated sugar, eggs, and vanilla in a large mixing bowl and beat with an electric mixer on low speed until the ingredients are incorporated, 30 seconds. Stop the machine and scrape down the side of the bowl with a rubber spatula. Increase the mixer speed to medium and beat for 1½ to 2 minutes longer, scraping down the side of the bowl again if needed. The batter should look well blended.

4. Measure out 1 cup of the cupcake batter, stir this into the melted chocolate mixture, and set it aside. Using the rest of the batter, spoon or scoop a heaping ⅓ cup of batter into each lined cupcake cup, filling it three quarters of the way full. (You will get between 22 and 24 cupcakes; remove the empty liners, if any.)

5. Drop a generous tablespoon of the chocolate batter on top of each cupcake. Swirl it into the batter using a wooden skewer or dinner knife.

6. Place the pans in the oven and bake the cupcakes until they are golden and the tops spring back when lightly pressed with a finger, 23 to 28 minutes. Remove the pans from the oven and place them on wire racks to cool for 5 minutes. Run a dinner knife around the edge of the cupcake cups, lift the cupcakes up from the bottom of the pans using the end of the knife, and pick them out of the pans carefully with your fingertips. Place the cupcakes on a wire rack to cool for 15 minutes before frosting.

7. Meanwhile, make Martha's Chocolate Icing, if using.

8. Spoon a heaping tablespoon of frosting on top of each cupcake and spread it out with a short metal spatula or spoon, taking care to cover the top completely. If using Martha's Chocolate Icing, place the cupcakes on a rack so the icing can set, 10 minutes. The cupcakes are then ready to serve.

Keep It Fresh! Store these cupcakes, in a cake saver or under a glass dome, at room temperature for up to three days or for up to one week in the refrigerator. Freeze the cupcakes, in a cake saver or wrapped in aluminum foil, for up to three months. Let the cupcakes thaw overnight in the refrigerator before serving.

How Many Minis Will the Recipe Make?

I've heard this question a lot over the years. So here is the skinny on the minis, the regulars, and the grands. One batch of cupcake or muffin batter will make:

Thirty-six cupcakes 2 inches in diameter (minis); bake them 13 to 18 minutes.

Twenty to twenty-four cupcakes 2½ inches in diameter; bake them 18 to 28 minutes.

Twelve cupcakes 3 to 4 inches in diameter; bake them 25 to 30 minutes.

Chocolate Buttermilk Cupcakes with Chocolate Fudge Marshmallow Frosting

makes:
22 to 24 cupcakes (2½ inches in diameter)

prep:
15 minutes

bake:
20 to 25 minutes

cool:
20 minutes

JUST LIKE THAT PAIR of faithful jeans or the little black dress that takes you anywhere, this cupcake recipe is versatile and adored. You can use a chocolate cake mix that is plain or has pudding in it, but you've got to add buttermilk, the secret ingredient that keeps these cupcakes moist. And you add a little flour, too, which gives the cupcakes more structure so they're able to handle one of my favorite frostings. Thick and fudgy, the frosting is a natural for cupcakes.

24 paper liners for cupcake pans (2½-inch size)
1 package (18.25 ounces) chocolate cake mix, plain or with pudding
¼ cup all-purpose flour
2 tablespoons unsweetened cocoa powder
1½ cups buttermilk
½ cup vegetable oil
3 large eggs
2 teaspoons pure vanilla extract
Chocolate Fudge Marshmallow Frosting (page 479)

1. Place a rack in the center of the oven and preheat the oven to 350°F. Line 24 cupcake cups with paper liners and set the pans aside.

2. Place the cake mix, flour, cocoa powder, buttermilk, oil, eggs, and vanilla in a large mixing bowl and beat with an electric mixer on low speed until the ingredients are incorporated, 30 seconds. Stop the machine and scrape down the side of the bowl with a rubber spatula. Increase the mixer speed to medium and beat for 1½ to 2 minutes longer, scraping down the side of the bowl again if needed. The batter should look well blended.

3. Spoon or scoop a heaping ¼ cup of cupcake batter into each lined cupcake cup, filling it two thirds of the way full. (You will get between 22 and 24 cupcakes; remove the empty liners, if any.)

4. Place the pans in the oven and bake the cupcakes until the tops spring back when lightly pressed with a finger, 20 to 25 minutes. Remove the pans from the oven and place them on wire racks to cool for 5 minutes. Run a dinner knife around the edge of the cupcake cups, lift the cupcakes up from the bottom of the pans using the end of the knife, and pick them out of the pans carefully with your fingertips. Place the cupcakes on a wire rack to cool for 15 minutes longer before frosting.

5. Meanwhile, make the Chocolate Fudge Marshmallow Frosting.

6. Spoon a heaping tablespoon of frosting on top of each cupcake and swirl it with a short metal spatula or spoon to spread it out, taking care to cover the top completely. The cupcakes are then ready to serve.

Keep It Fresh! Store these cupcakes, in a cake saver or under a glass dome, at room temperature for up to three days or for up to one week in the refrigerator. Freeze the cupcakes, in a cake saver or wrapped in aluminum foil, for up to three months. Let the cupcakes thaw overnight in the refrigerator before serving.

Recipe Reminders

MADE FOR

PREP NOTES

DON'T FORGET

SPECIAL TOUCHES

German Chocolate Cupcakes

makes:
22 to 24 cupcakes (2½ inches in diameter)

prep:
25 minutes

bake:
19 to 23 minutes

cool:
20 minutes

IT'S FUNNY WHAT YOU LEARN about cakes when you write a book about them and travel on a book tour! I knew apple and pumpkin pies were the way to a man's heart, but German chocolate cake . . . I had no idea. At bookstore signings men of all ages lined up for samples of the German chocolate cake. On air, male TV hosts gushed about their mom's German chocolate cake. So here you have a cupcake for Valentine's Day or for birthdays or for any special occasion for that man in your life. This is the real deal, a moist cake with the legendary coconut and pecan frosting.

24 paper liners for cupcake pans (2½-inch size)
1 bar (4 ounces) German's sweet chocolate (see Note)
1 package (18.25 ounces) plain German chocolate cake mix
3 tablespoons vanilla instant pudding mix
1 cup reduced-fat sour cream, or 1 cup buttermilk
½ cup water
½ cup vegetable oil
4 large eggs
1 teaspoon pure vanilla extract
My Coconut Pecan Frosting (page 484)

1. Place a rack in the center of the oven and preheat the oven to 350°F. Line 24 cupcake cups with paper liners and set the pans aside.

2. Grate the chocolate bar: Break the bar into pieces and drop them, one at a time, through the feed tube of a food processor while it is running. Or, carefully rub the chocolate bar with a hand-held coarse cheese grater, such as a Microplane. Set the grated chocolate aside.

3. Place the cake mix, pudding mix, sour cream or buttermilk, water, oil, eggs, and vanilla in a large mixing bowl and beat with an electric mixer on low speed until the ingredients are incorporated, 30 seconds. Stop the machine and scrape down the side of the bowl with a rubber spatula. Increase the mixer speed to medium and beat for 1½ to 2 minutes longer, scraping down the side of the bowl again if needed. The batter should look well blended. Fold in the grated chocolate.

4. Spoon or scoop ⅓ cup of cupcake batter into each lined cupcake cup, filling it three quarters of the way full. (You will get between 22 and 24 cupcakes; remove the empty liners, if any.)

5. Place the pans in the oven and bake the cupcakes until the tops spring back when lightly pressed with a finger, 19 to 23 minutes. Remove the pans from the oven and place them on wire racks to cool for 5 minutes. Run a dinner knife around the edge of the cupcake cups, lift the cupcakes up from the bottom of the pans using the end of the knife, and pick them out of the pans carefully with your fingertips. Place the cupcakes on a wire rack to cool for 15 minutes longer before frosting.

6. Meanwhile, make the coconut pecan frosting.

Recipe Reminders

MADE FOR

PREP NOTES

DON'T FORGET

SPECIAL TOUCHES

7. Spoon a heaping tablespoon of frosting on top of each cupcake and spread it out with a short metal spatula or spoon, taking care to cover the top completely. The cupcakes are then ready to serve.

Keep It Fresh! Store these cupcakes, in a cake saver or under a glass dome, at room temperature for one day or for up to one week in the refrigerator. Freeze the cupcakes, in a cake saver or wrapped in aluminum foil, for up to three months. Let the cupcakes thaw overnight in the refrigerator before serving.

Note: You may omit the German's chocolate if you like. Or, you can substitute 1 cup of miniature semisweet chocolate chips for the grated German's chocolate.

Red Velvet Peppermint Cupcakes

makes:
22 to 24 cupcakes (2½ inches in diameter)

prep:
10 minutes

bake:
20 to 25 minutes

cool:
20 minutes

RED VELVET CAKE enjoys a cultlike following. People just go gaga over this cake, and everyone has their philosophy as to how the cake should taste and what frosting is appropriate for it. In much of the Midwest a cooked flour and sugar frosting is spread over red velvet cakes, but everyone else agrees that a cream cheese frosting works well. I may be creating a real red velvet faux pas here, adding a dash of peppermint extract to the batter, but try it and see for yourself. Now I can't decide which frosting works best—cream cheese or chocolate pan frosting. To make these party ready, crush peppermint candies and sprinkle them on top of the cupcakes before the frosting sets.

24 paper liners for cupcake pans (2½-inch size)
1 package (18.25 ounces) German chocolate cake mix, with or without pudding
1 cup sour cream or buttermilk (see Note)
½ cup water
½ cup vegetable oil
3 large eggs
1 bottle (1 ounce) red food coloring
½ teaspoon pure peppermint extract, or to taste
Cream Cheese Frosting (page 471), or Chocolate Pan Frosting (make the amount for cupcakes; page 476)
Crushed peppermint candies (optional)

Recipe Reminders

MADE FOR

PREP NOTES

DON'T FORGET

SPECIAL TOUCHES

1. Place a rack in the center of the oven and preheat the oven to 350°F. Line 24 cupcake cups with paper liners and set the pans aside.

2. Place the cake mix, sour cream, water, oil, eggs, food coloring, and peppermint extract in a large mixing bowl and beat with an electric mixer on low speed until the ingredients are incorporated, 30 seconds. Stop the machine and scrape down the side of the bowl with a rubber spatula, then taste the batter and add more peppermint extract, if desired. Increase the mixer speed to medium and beat for 1½ to 2 minutes longer, scraping down the side of the bowl again if needed. The batter should look well blended.

3. Spoon or scoop a heaping ¼ cup of cupcake batter into each lined cupcake cup, filling it two thirds of the way full. (You will get between 22 and 24 cupcakes; remove the empty liners, if any.)

4. Place the pans in the oven and bake the cupcakes until the tops spring back when lightly pressed with a finger, 20 to 25 minutes. Remove the pans from the oven and place them on wire racks to cool for 5 minutes. Run a dinner knife around the edge of the cupcake cups, lift the cupcakes up from the bottom of the pans using the end of the knife, and pick them out of the pans carefully with your fingertips. Place the cupcakes on a wire rack to cool for 15 minutes longer before frosting.

5. Meanwhile, make the Cream Cheese Frosting or the Chocolate Pan Frosting.

6. Spoon a heaping tablespoon of frosting on top of each cupcake and spread it out with a short metal spatula or spoon, taking care to cover the top completely. Sprinkle the tops with some of the candy pieces, if using, then place the cupcakes, uncovered or in a cake saver, in the refrigerator until the frosting sets, 20 minutes. The cupcakes are then ready to serve.

Keep It Fresh! Store these cupcakes, in a cake saver or under a glass dome, at room temperature for up to three days or for up to one week in the refrigerator. Freeze the cupcakes, in a cake saver or wrapped in aluminum foil, for up to six months. Let the cupcakes thaw overnight in the refrigerator before serving.

Note: You can use either sour cream or buttermilk—or a combination of the two—in this recipe. For a lower fat version, use plain yogurt.

Strawberry Cheesecake Cupcakes

makes:
26 to 28 cupcakes (2½ inches in diameter)

prep:
20 minutes

bake:
20 to 25 minutes

cool:
20 minutes

THIS FUN RECIPE comes from Nadine Ballard of Centerville, Ohio. Her daughter's volleyball and crew teams recruit her to bake for everyone's birthday, and she came up with this recipe. I love the creamy cheesecake filling and the classic strawberry cake in these cupcakes. I added the lemon-flavored buttercream frosting but Nadine favors a cream cheese frosting. We both agree the best garnish is a slice of strawberry.

For the cupcakes

28 paper liners for cupcake pans (2½-inch size)
1 package (18.25 ounces) plain white cake mix
1 package (3 ounces) strawberry gelatin
4 tablespoons all-purpose flour
1 cup milk
½ cup vegetable oil
½ cup crushed fresh strawberries (5 to 6 large berries; see Note)
3 large eggs

For the filling

1 package (8 ounces) cream cheese, at room temperature
⅓ cup granulated sugar
1 large egg
Lemony Buttercream Frosting (page 469), or Buttercream Frosting (page 468)

1. Place a rack in the center of the oven and preheat the oven to 350°F. Line 28 cupcake cups with paper liners and set the pans aside.

2. Make the cupcake batter: Place the cake mix, strawberry gelatin, and flour in a large mixing bowl and stir to combine. Add the milk, oil, strawberries, and 3 eggs and beat with an electric mixer on low speed until the ingredients are incorporated, 30 seconds. Stop the machine and scrape down the side of the bowl with a rubber spatula. Increase the mixer speed to medium and beat for 1½ to 2 minutes longer, scraping down the side of the bowl again if needed. The batter should look well blended. Set the batter aside.

3. Make the filling: Place the cream cheese, granulated sugar, and 1 egg in a medium-size mixing bowl and beat with an electric mixer on low speed until the mixture is creamy, 1 minute.

4. Spoon or scoop a heaping ¼ cup of cupcake batter into each lined cupcake cup, filling it two thirds of the way full. (You will get between 26 and 28 cupcakes; remove the empty liners, if any.) Spoon a generous tablespoon of the cheesecake filling over each cupcake.

5. Place the pans on the center rack of the oven. If both pans do not fit on one oven rack, it's fine to let a pan sit on the counter while the first batch of cupcakes bake. Bake the cupcakes

Recipe Reminders

MADE FOR

____
____
____
____

PREP NOTES

____
____
____
____

DON'T FORGET

____
____
____
____

SPECIAL TOUCHES

____
____
____
____
____
____
____
____
____

until the tops spring back when lightly pressed with a finger, 20 to 25 minutes. Remove the pans from the oven and place them on wire racks to cool for 5 minutes. Run a dinner knife around the edge of the cupcake cups, lift the cupcakes up from the bottom of the pans using the end of the knife, and pick them out of the pans carefully with your fingertips. Place the cupcakes on a wire rack to cool for 15 minutes longer before frosting.

6. Meanwhile, make the Lemony Buttercream Frosting.

7. Spoon a tablespoon of frosting on top of each cupcake and spread it out with a short metal spatula or spoon, taking care to cover the top completely. The cupcakes are then ready to serve.

Keep It Fresh! Store these cupcakes, in a cake saver or under a glass dome, at room temperature for up to two days or for up to one week in the refrigerator. Freeze the cupcakes, in a cake saver or wrapped in aluminum foil, for up to three months. Let the cupcakes thaw overnight in the refrigerator before serving.

Note: You can use frozen strawberries for these cupcakes. Measure a generous ½ cup of unsweetened frozen strawberries, place them in a small microwave-safe glass bowl, and microwave on high power for 1 minute. Remove the bowl and crush the berries with a potato masher or the back of a fork. Drain off some of the liquid before measuring the berries again.

Turn a White Mix into Chocolate

If you've got a white cake mix and want to make chocolate cupcakes, don't fret. Stir a quarter cup of unsweetened cocoa into the white cake mix before beating it with the other ingredients. You may need to add a little extra liquid, say another tablespoon or two, because cocoa can dry out a batter. And, make sure you pick a sweet and creamy frosting for the top.

Lemon Cupcakes with a Lemony Buttercream Frosting

THERE IS ALWAYS A PLACE for a lemon cake and so it goes with lemon cupcakes. Take them to a potluck and those who don't love chocolate will thank you. Bring them to a bake sale and you'll have buyers young and old. There isn't a season or a time or a place that doesn't welcome the flavor of fresh lemons. All you need for this recipe—besides the basics—are lemons! Use a large one for the cupcakes and a medium-size lemon to make the frosting.

makes:
22 to 24 cupcakes (2½ inches in diameter)

prep:
15 minutes

bake:
20 to 25 minutes

cool:
20 minutes

24 paper liners for cupcake pans (2½-inch size)
1 large or 2 small lemons
1 package (18.25 ounces) plain yellow cake mix
3 tablespoons vanilla instant pudding mix
1 tablespoon granulated sugar
1 cup warm water
½ cup vegetable oil
3 large eggs
Lemony Buttercream Frosting (page 469)

1. Place a rack in the center of the oven and preheat the oven to 350°F. Line 24 cupcake cups with paper liners and set the pans aside.

2. Rinse the lemon and pat it dry with paper towels. Grate enough zest to measure about 1 tablespoon. Cut the lemon in half and squeeze ⅓ cup of lemon juice into a small bowl.

Recipe Reminders

MADE FOR

____

____

____

____

PREP NOTES

____

____

____

____

DON'T FORGET

____

____

____

____

SPECIAL TOUCHES

____

____

____

____

____

____

____

____

3. Place the lemon zest and juice in a large mixing bowl. Add the cake mix, pudding mix, granulated sugar, water, oil, and eggs and beat with an electric mixer on low speed until the ingredients are incorporated, 30 seconds. Stop the machine and scrape down the side of the bowl with a rubber spatula. Increase the mixer speed to medium and beat for 1½ to 2 minutes longer, scraping down the side of the bowl again if needed. The batter should look well blended.

4. Spoon or scoop about ⅓ cup of cupcake batter into each lined cupcake cup, filling it three quarters of the way full. (You will get between 22 and 24 cupcakes; remove the empty liners, if any.)

5. Place the pans in the oven and bake the cupcakes until they are golden and the tops spring back when lightly pressed with a finger, 20 to 25 minutes. Remove the pans from the oven and place them on wire racks to cool for 5 minutes. Run a dinner knife around the edge of the cupcake cups, lift the cupcakes up from the bottom of the pans using the end of the knife, and pick them out of the pans carefully with your fingertips. Place the cupcakes on a wire rack to cool for 15 minutes longer before frosting.

6. Meanwhile, make the Lemony Buttercream Frosting.

7. Spoon a heaping tablespoon of frosting on top of each cupcake and spread it out with a short metal spatula or spoon, taking care to cover the top completely. The cupcakes are then ready to serve.

Keep It Fresh! Store these cupcakes, in a cake saver or under a glass dome, at room temperature for up to three days or for up to one week in the refrigerator. Freeze the cupcakes, in a cake saver or wrapped in aluminum foil, for up to three months. Let the cupcakes thaw overnight in the refrigerator before serving.

White Sour Cream Cupcakes

EITHER SOUR CREAM OR YOGURT works well in this simple recipe—as does your choice of a liquid, whether it's water or orange juice. Bake these and frost them with Cream Cheese Frosting for serving at home. Top the cupcakes with a thin smear of orange marmalade before frosting them for a cupcake perfect for afternoon tea or a bridal luncheon. Flavor the batter with a bit of almond extract or use orange juice as the liquid to turn them into cupcakes custom-made for a wedding, especially if arranged on a cupcake tree. The garnishes are limitless—try white chocolate shavings, toasted almonds, or pomegranate seeds.

makes:
22 to 24 cupcakes (2½ inches in diameter)

prep:
15 minutes

bake:
18 to 23 minutes

cool:
20 minutes

24 paper liners for cupcake pans (2½-inch size)
1 package (18.25 ounces) plain white cake mix
3 tablespoons vanilla instant pudding mix
1 cup sour cream or plain low-fat yogurt
½ cup vegetable oil
½ cup water or orange juice
3 large eggs
1 teaspoon pure vanilla extract
Cream Cheese Frosting (page 471)

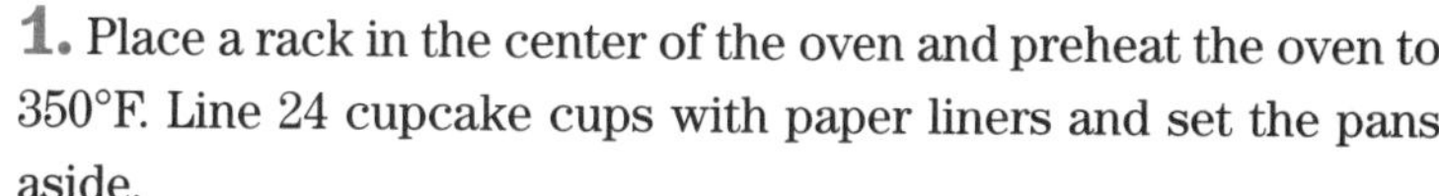

1. Place a rack in the center of the oven and preheat the oven to 350°F. Line 24 cupcake cups with paper liners and set the pans aside.

2. Place the cake mix, pudding mix, sour cream or yogurt, oil, water or orange juice, eggs, and vanilla in a large mixing bowl and

Recipe Reminders

MADE FOR

PREP NOTES

DON'T FORGET

SPECIAL TOUCHES

beat with an electric mixer on low speed until the ingredients are incorporated, 30 seconds. Stop the machine and scrape down the side of the bowl with a rubber spatula. Increase the mixer speed to medium and beat for 1½ to 2 minutes longer, scraping down the side of the bowl again if needed. The batter should look well blended.

3. Spoon or scoop a heaping ¼ cup of cupcake batter into each lined cupcake cup, filling it two thirds of the way full. (You will get between 22 and 24 cupcakes; remove the empty liners, if any.)

4. Place the pans in the oven and bake the cupcakes until they are golden and the tops spring back when lightly pressed with a finger, 18 to 23 minutes. Remove the pans from the oven and place them on wire racks to cool for 5 minutes. Run a dinner knife around the edge of the cupcake cups, lift the cupcakes up from the bottom of the pans using the end of the knife, and pick them out of the pans carefully with your fingertips. Place the cupcakes on a wire rack to cool for 15 minutes longer before frosting.

5. Meanwhile, make the Cream Cheese Frosting.

6. Spoon a heaping tablespoon of frosting on top of each cupcake and spread it out with a short metal spatula or spoon, taking care to cover the top completely. Place the cupcakes, uncovered or in a cake saver, in the refrigerator until the frosting sets, 20 minutes. The cupcakes are then ready to serve.

Keep It Fresh! Store these cupcakes, in a cake saver or under a glass dome, at room temperature for up to three days or for up to one week in the refrigerator. Freeze the cupcakes, wrapped in aluminum foil, for up to three months. Let the cupcakes thaw overnight in the refrigerator before serving.

Holiday Cupcake Ideas

Some moms seem to have a cupcake for every occasion, don't they? Here are five ideas for creating cupcakes for your next holiday party. Move over supermoms!

Halloween—Bake chocolate cupcakes and prepare a plain buttercream or cream cheese frosting. Tint the frosting orange. Take a tube of black or brown frosting and pipe out a spooky face or a big jack-o'-lantern smile on each cupcake. Or do as my daughter Litton did at a recent Halloween and arrange the orange cupcakes on a big platter in the shape of a pumpkin. She piped a pumpkin face over the cupcakes and with a green icing tube piped out the stem at the top.

New Year's—I'm thinking of an elegant black, white, gold, and silver combination to ring in the New Year. Bake white cupcakes and frost half of them with plain buttercream and the other half with chocolate frosting—the sour cream ganache would be nice. Buy gold and silver edible glitter and sprinkle this over the frosted cupcakes.

Mardi Gras—The colors of this holiday are purple, gold, and green, symbolizing justice, power, and faith, in that order. To make multicolored Mardi Gras cupcakes mix together a white cupcake batter and divide it into three bowls. Add purple food coloring to one bowl (mix blue with a little red to get purple); to another bowl add yellow food coloring, and to the last, add green. For each cupcake, place a small scoop of each colored batter in the cupcake liner. Bake the cupcakes, then frost them with plain cream cheese frosting and decorate them with purple, gold, and green sprinkles. This same method can be used for Easter egg cupcakes—choose the springtime colors pink, green, and yellow.

Valentine's Day—Make "Sweetheart" cupcakes using heart-shaped baking pans and a red velvet or white cupcake batter. Frost the cupcakes with a plain cream cheese frosting. Then, using a tube of icing, pen the mottoes found on those Sweetheart candies, like "Be mine."

Fourth of July—Last summer my older daughter Kathleen and her friend Marybeth baked their annual July Fourth cupcakes together. They often rely on the Pillsbury confetti cupcake mix, but without one at hand, they created their own. They folded "confetti" flattened colored sugar sprinkles into my White Sour Cream Cupcakes batter (see page 371) before baking. They frosted the cupcakes with plain cream cheese frosting. And then they went wild with the red, white, and blue decorations. When creativity wanes, enlist teens to help out!

10 Big Bake Sale Secrets

You baked it and homemade is always a big hit. But these plan-ahead tips should help you bring in even more money at the bake sale table.

1. Think whole cakes and whole pies. Think of a pan of brownies someone can stash in the freezer. With less time to bake at home, people love bake sales for stocking up on dinner party cakes they can freeze and for whole pies and batches of brownies and cookies they can take to a neighbor or to the office.

2. When it comes to cakes, go with the mainstream favorites—chocolate layer cakes, cozy pound cakes, and nostalgic carrot cakes.

3. Also think small. Parents may give kids money to spend at the sale and kids will enjoy a frosted cupcake or small plastic bags filled with homemade cookies.

4. The best cookies for selling are such classics as oatmeal-raisin and chocolate chip or cookies that are a specialty of one of the bake sale bakers. These can be heirloom holiday cookies, old-fashioned snickerdoodles, or some cookies that are rare and delicious and not available at any other time and place. Write the name of the baker on the tag, such as "Judy's Snickerdoodles."

5. No wrapping is needed for cupcakes. The favorite flavor of all time is vanilla frosted with chocolate and dusted with sugar sprinkles.

6. You've got to have pies—fudge, lemon meringue, chess, apple, or pecan. A cake may woo a woman, but the pie is the way to a man's heart. And you can sell fruit cobblers and crisps ready to take home and heat for dessert.

7. Love the loaves, too. When it comes to whole loaves of sweet breads, banana and pumpkin are the most coveted. Fall is also the time for apple cinnamon and zucchini breads.

8. Sell homemade rolls right in the pan or a dozen cornbread muffins or bran muffins for breakfast—breads are beloved but not often baked.

9. To jazz up brownie sales, don't just bake plain ones. Fill them with mint candies or brush them with Kahlúa as they cool in the pan. Frost the top with a homemade icing. Don't forget butterscotch brownies and peanut butter bars. Bake these in disposable aluminum pans and sell them by the panful.

10. And last, but not least, have candy makers prepare toffee, divinity, and peanut brittle. Bag them in clear plastic and tie them with a pretty bow. These are both a delicacy and a really sweet deal.

Bake Sale Caramel Cupcakes

I F YOU'VE READ MY BOOKS you know I love homemade caramel frosting. I'm especially fond of the recipe I share here because it is one my mother gave me years ago. What makes caramel frosting on a vanilla cupcake special is its delicious simplicity. And, what makes the frosting perfect for bake sales is that it isn't affected by heat or humidity, it travels well without smudging, and most important, it is beloved by all.

makes:
22 to 24 cupcakes (2½ inches in diameter)

prep:
15 minutes

bake:
20 to 25 minutes

cool:
20 minutes

24 paper liners for cupcake pans (2½-inch size)
1 package (18.25 ounces) plain yellow cake mix
3 tablespoons vanilla instant pudding mix
1¼ cups milk
½ cup vegetable oil
4 large eggs
1 teaspoon pure vanilla extract
Quick Caramel Frosting (page 485)

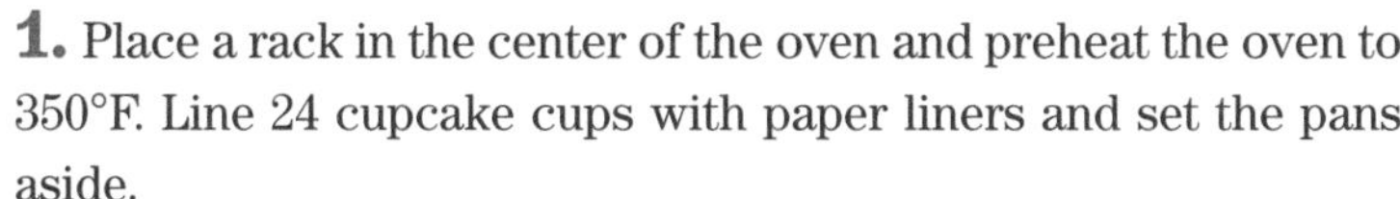

1. Place a rack in the center of the oven and preheat the oven to 350°F. Line 24 cupcake cups with paper liners and set the pans aside.

2. Place the cake mix, pudding mix, milk, oil, eggs, and vanilla in a large mixing bowl and beat with an electric mixer on low speed until the ingredients are incorporated, 30 seconds. Stop

Recipe Reminders

MADE FOR

PREP NOTES

DON'T FORGET

SPECIAL TOUCHES

the machine and scrape down the side of the bowl with a rubber spatula. Increase the mixer speed to medium and beat for 1½ to 2 minutes longer, scraping down the side of the bowl again if needed. The batter should look well blended.

3. Spoon or scoop a heaping ¼ cup of cupcake batter into each lined cupcake cup, filling it two thirds of the way full. (You will get between 22 and 24 cupcakes; remove the empty liners, if any.)

4. Place the pans in the oven and bake the cupcakes until they are golden and the tops spring back when lightly pressed with a finger, 20 to 25 minutes. Remove the pans from the oven and place them on wire racks to cool for 5 minutes. Run a dinner knife around the edge of the cupcake cups, lift the cupcakes up from the bottom of the pans using the end of the knife, and pick them out of the pans carefully with your fingertips. Place the cupcakes on a wire rack to cool for 15 minutes longer before frosting.

5. Meanwhile, make the Quick Caramel Frosting.

6. Spoon a heaping tablespoon of frosting on top of each cupcake and spread it out with a short metal spatula or spoon, taking care to cover the top completely. The cupcakes are then ready to serve.

Keep It Fresh! Store these cupcakes, in a cake saver or under a glass dome, at room temperature for up to five days or for up to one week in the refrigerator. Freeze the cupcakes, in a cake saver or wrapped in aluminum foil, for up to three months. Let the cupcakes thaw overnight on the counter before serving.

Sock-It-To-Me Muffins

SOME OF MY FAVORITE COFFEE CAKES are the ones that begin with a yellow cake mix that you sprinkle with streusel layers of cinnamon, brown sugar, and pecans. I shared the Sock-It-To-Me Cake, all the rage in the 1970s, in the first book. These muffins are a take-off on that legendary cinnamon cake. Bake the muffins ahead of time for brunches and parties and freeze them until needed.

makes:
20 muffins (2½ inches in diameter)

prep:
20 minutes

bake:
20 to 25 minutes

cool:
25 minutes

For the streusel

⅓ cup packed light brown sugar
2 teaspoons ground cinnamon
½ cup finely chopped pecans

For the muffins

Vegetable oil spray, for misting the pans
1 package (18.5 ounces) plain butter recipe golden cake mix
2 tablespoons all-purpose flour
1 cup sour cream or buttermilk
⅓ cup vegetable oil
¼ cup water
3 large eggs
1 teaspoon pure vanilla extract

Recipe Reminders

MADE FOR

PREP NOTES

DON'T FORGET

SPECIAL TOUCHES

1. Make the streusel: Place the brown sugar, cinnamon, and pecans in a small bowl and stir to combine. Set the streusel aside.

2. Make the muffins: Place a rack in the center of the oven and preheat the oven to 375°F. Lightly mist 20 cupcake cups with vegetable oil spray and set the pans aside.

3. Place the cake mix and flour in a large mixing bowl. Whisk out any lumps with a small wire whisk. Add the sour cream or buttermilk, oil, water, eggs, and vanilla to the bowl and stir with a wooden spoon until the eggs are beaten and the ingredients are just incorporated, 40 to 50 strokes. There may still be lumps in the batter.

4. Spoon or scoop a couple of tablespoons of muffin batter into each of the prepared cupcake cups. Add a generous teaspoon of streusel mixture to each. Spoon or scoop another couple of tablespoons of batter into each cup, then top with another teaspoon of streusel, filling it three quarters of the way full.

5. Place the pans in the oven and bake the muffins until they are golden and the tops spring back when lightly pressed with a finger, 20 to 25 minutes. Remove the pans from the oven and place them on wire racks to cool for 5 minutes. Run a dinner knife around the edge of the muffins, lift them up from the bottom of the pans using the end of the knife, and pick them out of the pans carefully with your fingertips. Place the muffins on a wire rack to cool for 20 minutes longer, then serve.

Keep It Fresh! Store these muffins, in a cake saver or under a glass dome, at room temperature for up to five days. Freeze the muffins, in a cake saver or wrapped in aluminum foil, for up to three months. Let the muffins thaw overnight on the counter before serving.

Chocolate Chip Muffins

MY DAUGHTER LITTON loves to bake muffins and her favorites are chocolate chip muffins. They're great for a snack, dessert in a lunch box, or even for a dinner dessert. This muffin recipe is a lot better than the chocolate chip muffin mixes out there on supermarket shelves. It's easy to assemble with ingredients you've got on hand. The mini chips fold in nicely and don't sink to the bottom as larger chips often do. As always when baking muffins, bake them in an oven that's a little hotter than you would usually use—375°F—so they bake quickly and develop a nice crunchy crust.

makes:
20 to 22 muffins (2½ inches in diameter)

prep:
10 minutes

bake:
17 to 22 minutes

cool:
25 minutes

Vegetable oil spray, for misting the pans
1 package (18.5 ounces) plain butter recipe golden cake mix, or 1 package (18.25 ounces) yellow or vanilla cake mix with pudding
2 tablespoons all-purpose flour
1 cup vanilla low-fat yogurt
½ cup vegetable oil
½ cup water
3 large eggs
1 cup (6 ounces) miniature semisweet chocolate chips

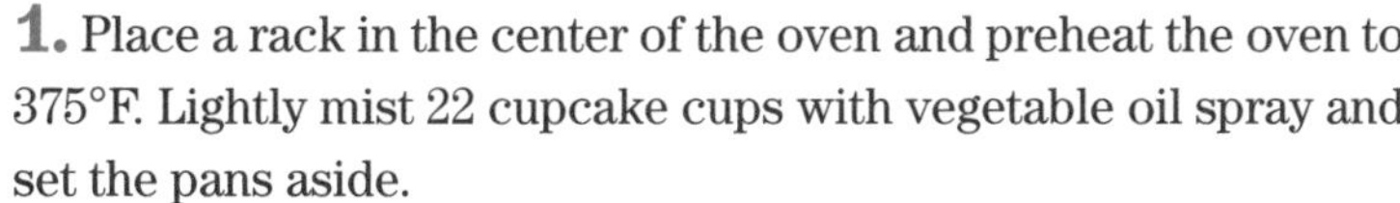

1. Place a rack in the center of the oven and preheat the oven to 375°F. Lightly mist 22 cupcake cups with vegetable oil spray and set the pans aside.

Recipe Reminders

MADE FOR

PREP NOTES

DON'T FORGET

SPECIAL TOUCHES

2. Place the cake mix and flour in a large mixing bowl. Whisk out any lumps with a small wire whisk. Add the yogurt, oil, water, and eggs to the bowl and stir with a wooden spoon until the eggs are beaten and the ingredients are just incorporated, 40 to 50 strokes. There may still be lumps in the batter. Fold in the chocolate chips.

3. Spoon or scoop ⅓ cup of muffin batter into the prepared cupcake cups, filling them three quarters of the way full. (You will get between 20 and 22 muffins.)

4. Place the pans in the oven and bake the muffins until they are golden and the tops spring back when lightly pressed with a finger, 17 to 22 minutes. Remove the pans from the oven and place them on wire racks to cool for 5 minutes. Run a dinner knife around the edge of the muffins, lift them up from the bottom of the pans using the end of the knife, and pick them out of the pans carefully with your fingertips. Place the muffins on a wire rack to cool 20 minutes longer, then serve.

Keep It Fresh! Store these muffins, in a cake saver or under a glass dome, at room temperature for up to five days. Freeze the muffins, in a cake saver or wrapped in aluminum foil, for up to three months. Let the muffins thaw overnight on the counter before serving.

Apple Spice Muffins

Years ago Diana Crawford, a resident of Martinsburg, West Virginia, sent me a wonderful apple spice Bundt cake recipe that ended up winning my recipe contest. I remembered that cake when creating this muffin recipe. Diana's cake begins with a spice mix to which she adds maple flavoring and buttermilk, and so does this batter. And it also includes chopped fresh apple; use whatever you've got—the more tart and crisp the apple, the better the muffin flavor will be.

makes:
20 muffins (2½ inches in diameter)

prep:
20 minutes

bake:
20 to 25 minutes

cool:
25 minutes

Vegetable oil spray, for misting the pans
1 package (18.25 ounces) plain spice cake mix
1⅓ cups buttermilk
½ cup vegetable oil
3 large eggs
1 teaspoon maple flavoring
1 cup finely chopped apple
¼ cup packed light brown sugar
¼ cup finely chopped pecans, plus additional for sprinkling
½ teaspoon ground cinnamon

1. Place a rack in the center of the oven and preheat the oven to 375°F. Lightly mist 22 cupcake cups with vegetable oil spray and set the pans aside.

Recipe Reminders

MADE FOR

PREP NOTES

DON'T FORGET

SPECIAL TOUCHES

2. Place the cake mix, buttermilk, oil, eggs, and maple flavoring in a large mixing bowl and stir with a wooden spoon until the eggs are beaten and the ingredients are just incorporated, 40 to 50 strokes. There may still be lumps in the batter. Set the batter aside.

3. Place the apple in a small bowl along with the brown sugar, the ¼ cup pecans, and the cinnamon. Stir to combine.

4. Spoon or scoop a couple of tablespoons of muffin batter into the prepared cupcake cups, then top with a heaping teaspoon of the apple mixture. Spoon or scoop another couple of tablespoons of batter into the filled cups, then top with another heaping teaspoon of apple mixture. Sprinkle the tops with the additional pecans.

5. Place the pans in the oven and bake the muffins until the tops spring back when lightly pressed with a finger, 20 to 25 minutes. Remove the pans from the oven and place them on wire racks to cool for 5 minutes. Run a dinner knife around the edge of the muffins, lift them up from the bottom of the pans using the end of the knife, and pick them out of the pans carefully with your fingertips. Place the muffins on a wire rack to cool for 20 minutes longer, then serve.

Keep It Fresh! Store these muffins, in a cake saver or under a glass dome, at room temperature for up to three days. Freeze the muffins, in a cake saver or wrapped in aluminum foil, for up to three months. Let the muffins thaw overnight on the counter before serving.

Cake Mix Cinnamon Rolls

MINNEAPOLIS WAS ONE of the first wintry stops I made on the book tour for the first *Cake Mix Doctor* book. My media escort Lois Lee and I trudged through the snow from TV station to TV station. We had a good time getting to know each other, and by the end of my visit Lois mentioned a recipe she just had to send me. It was for cinnamon rolls that begin, believe it or not, with a box of cake mix. I baked those rolls up when I returned home and loved the recipe. Every time I take a bite of these I think of Lois and the frozen tundra of the north! Keep in mind that you will need two 13 by 9–inch metal baking pans to make the cinnamon rolls.

makes:
about 30 rolls

prep:
2½ to 3 hours

bake:
28 to 32 minutes

cool:
2 to 3 minutes

2½ cups warm water (105° to 115°F)
About 2 packages (½ ounce total) active plain dry yeast
1 teaspoon pure vanilla extract
1 teaspoon salt
1 package (18.25 ounces) plain yellow cake mix
5 cups all-purpose flour, plus ⅓ cup flour for rolling out the dough
2 cups packed light brown sugar
16 tablespoons (2 sticks) butter, plus 4 tablespoons (½ stick) butter, melted
2 tablespoons light corn syrup
1 cup chopped pecans
½ cup granulated sugar
1 tablespoon ground cinnamon

Recipe Reminders

MADE FOR

PREP NOTES

DON'T FORGET

SPECIAL TOUCHES

1. Pour the warm water into a large mixing bowl, add the yeast, and stir until it dissolves. Stir in the vanilla and salt, then stir in the cake mix and the 5 cups of flour until well combined. Cover the bowl with a clean kitchen towel, place it in a warm place, and let the dough rise for 1 hour.

2. Meanwhile, make a caramel sauce: Place the brown sugar, 16 tablespoons of butter, and the corn syrup in a small saucepan over low heat. Stir until the brown sugar dissolves, then stir in the pecans. Divide the caramel sauce between two 13 by 9–inch metal baking pans and set the pans aside.

3. After an hour, uncover the dough and punch it down with your fist. Divide the dough in half. Use half of the remaining ⅓ cup of flour to dust a large work surface and flour a rolling pin. Roll one half of the dough into a rectangle about 12 by 18 inches and about ¼ inch thick. Brush the rectangle of dough with 2 tablespoons of the melted butter. Stir the granulated sugar and cinnamon together in a small bowl and sprinkle half of this over the melted butter on the rectangle of dough. Starting at one of the long sides, roll the dough rectangle up like a jelly roll.

4. Using a floured knife, cut the roll of dough crosswise into roughly 1-inch-thick slices; the log will make about 15 slices. Arrange the slices of dough cut-side-down and side by side on top of the caramel mixture in one of the baking pans.

5. Using the remaining flour, dust the work surface again and roll out the remaining dough into a 12 by 18–inch rectangle. Brush the rectangle of dough with the remaining 2 tablespoons of melted butter, sprinkle the remaining sugar and cinnamon mixture on top, then roll up the dough and cut it into 1-inch-thick slices. Arrange the rolls in the second baking pan. Cover each baking pan with a kitchen towel, place the pans in a warm place, and let the rolls rise for 30 minutes.

6. Meanwhile, place a rack in the center of the oven and preheat the oven to 350°F.

7. Place the baking pans in the oven side by side and bake the rolls until they spring back when lightly pressed with a finger, 28 to 32 minutes. Remove the pans from the oven and place them on wire racks to cool for 2 to 3 minutes. Run a dinner knife around the edge of the rolls and then invert them onto a rectangular serving platter. Serve the rolls warm.

Keep It Fresh! Store these rolls, covered with aluminum foil, at room temperature for up to three days. Freeze the rolls, wrapped in foil, for up to six months. Let the rolls thaw overnight on the counter before serving. Reheat the rolls, covered with foil, in a 350°F oven for 10 minutes.

Whoopie Pies

makes:
about 18 whoopie pies

prep:
20 minutes

bake:
10 to 12 minutes

cool:
35 minutes

THROUGH THE YEARS readers have told me about a dessert called a whoopie pie. Some of them say it is Midwestern in origin, others say from southwestern Pennsylvania. They have tempted me with the description—two soft little chocolate cakes between which you sandwich a creamy vanilla filling. One reader kindly called them Oreos on steroids! Well, I was curious to find the recipe and bake them. Thanks to Joan Linthicum of Raleigh, North Carolina, for sending me her recipe. These buttery, soft cakes are something Joan has been baking for more than twenty years.

For the cakes

1 package (18.25 ounces) plain chocolate cake mix
8 tablespoons (1 stick) butter, melted
1 large egg

For the filling

2 cups confectioners' sugar, sifted
¼ cup vegetable shortening
1 large pasteurized egg white (see Notes)
½ teaspoon pure vanilla extract

1. Make the cakes: Place a rack in the center of the oven and preheat the oven to 350°F. Set aside 2 ungreased baking sheets.

2. Place the cake mix, butter, and egg in a large mixing bowl and beat with an electric mixer on low speed until the ingredients come together in a stiff mass, 1 to 2 minutes. Form the dough into 1-inch balls with your hands or scoop the dough into balls. Place the balls of dough on baking sheets 2 inches apart.

3. Place the baking sheets in the oven and bake the cakes until they are still a little soft, 10 to 12 minutes. If your oven cannot accommodate both baking sheets on the center rack, place one on the top rack and one on the center rack and rotate them halfway through the baking time. Remove the baking sheets from the oven and let the cakes cool on them for 5 minutes. Then, using a metal spatula, transfer the cakes to wire racks to cool completely, 30 minutes longer.

4. Make the filling: Place the confectioners' sugar, shortening, egg white, and vanilla in a medium-size mixing bowl and beat with an electric mixer on low speed until just combined, 1 minute. Spoon about 1 teaspoon onto the flat side of one cake. Top the filling with a second cake to make a sandwich. Repeat with the remaining cakes and serve.

Keep It Fresh! Store the Whoopie Pies, covered with plastic wrap, at room temperature for up to three days. Freeze the Whoopie Pies, wrapped in aluminum foil, for up to three months. Let the Whoopie Pies thaw at room temperature overnight before serving.

Notes: The filling in this recipe is uncooked and uses a raw egg. Whenever you use raw eggs, make sure they are pasteurized eggs (available at the supermarket).

Or, if you prefer, sandwich soft ice cream between the cakes and store them in the freezer. Coffee, mint chocolate chip, and vanilla are all delicious in these chewy cakes.

Recipe Reminders

MADE FOR

____

____

____

____

PREP NOTES

____

____

____

____

DON'T FORGET

____

____

____

____

SPECIAL TOUCHES

____

____

____

____

____

____

____

____

____

How to Tote Cupcakes: Clever Carriers

Cupcake cooks devised their own ways for getting the cute cakes to bake sales and parties long before cupcake carriers were invented. I used to (and still do!) use cardboard shirt boxes lined with waxed paper. But, there are many ways to make the journey a little easier on your frosted and decorated cupcakes.

1. A plastic 13 by 9-inch carrying case with a locking lid: This would be the best of your options—an investment in the beginning but with you for life.

2. Baking pans with snap-on plastic lids: These are useful not only for baking but also for toting cupcakes. Their three-inch depth seems just the right height to not mess up the top of the cupcakes. They come in a 13 by 9-inch (brownie) size as well as the 9-inch square. Choose from either the sturdy metal pans sold in cookware stores or the more disposable aluminum pans with lids sold at supermarkets.

3. A plastic or woven picnic basket with a pie stand: The pie stand splits the space inside the basket, allowing you to carry cupcakes on both the bottom and the upper level.

4. A plastic cake carrier: It will hold about a dozen cupcakes.

5. For lunch boxes, try plastic one-cup containers with snap-on lids.

6. Right on the serving platter: Place toothpicks in the center of a half dozen cupcakes and then drape plastic wrap on top. The toothpicks will act as poles, preventing the plastic from messing up the frosting.

Brownies, Bars, and Cookies

◆◆◆◆◆◆

The Brownie Doctor is in! This chapter is all about brownies, bars, and cookies, those satisfying treats you can create from cake and brownie mixes. Let's face it, brownie mixes are everywhere. We might make homemade brownies once or twice a year, but keeping a box of brownie mix on the pantry shelf is culinary insurance when life gets busy. It's simple to top brownies baked straight from the box with a homemade icing and toasted pecans, or they can become adult dinner party fare with a touch of rum or a fancy mascarpone topping.

The bars in this chapter are versatile and ready to go when you are. And cookies are so easy that you can stir them together with your kids or grandkids in the time it takes for the oven to preheat.

Testing all the recipes in this chapter was sheer heaven! I fell for the Cranberry Almond Brownies with sweetened dried cranberries folded into the batter and also the Rum-Soaked Apricot Brownies with dried apricots plumped in warm rum. My daughter loved the Cookies and Cream Brownies made with chopped Oreo cookies. And Old-Fashioned Pan Brownies remind me of the frosted fudge cake of my youth—except the brownies are a lot faster to prepare. As for decadent desserts, try the Gooey Pecan Pie Brownies, with chunks of pecan pie folded in, or the Tiramisu Brownies, smooth, creamy, and so good you'd swear you were in Italy.

As for the bars, you will adore the cheesecake-like Houdini Bars, the Turtle Bars, a favorite of my children, and my new version of an old favorite, the peanut butter chocolate bars. You'll find several variations of bars cut from a classic gooey butter cake in this chapter—Aimee's Chess Cake, Lemon Gooey Butter Cake, and a Chocolate Walnut Gooey Butter Cake. With a crisp crust on the bottom and a soft center, these bars are perfect for baking and serving warm or for stashing in the freezer. And I've got bars that have more spongy cakelike texture, such as the Applesauce Bars with a Light Cream Cheese Frosting.

Cake mix cookies are quick to fix, and I have included a handful of recipes, including my favorites, the Easy Chocolate Cookies, the Spice Drop Cookies, and Angel Food Macaroons.

Before you begin, here is a little advice. Brands of brownie mixes differ in quality and outcome, and their availability varies across the country. If you haven't already chosen a favorite, buy a handful of different brownie mixes and bake them according to the package directions. Choose the plainest, best-tasting brownie mix because you'll be doctoring it according to my recipes. As long as the mix is between 18 and 21 ounces it will work in my recipes.

I have come to like unsalted butter better than lightly salted in these recipes because it gives a more homemade taste. I add nuts on top just before baking so they have a chance to crisp up and develop flavor while they're in the oven. And lastly, I don't overbake brownies and bars. If you tend to forget what's in the oven, set a timer!

That's it. Many recipes will call for a baking temperature of 350°F, while others call for 325°F. I have suited the temperature to the recipe. You'll have nicer bars that bake more evenly and have a crisper exterior if you bake them in a metal pan, not a glass one. Other than that, pour a glass of milk and enjoy this assortment of easy bars, brownies, and cookies. No one will ever know they began with a box.

◆◆◆◆◆

Old-Fashioned Pan Brownies

THIS IS THE WAY WE MADE BROWNIES when I was growing up—big and cakey with a homemade pan frosting poured on top. You had to let the frosting set before you sliced the brownies and this was the hardest thing to do! It took willpower to walk out of the kitchen and let that frosting harden. But the wait was worth it. If you are traveling with these, let the pan cool, cover it with a snap-on lid or with aluminum foil, and you're ready to go.

makes:
at least 30 brownies

prep:
15 minutes

bake:
45 to 50 minutes

cool:
30 minutes

Vegetable oil spray, for misting the pan
Flour, for dusting the pan
2 packages (about 20 ounces each) brownie mix
12 tablespoons (1½ sticks) butter, melted
½ cup buttermilk
4 large eggs
2 teaspoons pure vanilla extract
Chocolate Pan Frosting (make the amount for a sheet cake; page 476)
½ cup chopped pecans (optional)

1. Place a rack in the center of the oven and preheat the oven to 325°F. Lightly mist the bottom of a 13 by 9–inch metal baking pan with vegetable oil spray, then dust it with flour. Shake out the excess flour and set the pan aside.

Recipe Reminders

MADE FOR

PREP NOTES

DON'T FORGET

SPECIAL TOUCHES

2. Place the brownie mix, butter, buttermilk, eggs, and vanilla in a large mixing bowl and stir with a wooden spoon until moistened, about 40 strokes. Transfer the batter to the prepared baking pan and place the pan in the oven.

3. Bake the brownies until the edges have set and the center is still a little soft (press it lightly with a finger), 45 to 50 minutes. Transfer the baking pan to a wire rack and let the brownies cool for 20 minutes before frosting.

4. Meanwhile, make the Chocolate Pan Frosting.

5. Pour the frosting over the top of the brownies, spreading it evenly with a metal spatula. If desired, sprinkle the pecans over the frosting before it sets. Let the frosting set for 10 minutes before cutting the brownies into bars (see page 400) and serving.

Keep It Fresh! Store the brownies, covered with plastic wrap or aluminum foil, at room temperature for up to three days or for up to one week in the refrigerator. Freeze the uncut brownies in the pan, covered with aluminum foil, for up to three months. Let the brownies thaw overnight on the counter before serving.

Yummy Yogurt Brownies

An easy and delicious way to cut the fat in a brownie recipe is to substitute nonfat vanilla yogurt for the oil and liquid called for in your recipe. If a recipe calls for a stick of butter use a half cup of yogurt instead. The brownies will be more cakelike in texture but just as yummy. Dust them with confectioners' sugar before serving.

Mireille's Brownies

After sharing online my way of making brownies, Mireille McKell of Chillicothe, Ohio, quickly sent me her recipe. She, too, begins with a mix but spreads marshmallow creme over the top of the baked brownies when they emerge from the oven and then pours a satiny chocolate icing on top. This is one big pan of brownies, using two boxes of mix, and it is perfect for toting to a covered dish supper when you need to feed a crowd. Or bake these and freeze half for a dessert down the road. Just thinking about these brownies makes me very hungry!

makes:
at least 30 brownies

prep:
20 minutes

bake:
45 to 50 minutes

cool:
20 minutes

For the brownies

Vegetable oil spray, for misting the pan
2 packages (about 20 ounces each) brownie mix
⅔ cup water
⅔ cup vegetable oil
4 large eggs

For the icing

6 tablespoons (¾ stick) butter
5 tablespoons milk
3 tablespoons unsweetened cocoa powder
1 teaspoon pure vanilla extract
3¾ cups confectioners' sugar (about 1 box), sifted
1 jar (7 ounces) marshmallow creme

Recipe Reminders

MADE FOR

PREP NOTES

DON'T FORGET

SPECIAL TOUCHES

1. Make the brownies: Place a rack in the center of the oven and preheat the oven to 325°F. Lightly mist a 13 by 9–inch baking pan with vegetable oil spray. Set the pan aside.

2. Place the brownie mix, water, oil, and eggs in a large mixing bowl and stir with a wooden spoon until the ingredients are incorporated, about 50 strokes, or beat with an electric mixer on low speed for 30 seconds. Transfer the batter to the prepared baking pan, smoothing the top with a rubber spatula.

3. Place the pan in the oven and bake the brownies until the edges have set and the center is still a little soft (press it lightly with a finger), 45 to 50 minutes.

4. Meanwhile, make the icing: Melt the butter in a saucepan over medium heat. Add the milk and cocoa powder, stirring constantly until just boiling, 2 to 3 minutes. Remove the pan from the heat and add the vanilla and confectioners' sugar, stirring until smooth. Keep the icing warm over low heat.

5. As soon as the brownies come out of the oven, spread the marshmallow creme over the top. Let the creme soften on top of the hot brownies. Then, slowly pour the warm icing evenly over the top of the marshmallow creme and spread with a knife to smooth it out. It does not matter if the marshmallow creme mixes with the icing. Let the brownies cool for 20 minutes before cutting them into bars (see page 400) and serving.

Keep It Fresh! Store the brownies, covered with plastic wrap or aluminum foil, at room temperature for up to four days. Freeze the uncut brownies in the pan, covered with aluminum foil, for up to three months. Let the brownies thaw overnight on the counter before serving.

10 Wonderful Ways to Doctor Up a Brownie Mix

No time for a recipe? Feel like winging it? Here are some easy add-ins for a box of brownie mix.

1. Fold in one cup of semisweet chocolate, white chocolate, or butterscotch chips.

2. Sprinkle a half cup of finely chopped walnuts or pecans over the top before baking.

3. Add one teaspoon of almond extract to the batter and scatter a quarter cup of sliced almonds over the top.

4. Add one cup of chopped peanut butter cups.

5. Add a half cup of chopped chocolate-covered toffee bar.

6. Add a quarter cup of brewed coffee or espresso; be sure it's cooled.

7. Add one tablespoon of rum, brandy, or coffee liqueur.

8. Add a handful of fresh cranberries or raisins.

9. Add a dash of mint extract or a handful of mint chocolate chips.

10. Dollop the top with your favorite fruit preserves before baking; raspberry, cherry, or orange marmalade are all good.

Cookies and Cream Brownies

makes:
16 brownies

prep:
15 minutes

bake:
40 to 42 minutes

cool:
20 minutes

I **JUST HAVE NO WILLPOWER** when these brownies are in the house! And whereas I seldom mention a food product by name, there is one and only one Oreo cookie and that's what I call for here. Bake these brownies ahead and freeze them covered in the pan. Or cover and stash them in an out-of-the-way place; if any one finds them they will be eaten.

For the brownies

Vegetable oil spray, for misting the pan
1 package (about 20 ounces) brownie mix
8 tablespoons (1 stick) butter, melted
2 large eggs
4 Oreo cookies, coarsely chopped (½ cup)

For the frosting

4 ounces cream cheese, at room temperature
2 tablespoons (¼ stick) unsalted butter, at room temperature
1 cup confectioners' sugar, sifted
8 Oreo cookies, coarsely chopped (1 cup)

1. Make the brownies: Place a rack in the center of the oven and preheat the oven to 325°F. Lightly mist the bottom of an 8-inch square metal baking pan with vegetable oil spray and set the pan aside.

Speed It Up!

Don't have 20 minutes for the brownies to cool? Place the pan in the refrigerator and they'll be cool in half the time.

2. Place the brownie mix, melted butter, and eggs in a large mixing bowl and stir with a wooden spoon until moistened, about 40 strokes. Transfer the batter to the prepared baking pan and press the ½ cup of chopped Oreos onto the top of the batter. Place the pan in the oven.

3. Bake the brownies until the edges have set and the center is still a little soft (press it lightly with a finger), 40 to 42 minutes. Transfer the baking pan to a wire rack and let the brownies cool for 20 minutes before frosting.

4. Make the frosting: Place the cream cheese and room temperature butter in a large mixing bowl and beat with an electric mixer on low speed until soft, 30 seconds. Turn off the machine and add the confectioners' sugar. Beat on low speed until the confectioners' sugar is incorporated, 30 seconds longer. Fold in the 1 cup of chopped Oreos.

5. Spoon the frosting on top of the cooled brownies in the pan. Using a small metal spatula, spread the frosting evenly over the top of the brownies. Place the brownies in the refrigerator for 10 minutes until the frosting sets before cutting them into 2-inch square bars and serving.

Keep It Fresh! Store the brownies, covered with plastic wrap or aluminum foil, in the refrigerator for up to five days. Freeze the brownies in the pan, covered with aluminum foil, for up to three months. Let the brownies thaw overnight in the refrigerator before serving.

Recipe Reminders

MADE FOR

____

____

____

____

PREP NOTES

____

____

____

____

DON'T FORGET

____

____

____

____

SPECIAL TOUCHES

____

____

____

____

____

____

____

____

____

Gooey Pecan Pie Brownies

makes:
at least 30 brownies

prep:
15 minutes

bake:
50 to 55 minutes

cool:
1 hour

MANY YEARS AGO a cheesecake into which a chopped pecan pie had been folded was a winning recipe in the *Southern Living* cooking contest. I could never get this idea out of my head—I could taste that pecan pie baked into the cheesecake. And then when testing brownies, the memory came back to me and I wanted to taste that pecan pie in a pan of brownies. I tried it, and I'll have to say this is one of the best brownie recipes that has come out of my kitchen. The pie crust almost disappears in the brownie batter and the filling creates gooey/crunchy pockets of pecan pie wonder. Granted, it is not low-cal. And using two boxes of brownie mix, plus a pecan pie, makes for a big pan—enough for thirty or more people. Bake this when you've got a crowd—for Super Bowl parties and covered dish suppers and bake sales.

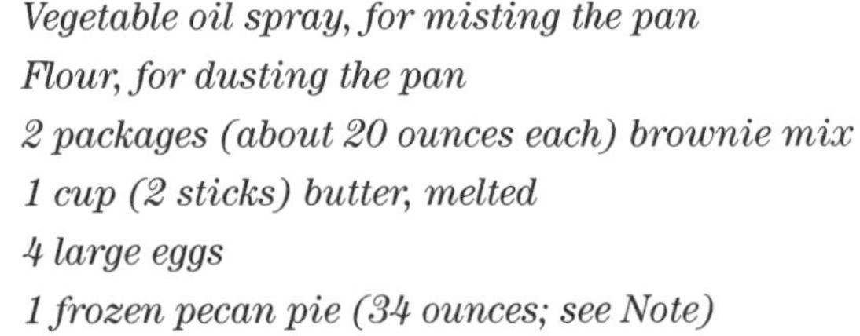

Vegetable oil spray, for misting the pan
Flour, for dusting the pan
2 packages (about 20 ounces each) brownie mix
1 cup (2 sticks) butter, melted
4 large eggs
1 frozen pecan pie (34 ounces; see Note)

1. Place a rack in the center of the oven and preheat the oven to 325°F. Lightly mist a 13 by 9–inch metal baking pan with vegetable oil spray, then dust it with flour. Shake out the excess flour and set the pan aside.

2. Place the brownie mix, butter, and eggs in a large mixing bowl and stir with a wooden spoon until the ingredients are incorporated, about 40 strokes, or beat with an electric mixer on low speed for 30 seconds. If necessary, scrape down the side of the bowl with a rubber spatula. Set the brownie batter aside.

3. Remove the pecan pie from the freezer, remove the pie from the pie pan, and place the pie on a cutting board. Cut the pecan pie into ¾- to 1-inch pieces (you'll find it isn't frozen solid). Fold the pieces of pie into the brownie batter until just combined. Transfer the batter to the prepared baking pan, smoothing the top with a rubber spatula.

4. Place the pan in the oven and bake the brownies until the edges have set and the center is still a little soft (press it lightly with a finger), 50 to 55 minutes. Transfer the baking pan to a wire rack and let the brownies cool completely, about 1 hour, before cutting them into bars (see page 400) and serving.

Keep It Fresh! Store the brownies, covered with plastic wrap or aluminum foil, at room temperature for up to three days or for up to one week in the refrigerator. Freeze the uncut brownies in the pan, covered with aluminum foil, for up to three months. Let the brownies thaw overnight on the counter before serving.

Note: If you really love pecans, top the brownie batter with ¾ to 1 cup of pecan halves before baking. Store-bought pecan pies don't contain enough pecans for pecan lovers.

Recipe Reminders

MADE FOR

____

____

____

____

PREP NOTES

____

____

____

____

DON'T FORGET

____

____

____

____

SPECIAL TOUCHES

____

____

____

____

____

____

____

____

____

Raise the Bar!
Get Out the Ruler and Start Slicing

There is really no exact way to cut brownies or bars baked in 13 by 9-inch pans. Sometimes I get out the ruler, but often I just eyeball it. To make things more confusing not all of these pans are exactly the same size—I have a true 13 by 9-inch metal baking pan but also one that measures slightly smaller at 12 by 8¾ inches. If you use the smaller pan, allow a little extra baking time. The bars will turn out slightly taller, which is nice. To measure your pan, place the ruler just inside the edges.

When I cut a pan of brownies I usually make the pieces as small as is reasonably possible. I have two reasons: One, this makes a pan of brownies go a lot further; and two, people often don't want a big serving. They might eat two smaller pieces but only half of a larger piece—go figure!

I can cut thirty, thirty-two, or forty bars from a 13 by 9-inch pan and here is how.

◆ For thirty long bars: Starting at a short end of the pan, make two lengthwise cuts that divide the pan into three equal three-inch-wide strips. Then make a cut down the center of the long side. On each side of this cut make four more equidistant parallel cuts. You will end up with three long rows of ten brownies or bars—thirty in all.

◆ For thirty-two bars: Make a cut crosswise down the center of the brownies or bars, then cut them in half lengthwise; you will have four large pieces. Cut each of these pieces in quarters along the long side of the pan, then cut these smaller pieces in half crosswise. You will have a total of thirty-two brownies or bars.

◆ For the most bars of all, forty bite-size portions: Starting at the short end, make four lengthwise cuts, each about 1¾ inches wide. Then make seven crosswise cuts, each about 1¾ inches wide, for a total of forty brownies or bars.

With this math in mind, you can turn out your favorite size bar just by using a ruler and your eye. No matter what size you slice, to keep the edges nice and straight run the knife under warm water before making each cut.

Cranberry Almond Brownies

PUBLICIST RON LONGE shared with me the way he adds fresh cranberries to brownies he serves at holiday parties. The idea intrigued me, but instead of using fresh cranberries, I opted for the sweetened dried cranberries that are available all the time, which means I can make this recipe year-round! Cranberries and almonds are natural flavor partners. This is such a decadent recipe no one will ever guess it started with a mix. Substitute a scattering of white chocolate chips for the chocolate ones for an even more festive look.

makes:
at least 30 brownies

prep:
15 minutes

bake:
45 to 50 minutes

cool:
about 20 minutes

Vegetable oil spray, for misting the pan
Flour, for dusting the pan
2 packages (about 20 ounces each) brownie mix
1 cup (2 sticks) butter, melted
4 large eggs
1 teaspoon pure vanilla extract
½ teaspoon pure almond extract
¼ teaspoon ground cinnamon
1 cup dried sweetened cranberries (see Note)
½ cup (3 ounces) semisweet chocolate chips
2 tablespoons sliced almonds

1. Place a rack in the center of the oven and preheat the oven to 325°F. Lightly mist a 13 by 9–inch metal baking pan with vegetable oil spray, then dust it with flour. Shake out the excess flour and set the pan aside.

Recipe Reminders

MADE FOR

PREP NOTES

DON'T FORGET

SPECIAL TOUCHES

2. Place the brownie mix, butter, eggs, vanilla and almond extracts, and cinnamon in a large mixing bowl and beat with an electric mixer on low speed until the ingredients are incorporated, 30 seconds. Stop the machine and scrape down the side of the bowl with a rubber spatula. Increase the mixer speed to medium and beat until the mixture is smooth, about 30 seconds longer. Fold in the cranberries. Transfer the batter to the prepared baking pan, smoothing the top with the rubber spatula. Scatter the chocolate chips and almonds on top.

3. Place the pan in the oven and bake the brownies until the edges have set and the center is still a little soft (press it lightly with a finger), 45 to 50 minutes. Transfer the baking pan to a wire rack and let the brownies sit until nearly cool, about 20 minutes.

4. Cut the brownies into bars (see page 400) and serve warm or let cool to room temperature, 10 minutes longer.

Keep It Fresh! Store the brownies, covered with plastic wrap or aluminum foil, at room temperature for up to three days or for up to one week in the refrigerator. Freeze the brownies in the pan, covered with aluminum foil, for up to three months. Let the brownies thaw overnight on the counter before serving.

Note: If you like, substitute dried cherries for the cranberries in this recipe. And if you want to use fresh cranberries, add 1 cup rinsed, drained fresh cranberries instead of the dried ones. They pop open while baking and because the brownies are plenty sweet, no additional sugar is necessary.

Music To My Mouth Brownies

I MIGHT NOT GO SO FAR as to say this recipe has a cult-like following, but it's pretty close! This is one of those supereasy recipes that travel by word of mouth, and I had to share it with you here. It is essentially a plain brownie into which you fold chopped Symphony candy bars, the kind with the almonds and toffee. When it bakes the candy becomes creamy and mousselike. So you bite into these soft pockets of chocolate loveliness—get the picture? You can use any mix you like for the brownies, but make sure you do not refrigerate them because if you do the creamy candy bars will harden and won't soften even if you bring the brownies back to room temperature.

makes:
16 brownies

prep:
10 minutes

bake:
38 to 42 minutes

cool:
20 minutes

Vegetable oil spray, for misting the pan
1 package (about 20 ounces) brownie mix
8 tablespoons (1 stick) butter, melted
2 large eggs
2 Hershey's Symphony chocolate bars with almonds and toffee (4.25 ounces each), coarsely chopped

1. Place a rack in the center of the oven and preheat the oven to 325°F. Lightly mist the bottom of an 8-inch square metal baking pan with vegetable oil spray and set the pan aside.

2. Place the brownie mix, butter, and eggs in a large mixing bowl and stir with a wooden spoon until moistened, about 40 strokes. Fold in the chopped chocolate bars. Transfer the batter to the

Candy Bar Brownies

You can follow the same recipe and replace the Symphony bars with four chopped Milky Way bars (2.05 ounces each) or four Baby Ruth bars (2.1 ounces each), too. All brownies that have candy bars folded in taste best when kept at room temperature. And to make slicing neater, wipe off the knife between cuts.

Recipe Reminders

MADE FOR

PREP NOTES

DON'T FORGET

SPECIAL TOUCHES

prepared baking pan, smoothing the top with a rubber spatula, and place the pan in the oven.

3. Bake the brownies until the edges have set and the center is still a little soft (press it lightly with a finger), 38 to 42 minutes. Transfer the baking pan to a wire rack and let the brownies cool for 20 minutes before cutting them into 2-inch square bars and serving.

Keep It Fresh! Store the brownies, covered with plastic wrap or aluminum foil, at room temperature for up to five days. Freeze the brownies in the pan, covered with aluminum foil, for up to three months although the candy bars will get hard after freezing. Let the brownies thaw overnight on the counter before serving.

Five More Bake Sale Tips

1. Buy ingredients in bulk at wholesale clubs to save money. The larger size mixes are perfect for bake sale portions.

2. Most recipes can be doubled in the same (large) bowl with success. You may not want to more than double up as it becomes difficult to blend ingredients in very large amounts. Instead, make two batches at a time and then begin again with another two batches.

3. Buy disposable pans to speed prep time. Breads that benefit from reheating can be sold right in the pan.

4. Begin baking several weeks ahead of time and freeze things. Breads, cakes, cookies, and bars all freeze well in resealable plastic freezer bags.

5. Many people are allergic to nuts, so if you're baking with them or nut oils, label the item accordingly.

Marbled Ricotta Cheesecake Brownies

Nothing is more delicious than a cheesecake brownie—you know the kind with the brownie on the bottom and a creamy cheesecake layer on top or marbled throughout. This is an Italian take on that classic using part-skim ricotta cheese instead of cream cheese. Have fun with the flavoring here, adding a little grated orange peel to the cheesecake layer or a pinch of cinnamon. You'll love the richness ricotta brings to this recipe.

makes:
16 brownies

prep:
15 minutes

bake:
40 to 45 minutes

cool:
1 hour

Vegetable oil spray, for misting the pan
1 package (about 20 ounces) brownie mix
3 large eggs
⅓ cup cool strong brewed coffee, or ⅓ cup water
⅓ cup vegetable oil
2 teaspoons pure vanilla extract
15 ounces part-skim ricotta cheese (see Note)
½ cup granulated sugar
1 tablespoon cornstarch
½ teaspoon pure almond extract

1. Place a rack in the center of the oven and preheat the oven to 350°F. Lightly mist the bottom of an 8-inch square metal baking pan with vegetable oil spray and set the pan aside.

2. Place the brownie mix, 1 egg, coffee, oil, and 1 teaspoon of vanilla in a large mixing bowl and stir with a wooden spoon until moistened, about 40 strokes. Transfer the batter to the

Recipe Reminders

MADE FOR

PREP NOTES

DON'T FORGET

SPECIAL TOUCHES

prepared baking pan, smoothing the top with a rubber spatula. Set the pan aside.

3. Place the ricotta cheese, granulated sugar, cornstarch, the remaining 2 eggs, and 1 teaspoon of vanilla, and the almond extract in a medium-size mixing bowl and beat with an electric mixer on medium speed until combined, 1 minute. Slowly pour the ricotta mixture over the brownie batter. Using a knife or small spatula, swirl the batter up and over the ricotta mixture to give it a marbled look. Place the baking pan in the oven.

4. Bake the brownies until the edges have set and the center is still a little soft (press it lightly with a finger), 40 to 45 minutes. Transfer the baking pan to a wire rack and let the brownies cool to room temperature, 1 hour, before cutting them into 2-inch square bars and serving.

Keep It Fresh! Store the brownies, covered with plastic wrap or aluminum foil, in the refrigerator for up to five days. Freeze the brownies in the pan, covered with aluminum foil, for up to three months. Let the brownies thaw overnight in the refrigerator before serving.

Note: Part-skim ricotta is the best choice for these brownies because you don't need the added fat of whole-milk ricotta, and part-skim ricotta has a better flavor and texture than fat-free.

Chocolate Mint Brownies

ABSOLUTELY THE BEST PARTNER for chocolate is mint; they were made for each other. And adding mint—whether it be a little peppermint extract or chopped peppermint candy—is the easiest way to doctor up a box of brownie mix. People won't believe these brownies weren't made from scratch.

makes:
16 brownies

prep:
10 minutes

bake:
38 to 42 minutes

cool:
20 minutes

Vegetable oil spray, for misting the pan
1 package (about 20 ounces) brownie mix
8 tablespoons (1 stick) butter, melted
2 large eggs
½ teaspoon pure peppermint extract
1 cup chopped Andes chocolate mint candies, or 1 cup chopped Hershey's mint chocolate Kisses

1. Place a rack in the center of the oven and preheat the oven to 325°F. Lightly mist the bottom of an 8-inch square metal baking pan with vegetable oil spray and set the pan aside.

2. Place the brownie mix, butter, eggs, and peppermint extract in a large mixing bowl and stir with a wooden spoon until moistened, about 40 strokes. Transfer the batter to the prepared baking pan. Scatter the chopped mint chocolate candy on top of the batter and place the pan in the oven.

3. Bake the brownies until the edges have set and the center is still a little soft (press it lightly with a finger), 38 to 42 minutes.

Double Up!

You can bake a big batch of mint brownies by using two packages of brownie mix, two sticks of butter, four eggs, one teaspoon of pure peppermint extract, and two cups of chopped chocolate mint candy. Bake the brownies in a 13 by 9-inch pan for 45 to 50 minutes at 325°F.

Recipe Reminders

MADE FOR

PREP NOTES

DON'T FORGET

SPECIAL TOUCHES

Transfer the baking pan to a wire rack and let the brownies cool for 20 minutes before cutting them into 2-inch square bars and serving.

Keep It Fresh! Store the brownies, covered with plastic wrap or aluminum foil, at room temperature for up to five days. Freeze the brownies in the pan, covered with aluminum foil, for up to three months. Let the brownies thaw overnight on the counter before serving.

Worth the Fuss Peppermint Brownies

Bake the Chocolate Mint Brownies as the recipe suggests and let them cool. Then, make a small batch of the Chocolate Pan Frosting (page 476). Stir in a quarter teaspoon of pure peppermint extract as the frosting cools. Spread this frosting over the cooled brownies, then top them with two tablespoons of crushed hard peppermint candies while the frosting is still soft. Serve the brownies with a scoop of vanilla ice cream.

Peanut Butter Brownies

makes: at least 30 bars

prep: 20 minutes

bake: 28 to 32 minutes

cool: 20 minutes

SIMILAR TO Our Favorite Peanut Butter Chocolate Bars on page 429, this recipe has an ooey-gooey chocolate filling made with sweetened condensed milk and chocolate chips. But instead of the golden cake mix, this uses a brownie mix, to which you add crunchy peanut butter. This is one of my family's new favorite recipes and I know it will be one of yours.

1 package (about 20 ounces) brownie mix
1 cup crunchy peanut butter
8 tablespoons (1 stick) butter, melted
2 large eggs
1 package (12 ounces; 2 cups) semisweet chocolate chips (see Note)
1 can (14 ounces) sweetened condensed milk
2 teaspoons pure vanilla extract

1. Place a rack in the center of the oven and preheat the oven to 350°F. Set aside an ungreased 13 by 9–inch metal baking pan.

2. Place the brownie mix, peanut butter, butter, and eggs in a large mixing bowl and beat with an electric mixer on low speed for 1 minute. Stop the machine and scrape down the side of the bowl with a rubber spatula. The mixture will be thick. Set aside about 1½ cups for the topping. Place the remaining brownie mixture in the baking pan, pressing it over the bottom of the pan with your fingertips so that it reaches all sides. Set the pan aside.

Recipe Reminders

MADE FOR

PREP NOTES

DON'T FORGET

SPECIAL TOUCHES

The Big Chill! Freezing Tips for Brownies and Bars

Brownies and bars may be delicious freshly baked and eaten straight from the pan but they are just as tasty after being frozen. I love to keep brownies in the freezer, because I can pull them out when I need a quick dessert or just have that late-afternoon chocolate craving! Here are things you need to remember when freezing brownies and other bars.

◆ For best results, freeze brownies and bars in a freezer that you do not open and close often.

◆ It's best to freeze brownies and bars uncut in the pan in which they were baked. Cover the top of the pan with heavy-duty aluminum foil before freezing.

◆ If you are freezing cut bars, wrap them in aluminum foil then place the foil package in a resealable plastic freezer bag.

◆ Cut bars can also be frozen in plastic containers with tight-fitting lids.

◆ Although brownies and bars can be frozen frosted or unfrosted, for best results, freeze them unfrosted, thaw them, then frost before serving.

◆ For convenience, you can pull individual frozen bars from the freezer, place them on a microwave-safe plate, and speed thaw the bars in the microwave before serving.

◆ Brownies and bars keep frozen for two to six months in the freezer.

3. Place the chocolate chips and condensed milk in a medium-size microwave-safe glass bowl and microwave on high power for 1 minute. Stir in the vanilla and continue stirring until the chocolate has melted and the mixture is smooth and creamy. Pour the chocolate mixture into the baking pan, spreading it evenly with the rubber spatula so that it reaches the sides of the pan. Using your fingertips, crumble the reserved topping and scatter it over the chocolate mixture. Place the pan in the oven.

4. Bake the brownies until the edges have set and the top crust springs back when lightly pressed with a finger, 28 to 32 minutes. Transfer the baking pan to a wire rack and let the brownies cool for 20 minutes before cutting them into bars (see page 400) and serving.

Keep It Fresh! Store the brownies, covered with plastic wrap or aluminum foil, at room temperature for up to three days or for up to a week in the refrigerator. Freeze the brownies in the pan, wrapped in aluminum foil, for up to three months. Let the brownies thaw overnight on the counter before serving.

Note: If you use white chocolate chips instead of semisweet you will have the most beautiful bars.

Beth's Unbelievable Brownies

My friend Beth Meador is a good cook who passed along her secret for making the best brownies. She starts with any good brownie mix and follows the directions on the package. "But you've got to underbake it." Then she frosts the brownies with a homemade chocolate icing, such as Martha's Chocolate Icing (page 480).

Rum-Soaked Apricot Brownies

makes:
16 brownies

prep:
10 minutes

bake:
40 to 45 minutes

cool:
20 minutes

I **ADORE THE RUM AND APRICOT** flavor duo. Add chocolate and that may be the most winning dessert triumvirate of flavors imaginable. So with that in mind I created a brownie that is dazzling enough to serve at your next dinner party. We adults deserve something all our own once in a while.

Vegetable oil spray, for misting the pan
Flour, for dusting the pan
½ cup finely chopped dried apricots (8 to 10 apricots)
¼ cup plus 2 tablespoons dark rum
1 package (about 20 ounces) brownie mix
8 tablespoons (1 stick) butter, melted
2 large eggs
Chocolate Pan Frosting (optional; page 476, see Note)

1. Place a rack in the center of the oven and preheat the oven to 325°F. Lightly mist the bottom of an 8-inch square metal baking pan with vegetable oil spray, then dust it with flour. Shake out the excess flour and set the pan aside.

2. Place the apricots and ¼ cup of rum in a 2-cup glass measuring cup and heat in the microwave on high power for 1 minute. Remove the measuring cup from the microwave and let cool for 10 minutes; the apricots will soak up the rum as they cool.

3. Place the brownie mix, butter, and eggs in a large mixing bowl and stir with a wooden spoon until moistened, about 40 strokes. Fold in the rum-soaked apricots. Transfer the batter to the prepared baking pan and place the pan in the oven.

4. Bake the brownies until the edges have set and the center is still a little soft (press it lightly with a finger), 40 to 45 minutes. Transfer the baking pan to a wire rack and brush the brownies with the remaining 2 tablespoons of rum while they are hot. Let the brownies cool for 20 minutes before cutting them into bars (see page 400) or frosting them, if desired.

Keep It Fresh! Store the brownies, covered with plastic wrap or aluminum foil, at room temperature for up to five days. Freeze the brownies in the pan, covered with aluminum foil, for up to three months. Let the brownies thaw overnight on the counter before serving.

Note: If you use the Chocolate Pan Frosting—and I highly recommend it—be sure to make just a small amount, the same amount needed to top a Bundt cake.

Recipe Reminders

MADE FOR

PREP NOTES

DON'T FORGET

SPECIAL TOUCHES

Tiramisu Brownies

makes:
at least 30 bars

prep:
15 minutes

bake:
45 to 50 minutes

cool:
40 to 50 minutes

What could possibly be better tasting than ladyfingers soaked in sherry and layered in a fluffy tiramisu? A brownie version of the perennial Italian dessert favorite. And this is such an easy recipe to prepare ahead of time for company. I say prepare ahead because the topping needs to chill and the flavors get even better after a day in the refrigerator. Just before serving dust the top of the brownies with unsweetened cocoa powder or chocolate shavings. Pour the coffee and you are in for a treat!

For the brownies

Vegetable oil spray, for misting the pan
2 packages (about 20 ounces each) brownie mix
⅔ cup vegetable oil
½ cup cooled brewed coffee
4 large eggs
2 tablespoons cream sherry or marsala wine

For the tiramisu topping

1 cup heavy (whipping) cream or evaporated milk
¼ cup granulated sugar
1 teaspoon instant coffee granules
1 teaspoon pure vanilla extract
8 ounces mascarpone cheese
2 tablespoons cream sherry or marsala wine
1 teaspoon unsweetened cocoa powder, for dusting

1. Make the brownies: Place a rack in the center of the oven and preheat the oven to 325°F. Lightly mist a 13 by 9–inch metal baking pan with vegetable oil spray and set the pan aside.

2. Place the brownie mix, oil, coffee, and eggs in a large mixing bowl and stir with a wooden spoon until the ingredients are incorporated, about 50 strokes, or beat with an electric mixer on low speed for 30 seconds. Transfer the batter to the prepared baking pan, smoothing the top with a rubber spatula.

3. Place the pan in the oven and bake the brownies until the edges have set and the center is still a little soft (press it lightly with a finger), 45 to 50 minutes. Transfer the baking pan to a wire rack and brush the top of the brownies very lightly with the 2 tablespoons of the sherry or marsala. Let the brownies cool on the wire rack for 10 minutes, then place them in the refrigerator to cool completely, 30 minutes longer.

4. Meanwhile, make the tiramisu topping: Place the cream in a large microwave-safe glass mixing bowl along with the granulated sugar and coffee powder and stir to mix. Microwave on high power for 1 minute. Remove the bowl from the microwave oven and stir until the sugar and coffee powder dissolve. Stir in the vanilla. Place the bowl in the refrigerator to chill for at least 30 minutes.

5. When the cream and the brownies have chilled, remove the bowl of cream from the refrigerator and beat it with an electric mixer on high power until nearly stiff peaks form, 2 minutes. Place the mascarpone in a separate bowl, and using the same beaters, beat on low speed until fluffy, then pour in the 2 tablespoons of sherry or marsala. Continue to beat until smooth. Fold the mascarpone mixture into the whipped cream and beat on medium-high speed until just combined.

Recipe Reminders

MADE FOR

PREP NOTES

DON'T FORGET

SPECIAL TOUCHES

6. Remove the pan of brownies from the refrigerator and spoon the topping over them, smoothing the top with a rubber spatula. Just before serving, sift the cocoa powder over the top of the brownies, then cut them into bars (see page 400) and serve.

Keep It Fresh! Store the brownies, covered with plastic wrap or aluminum foil, in the refrigerator for up to three days. You can bake the brownie layer ahead of time and freeze it in the pan, covered with aluminum foil, for up to three months. Let the brownies thaw overnight on the counter, then make the topping.

How to Tell When Brownies Are Done

It's best to slightly undercook brownies rather than overcook them. Brownies continue to cook in a hot pan, so undercooking helps to prevent them from drying out. The trick is to check the outside edges—when they are firm but the center is still a little soft, stick a toothpick in the center. It should come out with a few moist crumbs attached.

If you are worried about overbaking brownies, set a timer for five minutes less than the recipe suggests, turn on the light inside the oven, and look for signs of doneness. This is especially helpful if you think your oven tends to bake hotter than it should.

And to make brownies easier to slice—especially if you intentionally undercook them—place the cooled pan in the freezer or refrigerator until the brownies are firm, then slice them, arrange them on a plate, and let them come back to room temperature before serving.

Night and Day Brownie Bites

OKAY, I HAVE A WEAKNESS for brownies and for cheesecake. I also can't decide when I enjoy a bite of brownie best—in the late morning or late at night. So these little gems evolved as I tested new ways to bake up a brownie mix that would suit either morning or evening cravings. The secret is substituting brewed coffee for the water in the brownie batter. Take these to work with you and share them with coworkers. Or, serve them after a dinner party with friends.

makes: 24 brownie bites

prep: 20 minutes

bake: 22 to 26 minutes

cool: 15 minutes

Vegetable oil spray, for misting the cupcake tin(s)

For the brownie ("night") batter

1 package (about 20 ounces) brownie mix
⅓ cup vegetable oil
⅓ cup cooled brewed coffee
1 large egg
1 teaspoon pure vanilla extract

For the cream cheese ("day") batter

1 package (8 ounces) cream cheese, at room temperature
⅓ cup granulated sugar
1 tablespoon all-purpose flour
¼ teaspoon ground cinnamon (optional)
1 large egg

1 teaspoon confectioners' sugar (optional), for dusting

Recipe Reminders

MADE FOR

PREP NOTES

DON'T FORGET

SPECIAL TOUCHES

1. Place a rack in the center of the oven and preheat the oven to 350°F. Lightly mist one 24-cup or two 12-cup 1½- or 2-inch cupcake tins with vegetable oil spray or line it with paper liners. Set the cupcake tin(s) aside.

2. Make the brownie batter: Place the brownie mix, oil, coffee or water, 1 egg, and vanilla in a large mixing bowl and stir with a wooden spoon until the ingredients are well incorporated, 40 strokes. Set the bowl aside.

3. Make the cream cheese batter: Place the cream cheese in a large mixing bowl and beat with an electric mixer on low speed until fluffy, 30 seconds. Add the granulated sugar, flour, cinnamon, if using, and 1 egg and continue beating on low speed until well combined, 30 seconds to 1 minute.

4. To assemble the brownie bites in a yin and yang design of dark and light side by side, place a generous tablespoon of brownie batter into one cupcake well at the same time you add a generous tablespoon of the cream cheese batter, so that each batter takes up half of the well. Repeat filling the wells with the remaining brownie and cream cheese batters. For a layer of brownie on the bottom and a white layer on top, fill each cupcake well with one scoop of brownie batter and spoon a generous tablespoon of cream cheese batter over it.

5. Place the cupcake tin(s) in the oven and bake the brownie bites until the edges have set and the centers spring back when lightly pressed with a finger, 22 to 26 minutes. Remove the cupcake tin(s) from the oven and let the brownie bites cool for 10 minutes. Lift up the brownie bites in baked cupcake liners or run a sharp knife around the edges of those baked without liners and transfer them to a wire rack to cool for 5 minutes longer (if you can resist eating them at once).

6. To garnish the brownie bites, dust them with confectioners' sugar, if desired.

Keep It Fresh! Store the brownie bites, covered with plastic wrap, at room temperature for up to three days or for up to one week in the refrigerator. Freeze the brownie bites, covered with aluminum foil, for up to three months. Let the brownie bites thaw on the counter before serving.

How to Turn a Chocolate Cake Mix into a Brownie

First, place a rack in the center of the oven and preheat the oven to 350°F. Lightly mist a 13 by 9-inch cake pan with vegetable oil spray and dust it with flour. Shake out the excess flour and set the pan aside. Combine one package (18.25 ounces) of plain chocolate cake mix with two large eggs and eight tablespoons (one stick) of melted, unsalted butter in a large mixing bowl. Using a wooden spoon, stir until the mixture is thoroughly blended; it will be stiff. Fold in 1½ cups of miniature semisweet chocolate chips and stir until well blended. Transfer the batter to the prepared pan and, using a rubber spatula, spread it evenly. Place the pan in the oven and bake the brownies until the center is still soft and springs back when lightly pressed with a finger, 18 to 20 minutes. Remove the pan from the oven and place it on a wire rack to cool completely before slicing.

For quick little brownie cups: Scoop the batter into lightly misted miniature muffin tins. It will fill about three dozen. If desired, scatter finely chopped walnuts over the tops before baking. Bake at 350°F until still a little soft to the touch, 12 to 15 minutes, no more. Remove the pan from the oven and let the brownie cups cool in the pan for 3 to 4 minutes. Run a sharp knife around the edges, lift the brownie cups out, and place them on a wire rack to cool completely.

Slow Cooker Brownie Peanut Butter Pudding

serves:
16 to 20

prep:
10 minutes

bake:
2 hours

standing time:
30 minutes

TAKING A LITTLE CREATIVE LICENSE, this recipe is part brownie but also part pudding. It's one of the fun recipes that begins with a brownie mix and has all sorts of other goodies added—peanut butter, chocolate chips, and brown sugar. And then the pudding cooks in a slow cooker, which makes it rich and gooey and great to serve during cold weather. Thanks to Jill Conyer of Houston for sending it to me years ago.

Vegetable oil spray, for misting the slow cooker
1½ cups water
1 cup packed light brown sugar
3 tablespoons unsweetened cocoa powder
1 package (about 20 ounces) brownie mix
½ cup peanut butter
½ cup milk or buttermilk
2 tablespoons (¼ stick) butter, melted
2 large eggs
1 cup (6 ounces) semisweet chocolate chips
Vanilla ice cream, for serving

1. Lightly mist a 5-quart slow cooker with vegetable oil spray and set it aside.

2. Place the water, brown sugar, and cocoa powder in a small saucepan over medium-high heat and bring to a boil, stirring. Remove the pan from the heat and stir until the brown sugar dissolves. Set the hot water and brown sugar mixture aside.

3. Place the brownie mix, peanut butter, milk, butter, and eggs in a large mixing bowl and stir with a wooden spoon until the mixture is smooth, 40 strokes. Fold in the chocolate chips. Transfer the batter to the prepared slow cooker. Pour the hot water and brown sugar mixture over the top.

4. Cover the slow cooker and cook the pudding on high power until nearly set, 2 hours. Turn off the heat and let the pudding stand for 30 minutes. Uncover the slow cooker and spoon the pudding into serving bowls. Top with vanilla ice cream.

Keep It Fresh! Store the pudding, covered, in the refrigerator for two days. You can reheat individual portions by spooning them into microwave-safe serving bowls and heating these in the microwave oven on high power for 10 to 15 seconds.

Recipe Reminders

MADE FOR

PREP NOTES

DON'T FORGET

SPECIAL TOUCHES

Fudge Brownie Torte

serves:
8 to 12

prep:
15 minutes

bake:
40 to 45 minutes

cool:
30 minutes

Add **DRIED SWEETENED CRANBERRIES** or yellow raisins and a touch of brandy to a brownie mix and you have the beginning of an elegant dessert. Yes, it's a brownie but it is baked in a springform pan. Slice the torte and serve it with whipped cream and raspberries, then wait for the oohs and aahs.

Vegetable oil spray, for misting the pan
½ cup dried sweetened cranberries or yellow raisins
¼ cup brandy
¼ cup water
1 package (about 20 ounces) brownie mix
½ cup vegetable oil
1 large egg
Sweetened Whipped Cream (page 489), for serving
1 cup fresh raspberries, for serving

Want to Gild the Lily?

Dust everything—torte, whipped cream, and berries—with confectioners' sugar. Or, drizzle your favorite chocolate sauce over everything.

1. Place a rack in the center of the oven and preheat the oven to 350°F. Lightly mist a 10-inch springform pan with vegetable oil spray. Cover the bottom of the pan with aluminum foil and set the pan aside.

2. Place the cranberries or raisins in a small microwave-safe glass bowl, pour in the brandy and water, and microwave on high power until the mixture has warmed, 30 seconds.

3. Place the brownie mix, oil, and egg in a large mixing bowl. Pour in the brandy and cranberry mixture, then beat with an electric mixer on low speed until the ingredients just come together, 30 seconds. Stop the machine and scrape down the side of the bowl with a rubber spatula. Transfer the batter to the prepared springform pan and place the pan in the oven.

4. Bake the torte until the edges are crisp and the center has just set but is still moist, 40 to 45 minutes. Transfer the springform pan to a wire rack and let the torte cool for 30 minutes. Run a sharp knife around the edge of the pan, remove the outside of the springform pan, then slice and serve the torte with whipped cream and fresh raspberries.

Keep It Fresh! Store the torte, wrapped in aluminum foil, at room temperature for up to five days. Freeze the torte, wrapped in aluminum foil, for up to three months. Let the torte thaw on the counter overnight before serving.

Recipe Reminders

MADE FOR

____

____

____

____

PREP NOTES

____

____

____

____

DON'T FORGET

____

____

____

____

SPECIAL TOUCHES

____

____

____

____

____

____

____

____

____

Chocolate Chip Cookie Bars

makes:
at least 30 bars

prep:
10 minutes

bake:
43 to 48 minutes

cool:
30 minutes

IT'S A TOSS-UP as to what is more enjoyable, eating chocolate chip cookies or these delectable cookie bars. Crammed with brown sugar and semisweet chocolate chips, they resemble made from scratch cookies, except these bars are faster to assemble. Aviva Korngold of Hicksville, New York, shared this recipe for cookie fans who lack the time to make cookies.

Vegetable oil spray, for misting the pan
1 package (18.5 ounces) plain butter recipe golden cake mix
1 package (3.4 ounces) vanilla instant pudding mix
8 tablespoons (1 stick) butter, melted
⅔ cup milk
½ cup packed light brown sugar
3 large eggs
1 teaspoon pure vanilla extract
1 cup (6 ounces) semisweet chocolate chips

1. Place a rack in the center of the oven and preheat the oven to 350°F. Lightly mist the bottom of a 13 by 9–inch baking pan with vegetable oil spray and set the pan aside.

2. Place the cake mix, pudding mix, butter, milk, brown sugar, eggs, and vanilla in a large mixing bowl and beat on low speed with an electric mixer until the ingredients are incorporated, 30 seconds. Turn off the machine and scrape down the side of the bowl with a rubber spatula. Increase the mixer speed to medium and beat until the batter is well combined, 1 minute longer. Fold in the chocolate chips. Transfer the batter to the prepared baking pan, smoothing the top with the rubber spatula so that it reaches the sides. Place the pan in the oven.

3. Bake the cookie bar batter until the edges are well browned and the center is firm to the touch, 43 to 48 minutes. Transfer the baking pan to a wire rack and let cool for 30 minutes before cutting the bars (see page 400) and serving.

Keep It Fresh! Store the bars, covered with plastic wrap or aluminum foil, at room temperature for up to three days or for up to one week in the refrigerator. Freeze the bars in the pan, covered with aluminum foil, for up to three months. Let the bars thaw overnight on the counter before serving.

Recipe Reminders

MADE FOR

____

____

____

____

PREP NOTES

____

____

____

____

DON'T FORGET

____

____

____

____

SPECIAL TOUCHES

____

____

____

____

____

____

____

____

____

Orange Chocolate Chip Bars

makes:
at least 30 bars

prep:
25 minutes

bake:
35 to 40 minutes

cool:
40 minutes

I'VE LEARNED that some people love the combination of orange and chocolate and others don't get it. My younger daughter loves chocolate with orange. She always hopes for a "chocolate orange" in her Christmas stocking. Shaped like a small orange, the chocolate candy falls into sections just as an orange does, and it has a wonderful orange flavor. After one bite of these bars, I thought of the chocolate orange. Bake this during winter holidays to place on party trays with a selection of your favorite cookies.

For the crust and topping

Vegetable oil spray, for misting the pan
1 package (18.25 ounces) yellow or butter recipe golden cake mix with pudding
1 cup quick-cooking oats
4 tablespoons (½ stick) butter, at room temperature
1 large egg

For the filling and glaze

1 large orange
Orange juice from a carton, if needed
8 tablespoons (1 stick) butter
1 cup (6 ounces) semisweet chocolate chips
½ cup granulated sugar
2 large eggs
1 cup very finely chopped pecans (from 1½ cups pecan halves)
1½ cups confectioners' sugar, sifted

1. Place a rack in the center of the oven and preheat the oven to 350°F. Lightly mist a 13 by 9–inch metal baking pan with vegetable oil spray and set the pan aside.

2. Make the topping and crust: Place the cake mix, oats, and 4 tablespoons of butter in a large mixing bowl and beat with an electric mixer on low speed until the ingredients are incorporated, 30 seconds. Stop the machine and scrape down the side of the bowl with a rubber spatula. Measure 1 cup of this mixture and set it aside for the topping. Add the 1 egg to the remaining mixture in the bowl and beat on low speed until just blended. The dough will be stiff; press it into the prepared baking pan to form the crust. Set the pan aside.

3. Make the filling: Rinse the orange and pat it dry with paper towels. Grate enough zest to measure 2 to 3 teaspoons and set aside. Cut the orange in half and squeeze the juice into a small bowl. Measure ¼ cup of juice for the filling and set it aside. You will need 3 tablespoons more of orange juice for the glaze. If the orange does not yield sufficient juice, add enough orange juice from the carton to measure 3 tablespoons and set this juice aside.

Recipe Reminders

MADE FOR

PREP NOTES

DON'T FORGET

SPECIAL TOUCHES

4. Place the 8 tablespoons of butter and the chocolate chips in a medium-size saucepan over low heat and stir until they melt. Stir in the granulated sugar until smooth, 2 to 3 minutes. Remove the pan from the heat. Beat the 2 eggs in a small bowl with a fork and slowly add 1 tablespoon of the melted chocolate mixture to them, whisking to blend. Add this egg mixture to the chocolate in the saucepan, still off the heat, whisking to blend. Fold in the pecans, orange zest, and the ¼ cup of orange juice. Pour the filling over the crust, spreading it with a spatula to reach the edges. Scatter the reserved topping over the filling.

5. Place the pan in the oven and bake until the edges of the bars have set and the center is still a little soft (press it lightly with a finger), 35 to 40 minutes. Transfer the baking pan to a wire rack and let cool for about 30 minutes.

6. Make the glaze: Place the confectioners' sugar in a small bowl and stir in the 2 tablespoons of orange juice. Add the remaining 1 tablespoon of juice a little at a time if needed to make a thick drizzleable glaze. Drizzle the glaze over the bars. Let the glaze set for 10 minutes before cutting the bars (see page 400) and serving.

Keep It Fresh! Store the bars, covered with plastic wrap or aluminum foil, at room temperature for up to three days or for up to one week in the refrigerator. Freeze the bars in the pan, covered with aluminum foil, for up to three months. Let the bars thaw overnight on the counter before serving.

Our Favorite Peanut Butter Chocolate Bars

I HAVE MADE THESE PEANUT BUTTER BARS so many times that yes, you could blindfold me and I could bake them without looking. They are the bars my kids request when they come home from school or camp. They are the bar of choice at their parties. They are just plain good. A cross between a peanut butter cookie and creamy fudge, these bars satisfy a sweet tooth like no other. But through the years I have tinkered with the original recipe, making it even better. I no longer add the chopped pecans, coconut, and butter I first called for in the fudge layer because, frankly, you don't need them. I really prefer the color and flavor of a plain butter recipe golden cake mix for these bars because the yellow mixes often have too much food coloring in them. And now I bake the bars at 350°F to promote browning; you want to bake them long enough for the top to turn golden brown. Honestly, my children are not so picky, but I like them crunchy and golden on top. Enjoy!

makes:
at least 30 bars

prep:
20 minutes

bake:
30 to 35 minutes

cool:
20 minutes

1 package (18.5 ounces) plain butter recipe golden cake mix or 1 package (18.25 ounces) plain yellow or vanilla cake mix
1 cup smooth or crunchy peanut butter
8 tablespoons (1 stick) butter, melted
2 large eggs
1 package (12 ounces; 2 cups) semisweet chocolate chips
1 can (14 ounces) sweetened condensed milk
2 teaspoons pure vanilla extract

Recipe Reminders

MADE FOR

PREP NOTES

DON'T FORGET

SPECIAL TOUCHES

1. Place a rack in the center of the oven and preheat the oven to 350°F. Set aside an ungreased 13 by 9–inch metal baking pan.

2. Place the cake mix, peanut butter, butter, and eggs in a large mixing bowl and beat with an electric mixer on low speed until the ingredients are incorporated, 1 minute. Stop the machine and scrape down the side of the bowl with a rubber spatula. The mixture will be thick. Measure about 1½ cups of this mixture and set it aside for the topping. Place the remaining cake mix mixture in the baking pan, pressing it over the bottom of the pan with your fingertips so that it reaches all sides to form the crust. Set the pan aside.

3. Place the chocolate chips and condensed milk in a medium-size microwave-safe glass bowl and microwave on high power for 1 minute. Stir in the vanilla and continue stirring until the chocolate has melted and the mixture is smooth and creamy. Pour the chocolate mixture over the crust, spreading it evenly with the rubber spatula so that it reaches the sides. Using your fingertips, crumble the reserved topping and scatter it over the chocolate.

4. Place the pan in the oven and bake the bars until they are golden brown around the edges and on top, 30 to 35 minutes. Transfer the baking pan to a wire rack and let cool for 20 minutes, before cutting the bars (see page 400) and serving.

Keep It Fresh! Store the bars, covered with plastic wrap, at room temperature for up to three days or uncut in the pan, covered with aluminum foil, in the refrigerator for up to five days. Freeze the bars in the pan, covered with aluminum foil, for up to three months. Let the bars thaw overnight on the counter before serving.

Houdini Bars

WHO CAN RESIST such an intriguing name and such a delicious and creamy bar? The magical recipe was sent to me several years ago by P. Jean Champoux, who lives in Westerville, Ohio. The cake mix, butter, and egg mixture forms a crust onto which you pour a cheesecake-like coconut mixture that bakes up tasting like a coconut cream pie. The story goes that these bars are so rich and delicious that they disappear quickly, thus the name.

makes:
at least 30 bars

prep:
15 minutes

bake:
45 to 50 minutes

cool:
30 minutes

1 package (18.25 ounces) plain yellow cake mix, or 1 package (18.5 ounces) plain butter recipe golden cake mix
8 tablespoons (1 stick) butter, melted
3 large eggs
1 package (8 ounces) reduced-fat cream cheese, at room temperature
1 teaspoon pure vanilla extract
2 cups confectioners' sugar, sifted (see Note)
½ cup sweetened flaked coconut
½ cup chopped pecans (optional)

1. Place a rack in the center of the oven and preheat the oven to 350°F. Set aside an ungreased 13 by 9–inch metal baking pan.

2. Place the cake mix, butter, and 1 egg in a large mixing bowl and beat on low speed with an electric mixer until the ingredients are incorporated, 1 minute. Press the batter into the bottom and partially up the sides of the baking pan and set the pan aside.

Recipe Reminders

MADE FOR

PREP NOTES

DON'T FORGET

SPECIAL TOUCHES

3. Place the cream cheese in the same mixing bowl and beat with an electric mixer on low speed until fluffy, 30 seconds. Add the remaining 2 eggs and the vanilla and confectioners' sugar and beat on low speed until smooth and combined, 1 minute. Fold in the coconut. Pour the mixture over the crust and smooth the top with a rubber spatula. Scatter the pecans, if using, over the top. Place the pan in the oven.

4. Bake the bars until the edges are well browned and the center is firm to the touch, 45 to 50 minutes. Transfer the baking pan to a wire rack and let cool for 30 minutes before cutting the bars (see page 400) and serving.

Keep It Fresh! Store the bars, covered with plastic wrap or aluminum foil, in the refrigerator for up to five days.

Note: I reduced the confectioners' sugar in P. Jean's recipe to 2 cups. If the cream cheese mixture is not sweet enough for you, add up to 1 cup more sugar.

Turtle Bars

When I'm testing recipes it really helps to get the baked goods out of the house! It so happened there was a dinner for the parents in my younger daughter's grade. Some of the moms were asked to bring dessert. I brought an assortment of bars, and at the end of the evening I noticed all the Turtle Bars were gone. I understand why—the gooey caramel center is irresistible, just as it is hard to beat in the chocolate candy by the same name.

makes:
at least 30 bars

prep:
25 minutes

bake:
40 to 45 minutes

cool:
35 minutes

Vegetable oil spray, for misting the pan
1 package (14 ounces) caramels (about 52)
4 tablespoons (½ stick) butter, plus 8 tablespoons (1 stick) butter, melted
½ cup heavy (whipping) cream or evaporated milk
1 package (18.25 ounces) plain German chocolate cake mix
1 tablespoon unsweetened cocoa powder
2 large eggs
1 cup (6 ounces) semisweet chocolate chips
1 cup chopped pecans or walnuts

1. Place a rack in the center of the oven and preheat the oven to 350°F. Lightly mist the bottom of a 13 by 9–inch metal baking pan with vegetable oil spray and set the pan aside.

2. Unwrap the caramels and place them in a heavy medium-size saucepan with the 4 tablespoons of butter and the cream. Cook,

Recipe Reminders

MADE FOR

PREP NOTES

DON'T FORGET

SPECIAL TOUCHES

stirring constantly, over low heat until the caramels melt and the sauce is smooth, 7 to 8 minutes. Remove the pan from the heat and set it aside.

3. Place the cake mix, cocoa powder, 8 tablespoons of melted butter, and the eggs in a large mixing bowl and beat on low speed with an electric mixer until the ingredients are incorporated, 30 seconds to 1 minute. Divide the batter in half. Place half of the batter in the prepared baking pan, pressing it evenly onto the bottom. Place the pan in the oven and bake until the cake begins to rise, 10 minutes. Remove the pan from the oven.

4. Stir the chocolate chips and nuts into the warm caramel mixture. Pour this over the cake in the pan and spread it to nearly reach the edges. Dollop the remaining batter in inch-size pieces over the caramel. Place the pan in the oven.

5. Bake the bars until the center is firm to the touch and the caramel is bubbling, 30 to 35 minutes. Transfer the baking pan to a wire rack and let cool completely, 35 minutes before cutting the bars (see page 400) and serving.

Keep It Fresh! Store the bars, covered with plastic wrap or aluminum foil, at room temperature for up to three days or for up to one week in the refrigerator. Freeze the bars in the pan, covered with aluminum foil, for up to three months. Let the bars thaw overnight on the counter before serving.

Butterscotch Bars

CHARLOTTE SHOPMEYER, who lives in Newburgh, Indiana, sent me this recipe several years ago. She takes the bars to church dinners and picnics and has given them as gifts. They're easy to make at the last minute from ingredients in your pantry. And they freeze well, too.

makes:
at least 30 bars

prep:
10 minutes

bake:
35 to 40 minutes

cool:
25 minutes

1 package (18.5 ounces) plain butter recipe golden cake mix
4 tablespoons (½ stick) butter, melted
2 large eggs
1 can (14 ounces) sweetened condensed milk
1 package (11 ounces) butterscotch chips
½ cup finely chopped pecans (optional)

1. Place a rack in the center of the oven and preheat the oven to 350°F. Set aside an ungreased 13 by 9–inch metal baking pan.

2. Place the cake mix, butter, and 1 egg in a large mixing bowl and beat on low speed with an electric mixer until the ingredients are incorporated, 30 seconds. The dough will be crumbly. Press it into the bottom of the prepared baking pan. Set the pan aside.

3. Place the condensed milk and the remaining egg in the same bowl and beat with the electric mixer on medium-low speed until just combined, 1 minute. Fold in the butterscotch chips. Pour the

Recipe Reminders

MADE FOR

PREP NOTES

DON'T FORGET

SPECIAL TOUCHES

mixture over the crust, smoothing the top with a spatula so that it reaches the sides. Scatter the pecans over the top, if using, and place the pan in the oven.

4. Bake the bars until the edges are golden brown and the center is nearly set, 35 to 40 minutes. Transfer the baking pan to a wire rack and let cool for 25 minutes before cutting the bars (see page 400) and serving.

Keep It Fresh! Store the bars, covered with plastic wrap or aluminum foil, at room temperature for up to three days or for up to one week in the refrigerator. Freeze the bars in the pan, covered with aluminum foil, for up to three months. Let the bars thaw overnight on the counter before serving.

Aimee's Chess Cake

AIMEE LUREY sent me this recipe many years ago. It was her grandmother's recipe, one she describes as "sweet and gooey." Since then I've received countless variations; some people call it "gooey butter cake." Aimee's recipe called for a half cup of oil but I substituted a stick of unsalted butter, melted. Either makes a crowd-pleasing dessert, best cut into small bars because it's so rich.

makes:
at least 30 bars

prep:
20 minutes

bake:
28 to 32 minutes

cool:
30 minutes

Vegetable oil spray, for misting the pan
Flour, for dusting the pan
1 package (18.25 ounces) plain yellow cake mix
8 tablespoons (1 stick) butter, melted
3 large eggs
4 cups confectioners' sugar, sifted
1 package (8 ounces) reduced-fat cream cheese, at room temperature
2 teaspoons pure vanilla extract

1. Place a rack in the center of the oven and preheat the oven to 350°F. Lightly mist a 13 by 9–inch metal baking pan with vegetable oil spray, then dust it with flour. Shake out the excess flour and set the pan aside.

2. Place the cake mix, butter, and 1 egg in a large mixing bowl and beat with an electric mixer on medium speed until just combined, about 30 seconds. Using your fingertips, press the mixture into the prepared baking pan and set the pan aside.

Recipe Reminders

MADE FOR

PREP NOTES

DON'T FORGET

SPECIAL TOUCHES

3. Place the remaining 2 eggs and the confectioners' sugar, cream cheese, and vanilla in the same mixing bowl; no need to wash the beaters. Beat with the electric mixer on medium speed until well combined and smooth, 3 to 4 minutes. Pour the batter over the cake mix mixture.

4. Place the pan in the oven and bake the cake until the edges have set and the top is light golden brown, 28 to 32 minutes. Transfer the baking pan to a wire rack and let cool completely, 30 minutes, before cutting the bars (see page 400) and serving.

Keep It Fresh! Store the bars, covered with plastic wrap or aluminum foil, at room temperature for up to three days or for up to one week in the refrigerator. Freeze the bars in the pan, covered with aluminum foil, for up to three months. Let the bars thaw overnight on the counter before serving.

Sugar, Sugar

How much sugar is in that bag or box? Here's a key.

1 pound of granulated sugar equals 2¼ cups.

A 1 pound box of brown sugar equals 2⅓ to 2⅔ packed cups.

A 1 pound box of confectioners' sugar equals 4 cups, unsifted.

A 2 pound bag of brown sugar equals about 5 packed cups.

A 2 pound bag of confectioners' sugar equals 8 cups, unsifted.

4 pounds of granulated sugar equal 9 cups.

5 pounds of granulated sugar equal 11¼ cups.

LEMON GOOEY BUTTER CAKE

I **SHARED A GOOEY BUTTER CAKE RECIPE** in the first *Cake Mix Doctor* book. But I didn't know I was sharing a recipe that was near and dear to the hearts of those in St. Louis until I went there on a book tour. This regional American cake has a crusty, cakey bottom and a gooey and sweet cream cheese filling, thus the name. It has been fun to learn about the cake through the years—that it was invented by accident by a baker in the 1930s who got his proportions mixed up and ended up with a gooey, and delicious, cake. It's popularity has spread outside of St. Louis. Many versions using a cake mix are circulated, but this one from reader Doris Johns of Hurst, Texas, is a favorite. She tipped me off that gooey butter cake tastes best when you put two eggs in both the crust and the filling and add a little vanilla to each layer.

makes:
at least 30 bars

prep:
20 minutes

bake:
42 to 45 minutes

cool:
30 minutes

For the crust

1 package (18.25 ounces) plain yellow or vanilla cake mix
8 tablespoons (1 stick) butter, melted
2 large eggs
1 teaspoon pure vanilla extract

For the filling

2 large lemons
1 package (8 ounces) cream cheese, at room temperature
2 large eggs
1 teaspoon pure vanilla extract
3¾ cups confectioners' sugar, sifted

1. Place a rack in the center of the oven and preheat the oven to 350°F. Set aside an ungreased 13 by 9–inch metal baking pan.

Recipe Reminders

MADE FOR

PREP NOTES

DON'T FORGET

SPECIAL TOUCHES

2. Make the crust: Place the cake mix, butter, 2 eggs, and 1 teaspoon of vanilla in a large mixing bowl and beat with an electric mixer on low speed until the ingredients are incorporated, 1½ to 2 minutes. Stop the machine and scrape down the side of the bowl with a rubber spatula. The batter should come together in a ball. Using your fingertips, pat the crust evenly over the bottom and ½ inch up the sides of the baking pan, smoothing it out with your fingers. Set the pan aside.

3. Make the filling: Rinse the lemons and pat them dry with paper towels. Grate enough zest to measure about 2 teaspoons. Cut the lemons in half and squeeze the juice into a small bowl; you will have about 6 tablespoons.

4. Place the cream cheese in the same mixing bowl that was used to make the crust and, using the same beaters (no need to clean either), beat with an electric mixer on low speed until fluffy, 30 seconds. Stop the machine and add the lemon juice, lemon zest, 2 eggs, and 1 teaspoon of vanilla and beat on medium speed for 1 minute. Stop the machine and add the confectioners' sugar. Beat on medium speed until the sugar is well incorporated, 1 minute. Stop the machine and scrape down the side of the bowl with a rubber spatula. Pour the filling into the baking pan and spread it with the rubber spatula so that it covers the entire surface and reaches the sides of the pan. Place the pan in the oven.

5. Bake the cake until it is well browned but the center still jiggles when you shake the pan, 42 to 45 minutes. Transfer the baking pan to a wire rack and let the cake cool for 30 minutes before cutting it into bars (see page 400) and serving.

Keep It Fresh! Store the bars, covered with plastic wrap or aluminum foil, at room temperature for up to three days or for up to one week in the refrigerator. Freeze the bars in the pan, covered with aluminum foil, for up to three months. Let the bars thaw overnight in the refrigerator before serving.

Chocolate Walnut Gooey Butter Cake

FAMOUS CAKES should have a chocolate version, right? So it goes with this cake, not so traditional as a plain gooey butter cake or one with lemon added, but just as delicious. I have learned that in Texas they call this the Neiman Marcus cake. Funny, any decadent chocolate confection from Texas seems to have a similar name! But with the chocolate chips and walnuts added, this does make an over-the-top gooey cake.

makes:
at least 30 bars

prep:
15 minutes

bake:
40 to 45 minutes

cool:
30 minutes

For the crust

1 package (18.25 ounces) plain chocolate cake mix

8 tablespoons (1 stick) butter, melted

2 large eggs

1 teaspoon pure vanilla extract

1 cup (6 ounces) semisweet chocolate chips

1 cup finely chopped walnuts

For the filling

1 package (8 ounces) cream cheese, at room temperature

2 large eggs

1 teaspoon pure vanilla extract

3¾ cups confectioners' sugar, sifted (see Note)

1. Place a rack in the center of the oven and preheat the oven to 350°F. Set aside an ungreased 13 by 9–inch metal baking pan.

2. Make the crust: Place the cake mix, butter, 2 eggs, and 1 teaspoon of vanilla in a large mixing bowl and beat with an electric mixer on low speed until the ingredients are incorporated, 1½ to 2 minutes. Stop the machine and scrape down the side of the bowl with a rubber spatula. The batter should come together in a ball. Using your fingertips, pat the crust evenly over the bottom and ½ inch up the sides of the baking pan, smoothing it out with your fingers. Scatter the chocolate chips and walnuts on top of the crust. Set the pan aside.

3. Make the filling: Place the cream cheese in the same mixing bowl that was used to make the crust and, using the same beaters (no need to clean either), beat with an electric mixer on low speed until fluffy, 30 seconds. Stop the machine and add the 2 eggs and 1 teaspoon of vanilla and beat on medium speed for 1 minute. Stop the machine and add the confectioners' sugar. Beat on medium speed until the sugar is well incorporated, 1 minute. Stop the machine and scrape down the side of the bowl with a rubber spatula. Pour the filling into the baking pan and spread it with the rubber spatula so that it covers the entire surface and reaches the sides of the pan. Place the pan in the oven.

4. Bake the cake until the edges have set but the center still jiggles when you shake the pan, 40 to 45 minutes. Transfer the baking pan to a wire rack and let the cake cool for 30 minutes, before cutting it into bars (see page 400) and serving.

Keep It Fresh! Store the bars, covered with plastic wrap or aluminum foil, at room temperature for up to three days or for up to one week in the refrigerator. Freeze the bars in the pan, covered with aluminum foil, for up to three months. Let the bars thaw overnight in the refrigerator before serving.

Note: Many recipes for gooey butter cake call for a box of confectioners' sugar. If you like a supersweet cake, add the whole box, which will measure about 4 cups. Sift the confectioners' sugar first to remove any lumps. I tend to like desserts that are a little less sweet, so I use just 3¾ cups of sugar. (I usually buy the plastic bags of confectioners' sugar because then I don't have to return to the store so often and because when tightly sealed the sugar stays fresher than sugar in the box.) Does ¼ cup less sugar make any difference in the flavor of this cake? It's a tad less sweet.

Recipe Reminders

MADE FOR

PREP NOTES

DON'T FORGET

SPECIAL TOUCHES

Pineapple Coconut Bars

makes:
at least 30 bars

prep:
30 minutes

bake:
35 to 40 minutes

cool:
30 minutes

INGRID MCGUIRE, who lives in Wilmette, Illinois, shared this recipe with me several years ago. It's her favorite cake mix recipe, one that turns the cake mix and oats, crushed pineapple, macadamia nuts, and white chocolate into festive bar cookies. If you like, drizzle a glaze on top—mix one and a half cups of confectioners' sugar with five tablespoons of pineapple juice. But I like the simplicity of the bars unadorned.

For the crust

Vegetable oil spray, for misting the pan
1 package (18.25 ounces) yellow or vanilla cake mix, plain or with pudding
1½ cups quick-cooking oats
8 tablespoons (1 stick) butter, melted
1 large egg

For the filling

½ cup all-purpose flour
1 can (14 ounces) sweetened condensed milk
1 can (8 ounces) crushed pineapple, lightly drained
¼ teaspoon ground nutmeg

For the topping

1 heaping cup chopped macadamia nuts (about 4.5 ounces)
1 cup sweetened flaked coconut
1 cup (6 ounces) white chocolate chips

1. Place a rack in the center of the oven and preheat the oven to 350°F. Lightly mist a 13 by 9–inch metal baking pan with vegetable oil spray and set the pan aside.

2. Make the crust: Place the cake mix, oats, butter, and egg in a large mixing bowl and beat with an electric mixer on low speed until the ingredients are incorporated, 1 minute. Measure 1½ cups of this mixture and set it aside for the topping. Press the remaining mixture evenly into the bottom of the prepared baking pan and set the pan aside.

3. Make the filling: Place the flour, condensed milk, pineapple, and nutmeg in the same mixing bowl and, using the same beaters (no need to clean either), beat with an electric mixer on low speed until the flour is just combined, 1 minute. Pour the filling into the baking pan.

4. Make the topping: Add the macadamia nuts, coconut, and white chocolate chips to the reserved topping mixture and stir until just combined. Scatter the topping over the filling. Place the pan in the oven and bake the bars until the edges have set and the center is golden brown, 35 to 40 minutes. Transfer the baking pan to a wire rack and let cool for 30 minutes before cutting the bars (see page 400) and serving.

Keep It Fresh! Store the bars, covered with plastic wrap or aluminum foil, at room temperature for up to five days. Freeze the bars in the pan, covered with aluminum foil, for up to three months. Let the bars thaw overnight on the counter before serving.

Recipe Reminders

MADE FOR

____

____

____

____

PREP NOTES

____

____

____

____

DON'T FORGET

____

____

____

____

SPECIAL TOUCHES

____

____

____

____

____

____

____

____

____

Applesauce Bars with a Light Cream Cheese Frosting

makes:
about 32 bars

prep:
20 minutes

bake:
25 to 30 minutes

cool:
45 minutes

OR SHOULD I CALL THIS SPANISH BAR CAKE? For years my newsletter readers sought out the recipe for Spanish bar cake, a spice cake that used to be baked in A&P grocery stores in the South. It was baked on Saturday mornings, and readers had wonderful childhood memories of shopping with their parents and looking forward to a slice of this cake. I remembered Spanish bar cake from my days in Atlanta. It was a dense spice cake with raisins. When I was testing this particular recipe, adapted from one sent to me by Ken King of Birmingham, Alabama, I had flashbacks of the A&P cake. So call this recipe what you like—the cake is dense with applesauce, spices, raisins, and walnuts. I frosted it with a light cream cheese frosting but you could certainly use a richer version. Run the tines of a fork through the icing in squiggles and the cake will look just as we all remember. Add a tablespoon of unsweetened cocoa powder to the batter should you want to add a deep mysterious flavor to this spice cake.

For the bars

Parchment paper, for lining the pan
1 package (18.25 ounces) plain spice cake mix
¼ cup lightly packed light brown sugar
¾ teaspoon ground cinnamon
½ teaspoon ground nutmeg
¼ teaspoon ground cloves
2 cups unsweetened applesauce (from a 23-ounce jar)
⅔ cup vegetable oil
4 large eggs
¾ cup raisins, chopped (see Notes)
½ cup finely chopped walnuts (optional)

For the frosting and garnish

4 ounces reduced-fat cream cheese, at room temperature
1 tablespoon milk
2½ cups confectioners' sugar, sifted
1 teaspoon pure vanilla extract
½ cup coarsely chopped walnuts (optional; see Notes)

1. Make the bars: Place a rack in the center of the oven and preheat the oven to 350°F. Line a 15 by 10 by 1–inch jelly roll pan with parchment paper and set the pan aside.

2. Place the cake mix, brown sugar, cinnamon, nutmeg, cloves, applesauce, oil, and eggs in a large mixing bowl and beat with an electric mixer on low speed until the ingredients are incorporated, 30 seconds. Stop the machine and scrape down the side of the bowl with a rubber spatula. Increase the mixer speed to medium and beat until the batter is smooth, about 1 minute longer. Fold in the raisins and ½ cup finely chopped walnuts, if using. Transfer the batter to the prepared baking pan, smoothing the top with the rubber spatula.

Recipe Reminders

MADE FOR

PREP NOTES

DON'T FORGET

SPECIAL TOUCHES

3. Place the pan in the oven and bake the bars until the edges have set and the center is still a little soft (press it lightly with a finger), 25 to 30 minutes. Transfer the baking pan to a wire rack and let cool for about 35 minutes.

4. Make the frosting: Place the cream cheese in a large mixing bowl and beat with an electric mixer on low until creamy, 1 minute. Stop the machine and add the milk, confectioners' sugar, and vanilla. Continue beating on low until the ingredients come together. Increase the mixer speed to medium low and beat until the frosting is creamy and light, 30 seconds longer. Spread the frosting evenly on top of the cooled cake. Run the tines of a fork through the icing to make squiggles or garnish it with the ½ cup of coarsely chopped walnuts, if desired. Let the frosting set for 10 minutes before slicing and serving the bars.

Keep It Fresh! Store the bars, covered with aluminum foil, in the refrigerator for up to one week. Freeze the bars in the pan, covered with aluminum foil, for up to three months. Let the bars thaw overnight in the refrigerator before serving.

Notes: For raisins reminiscent of those in the Spanish bar cake, use those labeled baking raisins—moist raisins found alongside the regular raisins. If you use baking raisins you don't need to chop them.

Toasted nuts always taste better than untoasted. If you want to toast the walnuts for the garnish, place them on a rimmed baking sheet in the oven while it preheats. It will take 4 to 5 minutes for the nuts to turn medium brown and become fragrant.

Pumpkin Spice Bars

SORT OF LIKE A CAKE, kind of like a cheesecake, and delicious chilled pretty much describes these easy to make bars. They are a wonderful do-ahead dessert for the holidays and a nice alternative to pumpkin pie. They're nice at fall and winter potlucks. And children love them, but you might want to omit the chopped nuts on top.

makes:
about 32 bars

prep:
20 minutes

bake:
30 to 35 minutes

cool:
1 hour

chill:
1 hour

For the crust

Vegetable oil spray, for misting the pan
1 package (18.25 ounces) plain spice cake mix
4 tablespoons (½ stick) butter, melted
1 large egg

For the filling

1 package (8 ounces) cream cheese, at room temperature
1 can (15 ounces) pumpkin, about 2 cups
1 can (14 ounces) sweetened condensed milk
2 large eggs
½ teaspoon ground pumpkin pie spice or cinnamon
1 cup finely chopped pecans, for garnish (optional; see Note)

Recipe Reminders

MADE FOR

PREP NOTES

DON'T FORGET

SPECIAL TOUCHES

1. Place a rack in the center of the oven and preheat the oven to 350°F. Lightly mist a 15 by 10 by 1–inch jelly roll pan with vegetable oil spray and set the pan aside.

2. Make the crust: Place the cake mix, butter, and 1 egg in a large mixing bowl and beat with an electric mixer on low speed until the ingredients are incorporated, 30 seconds. The mixture will be dry. Press it into the bottom of the prepared baking pan and set the pan aside.

3. Make the filling: Place the cream cheese in the same mixing bowl and, using the same beaters (no need to clean either), beat with an electric mixer on low speed until creamy, 30 to 40 seconds. Stop the machine and scrape down the side of the bowl with a rubber spatula. Add the pumpkin, condensed milk, 2 eggs, and pumpkin pie spice or cinnamon. Increase the mixer speed to medium-low and beat until the mixture is smooth, about 1 minute. Transfer the batter to the baking pan, smoothing the top with the rubber spatula. Top with the chopped pecans, if using.

4. Place the pan in the oven and bake the bars until the edges have set and the center is still a little soft (press it lightly with a finger), 30 to 35 minutes. Transfer the baking pan to a wire rack and let cool for 1 hour. Lightly wrap the pan with plastic wrap and refrigerate it for at least 1 hour before cutting and serving the bars.

Keep It Fresh! Store the bars, covered with plastic wrap or aluminum foil, in the refrigerator for up to five days. They do not freeze well.

Note: For a tasty variation, finely chop the pecans and fold them into the crust mixture instead of using them as a garnish.

Chocolate Italian Cookies

THIS IS A RECIPE that was making the rounds many years ago. It begins with a chocolate cake mix, then you add some flour and spices, and drop the batter onto baking sheets. There is nothing really Italian about the cookies, but they are exotic and festive. Feel free to fold in whatever dried fruit suits you.

makes:
5 dozen cookies

prep:
15 minutes

bake:
8 to 10 minutes

cool:
15 minutes

For the cookies

1 package (18.25 ounces) plain chocolate cake mix
1 cup all-purpose flour
1 tablespoon ground cinnamon
1 teaspoon ground nutmeg
1 teaspoon ground cloves
¾ cup vegetable oil
½ cup water
2 large eggs
1 teaspoon pure vanilla extract
1 cup finely chopped walnuts
1 cup golden raisins or dried sweetened cranberries

For the glaze

1½ cups confectioners' sugar
4 to 5 tablespoons milk

Recipe Reminders

MADE FOR

PREP NOTES

DON'T FORGET

SPECIAL TOUCHES

1. Make the cookies: Place a rack in the center of the oven and preheat the oven to 325°F. Set aside 2 ungreased baking sheets.

2. Place the cake mix, flour, cinnamon, nutmeg, and cloves in a large mixing bowl and stir to combine. Add the oil, water, eggs, and vanilla and stir with a wooden spoon until the dough is smooth, about 45 strokes, or beat with an electric mixer on low speed for 1 minute. Fold in the walnuts and raisins.

3. Drop the cookie dough by tablespoonfuls about 2 inches apart onto the ungreased baking sheets. Place the baking sheets in the oven; if your oven cannot accommodate both baking sheets on the center rack, place one on the top rack and one on the center rack and rotate them halfway through the baking time.

4. Bake the cookies until they are firm around the edges but still soft in the center, 8 to 10 minutes. Transfer the cookies to wire racks to cool for 5 minutes. Repeat with the remaining cookie dough.

5. Make the glaze: Place the confectioners' sugar in a large mixing bowl and stir in the milk until smooth. Using a small spoon, drizzle the glaze over the cooled cookies. Let the cookies rest for 10 minutes before serving so that the glaze can set.

Keep It Fresh! Store the cookies, under a glass dome or in a tightly sealed tin or plastic container, at room temperature for up to five days. Freeze the cookies, wrapped in aluminum foil, for up to three months. Let the cookies thaw overnight on the counter before serving.

Easy Chocolate Cookies

THIS RECIPE IS SO SIMPLE you might not even need a recipe. Try it the first time plain. Then, the second time fold in one cup of chocolate chips or some chopped nuts. Add a pinch of cinnamon or a little instant coffee or espresso powder. Make sure the cream cheese is soft so the batter blends together easily. If the cream cheese is cold, place it in the microwave oven for thirty to forty seconds to warm it up. Serve these cookies with coffee or mint chocolate chip ice cream. Or sandwich ice cream between them, freeze them, and you have homemade ice cream sandwiches.

makes:
3 dozen cookies

prep:
10 minutes

bake:
10 to 12 minutes

cool:
3 to 4 minutes

1 package (18.25 ounces) plain chocolate cake mix
1 package (8 ounces) cream cheese, at room temperature
1 large egg
1 teaspoon pure vanilla extract
4 tablespoons (½ stick) butter, melted

Recipe Reminders

MADE FOR

PREP NOTES

DON'T FORGET

SPECIAL TOUCHES

1. Place a rack in the center of the oven and preheat the oven to 375°F. Set aside 2 ungreased baking sheets.

2. Place the cake mix, cream cheese, egg, vanilla, and butter in a large mixing bowl and beat with an electric mixer on low speed until the ingredients are just combined, about 30 seconds. Stop the machine and scrape down the side of the bowl with a rubber spatula. Increase the mixer speed to medium and beat until the dough is nearly smooth, 1 minute longer. The dough will be thick and may still have lumps of cake mix.

3. Using a small cookie scoop or a spoon, drop the cookie dough by generous tablespoonfuls about 2 inches apart on the ungreased baking sheets. Place the baking sheets in the oven; if your oven cannot accommodate both baking sheets on the center rack, place one on the top rack and one on the center rack and rotate them halfway through the baking time.

4. Bake the cookies until they are firm around the edges but still soft in the center, 10 to 12 minutes. Remove the baking sheets from the oven and let the cookies cool on them for 2 to 3 minutes. Then, using a metal spatula, transfer the cookies to wire racks and let them cool completely, 20 minutes longer. Repeat with the remaining cookie dough.

Keep It Fresh! Store the cookies, in an airtight container or wrapped in aluminum foil, at room temperature for up to one week. Freeze the cookies, wrapped in aluminum foil, for up to three months. Let the cookies thaw overnight on the counter before serving.

German Chocolate Thumbprint Cookies

HEIDI QUINN, who lives in Carolina, Rhode Island, mentioned this recipe in an e-mail, and I could not get the thought of it out of my mind. So, I asked Heidi to send me the recipe. My kids loved the classic combination of coconut, pecans, and German chocolate cake. Just like the cake, the cookies are gooey and stay moist for days.

makes:
5 dozen cookies

prep:
25 minutes

bake:
10 to 12 minutes

cool:
20 minutes

1 cup granulated sugar
1 cup evaporated milk
8 tablespoons (1 stick) butter or margarine, plus 5 tablespoons butter, melted
1 teaspoon pure vanilla extract
3 large egg yolks, slightly beaten
1 cup sweetened flaked coconut
1 cup finely chopped pecans
1 package (18.25 ounces) plain German chocolate cake mix

Recipe Reminders

MADE FOR

PREP NOTES

DON'T FORGET

SPECIAL TOUCHES

1. Place a rack in the center of the oven and preheat the oven to 350°F. Set aside 2 ungreased baking sheets.

2. Place the granulated sugar, milk, 8 tablespoons of butter, and the vanilla and egg yolks in a heavy 2-quart saucepan over low heat and stir to combine as the butter melts. Increase the heat to medium and cook, stirring, until the mixture thickens and is bubbly, 10 minutes. Stir in the coconut and pecans. Remove the pan from the heat and let cool for 15 minutes. Measure out 1¼ cups of the mixture for the filling and set it aside.

3. Place the cake mix, 5 tablespoons of melted butter, and the remaining sugar mixture from the pan in a large mixing bowl and stir with a wooden spoon until just combined.

4. Using a spoon and your fingers, shape the cookie dough into 1-inch balls and place them 2 inches apart on the ungreased baking sheets. Using your thumb, make an indentation in the center of each ball of dough and fill it with a half teaspoon of the reserved filling mixture.

5. Bake the cookies until they are browned and lightly set, 10 to 12 minutes. Remove the baking sheets from the oven and let the cookies cool for 5 minutes. Then, using a metal spatula, transfer the cookies to wire racks to finish cooling, 20 minutes longer. Repeat with the remaining cookie dough and filling.

Keep It Fresh! Store the cookies, in an airtight container or wrapped in aluminum foil, at room temperature for up to three days. Freeze the cookies, wrapped in aluminum foil, for up to three months. Let the cookies thaw overnight on the counter before serving.

Chocolate Espresso Biscotti with Walnuts

CHARLOTTE, NORTH CAROLINA, resident Janice Elder uses a brownie mix to make these biscotti, which she gives as gifts during the winter holidays. To decorate them, she dips one end in melted dark chocolate or drizzles white chocolate all over. But if you're short on time, dredge the biscotti in confectioners' sugar or simply eat them as is. Not a coffee lover? Omit the espresso powder and add a smidgen (a quarter teaspoon) of cinnamon instead.

makes:
24 to 30 biscotti

prep:
25 minutes

bake:
18 to 20 minutes first baking, 8 to 10 minutes second baking

cool:
25 minutes

Parchment paper (optional), for lining the baking sheet
Vegetable oil spray (optional), for misting the baking sheet
1 package (about 20 ounces) brownie mix
¾ cup finely chopped walnuts
⅓ cup all-purpose flour
2 tablespoons espresso powder or instant coffee granules
1 teaspoon baking powder
2 tablespoons vegetable oil
2 large eggs
1 teaspoon pure vanilla extract
1 cup confectioners' sugar (optional), sifted, for garnish
1 cup (6 ounces) white or semisweet chocolate chips (optional), melted, for garnish

1. Place a rack in the center of the oven and preheat the oven to 350°F. Line a 12 by 18–inch baking sheet with parchment paper or mist it with nonstick cooking spray. Set the baking sheet aside.

Recipe Reminders

MADE FOR

____

____

____

____

PREP NOTES

____

____

____

____

DON'T FORGET

____

____

____

____

SPECIAL TOUCHES

____

____

____

____

____

____

____

____

____

2. Place the brownie mix, walnuts, flour, espresso powder, and baking powder in a large mixing bowl and stir to combine. Make a well in the center and add the oil, eggs, and vanilla. Using a wooden spoon, stir the liquid ingredients together, then gradually stir the dry ingredients into the liquid, stirring until the batter is well combined. The dough will become very stiff and you may need to use your hands to mix. Divide the dough into three pieces.

3. Using your hands, shape each third of dough into an 8–inch long log. Place the logs of dough on the prepared baking sheet 2 to 3 inches apart and flatten them into rectangular loaves 1 inch thick and about 2½ inches wide. Place the pan in the oven.

4. Bake the biscotti loaves until they are almost baked through but still soft, 18 to 20 minutes. Remove the baking sheet from the oven and let the loaves cool on it for 5 minutes. Leave the oven on.

5. Transfer the loaves to a cutting board and, using a bread knife, cut them diagonally into ¾–inch thick slices. Using a metal spatula, carefully arrange the slices flat on the baking sheet. Return the baking sheet to the oven and bake the biscotti for 8 to 10 minutes longer.

6. Remove the baking sheet from the oven and transfer the biscotti to wire racks to cool for 20 minutes. Serve them as is or dust them with confectioners' sugar (place the sugar in a large resealable plastic bag, add a few biscotti at a time, shake and then remove them). Or dip one end of each into melted chocolate or drizzle melted chocolate over the tops of biscotti.

Keep It Fresh! Store the biscotti, in a tightly sealed container, at room temperature for up to a week. Freeze the biscotti, wrapped in aluminum foil, for up to three months. Let the biscotti thaw overnight on the counter before serving.

Laura's Fudgy Rum Balls

SOME CAKES ARE FOR DECORATING, and some are for crumbling up and turning into rum balls! Laura Cunningham, of Parsippany, New Jersey, shared this recipe, which she makes from devil's food cake, cocoa, finely chopped nuts, a little coconut, and rum, of course. These are perfect for a cookie swap, holiday buffet, or just giving to friends. For a more intense coconut flavor, use a cup and a half of coconut milk instead of the water and oil in the cake batter.

makes:
6 dozen rum balls

prep:
35 to 40 minutes

bake:
35 to 40 minutes

cool:
30 minutes

Vegetable oil spray, for misting the pan
Flour, for dusting the pan
1 package (18.25 ounces) plain devil's food cake mix
1 cup water
½ cup vegetable oil
3 large eggs
2½ cups confectioners' sugar, sifted
¼ cup unsweetened cocoa powder
½ cup finely chopped walnuts or pecans
½ cup sweetened flaked coconut (optional)
2 to 3 tablespoons rum

Recipe Reminders

MADE FOR

PREP NOTES

DON'T FORGET

SPECIAL TOUCHES

1. Place a rack in the center of the oven and preheat the oven to 350°F. Lightly mist a 13 by 9–inch baking sheet with vegetable oil spray, then dust it with flour. Shake out the excess flour and set the pan aside.

2. Place the cake mix, water, oil, and eggs in a large mixing bowl and beat with an electric mixer on low speed until the ingredients are just incorporated, 30 seconds. Stop the machine and scrape down the side of the bowl with a rubber spatula. Increase the mixer speed to medium and beat until the batter is smooth, 1½ minutes longer. Spoon the batter into the prepared pan and place the pan in the oven.

3. Bake the cake until the top just springs back when lightly pressed with a finger, 35 to 40 minutes. Transfer the baking pan to a wire rack and let the cake cool completely, 30 minutes.

4. When the cake has cooled crumble it into a large mixing bowl. Add 2 cups of the confectioners' sugar and the cocoa powder, chopped nuts, coconut, if using, and rum. Using a wooden spoon, stir until well combined. Spoon out 1 to 2 tablespoons of the cake mixture and roll them into balls. Dredge the balls in the remaining ½ cup of confectioners' sugar.

Keep It Fresh! Store the rum balls in a tightly sealed container at room temperature for up to four days. Freeze the rum balls, wrapped in aluminum foil, for up to three months. Let the rum balls thaw overnight on the counter before serving.

Butterscotch Walnut Brownie Drops

THE TASTE OF BUTTERSCOTCH takes me back to my childhood when my favorite dessert was a butterscotch bar or warm butterscotch pudding. In this easy to bake cookie, comfort meets the sheer sophistication of chocolate and walnuts. Most any brownie mix will do in this recipe. As the cookies bake they will rise, but it is natural for them to flatten out as they cool. The cookies are chewy and delicious, and they freeze well if you need to bake ahead.

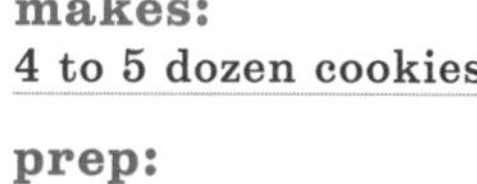

makes:
4 to 5 dozen cookies

prep:
15 minutes

bake:
8 to 10 minutes

cool:
5 minutes

1 package (about 20 ounces) brownie mix
8 tablespoons (1 stick) butter, melted
2 large eggs
½ teaspoon ground cinnamon
1 cup (6 ounces) butterscotch chips
1 cup chopped walnuts

Recipe Reminders

MADE FOR

PREP NOTES

DON'T FORGET

SPECIAL TOUCHES

1. Place a rack in the center of the oven and preheat the oven to 350°F. Set aside 2 ungreased baking sheets.

2. Place the brownie mix, butter, eggs, and cinnamon in a large mixing bowl and beat with an electric mixer on low speed until the ingredients come together, 30 seconds. Stop the machine and scrape down the side of the bowl with a rubber spatula. Add the butterscotch chips and walnuts. Beat on low speed until the dough is thick and well blended, 30 seconds longer.

3. Drop the cookie dough by generous tablespoons about 1 inch apart on the ungreased baking sheets. Place the baking sheets in the oven; if your oven cannot accommodate both baking sheets on the center rack, place one on the top rack and one on the center rack and rotate them halfway through the baking time.

4. Bake the cookies until they are crisp around the edges and puffed up but still a little soft in the center, 8 to 10 minutes. Remove the baking sheets from the oven and immediately transfer the cookies to wire racks to cool for 5 minutes. Repeat with the remaining cookie dough.

Keep It Fresh! Store the cookies, wrapped in aluminum foil or in an airtight container, at room temperature for up to one week. Freeze the cookies, wrapped in aluminum foil, for up to three months. Let the cookies thaw overnight on the counter before serving.

Spice Drop Cookies

makes:
4 to 5 dozen cookies

prep:
5 minutes

bake:
8 to 10 minutes

cool:
22 to 23 minutes

AN UNEXPECTED BONUS of baking is the memories. Memories you leave with your children as they enjoy your baked goods and memories of your own that come back to you when you're in the kitchen. I had one of these déjà vu experiences when I baked these spice cookies. The recipe was sent to me many years ago by Barb Fogg, who lives in New Smyrna Beach, Florida. They reminded me of a soft applesauce cookie my grandmother used to make. But this recipe is meant for today's busy kitchen, beginning with a spice cake mix to which you add eggs, oil, and prepared mincemeat. That's it. For glazing, stir together confectioners' sugar and orange juice until smooth, then drizzle it over the soft cookies. You could just as easily simply dust the cookies with confectioners' sugar.

For the cookies

1 package (18.25 ounces) plain spice cake mix
1 cup prepared mincemeat
½ cup vegetable oil
2 large eggs

For the glaze

1 cup confectioners' sugar, sifted
2 tablespoons orange juice

Recipe Reminders

MADE FOR

PREP NOTES

DON'T FORGET

SPECIAL TOUCHES

1. Make the cookies: Place a rack in the center of the oven and preheat the oven to 350°F. Set aside 2 ungreased baking sheets.

2. Place the cake mix, mincemeat, oil, and eggs in a large mixing bowl. Using a wooden spoon, stir until the ingredients are well incorporated, 45 strokes. Drop the cookie dough by tablespoonfuls 2 to 3 inches apart on the ungreased baking sheets. Place the baking sheets in the oven; if your oven cannot accommodate both baking sheets on the center rack, place one on the top rack and one on the center rack and rotate them halfway through the baking time.

3. Bake the cookies until they begin to brown around the edges and spring back when lightly pressed in the center, 8 to 10 minutes. Transfer the baking sheets to a wire rack to cool for 2 to 3 minutes. Using a metal spatula, transfer the cookies to wire racks to cool completely, 10 minutes longer. Repeat with the remaining cookie dough.

4. Make the glaze: Place the confectioners' sugar in a small bowl and stir in the orange juice. Using a teaspoon, drizzle the glaze over the cookies. Let the glaze set for 10 minutes before serving the cookies.

Keep It Fresh! Store the cookies, in a tightly sealed container or wrapped in aluminum foil, at room temperature for up to five days. Freeze the cookies, wrapped in aluminum foil, for up to three months. Let the cookies thaw overnight on the counter before serving.

Angel Food Macaroons

SEVERAL YEARS AGO in my newsletter I asked readers to help me find a macaroon recipe that began with a box of angel food cake mix. Many readers had that very recipe, and I am sharing it now. Making the macaroons is really easy, and you can eat them as is or dip them in chocolate before serving. For a variation, use just two cups of coconut and a little vanilla instead of the almond extract.

makes:
3 dozen cookies

prep:
10 minutes

bake:
10 to 12 minutes

cool:
10 minutes

Parchment paper, for lining the baking sheet
1 package (16 ounces) angel food cake mix
½ cup water
1½ teaspoons pure almond extract
3 cups (5 ounces) sweetened flaked coconut

1. Place a rack in the center of the oven and preheat the oven to 350°F. Line a baking sheet with parchment paper and set it aside.

2. Place the cake mix, water, and almond extract in a large mixing bowl and beat with an electric mixer on low speed until smooth, 30 seconds. Stop the machine and scrape down the side of the bowl with a rubber spatula. Increase the mixer speed to medium and beat for 1 minute longer. Fold in the coconut.

Recipe Reminders

MADE FOR

PREP NOTES

DON'T FORGET

SPECIAL TOUCHES

3. Drop the dough by rounded teaspoonfuls about 2 inches apart on the prepared baking sheet. Place the baking sheet in the oven and bake the macaroons until they are set and just beginning to brown, 10 to 12 minutes.

4. Remove the baking sheet from the oven and slide the parchment paper with the macaroons on top onto a wire rack to cool 5 for minutes. Using a small metal spatula, remove the macaroons from the parchment paper. You can reuse the parchment paper; place it back on the baking sheet and repeating the process with the remaining macaroon dough.

Keep It Fresh! Store the macaroons, in a tightly sealed container, at room temperature for up to three days or for up to one week in the refrigerator. Freeze the macaroons, wrapped in aluminum foil, for up to three months. Let the macaroons thaw overnight on the counter before serving.

Frostings

Frosting is the first and last taste you experience when forking into a slice of cake. It should never be an afterthought. My wonderful frostings—from the cooked chocolate icing to the fluffy buttercream—are the heart and soul of this book.

Homemade frostings have been my mantra for the last ten years. I find instant supermarket frostings subpar, not good enough for my cakes. As my mother said so many years ago, you can get away with a cake mix cake, but you must make your frosting from scratch. Homemade frosting might take a bit more time to assemble than opening a can, but it's worth it. Once you've made your first ganache, fluffy buttercream, or caramel frosting, you'll know what I mean. From the buttercreams to cream cheese frostings to new pan frostings to simple glazes, here are some stellar ways to dress up cakes. You'll find old favorites—my ganache and my buttercream—and also some improvements and new twists.

Throughout the book, in addition to the basic frostings in this chapter, there are myriad frostings, toppings, and glazes I developed just for a specific recipe. There are cream cheese frostings flavored with sherry or spices or brown butter and there are glazes custom-made for coffee cakes. While these appear with a particular recipe, feel free to mix and match frostings with any cake you like.

When making frosting, remember this: Use the best ingredients you've got—butter, chocolate, fresh confectioners' sugar. Sift out any lumps in confectioners' sugar before adding it. Make sure your butter and cream cheese are at room temperature for buttercreams and cream cheese frostings. And use a heavy saucepan to make the cooked icings, stirring them over low heat until they're smooth.

Frostings deserve consideration and care. They are what makes a good cake great.

Buttercream Frosting

makes:
3½ cups, enough to frost a 2- or 3-layer cake

prep:
5 minutes

Begin here on your frosting journey. This is the frosting that can go on every cake and cupcake you bake no matter what the flavor. It is especially nice on chocolate cupcakes, pink birthday cakes for little girls, and the Cinnamon Apple Spice Cake on page 62.

8 tablespoons (1 stick) butter, at room temperature
3¾ cups confectioners' sugar, sifted
3 to 4 tablespoons milk
2 teaspoons pure vanilla extract

Place the butter in a medium-size bowl and beat with an electric mixer on low speed until fluffy, 30 seconds. Stop the machine and add the confectioners' sugar, and 3 tablespoons of the milk, a bit at a time, beating with the mixer on low speed until the confectioner's sugar is well incorporated, 1 minute. Add the vanilla, then increase the mixer speed to medium and beat the frosting until it is light and fluffy, 1 minute longer. Add up to 1 tablespoon more milk if the frosting seems too stiff.

To frost 24 cupcakes, use:

4 tablespoons (½ stick) butter, at room temperature

3 cups confectioners' sugar, sifted

2 to 3 tablespoons milk

1 teaspoon pure vanilla extract

Lemony Buttercream Frosting

FROSTED WITH THIS FRESH TASTING FROSTING, the Lemon Cupcakes (page 369) or the Strawberry Cheesecake Cupcakes (page 366) are a treat to remember. The frosting is also good on the Old-Fashioned Pear and Ginger Cakes (page 57) and the Pineapple Carrot Cake (page 64).

makes:
2½ cups, enough to frost a 2-layer cake or 24 cupcakes

prep:
10 minutes

1 medium-size lemon
4 tablespoons (½ stick) butter, at room temperature
3 cups confectioners' sugar, sifted
Milk or water, if needed

1. Rinse and pat the lemon dry with paper towels, then grate enough zest to measure 1 teaspoon. Cut the lemon in half and squeeze the juice to yield 2 to 3 tablespoons.

2. Place the butter in a medium-size bowl and beat with an electric mixer on low speed until fluffy, 30 seconds. Stop the machine and add the confectioners' sugar and the lemon juice and zest a bit at a time, beating with the mixer on low speed until the confectioners' sugar is well incorporated, 1 minute. Increase the mixer speed to medium and beat the frosting until it is light and fluffy, 1 minute longer. If the frosting seems too stiff add a little milk or water to thin it.

Another Thing About Frostings

When matching the right frosting to a cake, consider consistency. Soft and delicate cakes can handle the hard, smooth texture of a caramel or penuche icing. These icings set, so they are like candy and they actually help the cake stay moist. And in summertime, the icings don't need refrigeration so this is the perfect choice for a potluck.

Heavier cakes, on the other hand, seem to do well with a richer frosting, such as a cream cheese frosting. Think of dark and moist devil's food, pumpkin, and red velvet cakes—all of these are perfect with a cream cheese frosting, and they will not dry out when stored in the refrigerator.

How to Make a Perfect Buttercream Frosting

Don't let the mystery of a simple buttercream frosting drive you to canned frosting! Here are my tips for success every time.

1. Soften the butter by leaving it out on the counter or by warming it in a microwave oven on high power for ten seconds.

2. Sift confectioners' sugar to rid it of lumps. You'll be glad you did.

3. For buttercreams, a good ratio is 1 tablespoon of liquid per cup of sugar used.

4. Don't add all of the liquid called for at once, just incorporate it as needed. Once you beat the soft butter, add a cup of sugar, then a little liquid; add another cup of sugar; add a tad more liquid; more sugar, more liquid, and the frosting should come to a creamy and spreadable consistency.

5. Now, rev up the mixer to whip the frosting full of air for ten seconds, and you're ready to frost.

Cream Cheese Frosting

A BIT LIGHTER than the cream cheese frosting from the first *Cake Mix Doctor* book, this one is just as delicious. It has half the butter as the original frosting, and I think this lets the cream cheese flavor come through more strongly. The frosting also needs less confectioners' sugar to pull it together, making it less sweet. It's perfect on the Cinnamon Streusel Layer Cake (page 92), the Better Banana Cake (page 27), or the Hummingbird Cake (page 280).

makes:
3 cups, enough to frost a 2-layer cake or 24 cupcakes

prep:
5 minutes

1 package (8 ounces) cream cheese, at room temperature (see Note)
4 tablespoons (½ stick) butter, at room temperature
3½ cups confectioners' sugar, sifted
2 teaspoons pure vanilla extract

Place the cream cheese and butter in a medium-size bowl and beat with an electric mixer on low speed until combined, 30 seconds. Stop the machine. Add the confectioners' sugar a bit at a time, beating with the mixer on low speed until the confectioners' sugar is well incorporated, 1 minute. Add the vanilla, then increase the mixer speed to medium and beat the frosting until fluffy, 1 minute longer. Use the frosting at once.

Cinnamon Cream Cheese Frosting

For a new take on an old favorite, add ½ teaspoon of ground cinnamon to the Cream Cheese Frosting.

To frost a 13 by 9-inch sheet cake, follow the steps but use:

4 ounces cream cheese, at room temperature

4 tablespoons (½ stick) butter, at room temperature

3 cups confectioners' sugar, sifted

1 teaspoon pure vanilla extract

To frost a 3-layer cake or to generously frost a 2-layer cake, follow the steps but use:

1 package (8 ounces) cream cheese, at room temperature

8 tablespoons (1 stick) butter, at room temperature

4 cups confectioners' sugar, sifted

1 tablespoon pure vanilla extract

Note: I'm all for using reduced-fat cream cheese. It *is* more watery than regular cream cheese, so save it for cooler weather. Or, place the frosted cake in the refrigerator to let the frosting set for 20 minutes before serving.

Confectioners' Sugar

What is confectioners' sugar? This was the question my eleven-year-old son posed as I dusted a stack of brownies to take to a party. Moms seem to have the answer for just about everything, but somehow I couldn't give him a good one for an ingredient I use every day. So, I did a little research.

Confectioners' sugar, also known as powdered sugar or icing sugar, is just a finely ground sugar that often contains cornstarch to make it easy to spoon and pour. The 10-X on the package means the sugar has been ground ten times.

Because confectioners' sugar absorbs moisture easily it needs to be kept sealed in a plastic bag or airtight jar. If it gets lumpy, sift it before baking.

Chocolate Cream Cheese Frosting

JUST THINKING ABOUT THIS FROSTING makes me hungry! Try it on the Chocolate Chip Layer Cake on page 111 or on just about anything else.

makes:
3 cups, enough to frost a 2-layer cake or 24 cupcakes

prep:
5 minutes

8 tablespoons (1 stick) unsalted butter, at room temperature
4 ounces cream cheese, at room temperature
⅓ cup unsweetened cocoa powder
3 cups confectioners' sugar, sifted
2 teaspoons pure vanilla extract

Place the butter and cream cheese in a medium-size bowl and beat with an electric mixer on low speed until combined, 30 seconds. Stop the machine. Add the cocoa powder and confectioners' sugar, a bit at a time, beating with the mixer on low speed until the confectioners' sugar is well incorporated, 1 minute. Add the vanilla, then increase the mixer speed to medium and beat the frosting until fluffy, 1 minute longer. Use the frosting at once.

Chocolate Notes

It's a funny thing—the longer you beat the Chocolate Cream Cheese Frosting, the lighter in color it will become.

If you fold in ¼ cup of miniature chocolate chips, you will have a delicious chocolate chip cream cheese frosting.

Orange Cream Cheese Frosting

makes:
3 cups, enough to frost a 2-layer cake or 24 cupcakes

prep:
5 minutes

THIS SIMPLE FROSTING—made with ingredients you most likely have in your kitchen—turns a plain vanilla cake into an orange cake. It makes any cake special, but you'll love it on the Fresh Orange Birthday Cake (page 37).

8 tablespoons (1 stick) butter, at room temperature
4 ounces cream cheese, at room temperature
1 teaspoon grated orange zest (see Note)
2 to 3 teaspoons fresh orange juice
3¾ cups confectioners' sugar, sifted

Place the butter and cream cheese in a medium-size bowl and beat with an electric mixer on low speed until combined, 30 seconds. Stop the machine. Add the orange zest, 2 teaspoons of the orange juice, and the confectioners' sugar, a bit at a time, beating with the mixer on low speed until the confectioners' sugar is well incorporated, 1 minute. Increase the mixer speed to medium and beat the frosting until fluffy, 1 minute longer. Add up to 1 teaspoon more orange juice if the frosting seems too stiff. Use the frosting at once.

Note: A small orange will yield a little more than 1 teaspoon of zest. And it will give you a tablespoon or two of juice, more than you need for this recipe.

10 Cream Cheese Frosting Easy Add-ins

Plain old cream cheese frosting speaks to me and satisfies me slathered on just about any cake. But even the most basic of frostings sometimes needs a little pick-me-up. So here are some ideas.

1. Add ¼ cup of crushed and drained fresh raspberries or strawberries.

2. The grated zest—just 1 teaspoon—of a rinsed lemon, lime, or orange adds intense flavor to the frosting.

3. For almond lovers, add ¼ cup of minced toasted almonds and ½ teaspoon of pure almond extract.

4. To top chocolate cake, fold ¼ cup of crushed peppermints into a cream cheese frosting.

5. Enrich the cream cheese frosting by folding in 6 ounces of white chocolate that has been chopped and melted in the microwave for about 1 minute.

6. Forgo the vanilla and add a dash of brandy, dark rum, or Irish whiskey.

7. Fold in ½ cup of miniature semisweet chocolate chips or ½ cup of crushed chocolate wafer cookies for the cookies and cream look.

8. Go tropical and add ¼ cup of drained, crushed, canned pineapple.

9. Make it mocha by adding 1 teaspoon of espresso powder or instant coffee granules and ¼ teaspoon of unsweetened cocoa powder.

10. Add a pinch of cinnamon—it's simple and always successful and perfect for carrot, spice, and chocolate cakes.

Chocolate Pan Frosting

makes:
4 cups, enough to frost a 2- or 3-layer cake

prep:
10 minutes

My **ALL-AROUND FROSTING,** this is what I turn to when I need a fabulous dessert in no time. It is my mom's recipe, a frosting I remember watching her stir with a wooden spoon and pour over brownies, cupcakes, and all sorts of layer cakes.

12 tablespoons (1½ sticks) butter
½ cup unsweetened cocoa powder
½ cup milk
About 5½ cups confectioners' sugar, sifted

1. Melt the butter in a medium-size saucepan over low heat, 2 to 3 minutes. Stir in the cocoa powder and milk. Cook, stirring, until the mixture thickens and just begins to come to a boil, 1 minute longer. Remove the pan from the heat. Stir in 5 cups of the confectioners' sugar, adding more if needed, until the frosting is thickened and smooth and the consistency of hot fudge sauce.

2. Ladle the warm frosting over the top of cooled cake layers, then spread the side of the cake with more frosting, smoothing it out with a long metal spatula as you go. The frosting will harden as it cools.

Never Run Out of Frosting

You won't run out as long as you have:

- ◆ At least 1 cup of frosting for every 12 cupcakes
- ◆ 1½ to 2 cups of frosting to cover the top of a cake in a 13 by 9-inch pan
- ◆ 1½ cups of frosting to glaze a Bundt or tube cake
- ◆ 2½ cups to 3 cups of frosting to frost the top and side of a cake from a 13 by 9-inch pan
- ◆ 3 to 4 cups of frosting for a two- or three-layer 9-inch cake or to completely cover a Bundt or tube pan cake.

Work quickly because this frosting sets up quickly. If the frosting becomes too thick, return the pan to low heat and stir the frosting to loosen it up.

To frost a 13 by 9-inch sheet cake, or 24 cupcakes follow the steps but use:

8 tablespoons (1 stick) butter

4 tablespoons unsweetened cocoa powder

⅓ cup milk

3½ cups confectioners' sugar, sifted

For enough frosting to pour over a Bundt cake, follow the steps but use:

4 tablespoons (½ stick) butter

2 tablespoons unsweetened cocoa powder

3 tablespoons milk

1½ cups confectioners' sugar, sifted

Fluffy Chocolate Frosting

makes:
3 cups, enough to frost a 2-layer cake or 24 cupcakes

prep:
10 minutes

ALSO KNOWN AS CHOCOLATE BUTTERCREAM, this is a great basic recipe that is hard to resist. You'll use it on yellow and chocolate cakes—and cakes of all shades in between.

8 tablespoons (1 stick) unsalted butter, at room temperature
⅔ cup unsweetened cocoa powder (see Notes)
3 cups confectioners' sugar, sifted, plus more confectioners' sugar if needed
⅓ cup milk, plus additional milk if needed (see Notes)
2 teaspoons pure vanilla extract

Place the butter and cocoa powder in a medium-size bowl and beat with an electric mixer on low speed until the mixture is soft and well combined, 30 seconds. Stop the machine and add the confectioners' sugar, ⅓ cup of milk, and the vanilla. Beat with the mixer on low speed until the frosting lightens and is fluffy, 2 to 3 minutes. Add 1 tablespoon at a time of more milk if the frosting is too thick or more confectioners' sugar if the frosting is too thin.

Notes: I use regular cocoa powder in this recipe. Dutch-processed cocoa has a more intense chocolate flavor, but its color is too dark to my eye for this frosting.

Use whatever milk you have in your refrigerator. If you have whole milk it will make a slightly richer frosting.

Chocolate Fudge Marshmallow Frosting

makes:
3 cups, enough to frost a 2-layer cake or 24 cupcakes

prep:
10 to 12 minutes

THIS OLD-FASHIONED FROSTING makes any layer cake memorable—especially the Classic Yellow Cake (page 67)—as well as any cupcakes, like the Chocolate Buttermilk Cupcakes (page 358).

2 cups granulated sugar
1 can (5 ounces) evaporated milk
10 large marshmallows
8 tablespoons (1 stick) butter
1 cup (6 ounces) semisweet chocolate chips
1 teaspoon pure vanilla extract

Place the granulated sugar, evaporated milk, and marshmallows in a large saucepan over medium heat and let come to a boil, stirring with a wooden spoon. Reduce the heat and let simmer for 6 minutes, stirring constantly. Remove the pan from the heat and stir in the butter, chocolate chips, and vanilla. Continue stirring until the frosting is thick and smooth and the chocolate and butter have melted, about 5 minutes. Use the frosting immediately; it sets up quickly.

Martha's Chocolate Icing

makes:
1½ cups, enough to frost a 2-layer cake, 24 cupcakes, or a 13 by 9-inch cake

prep:
8 to 10 minutes

To frost a Bundt or tube cake, follow the steps but use:

½ cup granulated sugar

3 tablespoons butter

3 tablespoons milk

1 tablespoon light corn syrup

½ cup semisweet chocolate chips

½ teaspoon pure vanilla extract

MY FRIEND AND RECIPE TESTER extraordinaire, Martha Bowden, passed this terrific chocolate frosting recipe along to me several years ago and I shared it with you in the *Chocolate from the Cake Mix Doctor*. But since that book was published, we've improved the icing a bit, adding a little light corn syrup to make it creamier and easier to spread. We also added a little vanilla to enhance the chocolate.

1 cup granulated sugar
5 tablespoons butter
⅓ cup milk
2 tablespoons light corn syrup
1 cup (6 ounces) semisweet chocolate chips
1 teaspoon pure vanilla extract

Place the granulated sugar, butter, milk, and corn syrup in a medium-size saucepan over medium-high heat and stir until the mixture comes to a boil, 3 to 4 minutes. Still stirring, let the mixture boil until the granulated sugar dissolves, 1 minute longer. Remove the pan from the heat and stir in the chocolate chips and vanilla. Continue stirring until the icing is smooth and the chocolate has melted. Use the icing immediately; it sets up quickly.

Martha's Milk Chocolate Icing

makes:
1½ cups, enough to frost 22 cupcakes or top a Bundt cake

prep:
15 minutes

Spoon this over the Peanut Butter Cookie Dough Cupcakes (page 348) or just about any cupcakes or Bundt cake you bake! This is a creamier and not so chocolaty version of Martha's regular icing on page 480. Kids love it.

¾ cup granulated sugar
5 tablespoons butter
¼ cup milk
1 cup milk chocolate chips

Place the granulated sugar, butter, and milk in a small saucepan over medium-high heat and stir until the mixture comes to a boil, 3 minutes. Still stirring, let the mixture boil until the granulated sugar dissolves, 1 minute longer. Remove the pan from the heat and stir in the chocolate chips. Continue stirring until the icing is smooth and the chocolate has melted. Let the icing cool in the pan for 5 minutes. When you spread the icing over a cake it will run down the side, then set up.

Chocolate Syrup Frosting

makes:
3 cups, enough to frost the top and center of a a 2- or 3-layer cake or 24 cupcakes

prep:
10 minutes

No chocolate frosting could be simpler or more sublime, with a silky, fudgy texture. It's a snap to make, since it requires no cooking. Thanks to Maryann Wilkerson of Little Rock, Arkansas, for sharing this recipe. Try it on Maryann's Chocolate Layer Cake (page 107).

8 tablespoons (1 stick) butter, at room temperature
½ cup unsweetened cocoa powder
½ cup chocolate syrup
4 cups confectioners' sugar, sifted
2 tablespoons milk, plus more if needed
1 teaspoon pure vanilla extract
Dash of salt

Place the butter, cocoa powder, and chocolate syrup in a large mixing bowl and beat with an electric mixer on low speed until just combined, 1 minute. Add the confectioners' sugar, 2 tablespoons of milk, and the vanilla and salt and beat on low speed until the confectioners' sugar is combined. Increase the mixer speed to medium-high and beat until smooth and spreadable, 1 minute longer. Add a little more milk if the frosting is too thick to spread.

Chocolate Ganache

ONE OF THE SIMPLEST FROSTINGS imaginable, ganache contains just two ingredients, hot cream and chopped semisweet chocolate. If you'd like to add a tablespoon of your favorite liqueur at the end, that makes just three ingredients. The right temperature is everything—make sure the cream heats long enough to be hot enough to melt the chocolate. As the ganache cools you'll see that it thickens and becomes more spreadable.

makes:
2 cups, enough to thinly frost a 2-layer cake or 24 cupcakes

prep:
5 minutes

cool:
45 minutes to 1 hour

8 ounces (1⅓ cups) semisweet chocolate chips
¾ cup heavy (whipping) cream
1 tablespoon liqueur of your choice, or 1 teaspoon pure vanilla extract (optional)

Place the chocolate chips in a large stainless steel mixing bowl. Pour the cream into a small heavy saucepan, place over medium heat, and bring to a boil, stirring. Remove the cream from the heat and pour it over the chocolate. Using a wooden spoon, stir until the chocolate is melted. Stir in the liqueur or vanilla, if using. Let the ganache cool at room temperature until spreadable, 45 minutes to 1 hour.

To generously frost a 2- or 3-layer cake, follow the steps but use:

16 ounces (2⅔ cups) semisweet chocolate chips

1½ cups heavy (whipping) cream

2 tablespoons liqueur of your choice, or 2 teaspoons pure vanilla extract (optional)

My Coconut Pecan Frosting

makes:
3 cups, enough to frost the top and center of a 2- or 3-layer cake or 24 cupcakes

prep:
35 minutes

cool:
20 minutes

THE CLASSIC FROSTING for a German chocolate cake, I love this frosting on cupcakes, too. It takes a little longer to make than some frostings because you've got to stir it carefully on the stove, but for special occasions it is worth it. For best results, toast the pecans and coconut separately for four to five minutes in a 350°F oven before adding them to the frosting. German chocolate cakes aren't frosted on the side—this frosting wouldn't stick—so the recipe makes just enough to frost between the layers and on top of the cake.

1 can (12 ounces) evaporated milk
1½ cups granulated sugar
12 tablespoons (1½ sticks) butter
4 large egg yolks, lightly beaten
1½ teaspoons pure vanilla extract
2 cups sweetened flaked coconut, toasted
1½ cups chopped pecans, toasted

Place the evaporated milk, granulated sugar, butter, and egg yolks in a large saucepan over medium heat. Cook, stirring constantly with a wooden spoon, until thickened and golden brown in color, 15 minutes. Remove from the heat. Stir in the vanilla. Let the frosting cool to room temperature, 20 minutes, then fold in the coconut and pecans.

Quick Caramel Frosting

I MAY BE PASSIONATE ABOUT CHOCOLATE, but this has to be my favorite frosting of all time. My mom passed along the recipe many years ago, and it has become our busy family's way of creating the caramel on our now famous caramel cake. I just don't have the time to caramelize sugar in a cast-iron skillet the way they did in the old days. And I don't think adding brown sugar to the recipe sacrifices the flavor at all. Use this frosting on everything!

makes:
3 cups, enough to frost a 2-layer cake or 24 cupcakes

prep:
15 minutes

8 tablespoons (1 stick) butter
½ cup packed light brown sugar
½ cup packed dark brown sugar
¼ cup milk
2 cups confectioners' sugar, sifted
1 teaspoon pure vanilla extract

Place the butter and brown sugars in a heavy medium-size saucepan over medium heat. Cook, stirring, until the mixture comes to a boil, about 2 minutes. Add the milk, stir, and let the mixture return to a boil, then remove the pan from the heat. Add about 1¼ cups of the confectioners' sugar and the vanilla. Beat with a wooden spoon or whisk until the frosting is smooth. Add ½ to ¾ cup confectioners' sugar, but not so much so that it thickens and hardens. Ladle the frosting over the cake layers while it is still warm. If you are frosting cupcakes, spoon the frosting on top while it is warm and it will set.

Tips for Trouble-Shooting the Quick Caramel Frosting

◆ **Spread the frosting on the cake while it is still warm; work quickly as it will set up fast.**

◆ **If the frosting hardens too soon, place the saucepan back over low heat and stir in a tablespoon or two of milk.**

◆ **Frost the top of the cake by pouring the frosting over it right from the pan.**

Penuche Icing

makes:
1 cup, enough to top a Bundt or tube pan cake

prep:
10 minutes

SORT OF A GLAZE, sort of a cooked icing, with a caramel flavor, this is wonderful stuff. Spread it over a zucchini or applesauce or gingerbread cake. This recipe makes just enough to top a Bundt cake.

½ cup packed light brown sugar
4 tablespoons (½ stick) butter
3 tablespoons milk
½ cup confectioners' sugar, sifted

Place the brown sugar and butter in a small saucepan and stir over medium heat until the butter melts and the mixture bubbles up, 2 to 3 minutes. Pour in the milk, stirring, and let the mixture come to a boil. Remove the pan from the heat and whisk in the confectioners' sugar until smooth. Spoon the icing over a cooled cake.

Caramel Glaze

CREAMY AND GOOEY, Caramel Glaze doesn't harden. I love it spooned over vanilla ice cream as well as on carrot cake and anything with apples and spice. This makes just enough to top a Bundt or tube pan cake.

makes:
½ cup, enough to lightly top a Bundt or tube pan cake

prep:
10 minutes

3 tablespoons butter
3 tablespoons packed light brown sugar
3 tablespoons granulated sugar
3 tablespoons heavy (whipping) cream
½ teaspoon pure vanilla extract

Place the butter, brown sugar, granulated sugar, and cream in a medium-size saucepan over medium heat and let come to a boil, stirring. Let the butter mixture boil for 1 minute, stirring constantly. Remove the pan from the heat and stir in the vanilla. Pour the glaze over a cooled cake.

White Chocolate Glaze

makes:
1 cup, enough to glaze a Bundt or tube cake

prep:
8 to 10 minutes

HERE'S A QUICK AND EASY WAY to dress up a Bundt or tube pan cake. Try it over the Pumpkin Spice Cake (page 88) or the Classic Darn Good Chocolate Cake (page 228). Look for white chocolate that contains cocoa butter as it tastes better.

½ cup granulated sugar
¼ cup milk
4 tablespoons (½ stick) butter
1 cup (6 ounces) white chocolate chips

Place the granulated sugar, milk, and butter in a small saucepan over medium heat and let come to a boil, stirring constantly, 2 minutes. Stir until the butter melts, 1 minute longer. Remove the pan from the heat and stir in the white chocolate chips until they are melted. Let the glaze cool for 2 to 3 minutes, then spoon it over a cooled cake.

Sweetened Whipped Cream

ANOTHER GREAT BASIC RECIPE from our kitchen, this sweetened whipped cream goes over warm chocolate cakes, alongside gingerbread, and on top of fresh strawberries when they are in season. I now add a little vanilla to it.

makes:
2 cups, enough to lightly frost a 2-layer cake or 24 cupcakes

prep:
5 minutes

1 cup heavy (whipping) cream, chilled
¼ cup confectioners' sugar
½ teaspoon pure vanilla extract

Place a large, clean mixing bowl and electric mixer beaters in the freezer for a few minutes while you assemble the ingredients. Pour the heavy cream into the chilled bowl and beat with an electric mixer on high speed until the cream has thickened, 1½ minutes. Stop the machine and add the confectioners' sugar and vanilla. Beat on high speed until stiff peaks form, 1 to 2 minutes longer.

Chocolate Sweetened Whipped Cream

For a real treat, melt 1 cup (6 ounces) of semisweet chocolate chips in a microwave oven on high power for 45 seconds or over low heat on the stove, then let the chocolate cool. Whip 2 cups (1 pint) heavy (whipping) cream until firm peaks form. Don't add sugar or vanilla, just fold the cooled chocolate into the whipped cream.

Conversion Tables

Liquid Conversions

U.S.	IMPERIAL	METRIC
2 tbs	1 fl oz	30 ml
3 tbs	1½ fl oz.	45 ml
¼ cup	2 fl oz	60 ml
⅓ cup	2½ fl oz.	75 ml
⅓ cup + 1 tbs	3 fl oz	90 ml
⅓ cup + 2 tbs	3½ fl oz.	100 ml
½ cup	4 fl oz	125 ml
⅔ cup	5 fl oz	150 ml
¾ cup	6 fl oz	175 ml
¾ cup + 2 tbs	7 fl oz	200 ml
1 cup	8 fl oz	250 ml
1 cup + 2 tbs	9 fl oz	275 ml
1¼ cups	10 fl oz	300 ml
1⅓ cups	11 fl oz	325 ml
1½ cups	12 fl oz	350 ml
1⅔ cups	13 fl oz	375 ml
1¾ cups	14 fl oz	400 ml
1¾ cups + 2 tbs	15 fl oz	450 ml
2 cups (1 pint)	16 fl oz	500 ml
2½ cups	20 fl oz (1 pint)	600 ml
3¾ cups	1½ pints	900 ml
4 cups	1¾ pints	1 liter

Weight Conversions

US/UK	METRIC	US/UK	METRIC
½ oz	15 g	7 oz	200 g
1 oz	30 g	8 oz	250 g
1½ oz	45 g	9 oz	275 g
2 oz	60 g	10 oz	300 g
2½ oz	75 g	11 oz	325 g
3 oz	90 g	12 oz	350 g
3½ oz	100 g	13 oz	375 g
4 oz	125 g	14 oz	400 g
5 oz	150 g	15 oz	450 g
6 oz	175 g	1 lb	500 g

Oven Temperatures

FAHRENHEIT	GAS MARK	CELSIUS
250	½	120
275	1	140
300	2	150
325	3	160
350	4	180
375	5	190
400	6	200
425	7	220
450	8	230
475	9	240
500	10	260

Note: Reduce the temperature by 20°C (68°F) for fan-assisted ovens.

Approximate Equivalents

1 stick butter = 8 tbs = 4 oz = ½ cup

1 cup all-purpose presifted flour or dried bread crumbs = 5 oz

1 cup granulated sugar = 8 oz

1 cup (packed) brown sugar = 6 oz

1 cup confectioners' sugar = 4½ oz

1 cup honey or syrup = 12 oz

1 cup grated cheese = 4 oz

1 cup dried beans = 6 oz

1 large egg = about 2 oz or about 3 tbs

1 egg yolk = about 1 tbs

1 egg white = about 2 tbs

Please note that all conversions are approximate but close enough to be useful when converting from one system to another.

Index

C

H

I

J

K

L

M

Q

R

S

T

U

V

Y

Z